LAW AND RELIGION IN THE COMMONWEALTH

This book examines law and religion from the perspective of its case law.

Each chapter focuses on a specific case from a Commonwealth jurisdiction, examining the history and impact of the case, both within the originating jurisdiction and its wider global context.

The book contains chapters from leading and emerging scholars from across the Commonwealth, including from the United Kingdom, Canada, Australia, Pakistan, Malaysia, India and Nigeria.

The cases are divided into four sections covering:

- Foundational Questions in Law and Religion
- Freedom of Religion around the Commonwealth
- Religion and state relations around the Commonwealth
- Rights, Relationships and Religion around the Commonwealth.

Like religion itself, the case law covers a wide spectrum of life. This diversity is reflected in the cases covered in this book, which include:

- *Titular Roman Catholic Archbishop of Kuala Lumpur v Home Minister* on the use of the Muslim name for God by non-Muslims in Malaysia
- *The Church of the New Faith v Commissioner of Pay-roll Tax* (Vic) which determined the meaning of religion in Australia
- *Eweida v UK* which clarified the application of Article 9 of the European Convention on Human Rights
- *R v Big M Drug Mart* on the individual protections of religious freedom under the Canadian Charter of Rights.

The book examines how legal disputes involving religion are among the most contested in the courts and shows that in these cases, passions run high and the outcomes can have significant consequences for all involved.

Law and Religion in the Commonwealth

The Evolution of Case Law

Edited by
Renae Barker
Paul T Babie
and
Neil Foster

•HART•
OXFORD • LONDON • NEW YORK • NEW DELHI • SYDNEY

HART PUBLISHING

Bloomsbury Publishing Plc

Kemp House, Chawley Park, Cumnor Hill, Oxford, OX2 9PH, UK

1385 Broadway, New York, NY 10018, USA

29 Earlsfort Terrace, Dublin 2, Ireland

HART PUBLISHING, the Hart/Stag logo, BLOOMSBURY and the Diana logo are trademarks of Bloomsbury Publishing Plc

First published in Great Britain 2022

A catalogue record for this book is available from the British Library.

A catalogue record for this book is available from the Library of Congress.

Library of Congress Control Number: 2022933983

ISBN: HB: 978-1-50995-014-0
ePDF: 978-1-50995-016-4
ePub: 978-1-50995-015-7

Typeset by Compuscript Ltd, Shannon

CONTENTS

PART III
RELIGION AND STATE RELATIONS AROUND THE COMMONWEALTH

PART IV
RIGHTS, RELATIONSHIPS, RESPONSIBILITIES AND RELIGION AROUND THE COMMONWEALTH

LIST OF CONTRIBUTORS

Craig Allen is a teaching fellow at the University of Birmingham, UK.

Azizat O Amoloye-Adebayo is a senior lecturer in the Department of Islamic Law, Faculty of Law, University of Ilorin, Nigeria.

Paul T Babie is Bonython Chair and Professor of Law, Associate Dean (International Development), and Director of the Research Unit for the Study of Society, Ethics and Law at the Adelaide Law School, University of Adelaide, Australia. He is also Adjunct Professor of Law at the Thomas More Law School, Australian Catholic University.

Renae Barker is Senior Lecturer in the School of Law and the University of Western Australia and Honorary Research Fellow at the Centre for Muslim States and Societies.

Luke Beck is Associate Professor of Constitutional Law and Associate Dean (Education) in the Faculty of Law at Monash University, Australia.

Iain T Benson is Professor of Law at the School of Law, University of Notre Dame Australia, Sydney, and Extraordinary Professor of Law at the Faculty of Law, University of the Free State, Bloemfontein, South Africa.

Kathryn Chan is Associate Professor of Law at the Faculty of Law, University of Victoria, Canada.

Michelle Flynn is a barrister at the Bar of Ireland and Associate Researcher at the Department of Law and Anthropology, Max Planck Institute for Social Anthropology, Germany.

Neil Foster is Associate Professor of Law at Newcastle Law School, Australia.

Mark Hill QC is a lecturer at the Open University Law School and an Associate Professor at Cardiff University (UK), the University of Pretoria (South Africa), King's College, London (UK) and University of Notre Dame Australia, Sydney. He is also Visiting Professor of Law and Distinguished Fellow of the University of Notre Dame London Law Programme.

Muhammad Kamaldeen Imam-Tamim is a senior lecturer at the Department of Islamic Law, Faculty of Law, University of Ilorin, Nigeria.

Ian Leigh is Emeritus Professor of Law at Durham University, UK.

Richard Moon is Distinguished University Professor at the University of Windsor, Canada.

Preeti Nalavadi is a lawyer from India and is an associate teacher of law and a PhD candidate at Adelaide Law School, University of Adelaide, Australia.

Joshua Neoh is Associate Professor of Law at the Australian National University.

Umar Rashid is a PhD candidate at the Adelaide Law School, University of Adelaide, Australia.

Russell Sandberg is Professor of Law at Cardiff University, UK.

Dian AH Shah is an assistant professor at the National University of Singapore.

Sawinder Singh is a PhD Candidate and an associate teacher at the Adelaide Law School, Australia, and a lawyer at the Punjab and Haryana High Court, Chandigarh (UT), India.

TABLE OF CASES

Australia

Canada

European Court of Human Rights

Hong Kong

India

Malaysia

New Zealand

Nigeria

Pakistan

South Africa

UK

US

1

Introduction

RENAE BARKER, PAUL T BABIE AND NEIL FOSTER

I. Introduction

Thomas Jefferson asserted that 'Christianity neither is, nor ever was a part of the common law'.[1] Whether you agree with Jefferson's assessment or that of Sir Matthew Hale, who asserted that 'Christianity is part of the Common Law of England',[2] it is hard to deny the importance of religion to law. Historically, many fundamental principles developed as part of the common law have rested upon religious foundations. Perhaps the most well known is the law of negligence. In *Donoghue v Stevenson*,[3] Lord Atkin drew upon the biblical story of the Good Samaritan[4] to develop his neighbourhood principle. While many Commonwealth countries now draw on more secular sources in developing the common law, there are of course those where religion still plays a direct role. In others, the role of religion may be less direct, but that does not mean it is completely absent from the case law; on the contrary, disputes about the role and place of religion in public and private life regularly make their way to the courtroom. This should surprise no one given that almost any aspect of human life can become the subject of religious belief and practice.[5] It is therefore hardly surprising that a wealth of judicial decisions in every jurisdiction deal with all manner of religious issues, interactions and disputes.

This volume examines those decisions dealing with law and religion in the legal systems of the Commonwealth of Nations (or, as we refer to it here, the Commonwealth). It includes cases from the UK, Canada, Australia, Malaysia, India, Pakistan, South Africa and Nigeria. While this represents just a sample of the rich jurisprudence on religion from the Commonwealth, the cases examined draw out many of the unique challenges faced by communities in working through disputes centred on religion as well as common challenges faced by many, if not all of those nations which comprise it.

[1] Letter from Thomas Jefferson to Thomas Cooper Monticello, 10 February 1814, www.let.rug.nl/usa/presidents/thomas-jefferson/letters-of-thomas-jefferson/jefl227.php.

[2] *Rex v Taylor* (27 and 28 Car II), 3 Keble 607; for a discussion of the case, see E Visconsi, 'The Invention of Criminal Blasphemy: *Rex v Taylor* (1676)' (2008) 103(1) *Representations* 30.

[3] *Donoghue v Stevenson* [1932] AC 562.

[4] See Luke 10:25–37.

[5] *Adelaide Company of Jehovah's Witnesses Inc v Commonwealth* (1943) 67 CLR 116, 124 (Latham CJ).

Some of the challenges addressed by the case law examined in this volume are recent – for example, the need to strike a balance between LGBTI+ rights and the rights of religious individuals and organisations whose beliefs and practices may not support same-sex relationships or marriage. Chapters 4, 5, 15 and 17 all examine cases that tackle this important issue from a number of different angles and jurisdictions. Other issues are somewhat older, although they have tended to recur in various guises over the decades or even centuries. For example, the role of the state in regulating blasphemy (Chapter 7) intra- and inter-religious disputes (Chapters 13 and 14), and religious marriage (Chapters 15 and 16) are all challenges which are long-standing and shared by jurisdictions across the Commonwealth.

The volume is divided into four parts. Part I, containing two chapters, considers cases that examine two foundational questions: the definition of religion and the nature and meaning of God. Part II, containing five chapters, examines a variety of freedom of religion issues found throughout the Commonwealth: religious dress at work, refusal of service on the basis of religious belief, Sunday trading laws, blasphemy laws, the enforcement of religious offences and the banning of religious organisations. Part III, containing seven chapters, concerns religion and state relationships. The cases examined consider religious federalism in Malaysia, the position of the Church of England in England and Wales, the meaning of 'establishment' in Australia, the role of courts in settling inter-religious disputes, the use of Islamic principles to expand the jurisdiction of the Supreme Court of Pakistan, the role of the state in internal religious disputes in Canada and the recognition of same-sex marriage in South Africa. The volume concludes with Part IV, containing four chapters, which explores the nature of rights, relationships and responsibilities. As with the previous three parts, Part IV draws on a wide range of examples, from Islamic marriage to undue influence and potential clashes between freedom of religion and other fundamental rights (most notably, and topically, LGBTI+ and women's rights).

II. Part I: Foundational Questions in Law and Religion

At the very heart of cases about law and religion lie questions about the definition of religion and the nature and meaning of God. Barker and Neoh explore these two important definitional concepts in Chapters 2 and 3. In the former, Barker examines the history and legacy of the Australian case *Church of the New Faith v Commissioner of Pay-roll Tax*.[6] The Australian High Court determined that the Church of Scientology was a religion for the purposes of the *Pay-roll Tax Act 1971* (Vic). However, as Barker argues, the impact of the case has been far-reaching. The definition(s) of religion set by the High Court have subsequently been applied and expanded in numerous Commonwealth jurisdictions, in Australia itself, as well as in New Zealand, Hong Kong and the UK. As Barker explains: '[B]y their very nature, definitions include and exclude.'[7]

[6] *Church of the New Faith v Commissioner of Pay-roll Tax (Vic)* (1983) 154 CLR 120.
[7] R Barker, ch 2 in this volume.

Neoh takes up this theme in Chapter 3 with the Malaysian case *Titular Roman Catholic Archbishop of Kuala Lumpur v Home Minister*.[8] There, the Malaysian Court of Appeal 'has done what generations of prophets have not dared to do: to name God, that is, to give God a proper name'.[9] Neoh argues that the approach of the Malaysian Court of Appeal in limiting the use of Allah to Muslims contains both legal and theological-philosophical errors, and demonstrates the inherent risk when secular judges attempt to 'play the role of theologian'.[10]

III. Part II: Freedom of Religion Around the Commonwealth

Some argue that freedom of religion is the oldest human right.[11] Today international, supranational and national law recognises this foundational right. Article 18 of the Universal Declaration of Human Rights, for instance, states:

> Everyone has the right to freedom of thought, conscience and religion; this right includes freedom to change his religion or belief, and freedom, either alone or in community with others and in public or private, to manifest his religion or belief in teaching, practice, worship and observance.[12]

However, freedom of religion is not absolute or unlimited. And where those limits are to be placed is often the source of conflict, requiring the careful balancing of competing interests. The breadth of issues which may be the source of case law dealing with freedom of religion is demonstrated in Part II.

Part II begins with an examination of two cases from the UK: *Eweida v UK*[13] and *Lee v Ashers Baking Company*.[14] In Chapter 4, Sandberg highlights both the promise and the limitations of the European Court of Human Rights' judgments in *Eweida v UK*. Sandberg's analysis highlights how the Strasbourg Court not only corrected the confused approach taken by the English judiciary to freedom of religion and discrimination, but also took the opportunity to elucidate an expansive new interpretation of its protection found in Article 9 of the European Convention on Human Rights.

In Chapter 5, Leigh examines *Lee v Ashers Baking Company*. This case began in the County Court in Northern Ireland before finding its way to the UK Supreme Court and, like *Eweida*, seemed destined for a decision in the European Court of Human Rights.[15]

[8] *Titular Roman Catholic Archbishop of Kuala Lumpur v Home Minister*, R1-25-28-2009 (High Court in Malaya, Lau Bee Lan J) (31 December 2009).

[9] J Neoh, ch 3 in this volume.

[10] ibid.

[11] M Kirby, 'Law, Human Rights and Religion – of Genocide, Sexuality and Apostasy' (2009) 9 *Macquarie Law Review* 3, 4; W Cole Durham, 'Freedom of Religion: The United States Model' (1994) 42 *American Journal of Comparative Law* 617, 618.

[12] *Universal Declaration of Human Rights*, GA Res 217A (III), UN GAOR, UN Doc A/810 (10 December 1948) art 18.

[13] *Eweida v UK* (2013) 57 EHRR 8.

[14] *Lee v Ashers Baking Company Ltd and Others* (Northern Ireland) [2018] UKSC 49.

[15] At the time of writing, the application is still pending before the Strasbourg Court.

Leigh examines the case from the perspective of the ongoing 'Culture Wars' between religion and LGBTI+ rights. He argues that the case has important implications in the 'harms race' – in which each side employs increasingly ambitious notions of harm to contest the other's claim to legal protection under equality and human rights law.

Chapter 6 takes us across the Atlantic to Canada, where Moon considers the first freedom of religion case to reach the Supreme Court of Canada following the enactment of the Canadian Charter of Rights and Freedoms in 1982. In *R v Big M Drug Mart*,[16] the Supreme Court took the opportunity to 'set out what it saw as the purpose or foundation of the Charter right'.[17] As Moon argues, in this early decision were the seeds of two competing concepts of freedom of religion both requiring the state to act neutrally, although on different bases.

In Chapter 7, Amoloye-Adebayo and Immam-Tamim examine the position of blasphemy under Nigerian law as found in *Shalla v State*.[18] They critique the United Nations Human Rights Committee position on blasphemy and argue that blasphemy should continue to be recognised as a crime in Nigeria. Their analysis highlights the need for the scope and protection of freedom of religion to be decided through taking account of local conditions and cultures rather than simply relying on purportedly universal norms.

Finally, in Chapter 8, Babie examines the Australian case *Adelaide Company of Jehovah's Witnesses v The Commonwealth*.[19] Babie argues for a 'a purposive, large, liberal approach'[20] to freedom of religion in Australian constitutional law, which would move away from the Australian High Court's, and commentators', traditionally narrow interpretation of section 116 of the *Australian Constitution*. Such an approach would open up new opportunities for the interpretation and application of freedom of religion in Australian jurisprudence.

IV. Part III: Religion and State Relations Around the Commonwealth

With varying degrees of success, scholars regularly attempt to define the width and breadth of the state–religion or state–church relationship.[21] Theory aside, in practice, each state must determine the ways in which the state and religion will interact in the particular circumstances of that jurisdiction. What works in one particular system may not work in another. As a result, the case law from around the Commonwealth reveals a

[16] *R v Big M Drug Mart* [1985] 1 SCR 295.

[17] R Moon, ch 6 in this volume.

[18] *Shalla v The State* [2007] 12 SCM (Pt 2), 603–45, SC.245/2004 (Supreme Court of Nigeria) (5 October 2007).

[19] *Adelaide Company of Jehovah's Witnesses v The Commonwealth* (1943) 67 CLR 116.

[20] P Babie, ch 8 in this volume.

[21] For just two examples, see W Cole Durham Jr, 'Perspectives on Religious Liberty: A Comparative Framework' in JD van der Vyver and J Witte Jr (eds), *Religious Human Rights in Global Perspective: Legal Perspectives* (Martinus Nijhoff, 1996) 1–44; and R Ahdar and I Leigh, *Religious Freedom in the Liberal State*, 2nd edn (Oxford University Press, 2013) 87–124. For a more extensive list, see R Barker, 'Pluralism verses Separation: Tension in the Australian Church State Relationship' (2021) 16(1) *Religion and Human Rights* 1, fn 43.

rich source of jurisprudence examining this complex interplay of individual and collective interests. Part III contains just a sample of the Commonwealth law, as found in the UK, Malaysia, Australia, India, Pakistan, South Africa and Canada.

Importantly, this provides an opportunity to juxtapose the different approaches of jurisdictions with differing majority faiths. The chapters in this part come from jurisdictions with majority Christian, Muslim and Hindu populations, with varying degrees of multiculturalism and religious plurality, as well as those with sizeable populations who identify as having no religion.

Part III begins, in Chapter 9, with an examination of the Malaysian case *Iki Putra Mubarrak v Kerajaan Negeri Selangor and Others*.[22] Here Shah explores the nature of Malaysia's religious federalism, explaining that while the case itself is ostensibly about laws prohibiting homosexual acts, the implications of the case and its progress through the Malaysian courts goes much deeper – 'mark[ing] a major step in recalibrating state–religion relations in Malaysia'.[23]

Hill's examination of the UK case *Aston Cantlow v Wallbank*[24] in Chapter 10 demonstrates that, like *Iki Putra Mubarrak*, while the issue raised is ostensibly about one thing, cases which deal with it have much wider implications. In *Aston Cantlow*, the UK House of Lords faced an otherwise unremarkable issue: 'the enforceability of a landowner's obligation to fund costly works to the fabric of a parish church under the archaic provisions of the *Chancel Repair Act 1932*'.[25] However, the consequences of the case, in terms of state–religion relationships, have been much more significant than this rather bland issue suggests. As Hill argues, the case makes clear that, despite being the established church, 'the Church of England is, essentially, a religious organisation and not a limb of government'.[26]

In Chapter 11, Beck examines the seminal Australian case on the separation of state and religion: *Attorney-General (Vic) ex rel Black v Commonwealth*.[27] He argues that while the outcome of the case – confirming the constitutional validity of federal funding of religious schools – is correct, the reasoning and interpretation given to the so-called establishment clause of section 116 of the *Australian Constitution* is deeply flawed. Despite this, the case remains the only exploration by the High Court of this limb of section 116 of the *Constitution*.

Religious conflict is a common theme around the Commonwealth, with varying approaches found in the treatment of the courts in every state. In Chapter 12, Singh considers an example from India. In *M Siddiq (D) Thr Lrs v Mahant Suresh Das and Others*,[28] the Supreme Court of India ostensibly settled a long-running dispute over land claimed by both Hindu and Muslim groups dating back to the sixteenth century. The Court permitted the Hindu groups to retain land upon which a mosque had previously stood, while at the same time granting land to the Muslim group whose mosque

[22] *Iki Putra Mubarrak v Kerajaan Negeri Selangor and Others* [2021] 1 LNS 47 (Federal Court).
[23] DAH Shah, ch 9 in this volume.
[24] *Aston Cantlow and Wilmcote with Billesley Parochial Church Council v Wallbank* [2004] 1 AC 546, [2003] 3 WLR 283, [2003] 3 All ER 1213 (HL).
[25] M Hill QC, ch 10 in this volume.
[26] ibid.
[27] *Attorney-General (Vic) ex rel Black v Commonwealth* (1981) 146 CLR 559.
[28] *M Siddiq (D) Thr Lrs v Mahant Suresh Das and Others*, AIR (2019) SC 1420.

had been destroyed. Singh argues that while this outcome may have been expedient, it is inconsistent with India's secular *Constitution*.

In Chapter 13, Rashid examines the Supreme Court of Pakistan decision in *Benazir Bhutto v Federation of Pakistan*.[29] His analysis provides an example of tension between different organs of state – in this case, the judiciary and the legislature – over issues of fundamental rights and religion. In this landmark case, the Supreme Court established its activist jurisdiction, invoking the role of Islam in the Constitution of Pakistan as well as references to Islamic principles.

A thorny issue in every Commonwealth jurisdiction concerns the state's role in resolving disputes within religious communities. In Chapter 14, Chan examines the Canadian case of *Lakeside Colony v Hofer*,[30] which involved elements of two common internal religious disputes: the ownership of religious community property and the ejection of members from religious communities. As Chan highlights, *Lakeside Colony v Hofer* engages with two questions that are central to state–religion relationships: on the one hand, the relationship between justiciability and jurisdiction; and, on the other hand, the juridical status of non-state legal norms.

Legal disputes about the recognition of same-sex marriage have occurred across the Commonwealth.[31] South Africa's contribution to this body of law came in *Minister of Home Affairs and Another v Fourie and Another; Lesbian and Gay Equality Project and Others v Minister of Home Affairs and Others*.[32] However, as Benson argues in Chapter 15, like many of the cases in Part III of this volume, the South African case is about more than same-sex marriage; it also 'provides … a jurisprudence that attempts to address the difficult philosophical and practical questions of pluralism, accommodation, and the nature of an open society'.[33]

V. Part IV: Rights, Relationships, Responsibilities and Religion around the Commonwealth

Central to many law and religion disputes are rights, relationships and responsibilities. The rights that individuals may hold as members of their communities are vast and increasingly complex. These complexities only increase where these rights interact with religion and the right to freedom of religion. As well as being rights holders, each individual is also interconnected with those in their community via a series of relationships and responsibilities. Part IV examines four examples: marriage; the right not to be discriminated against; women's rights; and undue influence.

[29] *Benazir Bhutto v Federation of Pakistan* [1988] PLD 416 (SC).

[30] *Lakeside Colony of Hutterian Brethren v Hofer* [1992] 3 SCR 165.

[31] See, eg, *Commonwealth v Australian Capital Territory* (2013) 250 CLR 441; *M v H* [1999] 2 SCR 3; *Reference re Same-Sex Marriage* [2004] SCC 79; *Hendricks v Quebec (Attorney-General)* [2002] RJQ 2506; *Halpern v Canada (Attorney-General)* [2003] OJ No 2268 (10 June 2003) (Ontario Court of Appeal); *Eagle Canada Inc v Canada (Attorney-General)* (2003) 225 DLR (4th) 472. For an example of similar case law outside of the Commonwealth, see *Obergefell v Hodges*, 576 US 644 (2015).

[32] *Minister of Home Affairs and Another v Fourie and Another; Lesbian and Gay Equality Project and Others v Minister of Home Affairs and Others* [2005] ZACC 19.

[33] I Benson, ch 15 in this volume.

Part IV begins with an examination of a case concerning one of the central relationships in most societies: marriage. In Chapter 16, Flynn examines the English Court of Appeal judgment in *Her Majesty's Attorney-General v Akhter and Others*.[34] While the case is fascinating in itself as an examination of the status of an Islamic marriage or *nikah*, which did not comply with state law, as Flynn explains, the significance of the decision goes further. It highlights the very real legal and practical consequences for those from religious minorities, and in particular women and children, where their religious 'marriage' is outside the ambit of state law.

In Chapter 17, Foster considers the role of balancing clauses and exemptions for religious organisations in anti-discrimination legislation via an examination of the Australian case *Christian Youth Camps Ltd v Cobaw Community Health Service Ltd*.[35] As Foster argues, cases involving religious organisations and sexual orientation discrimination 'present these issues very sharply'. He suggests that in this case, 'a number of features of the decision do not adequately balance the various rights involved and suggests that clarification on these matters will need to be provided by Parliaments and the High Court of Australia in the future'.[36]

In Chapter 18, Nalavadi examines the intersection of freedom of religion and the rights of women and children in India in two leading cases: *Sabarimala (Indian Young Lawyers Association and Others v State of Kerala and Others)*[37] and *Shayara Bano v Union of India*.[38] Nalavadi argues that 'while the Indian judiciary has played an impressive role in protecting the rights of women, there remain disputes between the equality and anti-discrimination provisions and the free exercise protections of the *Indian Constitution* that remain unresolved'.[39]

Finally, in Chapter 19, Allen examines the seminal UK case on religious undue influence: *Allcard v Skinner*.[40] For Allen, *Allcard v Skinner*, despite being the oldest case examined in this volume, had a long-lasting effect on the doctrine in both the UK and in Australia. The case continues to retain significance; not only do courts in both jurisdictions regularly cite it, but the central question raised by the case – when does religious influence become undue – remains relevant to religious institutions today. Many religious groups continue to require vows of obedience, tithes, donations and other forms of financial contribution.

VI. Final Thoughts

Two final thoughts. First, a word about the diversity of views on various issues in this volume. As with other academic collections of this sort, the authors were all invited to give their own informed academic opinion on these important cases. This means that

[34] *Her Majesty's Attorney-General v Akhter and Others* [2020] EWCA Civ 122.

[35] *Christian Youth Camps Ltd v Cobaw Community Health Service Ltd* (2014) 50 VR 256, [2014] VSCA 75.

[36] N Foster, ch 17 in this volume.

[37] *Sabarimala* (2019) 11 SCC 1. See also 2018 (8) SCJ 609; *Indian Young Lawyers Association and Others v State of Kerala and Others*, Writ Petition (Civil) 373 of 2006.

[38] *Shayara Bano v Union of India*, AIR 2017 SC 4609.

[39] P Nalavadi, ch 18 in this volume.

[40] *Allcard v Skinner* (1887) 36 Ch D 154.

not all the authors will agree with all the views expressed by other authors. But that, of course, is to be expected in a volume intended to express the diversity and plurality of views on these significant issues.

Second, whether you dive in at the beginning and read it cover to cover or select specific chapters upon which to focus, this volume offers something for everyone interested in law and religion in the Commonwealth. The very nature of the common law and the doctrine of stare decisis mean that the cases examined herein will continue to form the foundation for future decisions about law and religion. Many of the cases considered already build upon one another,[41] and will be built upon in turn as each jurisdiction faces new disputes involving religion. We hope through this volume to contribute to that future development through the extensive and detailed examination of the leading cases presented by experts drawn together from the Commonwealth.

[41] This volume contains cases dating from 1887 to 2021.

PART I

Foundational Questions in Law and Religion

2

Church of the New Faith v Commissioner of Pay-roll Tax

Defining Religion for the World?

RENAE BARKER

I. Introduction

Judicial attempts to define religion have been variously described as 'called upon to ponder the imponderable',[1] an impossible task[2] and misguided.[3] While it is tempting to assert that 'I know it when I see it',[4] legal certainty demands that a term essential to a myriad of legal rights and privileges be defined.[5] The High Court of Australia confronted the challenge of defining religion in *The Church of the New Faith v Commissioner of Pay-roll Tax* (Vic).[6] Like courts before and since, the High Court had to walk the fine line between the struggle 'to avoid, on the one hand, the Scylla of hard, sharp, particularistic definition and, on the other hand, the Charybdis of meaningless generalities'.[7] The three judgments came up with three separate definitions, spanning the spectrum of typologies of legal definitions of religion. This chapter examines both the history and legacy of the *Scientology Case*.

II. Facts and Background

In 1983, the High Court of Australia held that the beliefs and practices of the Church of the New Faith, also known as the Church of Scientology, were a religion in the state of Victoria. The path to this decision began many years earlier.

[1] *Jacques v Hilton*, 569 F Supp 730, 731 (D NJ 1983) (Sarokin J).
[2] *Alvarado v City of San Jose*, 94 F 3d 1223, 1227 (9th Cir 1996).
[3] GC Freeman, 'The Misguided Search for the Constitutional Definition of "Religion"' (1983) 71 *Georgetown Law Journal* 1519.
[4] *Jacobellis v Ohio*, 378 US 184, 197 (1964) (Stewart J).
[5] WC Durham Jr and BG Scharffs, *Law and Religion: National, International and Comparative Perspectives* (Aspen Publishers, 2010) 40.
[6] *The Church of the New Faith v Commissioner of Pay-roll Tax (Vic)* (1983) 154 CLR 120 (hereinafter '*Scientology Case*').
[7] Gale Virtual Reference Library, 'Religion' in *Encyclopaedia of Religion* (Gale, 2019) 7693.

On 19 November 1963, Labour leader John Galbally called for action 'against a group of charlatans who for monetary gain are exposing children of tender age, youths and adults to intimidation and blackmail, insanity and even suicide, family estrangement and bankruptcy, despite repeated warnings from the Mental Health Authority and other informed and responsible persons and bodies'.[8] The group in question was the Church of Scientology. The only reference in his long speech to the potential religiosity of Scientology was its registration in America, where 'they registered under the name of a religious organisation, the idea being that they could obtain certain taxation benefits when purchasing motor cars and such like'.[9]

John Galbally focused instead on the methods used by Scientology to recruit 'gullible people',[10] the large sums of money paid by individuals to Scientology, and the impact of association with Scientology on individual's careers, family ties and well-being.[11] While Galbally did not think much of any claim by the Church of Scientology to be a religion, others could see the similarity between them and other 'fringe' faith groups. Rupert Hamer, for example, commented that 'we are not faced locally with a gang of people who have set out on some conspiracy to fleece the public. They are devoted adherents and believers in this cult'.[12] The lack of reference to religion may be because Scientology did not necessarily see itself as religious.[13]

Scientology grew out of the Dianetics movement based on L Ron Hubbard's 1950 bestseller *Dianetics: The Modern Science of Mental Health*.[14] The first local Church of Scientology was founded in 1954 by Hubbard's followers with the Founding Church of Scientology being set up the following year in Washington DC.[15] However, as the title *Dianetics: The Modern Science of Mental Health* suggests, Dianetics itself did not begin life as a religious movement. In fact, Hubbard initially took his discoveries to the American Psychiatric Association and the American Medical Association, but, as J Gordon Melton put it: 'They declined to take Dianetics seriously.'[16] Within Scientology itself, the transition from 'science' to religion was far from uncontentious.[17] Even after Scientology began to describe itself as a religion, Scientology publications still described it as non-religious. For example, a publication referred to in the initial Victorian Supreme Court decision stated that: 'H.A.S.I. is non-religious – it does not demand any belief or faith nor is it in conflict with faith. People of all faiths use Scientology.'[18] In the same publication, Scientology is described as a 'precise science'.[19]

In response to Galbally's agitations, the Victorian government set up the Board of Inquiry into Scientology conducted by Keven Anderson QC.[20] Anderson was

[8] Victoria, *Parliamentary Debates*, Legislative Council, 19 November 1963, 2127 (John Galbally).
[9] ibid 2133.
[10] ibid 2131.
[11] ibid 2127–38. For the full debate, see 2127–59.
[12] ibid 2159 (RJ Hamer).
[13] R Barker, 'Scientology, the Test Case Religion' (2015) 40 *Alternative Law Journal* 275, 276–77.
[14] JG Melton, 'Birth of a Religion' in JR Lewis (ed), *Scientology* (Oxford University Press, 2009) 17, 21–23.
[15] ibid 23.
[16] ibid.
[17] HB Urban, *The Church of Scientology: A History of a New Religion* (Princeton University Press, 2011) 57–88; FK Flinn, 'Scientology as Technological Buddhism' in Lewis (n 14) 209, 213–16.
[18] *Church of the New Faith v Commissioner for Pay-roll Tax* [1983] VR 97, 99.
[19] ibid.
[20] R Barker, *State and Religion: The Australian Story* (Routledge, 2018) 202.

devastating in his assessment of Scientology from the very first line of his report: 'There are some features of Scientology that are so ludicrous that there may be a tendency to regard scientology as silly and its practitioners as harmless cranks.'[21] Later in the same paragraph, the report states that 'Scientology is evil; its techniques evil; its practice a serious threat to the community, medically, morally and socially; and its adherents sadly deluded and often mentally ill'.[22]

In a direct response to Anderson's report, the Victorian government passed the *Psychological Practices Act 1965* (Vic), which, inter alia, purported to restrict the practice of Scientology.[23] Western Australia and South Australia followed Victoria's lead with more targeted legislation aimed squarely at restricting the practice of Scientology.[24] The Australian *Companies Code* also included the terms 'Scientology' and 'Dianetics' on the Prohibited Names Directive.[25] This led the Church to rebrand itself as the Church of the New Faith. No successful prosecutions eventuated from the anti-Scientology legislation.[26] Despite inquiries into Scientology in England, New Zealand and South Africa, no other Commonwealth country passed similar legislation.[27] The English inquiry was particularly critical of Australia's approach as being 'discriminatory and contrary to all the best traditions of the Anglo-Saxon legal system'.[28]

In 1973, the then Attorney-General Lionel Murphy recognised Scientology as a religion for the purposes of the *Marriage Act 1961* (Cth).[29] This had the effect of nullifying some of the effect of the Victorian Act, as exemptions were given for 'any priest or minster of a recognised religion in accordance with the usual practice of that religion'.[30] The term 'recognised religion' was defined as a religion whose priests or ministers were recognised under the *Marriage Act 1961* (Cth).[31] Western Australia repealed its anti-Scientology Act in 1972, followed in 1973 by South Australia. Victoria finally repealed its anti-Scientology provisions in 1982.[32]

The *Scientology Case* itself arose out of a dispute over pay-roll tax. The Church of the New Faith Incorporated was assessed as liable to pay pay-roll tax by the Victorian Commissioner of Pay-roll Tax for the period 1 July 1975–30 June 1977.

[21] K Anderson, *Report of the Board of Inquiry into Scientology* (Government Printer, 1965) 1.

[22] ibid.

[23] Barker (n 20) 205–07.

[24] *Scientology Act 1968* (WA); *Scientology (Prohibition) Act 1968* (SA).

[25] A Possamai and A Possamai-Inesedy, 'Scientology Down Under' in Lewis (n 14) 345, 351; JT Richardson, 'Minority Religions ("Cults") and the Law: Comparisons of the United States, Europe and Australia' (1995) 18 *University of Queensland Law Journal* 183, 200.

[26] Barker (n 20) 207–08.

[27] ibid 208.

[28] JG Foster, *Enquiry into the Practice and Effects of Scientology* (Her Majesty's Stationery Office, 1971) 181. While the UK was critical of Australia's approach, there, too, restrictions were imposed on members of the Church of Scientology. For example, until the late 1980s, Scientologists were denied entry into the UK and were not recognised as a religion until 2014. See Barker (n 13).

[29] Barker (n 20) 206. Given that Murphy later sat on the *Scientology Case*, an argument could be made that he should have recused himself.

[30] *Psychological Practices Act 1965* (Vic), s 2(3).

[31] ibid s 2(4).

[32] Barker (n 20) 208–09.

The Church objected on the basis that it was exempt under section 10(1)(b) of the *Pay-roll Tax Act 1971* (Vic), which provided:

> (1) The wages liable to pay-roll tax under this Act do not include wages paid or payable –
>
> (b) by a religious or public benevolent institution, or a public hospital.[33]

The Church contended that it was a 'religious institution' and therefore exempt from pay-roll tax. At first instance, and on appeal to the Full Court of the Supreme Court of Victoria, the Church's claim to be a religion was unanimously dismissed.[34] At first instance, Crockett J expressed the opinion that the 'religious trappings' adopted by the Church of the New Faith/Scientology since the early 1960s were designed to gain the protection of laws such as the US First Amendment and section 116 of the *Australian Constitution*, and to take advantage of exemptions granted to religious organisations.[35] They considered 'whether scientology as it is now practices by those who were not party to the deception and whose belief in, and adherence to, the principles of scientology is undoubtable genuine can on that very account be a religious institution'.[36] Despite the fact that several Australian courts had held that Scientology was a religion,[37] Crockett J concluded that Scientology was not a religion and that its claim to be one was nothing more than a 'sham'.[38]

On appeal, the Full Court held that Scientology was not a religion. The Church of the New Faith advocated the approach taken by Adams J in the American case of *Malnak v Yogi*,[39] positing that defining religion was to compare the set of beliefs under consideration with existing religions using a set of indicia.[40] Young CJ applied the three indicia suggested by Adams J – the nature of the ideas,[41] comprehensiveness[42] and trappings (ceremonies and services)[43] – along with three of his own: public acceptance,[44] method of joining[45] and commercialism.[46] In each case, Young CJ determined that the Church of the New Faith did not meet the criteria. Kaye J determined that the definition of religion required the recognition of a Supernatural or Supreme Being or Power.[47] He based his determination on a series of dictionary definitions and English case law, all of which required recognition of a Supreme Being.[48] On assessing the evidence, Kaye J determined that the Church of the New Faith failed to demonstrate a general belief held

[33] *Scientology Case* (n 6) 128; *Pay-roll Tax Act 1971* (Vic), s 10(1)(b).
[34] *Church of the New Faith v Commissioner for Pay-roll Tax* (n 18).
[35] ibid 99–104, 106.
[36] ibid 104.
[37] See *Church of Scientology v Anderson* [1980] WAR 71.
[38] *Church of the New Faith v Commissioner for Pay-roll Tax* (n 18) 108, 111.
[39] *Malnak v Yogi*, 592 F 2d 197 (3d Cir 1979). For a discussion of *Malnak v Yogi*, see S Barringer, 'The New Age and the New Law' in L Griffin (ed), *Law and Religion: Cases in Context* (Aspen Publishers, 2010) 11.
[40] *Church of the New Faith v Commissioner for Pay-roll Tax* (n 18) 121–22.
[41] ibid 123–25.
[42] ibid 125.
[43] ibid 125–26.
[44] ibid 126.
[45] ibid 126–7.
[46] ibid 127–8.
[47] ibid 130.
[48] ibid 130–33.

by all of its members in a deity; as such, it was not a religious institution.[49] Brookings J did not analyse whether or not the Church of the New Faith was a religious institution; instead, he examined whether it was in breach of the *Psychological Practices Act 1965* (Vic). He concluded that the activities undertaken by the Church breached the Act and that many of the records held by them were liable for destruction.[50] As a result, the Church of the New Faith could not claim tax exemptions; to do so would be to benefit from its own criminal activity.[51]

III. Defining Religion: An Impossible and Perilous Task?

Defining religion appears to be a task which the judiciary either finds notoriously difficult or attempts to studiously avoid. For example, Bittker, Idleman and Ravitch note that in the US, 'religion appears to be one of the few key terms of the First Amendment, if not the only key term of that provision, that the contemporary Supreme Court has not authoritatively defined in a comprehensive or systemic manner'.[52] One of the primary difficulties in defining religion in the American context revolves around a need to articulate a definition which is workable under both the Free Exercise and Establishment limbs of the First Amendment.[53] The result is numerous lower court definitions which are inconsistent and in some cases contradictory. The challenge for courts attempting to wade through the myriad possible precedents was highlighted in *Friedman v Southern California Permanente Medical Group*:

> Complicating the answer to this question is that the expansive definition of religion in the pre-1970 conscientious objector cases, *Seeger* and *Welsh*, has been narrowed somewhat to a more specific test – one that compares a belief system to recognized, traditional religions – as typified by the plurality opinion in *Wisconsin v Yoder* … To further complicate matters, *Seeger* and *Welsh* were statutory interpretation cases, while *Yoder* is a free exercise clause decision … Moreover, *Malnak* and its progeny are efforts to define religion in the context of the Free Exercise Clause … Finally, many cases which have attempted to define or discuss religious belief have done so in the context of the *Religious Freedom Restoration Act*, which was invalidated by the United States Supreme Court in *City of Boerne v Flores*.[54]

The law in the UK exhibits a similarly confused approach to definition.[55] While numerous UK courts and tribunals have attempted to define religion, the definitions arrived at

[49] ibid 130–56.
[50] ibid 136–40.
[51] ibid 140–41.
[52] B Bittker, SC Idleman and FS Ravich, *Religion and the State in American Law* (Cambridge University Press, 2015) 331. See also *United States v Meyers*, 906 F Supp 1494 (D Wyo 1995).
[53] Bittker, Idleman and Ravich (n 52) 338–43.
[54] *Friedman v Southern California Permanente Medical Group*, 102 Cal App 4th 39, 69 (Cal App 2d Dist 2002).
[55] P Ridge, 'Not-for-Profit Law and Freedom of Religion' in M Harding (ed), *Research Handbook on Not-for-Profit Law* (Edward Elgar, 2018) 284, 292; R Sandberg, 'Clarifying the Definition of Religion under English Law: The Need for a Universal Definition' (2018) 20 *Ecclesiastical Law Journal* 132; PW Edge, 'Determining Religion in English Courts' (2012) 1 *Oxford Journal of Law and Religion* 402.

are inconsistent. Different definitions apply to different religious rights.[56] In comparison, the European Court of Human Rights has rarely considered the meaning of religion. This may be, at least in part, because Article 9 of the European Convention on Human Rights encompasses freedom of thought and conscience alongside freedom of religion, often making the need to separately define religion redundant.[57]

The state of confusion surrounding the attempt leads many to conclude that the judicial search for a definition of religion is impossible. In an oft-quoted passage from *Adelaide Company of Jehovah's Witnesses Inc v Commonwealth*,[58] Latham CJ opined that 'it would be difficult, if not impossible, to devise a definition of religion which would satisfy the adherents of all the many and various religions which exist, or have existed in the world'.[59] Latham CJ was not alone is this view – expressions on the impossibility of the task almost invariably accompany any judicial attempt to define the term. Consider just a few examples:

> Therefore the court is called upon to ponder the imponderable and define the indefinable and determine whether plaintiffs' beliefs and practices constitute a religion.[60]
>
> There has never been a universal legal definition of religion in English law, and experience across the common law world over many years has shown the pitfalls of attempting to attach a narrowly circumscribed meaning to the word. There are several reasons for this – the different contexts in which the issue may arise, the variety of world religions, developments of new religions and religious practices, and developments in the common understanding of the concept of religion due to cultural changes in society.[61]
>
> Indeed, a succinct and comprehensive definition of that concept would appear to be a judicial impossibility.[62]
>
> Attempting to define religion, in general and for the purposes of the Establishment Clause, is a notoriously difficult, if not impossible, task.[63]

Clearly, difficulties abound in defining religion.[64] By their very nature, definitions include and exclude. They 'demarcate the granting of benefits and burdens, of rights and duties: those included in the definition are recognised by law; those excluded are denied legal recognition'.[65] Therefore, the definition of religion must not be so wide as to encompass almost any form of belief such as to leave legal protections like freedom of religion 'in tatters',[66] while at the same time avoiding a definition that is so narrow as to exclude new, novel or unpopular belief systems.[67] The very act of defining religion can itself be 'a threat to religious freedom'.[68]

[56] Sandberg (n 55) 145–52.

[57] Ridge (n 55) 294. See also European Court of Human Rights, 'Guide to Article 9: Freedom of Thought, Conscience and Religion' (30 April 2019), www.echr.coe.int/Documents/Guide_Art_9_ENG.pdf [14].

[58] *Adelaide Company of Jehovah's Witnesses Inc v Commonwealth* (1943) 67 CLR 116.

[59] ibid 123.

[60] *Jacques v Hilton*, 569 F Supp 730, 731 (D NJ 1983) (Sarokin J).

[61] *R (Hodkin and Another) v Registrar-General of Births, Deaths and Marriages* [2014] 1 All ER 737, 747 (hereinafter '*Hodkin*').

[62] *Remmers v Brewer*, 361 F Supp 537, 540 (SD Iowa 1973).

[63] *Alvarado v City of San Jose*, 94 F 3d 1223, 1227 (9th Cir 1996).

[64] Bittker, Idleman and Ravich (n 52) 335.

[65] Edge (n 55).

[66] *Scientology Case* (n 6) 132.

[67] ibid 131–32; *Meyers* (n 52) 1499.

[68] *Scientology Case* (n 6) 150 (Murphy J); see also Barker (n 20) 15–16.

A legal definition of religion must be determined at a given point in time in response to a specific set of facts. This poses two particular difficulties. First, '[t]he task of defining "religion" poses a comparable risk of adverse retrospective judgment, especially as the … religious landscape increases in diversity and the collective sense of what constitutes inclusive or equal treatment continue to change'.[69] Second, there is a risk that the definition arrived at may be influenced by the facts of the case before the court. Arguably, there is a temptation to craft a definition in order to include or exclude a particular set of beliefs and practices based on a pre-conceived notion of whether or not they should qualify as a religion. High Court Justice Murphy may well have fallen prey to this temptation in his judgment in the *Scientology Case*. In 1973, in his role at the time as Attorney-General, he included Scientology on the list of religions recognised under the *Marriage Act 1961* (Cth). Having already determined that Scientology was a religion for the purposes of the *Marriage Act 1961* (Cth), he could come to no other conclusion when determining the definition of religion in the *Scientology Case*.

Regardless of these difficulties, it is incumbent upon courts to define religion. Failing to legally define religion also has inherent risks.[70] 'Religion', 'religious' and other derivatives of the word are legal terms the meaning of which carries important implications for individuals, groups and government.[71] In Australia, the concept of religion is relevant in interpreting myriad laws and regulations, including section 116 of the *Australian Constitution*, state and territory-based prohibitions against religious discrimination,[72] the guarantee of freedom of religion in the Australian Capital Territory, Victoria and Queensland charters of rights,[73] exemptions from various federal, state and local government taxes,[74] and registration as a religious charity under the *Charites Act 2013* (Cth), amongst many others.[75] Without a consistent legal definition, those administering and applying these laws may be tempted to 'manipulate the definition to include beliefs with which [they agree]', while a different decision maker 'with different leanings later might manipulate the definition to exclude beliefs with which [they disagree]'.[76]

One way in which the difficulties outlined above can, at least in part, be overcome is by remembering that the context in which a definition is propounded matters. Judges, politicians, theologians, philosophers, anthropologists, sociologists, psychologists and myriad other disciplines have attempted to define religion, with varying levels of success. Inevitably the definitions arrived at vary from discipline to discipline and from context to context.[77] What is a useful definition in one context will not work

[69] Bittker, Idleman and Ravich (n 52) 338.

[70] *Meyers* (n 52) 1501.

[71] Bittker, Idleman and Ravich (n 52) 343.

[72] *Discrimination Act 1991* (ACT), s 7; *Anti-Discrimination Act 1992* (NT), s 19(1); *Anti-Discrimination Act 1991* (Qld), s 7; *Equal Opportunity Act 1984* (SA), s 85T; *Anti-Discrimination Act 1998* (Tas), ss 14, 15, 16(o); *Equal Opportunity Act 2010* (Vic), s 6(n); *Equal Opportunity Act 1984* (WA), s 53.

[73] *Charter of Human Rights and Responsibilities Act 2006* (Vic), s 14; *Human Rights Act 2004* (ACT), s 14; *Human Rights Act 2019* (Qld), s 20.

[74] For an overview of tax exemptions to which religious organisations may be entitled in Australia, see GE Dal Pont, *Law of Charity* (LexisNexis Butterworths, 2010) 144–53.

[75] See generally I Ellis-Jones, 'What is Religion?' (2008) 13 *Local Government Law Journal* 168, 168.

[76] *Meyers* (n 52) 1501.

[77] R Crawford, *What is Religion?* (Routledge, 2003) 3; I Ellis-Jones, 'Beyond the Scientology Case' (PhD thesis, University of Technology Sydney, 2007) ch 1.

for other purposes.[78] Richard Dawkins' definition of religion as a virus is virtually useless to a judge trying to determine whether a particular set of beliefs is covered by section 116 of the *Australian Constitution*. On the other hand, it makes Dawkins' point very succinctly.[79]

In the *Scientology Case* – as, indeed, for all other judicial definitions – the definition of religion had a legal purpose: to determine the outer boundaries that the state, via the law (both legislation and case law), will recognise as religious. A particular set of beliefs and practices may well fit a non-legal definition of religion even if they do not amount to a religion for the purposes of law. In *United States v Meyers* (hereinafter '*Meyers*'), Brimmer J observed that 'there is no absolute causal link between the fact that [a party's] beliefs do not fit the criteria and the conclusion that his beliefs are not religious'.[80]

IV. An Australian Definition of Religion

Not only is there a need for a legal definition of religion, but there is also a need for a specific Australian definition of religion. As Mason ACJ and Brennan JJ recognised:

> The disadvantage in leaving the concept without examination by this Court was manifested by the course of the argument before us. Counsel for the corporation contended for a wide definition of religion in accordance with the indicia of a religion set out by Adams J in *Malnak v Yogi* … though it is clear that the formulation of those indicia owes much to the tests adopted by the Supreme Court of the United States in constructing particular Acts of the Congress. On the other hand, counsel for the Commissioner contended for a narrow definition which accorded with the test of a religion propounded by Dillon J in *In Re South Pacific Ethical Society; Barralet v A-G* … a test which confines the concept to theistic religions. It is undesirable that the clarification of a concept important to the law of Australia should be left to the courts of other countries when there is an appropriate opportunity for the concept to be clarified by this Court.[81]

Ultimately, the *Scientology Case* delivered Australia not one legal definition of religion, but three.[82] The final judgment is a boon to those who examine legal definitions of religion – in a single case, the court delivered a definition to fit each of the commonly discussed approaches to defining religion judicially: functional, substantive and analogical.[83] Yet the practical result is that the case does not have a clear *ratio*.[84] Despite this, Australia arguably leads the way, at least in terms of having a

[78] Durham Jr and Scharffs (n 5) 44.

[79] R Dawkins, 'Viruses of the Mind' in B Dahlbom (ed), *Dennett and His Critics* (Blackwell, 1993) 13.

[80] *Meyers* (n 52) 1502.

[81] *Scientology Case* (n 6) 130–31.

[82] Ellis-Jones (n 75) 178–82.

[83] Durham Jr and Scharffs (n 5); WC Durham and EA Sewell, 'Definition of Religion' in JA Serritella (ed), *Religious Organizations in the United States: A Study of Identity, Liberty, and the Law* (Carolina Academic Press, 2006) 3; R Ahdar and I Leigh, *Religious Freedom in the Liberal State*, 2nd edn (Oxford University Press, 2013) 145; Barker (n 20) 16–21.

[84] Ellis-Jones (n 75) 182.

binding authoritative definition of religion from a superior court. The strength of the Australian approach has been recognised by numerous courts around the world, with one witness in a New Zealand case describing the *Scientology Case* as 'a first class theological essay'.[85]

A. Functional

Justice Murphy provides a functional definition of religion. This form defines religion from the viewpoint of an individual adherent, focusing on the role religion plays in one's life. For Murphy J, this meant that:

> [A]ny body which claims to be religious, whose beliefs or practices are a revival of, or resemble earlier cults, is religious. Any body which claims to be religious and to believe in a supernatural Being or Beings, whether physical and visible … or a physical invisible God or spirit, or an abstract God or entity, is religious … Any body which claims to be religious, and offers a way to find meaning and purpose in life, is religious.[86]

The most well-known functional definitions come from American conscientious objector cases. In *United States v Seeger* (hereinafter '*Seeger*'), the US Supreme Court concluded that religion should include any sincere belief that is 'based upon a power or being, or upon a faith, to which all else is subordinate or upon which all else is ultimately dependent' and that 'occupies in the life of its possessor a place parallel to that filled by the God of those admittedly qualifying for the exemption'.[87] In *Welsh v United States* (hereinafter '*Welsh*'), the Court found that a conscientious objector who himself did not view his beliefs as religious could nevertheless qualify for exemption on the basis of religious belief if his 'opposition to war stem[med] from … moral, ethical, or religious beliefs about what is right and wrong' and if 'these beliefs … [were] held with the strength of traditional religious conviction' and 'imposed[d] upon him a duty of conscience to refrain from participating in any war at any time' thus 'occupy[ing] in the life of that individual a place parallel to that filled by … God in traditionally religious people'.[88] Arguably, these definitions were influenced by their context as relevant to exemptions from military service during the Vietnam War through the application of relevant legislation. However, the definitions from both *Seeger* and *Welsh* influenced later definitions, including that of Murphy J in the *Scientology Case*.[89]

Still, functional definitions are often criticised as being too wide.[90] The main difficulty with functional definitions is that they include beliefs 'parallel' to 'orthodox belief systems'. As Dillon J pointed out in *Barralet v Attorney-General*, 'parallels, by definition, never meet'.[91]

[85] *Centrepoint Community Growth Trust v Commissioner of Inland Revenue* [1985] 1 NZLR 673, 697 (hereinafter '*Centrepoint*').
[86] *Scientology Case* (n 6) 151.
[87] *United States v Seeger*, 380 US 163, 176 (1965).
[88] *Welsh v United States*, 398 US 333, 340 (1970).
[89] See Bittker, Idleman and Ravich (n 52) 354–55.
[90] Barker (n 20) 17; Durham Jr and Scharffs (n 5) 24; Ahdar and Leigh (n 83) 146–48.
[91] *Barralet v Attorney-General* [1980] 3 All ER 918, 924 (Dillon J).

B. Substantive

Substantive definitions lie at the opposite end of the definition spectrum to functional definitions,[92] and seek to identify the essence or core concepts of religion. In the *Scientology Case*, Mason ACJ and Brennan J distilled two key concepts:

> [F]or the purpose of the law, the criteria of religion are twofold, belief in a supernatural Being, Thing or Principle; and second, the acceptance of canons of conduct in order to give effect to that belief, although canons of conduct which offend against the ordinary laws are outside the area of any immunity, privilege or right conferred on the grounds of religion.[93]

Historically substantive definitions have tended to be theistic, requiring belief in a god or other supreme being.[94] In Mason ACJ and Brennan J's definition, the supernatural replaces God. More recent substantive definitions have moved further away from the need for a God or Gods. In *Syndicate Northcrest v Anselem*, the Supreme Court of Canada held that:

> Defined broadly, religion typically involves a particular and comprehensive system of faith and worship. Religion also tends to involve the belief in a divine, superhuman or controlling power. In essence, religion is about freely and deeply held personal convictions or beliefs connected to an individual's spiritual faith and integrally linked to one's self-definition and spiritual fulfilment, the practices of which allow individuals to foster a connection with the divine or with the subject or object of that spiritual faith.[95]

In the UK, in *R v Registrar General of Births, Deaths and Marriages*, Lord Toulson determined that religion is:

> [A] spiritual or non-secular belief system held by a group of adherents, which claims to explain mankind's place in the universe and relationship with the infinite, and to teach its adherents how they are to live their lives in conformity with the spiritual understanding associated with the belief system.[96]

If functional definitions are too wide, substantive definitions are too narrow. In focusing on the essence of religion, they risk missing religious beliefs and practices at the margin which may not share that essence. Substantive definitions are also criticised for attempting to find a single essence or core idea which is common to all religions. Critics argue that such attempts are misconceived because no such single characteristic exists.[97]

C. Analogical

Analogical definitions posit a set of indicia for the determination of the existence of a religion.[98] Rather than insisting upon an essential core that all religions share, the

[92] Also called essentialist definitions.
[93] *Scientology Case* (n 6) 136 (Mason ACJ and Brennan J).
[94] See *Barralet v Attorney-General* (n 91) 924 (Dillon J); *R v Registrar-General ex parte Segerdal* [1970] 2 QB 697, 707 (Denning MR); *Davis v Beason* 133 US 333, 341–42 (1890) (Field J); *United States v Macintosh* 283 US 605, 633–44 (1931) (Holmes J and Hughes CJ).
[95] *Syndicate Northcrest v Anselem* [2004] 2 SCR 551, 576 [39] (Iacobucci J).
[96] *Hodkin* (n 61) 752.
[97] Durham Jr and Scharffs (n 5) 45.
[98] Also called the family resemblance approach.

analytical approach accepts that not all religions will exhibit all of the characteristics, but the presence of one or more is a strong indication that the belief system under consideration is in fact a religion.[99] Wilson and Deane JJ took this approach in the *Scientology Case*, listing five indicia:

1. the particular collection of ideas and/or practices involves belief in the supernatural, that is to say, belief that reality extends beyond that which is capable of perception by the senses.
2. the ideas relate to man's nature and place in the universe and his relation to things supernatural.
3. the ideas are accepted by adherents as requiring or encouraging them to observe particular standards or codes of conduct or to participate in specific practices having supernatural significance.
4. however loosely knit and varying in beliefs and practices adherents may be, they constitute an identifiable group or identifiable groups.
5. the adherents themselves see the collection of ideas and/or practices as constituting a religion.[100]

Wilson and Deane JJ's definition drew and expanded upon that elucidated by Adams J in the US cases *Malnak v Yogi*[101] and *Africa v Commonwealth of Pennsylvania*.[102] Adams J outlined three indicia to determine whether a particular set of beliefs and practices constituted a religion:

> First, a religion addresses fundamental and ultimate questions having to do with deep and imponderable matters. Second, a religion is comprehensive in nature; it consists of a belief-system as opposed to an isolated teaching. Third, a religion often can be recognised by the presence of certain formal and external signs … that may be analogized to accepted religions. Such signs might include formal services, ceremonial functions, the existence of clergy, structure and organisation, efforts at propagation, observance of holidays and other similar manifestations associated with traditional religions.[103]

More recently, Brimmer J outlined a more extensive list of indicia in *Meyers*.[104] He determined that religion involves:

1. Ultimate Ideas: Religious beliefs often address fundamental questions about life, purpose, and death. As one court has put it, 'a religion addresses fundamental and ultimate questions having to do with deep and imponderable matters'. These matters may include existential matters, such as man's perception of life; ontological matters, such as man's sense of being; teleological matters, such as man's purpose in life; and cosmological matters, such as man's place in the universe.
2. Metaphysical Beliefs: Religious beliefs often are 'metaphysical', that is, they address a reality which transcends the physical and immediately apparent world. Adherents to many religions believe that there is another dimension, place, mode, or temporality, and they often believe that these places are inhabited by spirits, souls, forces, deities, and other sorts of inchoate or intangible entities.

[99] Durham Jr and Scharffs (n 5) 47.
[100] *Scientology Case* (n 6) 174.
[101] *Malnak v Yogi* (n 39). For a discussion of *Malnak v Yogi*, see Barringer (n 39) 11.
[102] *Africa v Pennsylvania*, 662 F 2d 1025 (3d Cir 1981).
[103] ibid 1032–35.
[104] *Meyers* (n 52) 1502–03.

3. Moral or Ethical System: Religious beliefs often prescribe a particular manner of acting, or way of life, that is 'moral' or 'ethical'. In other words, these beliefs often describe certain acts in normative terms, such as 'right and wrong', 'good and evil', or 'just and unjust'. The beliefs then proscribe those acts that are 'wrong', 'evil', or 'unjust'. A moral or ethical belief structure also may create duties – duties often imposed by some higher power, force, or spirit – that require the believer to abnegate elemental self-interest.
4. Comprehensiveness of Beliefs: Another hallmark of 'religious' ideas is that they are comprehensive. More often than not, such beliefs provide a telos, an overarching array of beliefs that coalesce to provide the believer with answers to many, if not most, of the problems and concerns that confront humans. In other words, religious beliefs generally are not confined to one question or a single teaching.
5. Accoutrements of Religion: By analogy to many of the established or recognized religions, the presence of the following external signs may indicate that a particular set of beliefs is 'religious':

   a. Founder, Prophet, or Teacher: Many religions have been wholly founded or significantly influenced by a deity, teacher, seer, or prophet who is considered to be divine, enlightened, gifted, or blessed.
   b. Important Writings: Most religions embrace seminal, elemental, fundamental, or sacred writings. These writings often include creeds, tenets, precepts, parables, commandments, prayers, scriptures, catechisms, chants, rites, or mantras.
   c. Gathering Places: Many religions designate particular structures or places as sacred, holy, or significant. These sites often serve as gathering places for believers. They include physical structures, such as churches, mosques, temples, pyramids, synagogues, or shrines; and natural places, such as springs, rivers, forests, plains, or mountains.
   d. Keepers of Knowledge: Most religions have clergy, ministers, priests, reverends, monks, shamans, teachers, or sages. By virtue of their enlightenment, experience, education, or training, these people are keepers and purveyors of religious knowledge.
   e. Ceremonies and Rituals: Most religions include some form of ceremony, ritual, liturgy, sacrament, or protocol. These acts, statements, and movements are prescribed by the religion and are imbued with transcendent significance.
   f. Structure or Organization: Many religions have a congregation or group of believers who are led, supervised, or counselled by a hierarchy of teachers, clergy, sages, priests, etc.
   g. Holidays: As is etymologically evident, many religions celebrate, observe, or mark 'holy', sacred, or important days, weeks, or months.
   h. Diet or Fasting: Religions often prescribe or prohibit the eating of certain foods and the drinking of certain liquids on particular days or during particular times.
   i. Appearance and Clothing: Some religions prescribe the manner in which believers should maintain their physical appearance, and other religions prescribe the type of clothing that believers should wear.
   j. Propagation: Most religious groups, thinking that they have something worthwhile or essential to offer non-believers, attempt to propagate their views and persuade others of their correctness. This is sometimes called 'mission work', 'witnessing', 'converting', or 'proselytizing'.

Importantly, all analogical definitions include a caution that it is not necessary for all of the indicia to be satisfied before a given set of beliefs and practices will be recognised. In the *Scientology Case*, Wilson and Deane JJ considered that: 'No one of the above indicia is necessarily determinative of the question whether a particular collection of ideas and/or practices should be objectively characterised as "a religion". They are no more than aids in determining that question and the assistance derived from them will vary according to the context in which the question arises.'[105] In *Meyers*, Brimmer J emphasised that 'no one of these factors is dispositive'.[106]

V. Application in Australia

Australian courts have had relatively few opportunities to apply and further develop the definitions from the *Scientology Case*. Only two cases have applied the *Scientology Case*'s definition: *RSSB Australia Pty Ltd v Ross*[107] and *Watkins v Commissioner for Corporate Affairs*.[108]

RSSB Australia Pty Ltd v Ross concerned an application for a permit to build a place of worship. Frankston City Council initially approved the permit, but this decision was later overturned by the Victorian Civil and Administrative Tribunal on the basis that Radha Soami Satsang Beas (RSSB) was not a religion and therefore the building it proposed was a place of assembly rather than a place of worship. As such, it did not fall within the requirements of the relevant Planning Scheme.[109] In coming to this conclusion, the Tribunal relied upon the Supreme Court of Victoria decision finding that Scientology was not a religion.[110] Given that this decision was later overturned by the High Court, Emerton J found that the Tribunal had erred in law in applying a much more restrictive definition of religion than required by the High Court.[111]

RSSB faced many of the same challenges as Scientology in terms of being recognised as a religion. RSSB did not have:

> '[U]nique sacred texts or a or set of values and belief systems regarding the person and divinity of god, and man's relationship to god' and/or engage in the persuasion of members and potential members that its set of ideas represents 'the true faith' or true answers to questions of ultimate concern.[112]

On its webpage, RSSB describes itself as 'a philosophical organisation' where attendees practise 'spiritual and meditation in addition to their religious backgrounds and beliefs, which could be varied'.[113]

Similarly, Scientology does not make exclusive claims over its adherents and historically describes itself as 'non-religious'.[114] Judge Emerton ultimately concluded that RSSB met both the definition proposed by Mason AJ and Brennan J and that proposed by

[105] *Scientology Case* (n 6) 174.
[106] *Meyers* (n 52) 1503.
[107] *RSSB Australia Pty Ltd v Ross* (2017) 224 LGERA 224.
[108] *Watkins v Commissioner for Corporate Affairs* [2021] SACAT 10 (4 January 2021).
[109] ibid 226.
[110] *Church of the New Faith v Commissioner for Pay-roll Tax* (n 18).
[111] *RSSB Australia Pty Ltd v Ross* (n 107) 230–31.
[112] ibid 231; see also 228–29.
[113] ibid 227.
[114] Barker (n 13) 276–78.

Deane and Wilson JJ.[115] Presumably, given that Murphy J's definition is the widest of the three, the beliefs and practices of RSSN would also satisfy that definition.

Watkins v Commissioner for Corporate Affairs concerned an application by the Church of the Flying Spaghetti Monster Australia (CFSMA) for incorporation pursuant to the *Associations Incorporation Act 1985* (SA).[116] The Commission of Corporate Affairs (hereinafter 'the Commission') rejected the CFSMA's application as an entity formed 'for a religious, educational, charitable or benevolent purpose' on the basis that it did not meet the eligibility criteria.[117] Central to the South Austrian Civil and Administrative Tribunal's review of the Commission's decision was whether the CFSMA was formed for a religious purpose.[118]

The Tribunal combined the reasoning of Mason ACJ and Brennan, Wilson and Deanne JJ from the *Scientology Case*, noting that the High Court had 'identified multiple indicia for determining if a set of beliefs constituted a religion', namely:

> [A] belief in a supernatural being, thing or principle, and an acceptance of canons of conduct in order to give effect to that belief … that the ideas must relate to humanity's nature and place in the universe and its relation to things supernatural; that adherents constitute an identifiable group or groups, however loose; and that the adherents themselves must see the collection of ideas and practices as constituting a religion.[119]

In concluding that the CFSMA was not formed for a religious purpose, the Tribunal focused on the distinction between a true religion and a sham or parody.[120] In particular, McEvoy SM drew attention to the purported religious texts of the CFSMA: *The Gospel of the Flying Spaghetti Monster* and *The Loose Canon: A Holy Book of the Church of the Flying Spaghetti Monster*.[121] These texts parody religious texts and rituals of other faiths[122] in what the applicant claimed was 'humour, for the purpose of generating curiosity'.[123] However, the Tribunal distinguished these texts from other religious texts, determining that they can 'only be read as parody or satire'.[124]

While the decision in *Watkins v Commissioner for Corporate Affairs* did not refer specifically to Murphy J's definition in the *Scientology Case*, Murphy J's more expansive approach was tacitly rejected by the Tribunal in its assertion that 'subjective belief does

[115] *RSSB Australia Pty Ltd v Ross* (n 107) 231. Justice Emerton also found that the tribunal had erred in focusing on whether or not RSSD was a religion rather than the proposed use of the building in determining whether or not it was a place of worship (at 231–32). She concluded that the building was a place of worship for the purposes of the relevant Planning Scheme. In coming to that conclusion, Emerton J commented that 'the applicant submitted that in determining whether the development is to be used as a "place of worship", a liberal approach to interpretation must be favoured over a narrow one, so as to respect standards of religious equality and tolerance in Australia. The Court should prefer a construction that permits persons to exercise their religion at the place where they wish over an interpretation or construction which prevents them from doing so. The common law supports the application of this interpretive approach to planning legislation. I accept this submission' (at 234).

[116] *Watkins v Commissioner for Corporate Affairs* (n 108) [2].

[117] ibid [50].

[118] ibid [51].

[119] ibid [56].

[120] ibid [57]–[70].

[121] ibid [54].

[122] In at times racist and sexist terms, see ibid [62].

[123] ibid [62].

[124] ibid [63].

not make the subject of the belief a religion for the purposes of the law in Australia'.[125] Instead, the Tribunal asserted that there are objective considerations which must be taken into account – namely, the indicia obtained by combining the judgments of Mason ACJ and Brennan, Wilson and Deanne JJ. While the CFSMA may have met the indicia taken from Mason ACJ and Brennan J's judgment, they did not have the requisite religious motivation and 'understanding that the beliefs or ideas relate to and help define humanity's nature and place in the universe and to things supernatural'.[126]

There have been a small number of other cases where the court has applied the definitions from the *Scientology Case* more briefly or in an indirect way. For example, the court has referred to the *Scientology Case* to confirm that 'religion' has a broad meaning for the purposes of Australian law,[127] that religious belief includes manifestation of that belief[128] and that the term 'religion' does not include 'no religion'.[129] There are also a number of cases which apply the definitions from the *Scientology Case* in a perfunctory way to confirm that Scientology is a religion for the purposes of law in Australia.[130] In *Lebanese Moslem Association v Minister for Immigration & Ethnic Affairs*, the court briefly referenced the *Scientology Case*, confirming that 'there can be no doubt that the ancient religion of Islam, with its close affinity with Judeo-Christin religion, is within the guarantee' of section 116 of the *Australian Constitution*.[131]

In *Federal Commissioner of Taxation v Word Investments Ltd*, the breadth of the term religious for the purposes of defining both 'charitable institution' and 'religious institution' in the context of sections 50–50(a) of the *Income Tax Assessment Act 1997* (Cth) was considered.[132] Kirby J found that the definition of religion was wide and would encompass not only 'Christian institutions that generally propound doctrines familiar to the courts', but also '[i]n a society such as Australia, the characterisation would have to extend to a very large range of "religious" beliefs'.[133] However, he was not prepared to include within the exemptions afforded by sections 50–50(a) 'investment and commercial business activities that are somehow linked with such institutions'.[134] In his view, 'if the expansion of the exemption to a company such as Word is to be sanctioned by law, it should be done by express legislation enacted for that purpose by the Parliament after a full debate about the issues of principle and policy that are raised'.[135] The majority[136]

[125] ibid [64].
[126] ibid [65].
[127] *Lebanese Moslem Association v Minister for Immigration & Ethnic Affairs* (1986) 11 FCR 543, 556; *North Coast Environment Council Inc v Minister for Resources* (1994) 55 FCR 492, 509–10.
[128] *Christian Youth Camps Ltd v Cobaw Community Health Services Ltd* (2014) 50 VR 256, 391–92, 403–04; *Minister for Immigration and Multicultural Affairs v Darboy* (1998) 52 ALD 44, 50–51.
[129] *Dixon v Anti-Discrimination Commissioner of Queensland* [2005] 1 Qld R 33 [19]. However, Douglas J went on to confirm that 'the question whether there has been discrimination against an atheist, for example, on the basis of religion is not, in my view, answered simply by the assertion that the attribute of religion does not include an absence of religion. What one must focus on principally is whether there has been discrimination either direct or indirect on the basis of that attribute'.
[130] *Hanna v Commissioner Community and Health Services Complaints Australian Capital Territory* (2002) 171 FLR 185 [11]; *NAVZ v Minister for Immigration and Multicultural and Indigenous Affairs* [2005] FCA 13 [50]; *Church of Scientology v Transmedia Productions Pty Ltd* (1987) Aust Torts Reports 80–101.
[131] *Lebanese Moslem Association v Minister for Immigration & Ethnic Affairs* (1986) 11 FCR 543, 556.
[132] *Federal Commissioner of Taxation v Word Investments Ltd* (2008) 236 CLR 204, 251–53.
[133] ibid 252.
[134] ibid.
[135] ibid 253.
[136] ibid (Gummow, Hayne, Heydon and Crennan JJ).

had no such difficulty finding that Word fell within the exemptions in sections 50–50(a) of the *Income Tax Assessment Act 1997* (Cth).[137]

In *Western Australia v Ward and Others*, Kirby J again made use of the *Scientology Case*, this time to consider the possibility that Indigenous Spirituality is covered by the definition of religion outlined in the *Scientology Case* and would therefore be protected by section 116.[138] He referred to comments by Murphy J that '[t]he Aboriginal religion of Australia and of other countries must be included'.[139] However, section 116 of the *Australian Constitution* had not been specifically argued in that case and Kirby J acknowledged his contention that it may apply to the *Native Title Act 1993* (Cth) via Indigenous Spirituality's inclusion in the definition of 'religion' to be purely speculative:[140]

> One thing is certain – the section speaks to all Australians and of all religions. It is not restricted to settlers, their descendants and successors, nor to the Christian or other organised institutional religions. It may be necessary in the future to consider s 116 of the Constitution in this context. At the least, it could influence the construction of the NTA so far as to avoid the possibility of invalidity by reason of s 116.[141]

Finally, there are a small number of cases where the *Scientology Case* has been referred to, usually by one of the parties, but where its inclusion is not entirely helpful.[142] In *Commonwealth Director of Public Prosecutions v Easton*, there is extensive reference to the case; however, far from illuminating matters, the use of the case by the Magistrate at first instance seems only to have confused the issues. The case concerned a failure to vote at an election on 2 July 2016 contrary to section 245(15) of the *Commonwealth Electoral Act 1918* (Cth).[143] At first instance, the Magistrate referred to the definition of religion in both the *Scientology Case* and the *Macquarie Dictionary* before concluding that:

> I am satisfied that his evidence shows an honestly held belief, a moral code that requires him not to vote. To vote would be to breach a truly held conscientious life viewpoint. Thus, the defendant in this case has a devout (but not religious) objection to voting. It would be simply nonsensical that were his deeply held moral objection subjectively connected to a recognised religion or a belief in god, that this would, of itself, be a valid and sufficient reason, but that a conscious agnostic well-developed moral faith as described by the defendant would not. The provision allows for a form of conscientious objection in my view, and that is what has been evidenced here.[144]

This led to some confusion on appeal and a lengthy discussion of the *Scientology Case* by Adams J,[145] who concluded that: 'Despite the reference to *Church of the New Faith* in

[137] The *Scientology Case* was also referred to for the purposes of defining 'religious institution' in *Pamas Foundation (Inc) v Deputy Federal Commissioner of Taxation* (1992) 35 FCR 117, 119 and *ACT Revenue Collections Commissioner v Council of the Dominican Sisters of Australia* (1991) 101 ALR 417, 424.

[138] *Western Australia v Ward and Others* (2002) 213 CLR 1.

[139] *Scientology Case* (n 6) 151.

[140] ibid.

[141] ibid.

[142] *Grace Bible Church v Reedman* [1984] 36 SASR 376, 380; *OV and OW v Members of the Board of Wesley Mission Council* (2010) 79 NSWLR 606, 611.

[143] *Commonwealth Director of Public Prosecutions v Easton* [2018] NSWSC 1516 [1]–[2].

[144] ibid [29].

[145] ibid [101]–[107].

his judgment, I am not satisfied his honour's reasons disclose that he actually found that Mr Easton believed it was his "religious duty" to abstain from voting nor that his belief system was a form of religion.'[146]

The relative paucity of cases applying the definition of religion is perhaps unsurprising, given Australia's religious demographic. In the 2016 census, 52.1 per cent of the population self-identified as Christian, while another 30.1 per cent identified as having no religion.[147] The remaining 17.8 per cent were split between those who did not answer the question (9.6 per cent) and other minority religions (8.2 per cent). It could therefore be expected that cases where the religiosity of a given set of beliefs or practices is in question will come from just 8.2 per cent of the population. This is of course a massive overestimation, as the vast majority of that 8.2 per cent comprises faiths that are already well recognised: Islam (2.6 per cent), Judaism (0.4 per cent), Hinduism (1.9 per cent) and Sikhism (0.5 per cent).[148] Even Buddhism (2.4 per cent),[149] a faith which arguably has some difficulties in meeting the traditional definitions of religion because of its non-theistic nature, has clearly been recognised for legal purposes as a religion.[150] The breadth of even the narrowest of the three definitions propounded by the High Court leave little scope for the exclusion of the vast majority of religions operating in Australia from the legal definition. It is therefore only those rare cases of new, novel or unpopular religion – those which challenge our understanding of religion or which our culture is predisposed to reject – in which the legal question will arise.[151]

VI. A World Leading Definition of Religion

As Pauline Ridge suggests, 'given the relative infrequency with which the issue comes before the courts, such definitions are inevitably influential outside their specific legal context'.[152] Ridge notes the impact of the American decision in *Malnak v Yogi*, which was referred to in both the *Scientology Case* and the UK case of *Hodkin*.[153] The *Scientology Case* itself drew upon decisions from both the UK[154] and the US.[155] It has in turn been

[146] ibid [106].

[147] Australian Bureau of Statistics, 'Census of Population and Housing: Reflecting Australia – Stories from the Census, 2016: Religion in Australia 2016' (Catalogue No 2071.0, 28 June 2017).

[148] Australian Bureau of Statistics, '2016 Census Data Reveals "No Religion" is Rising Fast' (Media Release 074.2017, 27 June 2017).

[149] ibid.

[150] See, eg, *Scientology Case* (n 6) 140.

[151] Barker (n 13) 276–78. See also the comments by Deputy Leader of the Opposition Queensland, Lawrence Springborg, during the debate to repeal anti-witchcraft laws: Queensland, *Parliamentary Debates*, Legislative Assembly, 10 November 2000, 4323 (Lawrence Springborg). See also Commonwealth of Australia, *Parliamentary Debates*, Senate, 13 March 1973, 351 (Edgar Prowse).

[152] Ridge (n 55) 292.

[153] ibid 292, fn 48.

[154] *Barralet v Attorney-General* (n 91); *R v Registrar-General ex parte Segerdal* (n 94).

[155] *Cantwell v Connecticut*, 310 US 296 (1940); *Davis v Beason*, 133 US 333 (1890); *Fellowship of Humanity v County of Alameda*, 315 P 2d 394 (Cal Dist Ct App 1957); *Gillette v United States*, 401 US 437 (1971); *Late Corp of the Church of Jesus Christ of Latter-Day Saints v United States*, 136 US 1 (1890); *Malnak v Yogi* (n 39); *Reynolds v United States*, 98 US 145 (1878); *Torcaso v Watkins*, 367 US 488 (1961); *United States v Ballard*, 322 US 78 (1944); *United States v Kauten*, 133 F 2d 703 (2d Cir 1943); *United States v Kuch*, 288 F Supp 439 (DDC 1968); *Seeger* (n 87); *Washington Ethical Society v District of Columbia*, 249 F 2d 127 (DC Cir 1957); *Watson v Jones*, 80 US 679 (1872); *Welsh* (n 88).

incredibly influential outside the specific legal context of exemptions to the Victorian *Pay-roll Tax Act 1971* (Vic).[156] The case has been cited by courts in the UK,[157] New Zealand,[158] Hong Kong,[159] Canada,[160] Northern Ireland,[161] Tuvalu[162] and Samoa.[163]

In 1985, just two years after the decision in the *Scientology Case*, the High Court of New Zealand applied its definitions in *Centrepoint Community Growth Trust v Commissioner of Inland Revenue* (hereinafter '*Centrepoint*').[164] In *Centrepoint*, the Court was asked to consider whether Centrepoint Community Growth Trust was a religion for the purposes of the exemption from conveyance duty pursuant to the *Cheque Duty Act 1971* (NZ).[165] Tompkin J was unaware of any New Zealand authority on the meaning of religion.[166] He canvassed a number of definitions from UK cases[167] before, as he put it, coming 'to what is, with respect, the particularly helpful judgment of the High Court of Australia'.[168] After outlining all three of the definitions from the *Scientology Case*, Tompkin J accepted 'the tests to which I have referred from the judgments of the High Court in the *Church of the New Faith* case – and for the reasons that are to me so persuasively set out in those judgments'.[169] He also made reference to expert evidence from Rev Dr Armstrong, a senior lecturer in systematic theology at the College of St John the Evangelist.[170] Justice Tompkin's considered the definition proposed by Rev Dr Armstrong to 'accord closely with the opinion of the High Court expressed in the judgment in the *Church of the New Faith* case'.[171] As Tompkin J noted, Rev Dr Armstrong had referred to the *Scientology Case* as 'a first class theological essay'.[172]

While Tompkin J did not formally express a preference for any one of the three definitions outlined in the *Scientology Case*, his analysis suggests a preference for Wilson and Deane JJ's approach. Justice Tompkin outlined a series of facts about the beliefs and

[156] Although as with references to the case in Australia, not all of these have been in relation to the definition of religion.

[157] *R v Secretary of State for Education and Employment ex parte Williamson* [2005] 2 AC 246; *Hodkin* (n 61); *United Grand Lodge of England v Revenue & Customs* [2014] UKFTT 164 (TC); *Re M (Children)* [2018] 4 WLR 60.

[158] *Centrepoint* (n 85) 673; *Re IC* [1999] NZFLR 471; Charities Registration Board of New Zealand, *Registration Decision: Jedi Society Incorporated (JED49458)* (Decision No 2015–2, 14 September 2015) (hereinafter '*Registration Decision: Jedi Society Incorporated*').

[159] *Chu Woan Chyi v Director of Immigration* [2007] HKCFI 267.

[160] *Bennett v Attorney-General for Canada and the Minister for Health for Canada* [2011] FC 1310.

[161] *Parsons, Re Application for Judicial Review* [2003] NICA 20 (6 June 2003, unreported).

[162] *Teonea v Pule o Kaupule of Nanumaga* [2009] TVCA 2; Court of Appeal Civil Appeal No 1 of 2005 (4 November 2009, unreported).

[163] *Lafaialii v Attorney-General* [2003] WSSC 8 (24 April 2003, unreported); *Sef v Lands and Titles Court* [2000] WSSC 46 (12 July 2000, unreported).

[164] *Centrepoint* (n 85).

[165] ibid 676–77.

[166] ibid 691.

[167] ibid 691–93; see *Keeren Kayemeth Le Jisroel Ltd v Inland Revenue Commissioners* [1931] 2 KB 465, 477; *United Grand Lodge of Ancient Free and Accepted Masons of England v Holborn Borough Council* [1957] 1 WLR 1080, 1090; *Thornton v Howe* (1862) 31 Beav 14, 19–20; *Re Watson* [1973] 3 All ER 678, 688; *Barralet v Attorney-General* (n 91) 924. Tompkins J also made brief reference to *Seeger* (n 87).

[168] *Centrepoint* (n 85) 693.

[169] ibid 695.

[170] ibid 696–97.

[171] ibid 697.

[172] ibid.

practices of Centrepoint as if applying a set of indicia. As the table below demonstrates his analysis echoes the language employed by Wilson and Deane JJ.[173]

Table 2.1 Comparison of Tompkin J's and Wilson and Deane JJ's criteria for religion

Tompkin J[174]	Wilson and Deane JJ[175]
The members of the trust ... have a belief in the supernatural ...	the particular collection of ideas and/or practices involves belief in the supernatural, that is to say, belief that reality extends beyond that which is capable of perception by the senses.
Included in those beliefs are concepts that relate not only to man's relationship to man but also to man's relationship to the supernatural ...	the ideas relate to man's nature and place in the universe and his relation to things supernatural.
The standard and codes of conduct that members expect to be observed involve not only the ceremonies and rites to which I have referred, but also the acceptance of total honesty in their relationships with each other and their commitment to Mr Potter and his teachings.	the ideas are accepted by adherents as requiring or encouraging them to observe particular standards or codes of conduct or to participate in specific practices having supernatural significance.
The members of the trust have an identification as a group.	however loosely knit and varying in beliefs and practices adherents may be, they constitute an identifiable group or identifiable groups.
the adherents to the principles, beliefs and objectives of the trust consider that they constitute a religion.	the adherents themselves see the collection of ideas and/or practices as constituting a religion.

Justice Tompkin ultimately concluded that 'the trust, both in its formal constitution and in the beliefs and practices of its adherents, has as one of its principal purposes the advancement of religion'.[176]

New Zealand courts and tribunals have applied the *Scientology Case* and *Centrepoint* on two further occasions.[177] In *Re IC*, the Mental Health Review Tribunal Southern Region quoted extensively from the judgment of Mason ACJ and Brennan J,[178] as well as quoting the definitions from the judgments of both Murphy J[179] and Wilson and Deane JJ.[180] The Tribunal also made reference to the definition of religion outlined by

[173] He also made specific reference to the fifth indicia of Wilson and Deane JJ.
[174] *Centrepoint* (n 85) 698.
[175] *Scientology Case* (n 6) 174.
[176] *Centrepoint* (n 85) 698.
[177] The New Zealand High Court also cited the *Scientology Case* in *Liberty Trust v Charities Commission* [2011] NZHC 68, 84 [58], fn 35, 91 [90], fn 55, 93 [97], fn 64.
[178] *Re IC* (n 158) 473–75.
[179] ibid 475–76.
[180] ibid 476–77.

Professor Ninian Smart[181] in his book *The World's Religions: Old Traditions and Modern Transformations*.[182] Smart outlines seven indicia of religion:

1) the practical and ritual dimension;
2) the experiential and emotional dimension;
3) the narrative and mythical dimension;
4) the doctrinal and philosophical dimension;
5) the ethical and legal dimension
6) the social and institutional dimension;
7) the material dimension.[183]

Before applying these seven indicia, the Tribunal stated that: 'These indicia set out by a leading professor of world religions do not vary in any material way from the indicia set out by the Australian High Court and followed by Tompkins J.'[184] It concluded that IC's beliefs did not fulfil any of the seven indicia and that they did not consider 'Mr IC's continuing preoccupation with his victim as constituting a religious belief'.[185]

In *Registration Decision: The Jedi Society Incorporated*, the New Zealand Charities Registration Board found that the Jedi Society Incorporated was not a religion for the purposes of registration as a charity under the *Charities Act 2005* (NZ).[186] The Board referred to both *Centrepoint* and the *Scientology Case*, the more recent UK case of *Hodkin*,[187] and decisions of the Charities Commission of England and Wales.[188] Unlike the earlier New Zealand decisions, the Board only made specific reference to the definition propounded by Mason ACJ and Brennan J. The Board was of the opinion that the definition from *Hodkin* was 'a useful modern reading of *Church of the New Faith* and confirms that this case is still current in terms of the law's definition of religion'.[189] Ultimately, the Board applied its own definition of religion, which appears to have been derived from combining definitions from decisions of the Charities Commission of England and Wales[190] with that from Mason ACJ and Brennan J.[191] The Board considered the following characteristics as demonstrating a religion:

A body of doctrines that:

- Concerns the place of humankind in the universe and its relationship with the infinite;
- Goes beyond that which can be perceived by the sense or ascertained through scientific method; and
- Contains canons of conduct around which adherents are to structure their lives

[181] In the judgment, Professor Smart is referred to as Professor Lilian Smart, JF Rowny Professor of Comparative Religions at the University of California and Professor Emeritus of Religious Studies, University of Lancaster, England.

[182] *Re IC* (n 158) 477.

[183] ibid.

[184] ibid 478.

[185] ibid.

[186] *Registration Decision: Jedi Society Incorporated* (n 158) [40].

[187] *Hodkin* (n 61).

[188] See Charity Commission for England and Wales, *Application for Registration of the Gnostic Centre* (16 December 2009).

[189] *Registration Decision: Jedi Society Incorporated* (n 158) [28].

[190] The Charity Commission for England and Wales rejected an application for registration as a charity by the Temple of the Jedi Order in 201. See Charity Commission for England and Wales, *The Temple of the Jedi Order – Application for Registration* (16 December 2016).

[191] For the definition of charity applied by the Charity Commission of England and Wales, see Ridge (n 55) 296–98.

> The doctrines and canons of conduct must also be sufficiently structured, cogent and serious so as to be capable of advancing religion.[192]

While the Board found that the Jedi Society Incorporated fulfilled the three criteria relating to a body of doctrines, it did 'not consider the doctrines and canons of conduct [to be] sufficiently structured, cogent and serious to advance religion in law'.[193] It found that 'the belief system is merely a collection of interconnected ideas based on the *Star Wars* universe, rather than structured, cogent and serious religion'.[194] However, it left the door open for the Jedi Society Incorporated to re-apply in the future, commenting 'in time … Jediism may develop the level of seriousness and structure necessary to advance religion'.[195]

The *Scientology Case* has also been directly applied by the High Court of Hong Kong in *Chu Woan Chyi and Other v Director of Immigration* in relation to the 'spiritual movement of Falun Dafa, commonly known as Falun Gong'.[196] In defining a religion, Hartmann J held that 'a religion … needs to be something more than a set of shared ethical beliefs. But it does not … certainly not in the Asian context, demand a belief in the existence of God or any intelligent first cause'.[197]

Hartmann J then adopted the definition outlined by Wilson and Deane JJ in the *Scientology Case*. In applying the indicia, he found that Falun Gong 'form an identifiable group, do accept a reality of the spirit that extends beyond the perceptions of our physical sense … acknowledge the supernatural … They seek to place themselves in harmony with this reality … they bind themselves to a code of ethical and moral behaviour which is integral to their spiritual aspirations'.[198] As such, he was 'satisfied that, under the Basic Law … the Falun Gong movement is to be recognised as a religious movement, its beliefs being religious beliefs'.[199] The only Wilson and Deane JJ indicia that Falon Gong was unable to satisfy was that 'the adherents themselves see the collection of ideas and/or practices as constituting a religion'.[200] Justice Hartman did not feel that this was detrimental to Falon Gong's case, as in his view: 'The real question is whether, however it wishes to see itself in comparative terms, it is, by reason of its belief structure, entitled to be recognised as a religion under the Basic Law'.[201]

Most recently, the UK Supreme Court considered the *Scientology Case* in *R (Hodkin and Another) v Registrar General of Births, Deaths and Marriages*.[202] Unlike the New Zealand and Hong Kong decisions, Lord Toulson formulated his own definition of religion. After surveying the definitions from the *Scientology Case* and *Malnak v Yogi*, he concluded that religion is:

> [A] spiritual or non-secular belief system held by a group of adherents, which claims to explain mankind's place in the universe and relationship with the infinite, and to teach its adherents how they are to live their lives in conformity with the spiritual understanding associated with the belief system.[203]

[192] *Registration Decision: Jedi Society Incorporated* (n 158) [29].
[193] ibid [31].
[194] ibid [40].
[195] ibid [41].
[196] *Chu Woan Chyi and Other v Director of Immigration* [2007] HKCFI 267 [1].
[197] ibid [55].
[198] ibid [57].
[199] ibid.
[200] ibid [52], [58]; *Scientology Case* (n 6) 174.
[201] *Chu Woan Chyi and Other v Director of Immigration* (n 196) [58].
[202] *Hodkin* (n 61).
[203] ibid 752.

In doing so, because both imported a theistic element, Lord Toulson rejected the previous UK definitions of religion from *Barralet v Attorney-General*[204] and *R v Registrar-General ex parte Segerdal*.[205] He commented that:

> [R]eligion should not be confined to religions which recognise a supreme deity. First and foremost, to do so would be a form of religious discrimination unacceptable in today's society. It would exclude Buddhism, along with other faiths such as Jainism, Taoism, Theosophy and part of Hinduism.[206]

Lord Toulson concluded that '[o]f the various attempts made to describe the characteristics of religion, [the] most helpful [is] that of Wilson and Deane JJ',[207] although he rejected their use of the term supernatural 'because it is a loaded word which can carry a variety of connotations'.[208]

VII. Conclusion

The Australian legal definitions of religion found in the *Scientology Case* have been criticised on a number of grounds. Ian Ellis-Jones criticised the *Scientology Case* for failing to provide clear dicta which can be easily applied by decision makers in both judicial and administrative roles. Similarly, Lord Toulson in *R v Registrar General of Births, Deaths and Marriages* felt the use of the word 'supernatural' was no longer appropriate. Yet, despite these critiques, the case continues to be referred to by both Australian and foreign courts. Unlike its UK and US counterparts, the Australian judiciary has not been tempted to develop myriad definitions of religion to suit different situations. Instead, the *Scientology Case* has stood as the single repository for Australia's legal definition of religion. While the existence of three separate definitions has the potential to cause confusion, this has not been the experience in practice. Courts which have sought to apply the definitions from the *Scientology Case* have generally found the religion under consideration to fall within all three definitions. Should the High Court of Australia have the opportunity to reconsider the legal definition of religion, it, too, like Lord Toulson, may reject the continued use of the term 'supernatural'.

[204] *Barralet v Attorney-General* (n 91) 924.
[205] *R v Registrar-General ex parte Segerdal* (n 94).
[206] *Hodkin* (n 61) 751.
[207] ibid 752.
[208] ibid.

3

Titular Roman Catholic Archbishop of Kuala Lumpur v Home Minister

What is the Name of God?

JOSHUA NEOH

The name of God is sacred. Although God is capitalised, God is not actually God's name. God is a common noun. If God has a name, that name would be a proper noun. In Judaism, God has a name that must not be pronounced. Where the Jewish tradition has the Tetragrammaton, the Christian tradition has the Trinitarian formula: In the Name of the Father, and of the Son, and of the Holy Spirit. Again, Father, Son and Spirit are common nouns, not proper nouns. In the Islamic tradition, insofar as Allah is simply the Arabic word for God, Allah too is a common noun, not a proper noun. But that is not so in Malaysia, after the case of the *Titular Roman Catholic Archbishop of Kuala Lumpur v Home Minister*. The Court of Appeal in that case has done what generations of prophets have not dared to do: to name God, that is, to give God a proper name. In Malaysia, the Islamic God has a proper name and that God's name is Allah. As Allah is the name of the Islamic God, no one else but Muslims can use that name to refer to God. Even if one disagrees with the court's judgment, one nonetheless has to admire its chutzpah.

This chapter will begin by setting out the facts of the case (section I) and the legal reasoning in the judgments of the High Court, the Court of Appeal and the Federal Court (section II). Section III will point out the hodgepodge of legal errors in the Court of Appeal's judgment. Section IV will focus on one particularly audacious proclamation in the judgment: the Court's attempt to name God. Section III will address the legal errors, while section IV will address the theological-philosophical errors. When the secular judiciary intervenes in matters of religion, there is necessarily a degree of presumptuousness, for what do secular judges know about divine law? The job of human judges is to judge human law, not God's law. Even accepting a degree of presumptuousness that is necessarily present in such cases, the Court of Appeal judgment has surpassed even that. The Court of Appeal in this case claims to know the name of God or, more audacious still, to name God. This chapter argues that the name that the Court of Appeal has purportedly given to God is not only wrong in law, but also wrong in fact.

I. The Facts

Politically, Malaysia has adopted the Westminster system of parliamentary democracy, in common with most Commonwealth countries. Legally, Malaysia is a common law jurisdiction, again in common with most Commonwealth countries.[1] Demographically, Malaysia is a Muslim majority country. Roman Catholics are a religious minority in the country. The Catholic Church publishes a weekly newsletter called the *Herald* in various languages, including in Malay, which is the national language in Malaysia. In the Malay-language edition of the publication, the *Herald* uses the term 'Allah' as the Malay translation for the word 'God'. This translation is consistent with the translation used in the Malay-language Bible, which goes as far back as 1629 when the first printed edition of the Gospel of Matthew appeared in the Malay language.

The Roman Catholic Archbishop of Kuala Lumpur was granted a permit to publish the *Herald* by the Home Minister under the *Printing Presses and Publications Act 1984*. However, the Minister imposed a *condition* that the publication must not use the term 'Allah' to refer to God. It is this condition that was the subject of litigation in this case. The Archbishop filed for judicial review of this ministerial decision. In the Malaysian legal system, judicial review of executive action is carried out based on standard common law principles in administrative law. Most immediately, this case raises the administrative law question of whether the Minister has the power to impose that condition under the *Printing Presses and Publications Act 1984*.

Beyond administrative law, this case also raises constitutional law issues, as the Archbishop had argued that the condition infringes, inter alia, the constitutional right of Roman Catholics to the freedom of religion. The key constitutional provisions that are directly relevant to this case are reproduced below for ease of reference:

> Article 3
>
> 3(1): Islam is the religion of the Federation; but other religions may be practised in peace and harmony in any part of the Federation.
>
> …
>
> 3(4): Nothing in this Article derogates from any other provision of this Constitution.
>
> Article 11
>
> 11(1): Every person has the right to profess and practise his religion and, subject to Clause (4), to propagate it.
>
> …
>
> 11(4): State law and in respect of the Federal Territories of Kuala Lumpur, Labuan and Putrajaya, federal law may control or restrict the propagation of any religious doctrine or belief among persons professing the religion of Islam.
>
> 11(5): This Article does not authorize any act contrary to any general law relating to public order, public health or morality.

As a matter of administrative law, the Archbishop's argument was that the Minister did not have the power to impose the impugned condition under the *Printing Presses and Publications Act 1984*. As a matter of constitutional law, the Archbishop's argument was

[1] On the history of the common law in Malaysia, see J Neoh, 'Legitimacy of the Common Law in Post-colonial Malaysia' [2010] *LAWASIA: Journal of the Law Association for Asia and the Pacific* 59.

that the impugned condition infringes the constitutional right to the freedom of religion that is protected under Article 11(1) of the Constitution. If either of these arguments was correct, then the condition would be null and void, either as a matter of administrative law or as a matter of constitutional law. The impugned condition, which is attached to the publication permit, is that the Catholic Church cannot use the word 'Allah' as the Malay-language translation for the word 'God' in its newsletter.

II. The Judgments

The judicial review application was filed at the High Court. The matter was heard at the High Court by a single judge, who ruled in favour of the Archbishop. The government appealed. The matter was then heard at the Court of Appeal by a panel of three judges, who ruled in favour of the government. The Archbishop appealed. The application for leave to appeal was heard at the Federal Court, which is the apex court in Malaysia. The application for leave to appeal was heard before a panel of seven judges, and by a 4:3 majority, the Federal Court denied leave to appeal, and the matter ended there. As the application for leave to appeal was denied, the Court of Appeal's judgment, which ruled in favour of the government, became the binding judgment.

As the Court of Appeal's judgment is the binding judgment, it will be focus of this chapter's analysis. However, for the sake of completeness, the following sections will briefly summarise the High Court's judgment (as a *prelude* to the Court of Appeal's judgment) and the Federal Court's judgment (as a *postscript* to the Court of Appeal's judgment). The High Court was overruled by the Court of Appeal. With the High Court and the Court of Appeal, we have two contrasting judgments, one in favour of the Archbishop and the other in favour of the government. The Federal Court denied leave to appeal by a 4:3 majority. With the Federal Court's split bench, we have also two contrasting positions, one refusing to grant leave to appeal and the other allowing leave to appeal.

A. Prelude: The High Court

The matter was first heard at the High Court in Kuala Lumpur before Lau J, who found the impugned condition to be illegal (under administrative law) and unconstitutional (under constitutional law). On the administrative law front, Lau J ruled that the decision maker committed numerous legal errors, including the failure to take into account relevant considerations, such as the fact that 'for 15 centuries, Christians and Muslims in Arabic-speaking countries have been using the word "Allah" in reference to the One God', the fact that 'the word "Allah" has been used continuously in the printed edition of the Matthew's Gospel in Malay in 1629, in the first complete Malay Bible in 1733 and in the second complete Malay Bible in 1879', and the fact that 'Munshi Abdullah who is considered the father of modern Malay literature had translated the Gospels into Malay in 1852 and he translated the word "God" as "Allah"'.[2]

[2] *Titular Roman Catholic Archbishop of Kuala Lumpur v Home Minister* (High Court in Malaya, Lau Bee Lan J, 31 December 2009) [12].

On the constitutional law front, Lau J ruled that the impugned condition contravened, inter alia, the freedom of religion provision in Article 11(1) of the Constitution. Lau J found that 'the use of the word "Allah" is an essential part of the worship and instruction in the faith of the Malay-speaking community of the Catholic Church in Malaysia'.[3] Although Article 11(4) does permit the government to 'control or restrict the propagation of any religious doctrine or belief among persons professing the religion of Islam', that permission is narrowly circumscribed. It only allows for restrictions to be imposed on propagation – specifically on propagation to Muslims. Therefore, propagation can be restricted, but the right to profess and practise one's religion cannot. In fact, that distinction is made explicit in the express terms of Article 11(1), which states that: 'Every person has the right to profess and practise his religion and, subject to Clause (4), to propagate it.' Clause (4) can only be used to restrict propagation. It cannot be used to restrict the profession and practice of a religion. Construing the right broadly and the restriction strictly, the state cannot ban the use of the word 'Allah' if it is used in the course of the profession of a religion, although the state may be able to ban it if it is used in the course of the propagation of a non-Islamic religion to Muslims. In this case, the use of the word 'Allah' is for internal worship and instruction *within* the Catholic Church, and not for propagation. That being the case, Article 11(4) cannot be relied upon to restrict the right under Article 11(1).[4]

Article 11(5) states that the freedom of religion protection under Article 11 'does not authorize any act contrary to any general law relating to public order, public health or morality'. The Home Minister sought to rely on Article 11(5) to justify the impugned condition on 'public order' grounds. The Home Minister submitted that 'the use of the word "Allah" is a security issue which is causing much confusion and which threatens and endangers public order',[5] but the Home Minister provided no supporting evidence to back up this claim. Consequently, Lau J rejected this 'public order' submission, finding that 'a mere statement by the 1st Respondent [ie, the Home Minister] that the exercise of power was necessary on the ground of national security without adequate supporting evidence is not sufficient in law'.[6] Lau J further took judicial notice of the fact that 'in other Muslim countries even in the Middle East where the Muslim and the Christian communities together use the word "Allah", one hardly hear of any confusion'.[7] In rejecting this submission, Lau J also warned that 'the Court has to consider the question of "avoidance of confusion" as a ground very cautiously so as to obviate a situation where a mere confusion of certain persons within a religious group can strip the constitutional right of another religious group', a right which is protected under Article 11(1).

B. The Three Judges at the Court of Appeal

The Home Minister appealed to the Court of Appeal. The matter was heard before a bench of three judges. The Court of Appeal overturned the High Court's judgment.

[3] ibid [15.5].
[4] ibid [18.4], [19.1].
[5] ibid [22.3].
[6] ibid.
[7] ibid [22.5].

All three judges at the Court of Appeal ruled in favour of the government. The three judges were Apandi JCA, Abdul Aziz JCA and Zawawi JCA.

It should be recalled that Article 3(1) states that 'Islam is the religion of the Federation; but other religions may be practised in peace and harmony in any part of the Federation'. Apandi JCA ruled that the first prong of Article 3 'places the religion of Islam at par with the other basic structures of the Constitution'.[8] This particular reading of the first prong of Article 3 bolsters his associated assertion that the insertion of the phrase 'in peace and harmony' in the second prong with regard to the practice of non-Islamic religions is meant 'to protect the sanctity of Islam as the religion of the country and also to insulate against … any possible and probable threat to the religion of Islam'.[9] Apandi JCA interpreted the phrase 'in peace and harmony' not as supporting the freedom of non-Muslims to practise their religion, but as a limitation on that freedom: that freedom is subject to the superiority of Islam in the Federation. Hence, if the government decides that the usage of the word 'Allah' by non-Muslims would constitute a possible and probable threat to Islam, it could impose the ban consistent with Article 3(1). The threat does not have to be actual, but only possible and probable, and the relevant threat here is to Islam as a religion, not to national security or public order. Even the freedom of religion guarantee under Article 11(1) is subject to the supposed superiority of Islam under Article 3(1). In the mind of Apandi JCA, Article 3 takes precedence over Article 11 for the simple and simplistic reason that Article 3 comes before Article 11. Article 3 is '3rd in the order of precedence of the Articles that were within the confines of Part I of the Constitution', while the fundamental liberties provisions, including the Article 11 provision for the freedom of religion, 'were grouped together subsequently under Part II of the Constitution',[10] so first come, first served.

Thereafter, the tone of the judgment switched from legal analysis to theological exposition. Apandi JCA claimed that 'to refuse to acknowledge the essential differences between religions will be an affront to the uniqueness of world religions[:] due recognition must be given to the names given to their respective Gods in their respective Holy books; such as "Yahweh" the God of the Holy Bible; "Allah" the God of the Holy al-Quran and "Vishnu" the God of the Holy Vedas'.[11] He deemed it appropriate and within his area of judicial competence to go around categorising and naming Gods, including the Gods of others. How did he know the name of God? Apparently he did some research of his own: 'For completeness, I note that from a quick research on the history of the language of the Bible, it is clear that the word "Allah" does not appear even once as the name of God or even of a man in the Hebrew Scriptures. The name "Allah" does not appear, even once in either the Old or New Testaments. There is no such word at all in the Greek New Testament.'[12]

The second judge on the bench of three, Abdul Aziz JCA, went a step further in theologising this matter. According to Aziz JCA, the name Allah 'is sacred to the Muslims

[8] *Home Minister v Titular Roman Catholic Archbishop of Kuala Lumpur* (Court of Appeal, Mohamed Apandi bin Ali JCA, 14 October 2013) [31].

[9] ibid [29].

[10] ibid [31].

[11] ibid [52].

[12] ibid [51].

and is placed on the highest position and its sanctity must be protected'. Allah 'refers to "oneness" and cannot be part of the concept of Trinity of Father, Son and the Holy Ghost of the Christian faith'; Allah is 'not just a mere word or translation of the word God as described in the Herald but it is a *special name* for the Muslim's God' (emphasis added).[13] Aziz JCA then returned to the recurrent theme of confusion: 'the use of the word "Allah" … to describe or refer to God among Christian[s] would create confusion among Muslims as the concept of God in Islam and in Christianity is world[s] apart – in the former it refers to the concept of oneness of God whereas in the latter it refers to the concept of Trinity of God'.[14]

The third judge, Zawawi JCA, extended the confusing logic of confusion further. According to him, if the word 'Allah' is to be employed by Christians, 'there will be a risk of misrepresentation of God within Christianity itself … in other words, the potential for confusion is not confined only to Muslims but also to Christians'.[15] It is difficult, for me at least, to understand what exactly is confusing here. Perhaps this 'potential for confusion' is akin to the following scenario: if I call my father 'Papa', and you call your father 'Papa', there is a risk that you will be confused that my Papa is your Papa, and your Papa is my Papa, or that we have the same Papa.[16] The state therefore has to protect not only Muslims, but also Christians from confusing their Gods. To prevent such confusion, Zawawi JCA had to step in to clear the air by proclaiming *ex cathedra* that 'Allah is not the God of the Bible; Allah is a *proper name* and the only God in Islam' (emphasis added).[17] How did he know the name of God? Apparently he, too, did some research of his own – on the internet. His judgment cited the following websites:

> See: http:/www.danielpipes.org/comments/185481
>
> See: http:/www.foxnews.com/story/0.2933, 293394,00.html
>
> See: http:/www.news.com.au/story/0.23599, 222540 – 13762,00.html
>
> See: answering – islam/org/Gilchrist/Vol 2/3B html.

C. Postscript: The Federal Court

After having won at the High Court but having lost at the Court of Appeal, the Archbishop filed for leave to appeal to the Federal Court, which is the apex court in the Malaysian judicial system. By a bare majority of 4:3, the Federal Court denied leave to appeal. The Archbishop posed a total of 28 leave questions under three categories: administrative law questions; constitutional law questions; and general questions.

The administrative law questions centred on the correct test that should be applied in a judicial review application concerning the exercise of ministerial discretion. Apandi JCA at the Court of Appeal claimed to have applied a test which he called 'subjectively objective'. As pointed out in the dissenting judgment by Zainun FCJ at the Federal Court,

[13] ibid (Court of Appeal, Abdul Aziz bin Abdul Rahim JCA, 14 October 2013) [92].

[14] ibid [36].

[15] ibid (Court of Appeal, Mohd Zawawi bin Salleh JCA, 14 October 2013) [28].

[16] See further J Neoh, 'The Name of God on Trial: Narratives of Law, Religion and State in Malaysia' (2014) 18 *Law Text Culture* 198, 215.

[17] *Home Minister v Titular Roman Catholic Archbishop of Kuala Lumpur* (Court of Appeal, Mohd Zawawi bin Salleh JCA, 14 October 2013) [26].

the idea of a 'subjective test' is 'old hat', while 'the term "subjectively objective" is paradoxical since they are two different concepts which negates one another'.[18] That then leaves only one correct test that should have been applied: the objective test. There is no such thing as a 'subjectively objective' test. The Court of Appeal has 'gone on a frolic of its own in applying this hybrid test'.[19] Zainun FCJ, dissenting, would have granted leave on this basis. The majority in the Federal Court affirmed the objective test as the correct test, but they refused to grant leave to appeal, as the majority claimed that although the Court of Appeal said it was applying the 'subjectively objective' test, it actually (perhaps even inadvertently) applied the correct test, ie, the objective test.[20] If that were the case, then it actually gives rise to a different problem, which was pointed out by Zainun FCJ in her dissent: 'the form and substance of the [Court of Appeal] judgment do not add up'.[21] The Court of Appeal said it was doing one thing, but it was actually doing another.

One of the key constitutional law questions that were posed by the Archbishop in the leave application concerned the correct interpretation of Article 3 of the Constitution. The Court of Appeal held that Article 3 of the Constitution, which makes Islam the religion of the Federation, takes precedence over the fundamental liberties provisions. The majority at the Federal Court denied leave to appeal these constitutional law questions on some technical procedural grounds, which were themselves open to question, but I shall wade into this particular procedural controversy in this chapter.[22] Dissenting, Malanjum CJSS would have granted leave to appeal, not least because 'it is disquieting in this case to note that in determining the ranking of importance of the various Articles in the FC [Federal Constitution] the Court of Appeal seems to have adopted the "first-come basis" approach'.[23] This 'first come, first served' approach to constitutional interpretation is clearly incorrect and, according to Malanjum CJSS, ought to be corrected on appeal, lest the error be perpetuated. Or as another dissenting judge, Tan FCJ, said: 'The constitutional questions should be answered by the Federal Court. They are too grave to be answered by any other'.[24]

The major issue in the general questions category concerned the theological pronouncements by the Court of Appeal judges based on their own internet research. The majority at the Federal Court refused to grant leave on this basis as they found these judicial-theological pronouncements to be 'mere obiter'.[25] Dissenting, Zainun FCJ would have granted leave to appeal as these judicial-theological pronouncements had 'escalated to a worrying level': 'the learned judges in the court below ought to have confined themselves strictly to the legal issues raised, since the question of the truth or otherwise of the disputed tenets of religious belief and faith … are all beyond the competence of judges of fact and law' – 'judges should not overreach themselves for

[18] *Titular Roman Catholic Archbishop of Kuala Lumpur v Home Minister* (Federal Court, Zainun Ali FCJ, 23 June 2014) [41], [98].

[19] ibid [99].

[20] ibid (Federal Court, Arifin Zakaria CJ, 23 June 2014) [33].

[21] ibid (Federal Court, Zainun Ali FCJ, 23 June 2014) [99].

[22] On the procedural point, see W Tay, 'The Use and Misuse of Article 4(3) and 4(4) of the Federal Constitution' (2015) 2 *Malayan Law Journal Articles* 154.

[23] *Titular Roman Catholic Archbishop of Kuala Lumpur v Home Minister* (Federal Court, Richard Malanjum CJSS, 23 June 2014) [64].

[24] ibid (Federal Court, Jeffrey Tan Kok Wha FCJ, 23 June 2014) [10].

[25] ibid (Federal Court, Arifin Zakaria CJ, 23 June 2014) [45].

we are not omniscient'.[26] Also dissenting, Malanjum CJSS would have granted leave to appeal to 'deal with the appropriateness of the learned judges of the Court of Appeal in conducting their own [theological] research via the Internet', without giving the parties 'any prior opportunity to submit on those materials obtained'.[27]

III. Legal Errors

With the denial of leave to appeal by the Federal Court, the theology-laden judgment of the Court of Appeal, which upheld the Allah ban, became the binding judgment. The Court of Appeal judgment will be the focus of analysis in this chapter. There are many errors, both of law and fact, in the Court of Appeal judgment. Let me pick off some low-hanging fruits first, before moving on to meatier issues.

To begin with, the 'first come, first served' approach to constitutional interpretation is obviously wrong. One simply has to look a few lines down from Article 3(1) to see the following provision in Article 3(4): 'Nothing in this Article derogates from any other provision of this Constitution.' This provision alone is sufficient to demolish any legal attempt to use the Article 3(1) proclamation of Islam as the religion of the Federation to qualify and restrict the Article 11(1) right to the freedom of religion. Nothing in Article 3 can be used to derogate from any other provision in the Constitution. That is explicitly stated in Article 3 itself. The numbering of the articles, which places Article 3 before Article 11, matters not one bit.[28]

Second, the Court of Appeal went on and on about Article 11(4), which allows for restrictions to be placed on the propagation of non-Islamic religions to Muslims, but that is entirely irrelevant to this case. This case had nothing to do whatsoever with the propagation of non-Islamic religions to Muslims; it was solely about Roman Catholics using a particular word in their *own* internal religious worship and instruction. While Article 11(4) is completely irrelevant to the case, Article 11(5) has some arguable relevance. Article 11(5) states that the freedom of religion protection under Article 11(1) 'does not authorize any act contrary to any general law relating to public order, public health or morality'. However, unlike Article 11(4), which allows the government to impose restrictions on propagation, Article 11(5) is not a restriction; rather, it is a clarification, and it is expressly phrased as a clarification. Article 11(5) simply makes it clear that the constitutional right to the freedom of religion is not a basis for an exemption from any *general* law relating to public order, public health or morality. Article 11(5) cannot be used specifically to restrict the right to the freedom of religion under Article 11(1). To recap, although Article 11(4) can be used to restrict the right to the freedom of religion under Article 11(1), it does not apply to the facts of this case. Conversely, although Article 11(5) arguably applies to the facts of this case, it cannot be

[26] ibid (Federal Court, Zainun Ali FCJ, 23 June 2014) [127], [128].

[27] ibid (Federal Court, Richard Malanjum CJSS, 23 June 2014) [68].

[28] For a more extensive analysis of art 3, see J Neoh, 'Islamic State and the Common Law in Malaysia: A Case Study of *Lina Joy*' (2008) 8 *Global Jurist* 4.

used to restrict the right to the freedom of religion under Article 11(1). It is a legal error to use either Article 11(4) or Article 11(5) to justify the impugned provision.[29]

Third, even assuming *arguendo* that Article 11(5) can be used to justify restrictions on the freedom of religion, it is still of no help to the government. The Court of Appeal referred to the protests that occurred right after the High Court initially ruled in favour of the Archbishop as evidence of a threat to public order, which is supposed to justify the Allah ban. These protests, which occurred after the High Court judgment, are irrelevant timewise. The material time was the time of the ministerial decision, when the Minister's delegate decided to attach the impugned condition to the publication permit. There were no protests then, and no threat to public order. The material time was not the time of the High Court decision. There were no public order disturbances at the material time when the Minister's delegate made the decision that was the subject of judicial review. To hold otherwise would be to allow one group's constitutional right to be held hostage by the willingness of another group to cause trouble: if one does not like a judicial decision in favour of a group, one could simply protest, thereby causing public order disturbances, which would then justify curtailing the rights of the group whose rights had just been vindicated by the court. That would make a mockery of the judicial process.

Fourth, Article 3(1) has two prongs: 'Islam is the religion of the Federation; but other religions may be practised in peace and harmony in any part of the Federation.' Hitherto, it has been widely understood and accepted that the second prong is meant to protect religious minorities, after the first prong made Islam the religion of the Federation. What the Court of Appeal did was to turn the second prong on its head by turning it from a protection of religious minorities into an imposition on religious minorities. According to the Court of Appeal, the insertion of the phrase 'in peace and harmony' in the second prong with regard to the practice of non-Islamic religions is meant 'to protect the sanctity of Islam as the religion of the country and also to insulate against … any possible and probable threat to the religion of Islam'.[30] On this errant reading of Article 3, the only way a religious minority can practise their religion 'in peace and harmony' is to practise it in such a way that pleases the majority. That is cold comfort for religious minorities. The Court of Appeal has turned a provision designed to protect religious minorities into a provision that imposes an obligation on the religious minorities to kowtow and tiptoe around the majority. This most bizarre interpretation goes against decades of settled understanding.[31]

Fifth, for the reasons that have been pointed out by Malanjum CJSS and Zainun FCJ at the Federal Court, it is legally wrong, let alone completely irrelevant, for the Court of Appeal to have engaged in the kind of pseudo-theological reasoning that it did. However, since they have done it, I shall endeavour in the next section to descend to

[29] For a more extensive analysis of art 11, see J Neoh, 'Apostasy and Freedom of Religion in Malaysia' in P Babie, N Rochow and B Scharffs (eds), *Freedom of Religion or Belief: Creating the Constitutional Space for Fundamental Freedoms* (Edward Elgar, 2020).

[30] *Home Minister v Titular Roman Catholic Archbishop of Kuala Lumpur* (Court of Appeal, Mohamed Apandi bin Ali JCA, 14 October 2013) [29].

[31] For an overview of the history of constitutionalism in Malaysia, see J Neoh, 'Snake with Two Heads: The Two Voices of the Malaysian Constitution' in S Farrar and P Subramaniam (eds), *Law and Justice in Malaysia: 2020 and Beyond* (Thomson Reuters, 2021).

their level and play their game in order to show why their pseudo-theological reasoning is faulty, which further shows why they should not have done it in the first place. Fools rush in where angels fear to tread.

IV. Theological-Philosophical Errors

Elsewhere, I have provided a political-philosophical analysis of the Court of Appeal judgment.[32] Here, in this section, I shall venture a theological-philosophical analysis of the judgment. All three of the Court of Appeal judges assert that Allah is the name of God. One judge said that 'Allah' is 'not just a mere word or translation of the word God as described in the Herald but it is a *special name* for the Muslim's God' (emphasis added).[33] Another judge said that 'Allah is a *proper name* and the only God in Islam' (emphasis added).[34] The first problem is that they have offered no analysis to justify this bold claim, so it is a bald assertion. The second problem is that it is wrong. Claiming that 'Allah' is God's name is like claiming that 'God' is God's name. It confuses a common noun with a proper noun.

The philosophical analysis of names is a subset of the philosophy of language, which is where I propose to begin the theological-philosophical analysis.[35] To do that, I have to introduce some technical terminology. A person's proper name is, usually, made up of proper nouns. My name is Joshua Neoh, which is a proper name with two proper nouns: Joshua and Neoh. If a person's proper name only has one proper noun, then that person is mononymous. European monarchs are often mononymous, like Elizabeth. Jesus is mononymous too. However, a mononymous proper name, which consists of only a proper noun, can be attached to a common noun. For example, Queen Elizabeth and Jesus Christ: Queen and Christ are common nouns. Christ is a title, just as Queen is a title. 'The Great' in Alexander the Great is, similarly, a title. His name is Alexander.

Proper names can have meanings, but the meaning of the name is irrelevant as far as the use of the name is concerned. A name refers to a person. It does not describe that person. Joshua means, roughly, 'God saves'. However, when someone calls me by my name, what matters is not the meaning of the word. They might not even know the meaning of the word 'Joshua'. They use that word to refer to me, not to describe who I am. I am not God and I have saved no one. The meaning of that name does not describe me. The meaning of a proper name does not limit or control the use of that name. Neither does the meaning of a proper name limit or control who or what it can refer to.

[32] Neoh (n 16).

[33] *Home Minister v Titular Roman Catholic Archbishop of Kuala Lumpur* (Court of Appeal, Abdul Aziz bin Abdul Rahim JCA, 14 October 2013) [92].

[34] ibid (Court of Appeal, Mohd Zawawi bin Salleh JCA, 14 October 2013) [26].

[35] For two excellent overviews of the philosophy of names and naming, see: S Cumming, 'Names' in E Zalta (ed), *Stanford Encyclopedia of Philosophy* (Metaphysics Research Lab, 2019); and G Forbes, 'Proper Names' in E Craig (ed), *Routledge Encyclopedia of Philosophy* (Routledge, 1998). The main philosophical divide in this field is between the 'sense theory' of names and the 'historical chain theory' of names. See G Frege, 'On Sense and Reference' (trans M Black) in PT Geach and M Black (eds), *Translations from the Philosophical Writings of Gottlob Frege* (Blackwell, 1980), who is the leading proponent of the 'sense theory'; and S Kripke, *Naming and Necessity* (Harvard University Press, 1980), who is the leading proponent of the 'historical chain theory'.

A proper name can have multiple referents. The same name can refer to multiple persons. A Google search reveals that there are several people currently living in the world who are called Joshua Neoh. I know of at least two persons by the name of Charles Taylor: the Canadian philosopher and the Liberian war criminal. When I refer to Charles Taylor, most people whom I speak to, unless they are simpletons, will be able to tell, from the context, whether I am referring to the philosopher or the war criminal. They will be able to match the proper name to the intended referent correctly and without fuss. As Wittgenstein states in his famous remark about the name 'Moses':

> Has the name 'Moses' got a fixed and unequivocal use for me in all possible cases? – Is it not the case that I have, so to speak, a whole series of props in readiness, and am ready to lean on one if another should be taken from under me, and vice versa?[36]

This section will argue that Allah is not a proper name for God, but *even if it is*, it is most unlikely that a person hearing the word 'Allah' will be confused as to which God the speaker is referring to. Most people, unless they are simpletons, will be able to match the proper name to the intended referent correctly and straightforwardly. It is commonplace for a proper name to have multiple referents, and it is not rocket science to figure out who the intended referent is. We do that all the time in a myriad of everyday conversations, which should put paid to the facetious worry that people will be confused when they hear the word 'Allah' as to which God the speaker is referring. The context will often make it abundantly clear. 'Allah' in a mosque refers to the Islamic God, while 'Allah' in a church refers to the Christian God. 'Allah' in the Quran refers to the Islamic God, while 'Allah' in the Bible refers to the Christian God. One proper name can refer to multiple persons and, conversely, one person can be referred to by multiple proper names. Names can co-refer to the same entity. Let's say, in some circles, I am called Joshua Neoh, but in other circles, I am simply called Neo. Both names – Joshua Neoh and Neo – can refer to the same person: me. This feature of name, too, is commonplace, and it is no cause for concern, least of all for confusion. The Christian God is sometimes called by this name, sometimes by that name and sometimes by the name 'Allah'. There is no reason to be confused on this score, for there is nothing unusual in this regard.

Even if Allah were to be a proper name for God, there is no reason to think that it will cause confusion when used by Christians alongside Muslims. But is Allah a proper name? A proper name is made up of proper nouns, which are distinct from common nouns. Proper nouns refer, while common nouns describe. The meaning of a proper noun does not matter in its use, while the meaning of a common noun does. 'Bachelor' is a common noun, and a bachelor means an unmarried man. The meaning of the word is a description of a bachelor. The description acts as a definition that limits the range of its application. Anyone, if they so wish, can call themselves Joshua, but not anyone can call themselves a bachelor without committing a linguistic mistake. A married man is, by definition, not a bachelor. A bachelor means an unmarried man, and that meaning matters. In contrast, although Joshua means 'God saves', that meaning does not matter. Someone who is not God and who has not saved anyone can still call themselves Joshua, but someone who is married cannot call themselves a bachelor. A married man who

[36] L Wittgenstein, *Philosophical Investigations* (trans GEM Anscombe) (Basil Blackwell, 1953) §79.

calls himself a bachelor is an incompetent user of the English language. If he is not an incompetent user of the English language, then he is a liar.

Allah has all the hallmarks of a common noun, not a proper noun. The word has a meaning that describes an entity. The description acts as a definition that limits the range of its application. A mere human is, by definition, not Allah, just as a married man is, by definition, not a bachelor. In the case of a bachelor, only if certain facts obtain is a particular person a bachelor. The relevant conditional facts are that one must be (i) unmarried, and (ii) a man. A similar linguistic structure applies to the word 'Allah' as well. The meaning of the word 'Allah' might be less settled than the meaning of the word 'bachelor', but that is not an impediment to the word being a common noun. Due to a phenomenon called the open texture of language, different people can employ slightly different descriptions in relation to a common noun. A degree of linguistic indeterminacy is to be expected. As Hart explains, a word will often have a core of settled meaning and a penumbra of uncertainty.[37] Let's suppose the core meaning of Allah as a common noun is, roughly, a supreme being who created the world. Those are the conditional facts. Any being that fits, or purports to fit, that description can be called Allah. One commits no linguistic mistake in calling that being Allah, be it Christian or Muslim.

It is possible for God to have a proper name, just as it is possible for anyone to have a proper name. However, not all religious traditions have given God a proper name, and it is not logically necessary for a religion to do so. It is logically possible, but not necessary, that God has a proper name. In biblical Hebrew, the common noun for God is Elohim. In addition to the common noun, the Jewish God also has a proper name, YHWH, which is sometimes known as the Tetragrammaton. That name is considered so sacred that it is not pronounced by observant Jews. 'The Tetragrammaton has revelatory significance': God naming himself YHWH is an act of divine self-revelation to the people of Israel.[38] God's revealing of his proper name to his chosen people is an expression of intimacy that forms a bond between the God of Israel and the people of Israel. Before God revealed his proper name to be YHWH, there was a common noun for the Jewish God in Hebrew, which is Elohim, but no proper noun. This example from Judaism illustrates clearly the difference between having a common noun and a proper noun for God. They are not the same thing.

By accepting Allah as a common noun, does it entail that anyone or anything can be called Allah? No. The meaning of a common noun determines the range of its application. One cannot call a mere human Allah without committing a linguistic mistake. Whether that linguistic mistake should be turned into a legal wrong is a separate matter. Abdul Aziz JCA claimed that Allah 'refers to "oneness" and cannot be part of the concept of Trinity of Father, Son and the Holy Ghost of the Christian faith'.[39] The most charitable way to make sense of this claim is to read it as saying that the meaning of the common noun 'Allah' includes the quality of oneness as part of its definitional

[37] HLA Hart, *The Concept of Law* (Oxford University Press, 2012) 128: 'Uncertainty at the borderline is the price to be paid for the use of general classifying terms in any form of communication concerning matters of fact. Natural languages [are] irreducibly open-textured.'

[38] M Byrne, *The Names of God in Judaism, Christianity, and Islam* (Continuum, 2011) 24.

[39] *Home Minister v Titular Roman Catholic Archbishop of Kuala Lumpur* (Court of Appeal, Abdul Aziz bin Abdul Rahim JCA, 14 October 2013) [92].

description. Oneness is one of its conditional facts. A being who does not satisfy, or purport to satisfy, this condition cannot be called Allah. Just as a married man is not a bachelor, so a plural being is not Allah, definitionally speaking.

As indicated earlier, due to the open texture of language, words often have a degree of linguistic indeterminacy. Some might think that the quality of oneness is part of the penumbra of the meaning of the word 'Allah', but not at the core of it. Abdul Aziz JCA seemed to think that it is at the core, so let's accept his definition *arguendo*. Even granting his more stringent description of the meaning of the word 'Allah', the Christian God still fits that description. It is a serious misunderstanding of Christian theology to think that it does not. The Trinity is called a trinity because it is three making up a unity, three-in-one. The first line of the Nicene Creed makes this point as plainly as possible: 'We believe in one God.' Therefore, even if a divine being has to be 'one' to be called Allah, per Abdul Aziz JCA, the Christian God is such a being.

V. Conclusion

A court of law is not a forum for theology. This case illustrates the dangers of secular judges playing the role of theologian and doing pseudo-theology. Why, then, did the Court of Appeal judges do it? Perhaps they did so for the following Nietzschean reason:

> The right of the masters to confer names extends so far that one should allow oneself to grasp the origin of language itself as the expression of the power of the rulers: they say 'this is such and such', they put their seal on each thing and event with a sound and in the process take possession of it.[40]

The naming of God in this case is simply an assertion of power. It is an attempt to assert dominance over a religious minority, which also explains the Court of Appeal's astonishing interpretation of Article 3. That interpretation places the freedom of religion of the minority at the sufferance of the majority. It sends a message to the minority to know their place. By putting their seal on the word 'Allah' and assuming exclusive possession of that word, it tells the religious minority who the master is in Malaysia.

For the Catholic minority in Malaysia, who have been deprived of their right to call their God 'Allah', there is not much that they can do, other than to take consolation in the following lines from Shakespeare:

> What's in a name? That which we call a rose
> By any other name would smell as sweet.[41]

[40] F Nietzsche, *On the Genealogy of Morals* (trans D Smith) (Oxford University Press, 1996) 13.
[41] W Shakespeare, *Romeo and Juliet* (Oxford University Press, 2000 [1597]).

PART II

Freedom of Religion Around the Commonwealth

4

Eweida v UK

Cross Words and the Reformulation of Religious Freedom

RUSSELL SANDBERG*

I. Introduction

In the early years of the twenty-first century, the legal framework concerning religion in England and Wales was transformed. Legislative changes led to religious freedom being seen as a human right and discrimination on the grounds of religion or belief became expressly forbidden. These new rights led to a plethora of high-profile cases, and restrictive and muddled case law. In *Eweida v UK*,[1] four of these judgments were considered by the European Court of Human Rights and for the first time the UK was found to be in breach of the Article 9 right to religious freedom. However, more importantly, the Strasbourg Court not only corrected the confused approach of the English judiciary, but also took the opportunity to elucidate an expansive new interpretation of Article 9. This chapter tells that story: how the confused and timid English approach ironically unlocked the full potential of Article 9.

The following discussion falls into four sections. Section II will examine the new legal framework regulating religion which had been developed by the early years of the twenty-first century and how it had been interpreted in a restrictive manner. Section III will then introduce the four claims that were ultimately considered by the European Court on Human Rights, focusing on the facts of each claim and how they had been dealt with under domestic law. Section IV will then focus on the European Court on Human Rights' judgment and how it corrected the restrictive English approach to Article 9. Section V examines the limitations of the judgment, particularly its application in relation to some of the four claims and also its legacy, contending that *Eweida v UK* provided a landmark step forward, but that the full potential of the decision is yet to be realised.

* Thanks to Joshua Neoh for his helpful comments on the first draft of this chapter.

[1] *Eweida v UK* (2013) 57 EHRR 8.

II. The New Legal Framework

The legal framework concerning the regulation of religion in England changed significantly at around the turn of the millennium. Although there had long been laws relating to religion, these mostly regulated religious groups.[2] From Magna Carta declaring that the English Church was free onwards, provisions generally protected religions as entities and their autonomy to perform certain tasks both social and legal, including notably in relation to education and marriage. Moreover, such provisions were ad hoc responses to particular issues or concerns. The grandstanding of Magna Carta was atypical: the absence of a single written constitution meant that principles of religious autonomy, religious toleration and later religious freedom were not articulated. This changed in the middle of the twentieth century with the advent of human rights treaties, but even then, such provisions were not enforceable by individuals under domestic law.

From the turn of the millennium onwards, such provisions became enforceable. First, the *Human Rights Act 1998* meant that from 2000 onwards, the provisions of the *European Convention on Human Rights* (*ECHR*) were enforceable in English courtrooms and public authorities were obligated to follow the *Convention*, including Article 9, which dealt with freedom of religion or belief. Second, from 2003, discrimination on the grounds of religion or belief became unlawful in England and Wales, with the *Employment Equality (Religion or Belief) Regulations 2003* prohibiting such discrimination in relation to employment and the *Equality Act 2006* then doing the same for the provision of goods and services. These rights, now consolidated in the *Equality Act 2010*, saw religion added as a protected characteristic alongside long-standing provisions concerning sex and race discrimination. The protection of religious freedom as a human right together with the prohibition of discrimination on the grounds of religion marked a significant change in how religion was recognised and regulated under English law. While the common law had traditionally taken a negative approach to freedoms, meaning that everything was permitted except that which was prohibited, the new legal framework took a positive approach protecting freedoms as rights.[3] This shift led to the 'juridification of religion', religion being framed as a legal right and the subject of litigation.[4] The new abstract way in which these new laws were expressed, including the need to weigh up the social justification, made new demands on the judiciary. Therefore, it was unsurprising that a restrictive approach was adopted, with judges being seemingly uncomfortable adjudicating such matters and keen to rely upon concrete legal tests.

Judges interpreting religious freedom claims under the *Human Rights Act 1998* found such concrete texts in the embryonic Article 9 case law of the *ECHR*.[5] It became understood by judges and commentators alike that three tests had to be met for Article 9(1) to be in play: first, the claim had to meet the definition of religion or belief, to which a wide

[2] See R Sandberg, *Law and Religion* (Cambridge University Press, 2011) ch 2.

[3] *Malone v Metropolitan Police Commissioner* [1979] Ch 344. See also *Attorney-General v Guardian Newspapers Ltd (No 2)* [1990] 1 AC 109, 178, per Donaldson MR: 'the starting point of our domestic law is that every citizen has a right to do what he likes, unless restrained by the common law … or by statute'.

[4] See Sandberg (n 1) 193–95.

[5] See ibid ch 5.

interpretation was given;[6] second, the claim had to be a manifestation of that religion or belief rather than being simply motivated by it;[7] and, third, what became known as the 'specific situation rule' applied, so that claimants who had voluntarily agreed to a situation which limited their religious freedom – such as by voluntarily signing a contract of employment that required them to work during times of prayer – could not subsequently bring an Article 9 claim.[8] The domestic judges relied heavily on these tests since if these were not met, then that would be fatal to the claim and so they would not need to consider the less technical and more contentious issue under Article 9(2) of whether the interference with Article 9 had been justified.

This was epitomised by the decision of what was then House of Lords[9] in *R (on the Application of Begum) v Headteacher and Governors of Denbigh High School.*[10] The case concerned a 13-year-old Muslim schoolgirl who had wished to wear a *jilbab* which was not allowed under the school rules.[11] When she was told to go home and change, she contended that she had been 'excluded/suspended' from the school in breach of her right to manifest her religion under Article 9. Although the court was unanimous in its disposal of Begum's claim, the reasoning of the judges differed. Lord Nicholls and Lady Hale held that there had been an interference with Article 9(1), but that it had been justified under Article 9(2). In contrast, Lords Bingham, Hoffmann and Scott held that there had been no interference with Article 9(1), clinging to and extending the 'specific situation rule'.[12]

Lords Bingham, Hoffmann and Scott proclaimed that interference with the right to religious freedom was 'not easily established'.[13] They declared that the right to manifest one's religion or belief did 'not require that one should be allowed to manifest one's religion at any time and place of one's own choosing';[14] rather, 'people sometimes have to suffer some inconvenience for their beliefs'. They said that for religious believers, there was an 'expectation of accommodation, compromise and, if necessary, sacrifice in the manifestation of religious beliefs'.[15] For Lord Bingham:

> The Strasbourg institutions have not been at all ready to find an interference with the right to manifest religious belief in practice or observance where a person has voluntarily accepted an employment or role which does not accommodate that practice or observance and there are other means open to the person to practise or observe his or her religion without undue hardship or inconvenience.[16]

[6] The focus here was on the concept of belief, not religion, and it became accepted in case law on art 2 of the first protocol to the *Convention* that a belief must be a worldview held with 'a certain level of cogency, serious reflection and importance': *Campbell and Cosans v UK* (1982) 4 EHRR 293.

[7] *Arrowsmith v UK* (1981) 3 EHRR 218.

[8] *Ahmad v UK* (1981) 4 EHRR 126.

[9] From 2009, the same body with the same powers became known as the Supreme Court and moved to premises separate to Parliament in a symbolic and expensive manifestation of the separation of powers.

[10] *R (on the Application of Begum) v Headteacher and Governors of Denbigh High School* [2006] UKHL 15. See further R Sandberg, *Religion, Law and Society* (Cambridge University Press, 2014) ch 1.

[11] Begum was aged 13 at the time of dispute and was 17 by the time of the House of Lords judgment. A *jilbab* was described in the judgment as 'a long shapeless dress ending at the ankle and designed to conceal the shape of the wearer's arms and legs'. By comparison, the permitted *shalwar kameez* was described as a sleeveless smock-like dress worn to between knee and mid-calf length (see *R (on the Application of Begum) v Headteacher and Governors of Denbigh High School* (n 11) [79]).

[12] Lord Bingham did note that art 9 was 'engaged or applicable', but by this he seems to simply recognise that the claimant was sincere: ibid [21].

[13] ibid [24] (Lord Bingham).

[14] ibid [50] (Lord Hoffmann).

[15] ibid [54] (Lord Hoffmann).

[16] ibid [23].

Lord Bingham held that the Article 9 case law of the European Court of Human Rights showed that 'there remains a coherent and remarkably consistent body of authority which our domestic courts must take into account and which shows that interference is not easily established'.[17] However, it is questionable whether this overstated the Strasbourg jurisprudence on the 'specific situation rule'. Lord Bingham's elucidation of the rule suggested that two requirements must be met in order for the rule to apply: first, the claimant must have 'voluntarily accepted an employment or role which does not accommodate' the religious manifestation they seek to exercise; and, second, there must be 'other means open to the person to practise or observe his or her religion without undue hardship or inconvenience'. However, their Lordships seem to have placed greater emphasis upon this second requirement. They focused on the issue of whether Begum could have gone to another school and gave rather less attention to the question of whether she voluntarily submitted to the system of norms.[18] By contrast, the Strasbourg case law focused on the first requirement.[19] The rule typically applied in relation to employment and similar situations where the claimant has voluntarily submitted themself to a system of norms.[20] By focusing on the second part of the rule, the judgment in *Begum* gave the 'specific situation rule' general effect: there was no interference with Article 9 'where the individual is left with a viable and voluntary choice to put themselves in a position where they can manifest their religion, even if this requires some personal sacrifice'.[21] For Lords Bingham, Hoffmann and Scott, this was sufficient to dismiss the claim: the school's refusal to allow Begum to wear a *jilbab* did not interfere with her religious freedom. This seems to be illogical: the refusal to allow Begum to attend school clearly prevented her from manifesting her religion in practice or observance. Moreover, deciding the case in this way meant that little attention was paid to the question of justification where a nuanced, fact-specific judgment could be reached.

The approach of Lords Bingham, Hoffmann and Scott proved to be influential. A series of lower court decisions concerning school uniforms regarded the *Begum* precedent as an 'insuperable barrier' to religious rights claims, which has erected 'a high threshold before interference can be established'.[22] Moreover, lower court decisions went even further than Lord Bingham by applying the 'specific situation rule' where only his second requirement was met.[23] In *X v Y School*,[24] Silber J held that there was no interference with Article 9 where the claimant was free to go to another school. The same conclusion was reached by the High Court in *Playfoot*,[25] where the Court deemed

[17] ibid [24].

[18] Note, by contrast, the speech of Baroness Hale, which suggested this is a significant issue based on the facts, given 'that the choice of secondary school is usually made by parents or guardians rather than by the child herself' (ibid 92).

[19] There is some limited support for this wider interpretation in *Jewish Liturgical Association Cha'are Shalom Ve Tsedek v France* (2000) 9 BHRC 27. However, this has not been followed in subsequent Strasbourg judgments.

[20] It has been applied in relation to those who voluntarily submit to military service (*Kalaç v Turkey* (1997) 27 EHRR 552), those who voluntarily enter into a contract of employment (*Stedman v UK* (1997) 5 EHRLR 544) and those who voluntarily enrol at a university (*Karaduman v Turkey* (1993) 74 DR 93).

[21] M Malik, 'Judgment: *R (SB) v Denbigh High School*' in R Hunter et al (eds), *Feminist Judgments: From Theory to Practice* (Hart Publishing, 2010) 336, 339.

[22] *R (on the Application of X) v Y School* [2006] EWHC (Admin) 298 [38], [100].

[23] Under this interpretation, the rule may be more accurately referred to as the 'contracting out doctrine'; see Malik (n 21) 336, 338.

[24] *R (on the Application of X) v Y School* (n 22).

[25] *R (on the Application of Playfoot (A Child) v Millais School Governing Body* [2007] EWHC Admin 1698.

itself competent to determine questions of Christian doctrine to develop a more restrictive version of the manifestation test. Supperstone QC, sitting as a High Court judge, held that although the claimant believed that she was wearing a 'purity ring' at school as a sign of her sexual restraint, this was not protected under Article 9, as she was not manifesting her Christian beliefs because she 'was under no obligation, by reason of her belief, to wear the ring; nor does she suggest that she was so obliged'.[26] Moreover, Supperstone QC held that even if the wearing of the ring was deemed to be a manifestation, the school's refusal to allow it to be worn did not represent an interference with Article 9 given that there were 'other means by which the Claimant [could] express her belief', such as by attaching the ring to her bag, wearing a badge or sticker instead, contributing to personal and social health education classes on the topic or by transferring to another school.[27] It was now established that there was no interference with Article 9 where it was possible for the claimant to manifest their religion elsewhere, even in ways which are inconvenient and require significant upheaval. If a believer could go to another school, leave their job or take their custom elsewhere, then they could not rely on Article 9. Even the Equality and Human Rights Commission expressed concern at this, concluding in its 2012 Human Rights Review that:

> Courts are setting too high a threshold for establishing 'interference' with the right to manifest a religion or belief, and are therefore not properly addressing whether limitations on Article 9 rights are justifiable.[28]

This restrictive interpretation discouraged litigants from bringing Article 9 claims under the *Human Rights Act 1998*.[29] Instead, for a while, claims were made under the new discrimination law provisions. A plethora of employment tribunal decisions followed, all of which would have been dismissed had they been argued on Article 9 grounds due to the 'specific situation rule'. However, while some claims succeeded under religious discrimination laws, others were unsuccessful and the suspicion arose that the restrictive legalistic approach found in the human rights case law had started to cross over to the religious discrimination decisions.[30] This was true of the four religious discrimination cases which were eventually brought to Strasbourg in *Eweida v UK*, as the next section will discuss.

III. The Four Cases under Domestic Law

Eweida v UK concerned whether the domestic courts (and, by extension, the UK) had failed to protect the Article 9 rights of four litigants who had brought religious discrimination claims before domestic courts and tribunals. These claims had concerned indirect religious discrimination, which exists where the claimant has suffered a disadvantage on

[26] ibid [23].
[27] ibid [3].
[28] https://www.equalityhumanrights.com/sites/default/files/human-rights-review-2012.pdf, 315.
[29] However, there were occasional exceptions, most notably *R (on the Application of Bashir) v The Independent Adjudicator and HMP Ryehull and the Secretary of State for Justice* [2011] EWHC 1108 (Admin).
[30] See Sandberg (n 2) ch 5.

the grounds of religion or belief[31] and this cannot be justified as being a proportionate means of achieving a legitimate aim. This is conceptually similar to the Article 9 case law, in that the first stage is a technical legal analysis, while the second stage is a contextual, sociological investigation concerning questions of policy and proportionality. The four claims in *Eweida v UK* fell into two groups. The first group of cases, *Eweida*[32] and *Chaplin*,[33] provided examples of claims of indirect religious discrimination which were dismissed on the basis that there was no disadvantage. Echoes of the reasoning in *Begum* and *Playfoot* could be clearly seen in the domestic court judgments in these two cases. The second group of cases, *Ladele*[34] and *McFarlane*,[35] were dismissed by domestic courts on questions of justification rather than disadvantage, but the little regard given to religious freedom in the decisions suggested that there was now a hierarchy of rights with religious discrimination coming below other equality strands.[36] The four claims were as follows.

Nadia Eweida, a part-time member of the check-in staff at British Airways (BA), sought to wear a silver cross in breach of BA's then uniform policy, which prohibited visible religious symbols, unless their wearing was mandatory. The Court of Appeal held that there was no indirect discrimination on the grounds of religion since the uniform policy did not put Christians at a particular disadvantage. There was no evidence that practising Christians considered the visible display of the cross to be a requirement of the Christian faith and no evidence that the provision created a barrier to Christians employed at BA.[37] Sedley LJ held that solitary disadvantage was not sufficient.[38] Quoting from *Begum*,[39] he suggested that 'the jurisprudence on [Article] 9 does nothing to advance the claimant's case'[40] and stated that if it had been held that there was indirect discrimination, then the claim would nevertheless be defeated by BA's case on justification.[41]

Shirley Chaplin, a nurse, was asked by her Senior Matron to remove the crucifix she wore around her neck at work on the grounds of health and safety. The Employment Tribunal held that the uniform policy did not 'place "persons" at a particular disadvantage'.[42] Despite evidence that another nurse, Mrs Babcock, had been asked to remove her cross and chain,[43] the Employment Tribunal held that Mrs Babcock had

[31] A disadvantage is suffered where the defendant applies a provision, criterion or practice (a PCP) against the claimant which is discriminatory in relation to the claimant's religion or belief. A PCP is discriminatory where it is: (i) applied equally to persons who do not share the claimant's religion or belief; (ii) puts persons of the claimant's religion or belief at a particular disadvantage compared with others; and (iii) actually puts the claimant at that disadvantage.

[32] *Eweida v British Airways* [2010] EWCA Civ 80.

[33] *Chaplin v Royal Devon & Exeter NHS Foundation Trust* [2010] ET Case Number: 17288862009 (6 April 2010).

[34] *Ladele v London Borough of Islington* [2009] EWCA Civ 1357.

[35] *McFarlane v Relate* [2010] EWCA Civ 880.

[36] As predicted by L Vickers, 'Religious Discrimination in the Workplace: An Emerging Hierarchy?' (2010) 12 *Ecclesiastical Law Journal* 280.

[37] *Eweida v British Airways* (n 33) [8].

[38] ibid [15].

[39] ibid [23].

[40] ibid [22].

[41] ibid [30]–[39].

[42] *Chaplin v Royal Devon & Exeter NHS Foundation Trust* (n 33).

[43] See ibid [15].

not been put at a particular disadvantage since the word 'particular' meant that the disadvantage suffered needed to be 'noteworthy, peculiar or singular', and this criteria had not been met, since Mrs Babcock's religious views were not so strong as to lead her to refuse to comply with the policy.[44] This was 'sufficient to dispose of the case', since the test for indirect discrimination referred 'to "persons" in the plural rather than the singular and here we have evidence that only one person, the claimant, was placed at a particular disadvantage'.[45] The Employment Tribunal added that if they had needed to decide whether the disadvantage was justified, they would have held that it was, since health and safety concerns provided a legitimate aim and the actions by the respondent were proportionate.[46]

Lillian Ladele, a registrar, refused on the grounds of conscience to perform civil partnership ceremonies. Both the Employment Appeal Tribunal[47] and the Court of Appeal[48] held that there had been a disadvantage, but that it had been justified.[49] The Court of Appeal held that the Council's policy decision to designate all registrars as civil partnership registrars had a legitimate aim: to fulfil the Council's policy to combat discrimination on the grounds of sexual orientation.[50] For Dyson LJ, the aim of the Council's 'Dignity for All' policy 'was of general, indeed overarching, policy significance [having] fundamental human rights, equality and diversity implications, whereas the effect on Ladele of implementing the policy did not impinge on her religious beliefs: she remained free to hold those beliefs, and free to worship as she wished'.[51] Further, Ladele was employed in a public job and was being 'required to perform a purely secular task, which was being treated as part of her job'.[52] Dyson LJ held that this conclusion was reinforced by Article 9.[53] Citing *Begum* and a number of Strasbourg decisions which had upheld the 'specific situation rule',[54] he concluded that 'Ladele's proper and genuine desire to have her religious views relating to marriage respected should not be permitted to override Islington's concern to ensure that all its registrars manifest equal respect for the homosexual community as for the heterosexual community'.[55]

Gary McFarlane, a counsellor at Relate, refused on the grounds of his Christian beliefs to counsel same-sex couples on sexual matters. Both the Employment Appeal Tribunal[56]

[44] ibid [27]. This was the decision of the majority. Mr Parkhouse, by contrast, held that both nurses had been placed at a disadvantage.

[45] ibid [28]. Article 9 was only mentioned in passing in the judgment when it was noted that art 9 was 'incorporated' into the Employment Equality Regulations (at [6]). Presumably the intention was to say that the Regulations were compatible with art 9.

[46] ibid [29]. This was the decision of the majority. Mr Parkhouse, by contrast, held the actions had not been proportionate.

[47] Employment Appeal Tribunal Case Number: UKEAT/0453/08/RN (10 December 2008).

[48] *Ladele v London Borough of Islington* (n 34).

[49] The original Employment Tribunal had held that there had been direct and indirect discrimination and harassment: [2008] Employment Tribunal 20–23 May 2008 (Case No 2203694/2007).

[50] *Ladele v London Borough of Islington* (n 34).

[51] ibid [51].

[52] ibid [52].

[53] See ibid [54]–[61].

[54] *Pichon and Sajous v France*, Application No 49853/99 (2 October 2001); *C v UK*, Application No 10358/83, 37 ECHR Dec & Rep 142; *Sahin v Turkey* (2007) 44 EHRR 5.

[55] *Ladele v London Borough of Islington* (n 34) [55].

[56] *McFarlane v Relate* [2009] UKEAT 0106/09/3011 (30 November 2009).

and the Court of Appeal[57] found *Ladele* to be definitive on this point. As Laws LJ noted, the two cases 'cannot sensibly be distinguished'.[58] It was held that although McFarlane had been disadvantaged, the employer's actions had had a legitimate aim (the provision of counselling services to all sections of the community regardless of their sexual orientation) and was proportionate.

Without questioning the decisions reached in these four cases that the claim of indirect religious discrimination failed, the way in which domestic courts and tribunals dealt with the claims was of concern. The speed with which they rejected the religious rights argument and their unwillingness to concede the relevance of the claimants' Article 9 rights were problematic. The domestic decisions in *Eweida* and *Chaplin* suggest that a restrictive interpretation was being taken to the question of whether there is a disadvantage, with proof being required that claimant's particular belief is shared by their co-religionists.[59] There would only be a disadvantage where their co-religionists agree that it is obligatory and, according to *Chaplin*, where at least one co-religionist is aggravated to the same extent as the claimant. Domestic courts and tribunals assumed that that all members of a particular religion share identical beliefs. Under their approach, manifestations of beliefs that are not regarded as obligatory according to co-religionists are denied protection; it does not matter what the individual claimant believes.

Although the approach in *Ladele* and *McFarlane* was preferable to that of *Eweida* and *Chaplin*, in that the indirect religious discrimination claims were dismissed on the basis of justification rather than disadvantage, in both *Ladele* and *McFarlane*, it is regrettable that in determining the question of justification, the courts and tribunals took a one-sided approach which paid little attention to religious rights. The courts and tribunals were correct to emphasise the importance of preventing sexual orientation discrimination, but were incorrect to underplay the importance of preventing religious discrimination. The courts were correct to stress that English law prohibits discrimination on the grounds of sexual orientation, but there was little recognition that English law also prohibits discrimination on the grounds of religion. The Court of Appeal in *Ladele* seemed to suggest that freedom of religion only included the right to hold beliefs and worship. The domestic courts did not seem to be balancing these two rights; rather, they gave the impression that religious rights are easily 'trumped' by other rights.[60] The approach of the domestic courts was to regard these cases as conflict of rights claims where a choice had to be made between preventing discrimination on the grounds of religion and discrimination on the grounds of sexual orientation.

[57] *McFarlane v Relate* (n 35). The application was also noteworthy because the case was supported by a witness statement by the former Archbishop of Canterbury, Lord Carey of Clifton, in which he argued for 'a specially constituted Court of Appeal of five Lords Justices who have a proven sensibility to religious issues'. See further R Sandberg, 'Laws and Religion: Unravelling *McFarlane v Relate Avon Ltd*' (2010) 12(3) *Ecclesiastical Law Journal* 361.

[58] *McFarlane v Relate* (n 35) [27].

[59] In *R (Eunice Johns and Owen Johns) v Derby City Council* [2011] EWHC Admin 375, the High Court subsequently confirmed that in indirect discrimination claims concerning Christians, it is now 'necessary to show "particular disadvantage" or "group" disadvantage to Christians or the particular denomination of Christianity' (at [101]).

[60] In *R (Eunice Johns and Owen Johns) v Derby City Council* (ibid), the High Court also confirmed that the result of *Ladele* and *McFarlane* is that the need not to discriminate on grounds of sexual orientation will always serve as justification for a religious discrimination claim (at [101]).

The treatment of all four of these claims also underlined how following *Begum*,[61] the specific situation rule was applied to cancel out any consideration of Article 9 in the workplace. Indeed, it might be questioned whether some of the claimants had voluntarily agreed to policies that restricted their religious rights. In particular, it is questionable whether Ladele voluntarily agreed to a contract of employment that included civil partnerships. When she applied for her job, there was no such thing as civil partnerships and unlike other councils, Islington Council had not been willing to compromise, but had designated all registrars as civil partnership registrars.[62] It was therefore unsurprising that the treatment of these four claims by domestic courts and tribunals raised the question of whether the UK's approach breached its obligations under Article 9 ECHR. It is this question which the Strasbourg decision in *Eweida v UK*[63] was concerned with and, as the next section will discuss, this judgment not only corrected a number of aspects that had been purported by the domestic courts, but also took the opportunity to re-draw some of the distinctions.

IV. The Promise of the Strasbourg Judgment

The decision of the European Court of Human Rights in *Eweida v UK* provides an important landmark in that it represents the first time that Strasbourg institutions have found the UK to be in breach of Article 9.[64] However, it is the reasoning of the Court and its interpretation of Article 9[65] which is of most importance rather than its particular decision that there was a violation of Article 9 in relation to *Eweida* and that there was no violation of Article 9 in relation to *Chaplin*, *Ladele* or *McFarlane*. The Court's statement of 'General Principles under Article 9 of the Convention' not only corrected the approach taken in the UK, but also provided an expansive new interpretation of Article 9 that had the potential to transform the understanding of religious freedom across the Council of Europe.[66]

This re-articulation was needed because the UK government's submission before the Court fully embraced the post-*Begum* restrictive interpretation of Article 9.[67] The UK government's submission was based upon very restrictive versions of two of the

[61] *R (on the Application of Begum) v Headteacher and Governors of Denbigh High School* (n 10).

[62] As Dyson LJ noted (*Ladele v London Borough of Islington* (n 34) [6]), s 29(2) of the *Civil Partnership Act 2004* required each 'registration authority to ensure that there is a sufficient number of civil partnership registrars for its area to carry out the functions of civil partnership registrars'. See further [75]–[76].

[63] *Eweida v UK* (n 2).

[64] This is particularly noteworthy given that Strasbourg 'seems to have been fairly reluctant to overturn local decisions about religious practice or religious symbols in relation to Article 9 rights – particularly in employment': J Garcia Oliva and F Cranmer, 'Education and Religious Symbols in the United Kingdom, Italy and Spain: Uniformity or Subsidiarity?' (2013) 19(3) *European Public Law* 555, 561.

[65] Eweida, Chaplin and McFarlane invoked art 9 of the *Convention*, taken alone and in conjunction with art 14, while Ladele complained only under Article 14 taken in conjunction with art 9. Article 14 prohibits discrimination on grounds, inter alia, of religion in the enjoyment of a *Convention* right. See *Eweida v UK* (n 1) [3].

[66] *Eweida v UK* (n 1) [79] et seq.

[67] Despite this, the then Prime Minister David Cameron stated that he welcomed the Court's decision and said that he would have legislated if there had been a different outcome: see 'British Airways Christian Employee Nadia Eweida Wins Case' *BBC News* (15 January 2013), www.bbc.co.uk/news/uk-21025332.

Article 9(1) tests: that behaviour needed to be a manifestation of rather than motivated by beliefs and the 'specific situation rule'. The UK government's submission was that the behaviour of the four claimants did not constitute a manifestation of their beliefs under Article 9. It was argued that their behaviour had been motivated or inspired by religion or belief, but it 'was not an act or practice of a religion in a generally recognised form' and so fell outside the protection of Article 9.[68] Alternatively, the government contended that even if the behaviour constituted a manifestation, there was still no interference with Article 9 since, following Lord Bingham's judgment in *Begum*, there was no interference 'where individuals voluntarily accept employment that does not accommodate religious practice, but where there are other means open to them to practise or observe their religion without undue hardship or inconvenience'.[69] The government emphasised that each of the applicants 'had been free to seek employment elsewhere' and this was considered to be sufficient to 'guarantee their Article 9 rights under domestic law'.[70]

The government's interpretation of Article 9 was rejected by the Strasbourg Court. In its elucidation of the 'general principles' that apply under Article 9, the Court re-articulated that although 'religious freedom is primarily a matter of individual thought and conscience', the text of Article 9(1) made it plain that 'freedom of religion also encompasses the freedom to manifest one's belief, alone and in private but also to practice in community with others and in public'.[71] The Court stressed that Article 9 protects 'views that attain a certain level of cogency, seriousness, cohesion and importance' and provided that this threshold was satisfied, 'the State's duty of neutrality and impartiality is incompatible with any power on the State's part to assess the legitimacy of religious beliefs or the ways in which those beliefs are expressed'.[72] Although most of these general principles were not new, this reference to the fact that the state had no role in assessing the ways in which beliefs are expressed can be seen as correcting the tendency of domestic courts to do just that in deciding that expressing belief in idiosyncratic ways is not protected. However, the Court clearly re-articulated the manifestation requirement and the 'specific situation rule'.

In clarifying the manifestation requirement, the Court accepted that it could not be said that 'every act which is in some way inspired, motivated or influenced by it constitutes a "manifestation" of the belief'.[73] This meant that 'acts or omissions which do not directly express the belief concerned or which are only remotely connected to a precept of faith fall outside the protection of Article 9'.[74] The Court re-articulated that in order to be a 'manifestation', the act must be 'intimately linked' to the applicant's religion or belief.[75] It was noted that an example of such a manifestation would be 'an act of worship or devotion which forms part of the practice of a religion or belief in a

[68] *Eweida v UK* (n 1) [58].

[69] ibid [59].

[70] ibid [60]. The government also submitted that in the alternative under art 9, measures taken by the employers had been proportionate to a legitimate aim in each case (at [61]).

[71] ibid [80].

[72] ibid [81].

[73] ibid [81]–[82].

[74] ibid [82].

[75] This formulation of the rule had been laid out by the Court before – eg, in *C v UK* (1983) 37 DR 142, 144; *Hasan and Chaush v Bulgaria* (2002) 34 EHRR 55.

generally recognised form'. However, the Court stressed that 'the manifestation of religion or belief is not limited to such acts'; rather, 'the existence of a sufficiently close and direct nexus between the act and the underlying belief must be determined on the facts of each case'. The Court was clear that 'there is no requirement on the applicant to establish that he or she acted in fulfilment of a duty mandated by the religion in question'.[76] Therefore, it rejected the submissions of the UK government on this point and made it clear that statements in the domestic case law which required actions to be obliged by the religion in question to be manifestations were incorrect. The judgment suggested that the manifestation requirement will only fail to be met if the action does not directly express the belief concerned or where the connection between the action and the belief is remote. The first limb of this test is easier to interpret than the second. It is difficult to find a clear example of an action which would fail the 'remote connection' test, especially where the 'direct expression' test has been met (given that the word 'or' is used in the judgment). This suggested that courts would now have to assess 'remoteness'. However, despite these difficulties, it is clear that the Strasbourg approach to manifestation is much more generous than that developed by the UK domestic courts.

In clarifying the ambit and role of the 'specific situation rule', the Court observed that the UK government had been correct to point out that, as Lord Bingham observed in *Begum*, the case law of the Strasbourg institutions had indicated that there would be no interference with Article 9(1) where 'a person is able to take steps to circumvent a limitation placed on his or her freedom to manifest religion or belief' and that in several employment cases, it had been held that 'the possibility of resigning from the job and changing employment meant that there was no interference with the employee's religious freedom'.[77] However, it was noted that this approach had not been taken by the Strasbourg Court in employment cases concerning other *Convention* rights and so this principle was no longer to be followed, 'given the importance in a democratic society of freedom of religion'.[78] Now, 'where an individual complains of a restriction on freedom of religion in the workplace, rather than holding that the possibility of changing job would negate any interference with the right, the better approach would be to weigh that possibility in the overall balance when considering whether or not the restriction was proportionate'. This meant that the 'specific situation rule' would no longer form part of the part of the Article 9(1) analysis, but would be a factor, and not a definitive one in weighing up the Article 9(2) question of justification. This would mean that cases like *Begum* would in future be decided on Article 9(2) grounds. It is also striking that the Strasbourg Court's interpretation of the 'specific situation rule' exclusively referred to the context of employment; this seems to suggest that *Begum* reasoning overstated the case law by applying the rule outside its original contractual setting.[79] Now, the fact that a child could go to another school to manifest their religion is now a factor that falls for consideration under Article 9(2) if it is relevant at all.

[76] *Eweida v UK* (n 1) [82]. The same point was expressed clearly in the partly dissenting opinion of Judges Bratza and Björgvinsson (at [2]).

[77] ibid [83].

[78] ibid [83]. The same point was expressed clearly in the partly dissenting opinion of judges Bratza and Björgvinsson (at [2]).

[79] As argued, for example, by M Hill and R Sandberg, 'Is Nothing Sacred? Clashing Symbols in a Secular World' [2007] *Public Law* 488; and Sandberg (n 2) 91.

This statement of general principles relating to Article 9 provided a significant step forward, at least in the context of the UK where the restrictive approach has now been discredited by Strasbourg. The judgment re-asserted that acts do not need to be obliged by the religion in question to be regarded as manifestations and marked a departure in Strasbourg jurisprudence away from the application of the specific situation rule. The focus was moved from the Article 9(1) issue of interference to the Article 9(2) question of justification. As Mark Hill noted, this new approach 'will not necessarily lead to a seismic shift in litigation outcomes' because 'shifting the theatre of dispute from Article 9(1) to Article 9(2) might well produce identical results but for different and more sophisticated reasoning'.[80] However, he also noted that 'there is a greater subjective element to Article 9(2)' and this has the effect that 'judicial outcomes may become less predictable'. This unpredictability is furthered by the way in which the judgment gives little guidance on how this balancing act is to be performed. As the next section will discuss, the brevity of the Court's analysis meant that there remain a number of unanswered questions, and this may have limited the subsequent influence and significance of *Eweida v UK*.

V. The Limitations of the Strasbourg Judgment

Writing shortly after the judgment, Mark Hill commented of *Eweida v UK* that 'the actual disposal of each of the four applications is of far less importance than the issues of principle and the revised judicial approach'. The previous section has shown this to be true, but the way in which the Strasbourg Court disposed of the four cases has proved to be of importance too. The brevity of the Court's reasoning has meant that the promise found in the Court's re-articulation of Article 9 has not been fully felt. This section will extrapolate this by first briefly considering the shortcomings and unanswered questions found in the way in which the four applications were dealt with, before surveying how *Eweida v UK* has had a limited impact upon the subsequent development of the interpretation of religious freedom in England and Wales.

The claim in *Eweida* was the only one of the four that succeeded. Unlike domestic courts, Strasbourg held that there had been an interference with Eweida's Article 9 right and that a fair balance had not been struck under Article 9(2).[81] Although the national courts operated within a margin of appreciation, they had afforded too much weight to the employer's wish to project a certain corporate image and not enough to the applicant's desire to manifest her religious belief.[82] For the majority,[83] there was a breach of Article 9 since inadequate attention had been given to whether the interference was proportionate. By contrast, in relation to *Chaplin*, the Court held that there had been an interference with Article 9, but that this was justified because of the need to protect

[80] M Hill, 'Religious Symbolism and Conscientious Objection in the Workplace' (2013) 15 *Ecclesiastical Law Journal* 191, 199, 200.

[81] *Eweida v UK* (n 1) [94].

[82] ibid [94].

[83] The partly dissenting opinion of judges Bratza and Björgvinsson dissented from the majority's opinion in relation to Eweida on the basis that they disagreed that they considered that the domestic courts had struck a fair balance: *Eweida v UK* (n 1) [5].

health and safety on a hospital ward and this 'was inherently of a greater magnitude than that which applied in respect of Ms Eweida'.[84]

This was a field where a 'wide margin of appreciation' was allowed, since the 'hospital managers were better placed to make decisions about clinical safety than a court, particularly an international court which has heard no direct evidence'. However, this ran the risk of writing a blank cheque wherever health and safety concerns are invoked, especially since the discussion of this issue had been obiter in the domestic decisions, which dispensed with the case by saying that there was no disadvantage. Moreover, the Court's judgment left unanswered the question of whether the test for indirect religious discrimination breaches Article 9 in requiring proof that the claimant's particular belief is shared by their co-religionists.[85] The logic of the Court's elucidation of general principles is that an individual's belief, which is shared by no one else, will still protected under Article 9. This would suggest that a rule under indirect discrimination law which requires evidence that the belief is shared would breach Article 9.[86]

The claims in *Ladele* and *McFarlane* were also dismissed on the grounds of justification under Article 9(2). In respect of *Ladele*, the Strasbourg Court held that the Council's actions had a legitimate aim and the means pursued was proportionate.[87] It was noted that the Court 'generally allows the national authorities a wide margin of appreciation when it comes to striking a balance between competing Convention rights'.[88] This wide margin of appreciation had not been exceeded in this case. However, the Court did note that the 'specific situation rule' was not fatal to Ladele's claim. The majority opinion stated that 'it cannot be said that, when she entered into her contract of employment, the applicant specifically waived her right to manifest her religious belief by objecting to participating in the creation of civil partnerships, since this requirement was introduced by her employer at a later date'.

This suggests that the weight of the 'specific situation rule' as a factor under Article 9(2) will be higher where the action that the claimant complains of were part of their contractual duties when they became an employee, and so they can be said to have specifically waived their Article 9 rights. The claim in *McFarlane* was dismissed in a similar manner. The Court again stressed that a wide margin of appreciation was afforded to states where 'the employer's action was intended to secure the implementation of its policy of providing a service without discrimination' and that this had not been exceeded in the present case.[89] The Court also emphasised again the new role of the 'specific situation rule' as a factor under Article 9(2) rather than being determinative under Article 9(1).[90] It is noticeable that even regarding *McFarlane* as a case where Article 9 rights were

[84] ibid [99].

[85] This point is noted but not dealt with in the partly dissenting opinion of Judges Bratza and Björgvinsson (ibid [9]).

[86] This does not necessarily mean that the statutory test is incorrect, but rather the judicial interpretation of it. Emphasis should be placed on the word 'would' in order to recognise, contrary to the Court of Appeal's decision in *Eweida*, that solitary disadvantage can be sufficient: *Eweida v UK* (2013) 57 EHRR 8, [2010] EWCA Civ 80 [15].

[87] *Eweida v UK* (n 1) [105]–[106].

[88] ibid [106].

[89] ibid [109].

[90] See ibid.

specifically waived by contract, the Court seemed adamant to stress that this is only a minor factor to be taken into account for the purposes of justification.[91]

However, it should be noted that despite the Court downplaying the importance of the 'specific situation rule', both of these claims were lost because they were constructed as involving the balancing of rights, with weight then being afforded to the need to combat discrimination on the grounds of sexual orientation rather than focusing on the complained case of religious discrimination. The wide deference given to the domestic courts is problematic, given that the domestic courts were operating under a restrictive understanding of Article 9 following *Begum*, which meant that the case was not argued on Article 9 grounds and that no real balancing of rights took place. The reliance on the margin of appreciation meant that the part of the judgment which applies the law was of little practical use to domestic courts and to employees. It would have been useful to see discussion of when and how employers might be expected to balance the rights not to discriminate on the grounds of sexual orientation with the right to religious freedom.

Therefore, it is perhaps unsurprising that the impact of *Eweida* upon the subsequent development of the interpretation of religious freedom in England and Wales has been mixed. On the one hand, *Eweida* has often been cited, typically as a part of the court or tribunal's articulation of what Article 9 protects. For instance, *Eweida* was cited in *R (on the Application of Harrison) v Secretary of State for Justice*[92] to support the conclusion that the current non-recognition of humanist marriage interfered with the applicant's human rights.[93] The *Eweida* rejection of the 'specific situation rule' has been accepted and followed by domestic courts. The Supreme Court in *Bull v Hall*[94] stated that in *Eweida*, 'the Strasbourg court abandoned its previous stance that there was no interference with an employee's right to manifest her religion if it could be avoided by changing jobs' and that this was now to be taken into account in the overall proportionality assessment.[95] The legacy of *Eweida* is that cases are not being dispensed with on the grounds of the 'specific situation rule'. However, the absence of cases applying the rule might also be attributable to the decline in such cases arguing Article 9 following *Begum*.

In most cases, *Eweida* has been cited rather than applied. However, some decisions have applied *Eweida* and this has not always led to the religious argument winning.[96] A strong example of this is the Employment Tribunal decision in *Gareddu v London Underground*,[97] which concerned the claim that a policy that stated that employees could not have more than 15 days off consecutively in August constituted indirect

[91] In contrast, the partly dissenting opinion of Judges Vučinić and De Gaetano (at [5]) stated that 'the reason why there was no violation of Article 9 in respect of the fourth applicant is that he effectively signed off or waived his right to invoke conscientious objection when he voluntarily signed up for the job'.

[92] *R (on the Application of Harrison) v Secretary of State for Justice* [2020] EWHC 2096 (Admin) [69].

[93] However, it was held that this was justified by the fact that the law was currently under review by the Law Commission. *Eweida* was similarly cited in *Re Smyth's Application for Judicial Review* [2018] NICA 25 to hold that humanist beliefs were within the ambit of art 9 in the context of marriage law in Northern Ireland.

[94] *Bull v Hall* [2013] UKSC 73 [47].

[95] *Eweida* has also been cited by the Employment Appeal Tribunal to insist that the art 9 understanding of belief is used for the purpose of discrimination law: *Harron v Chief Constable of Dorset Police* [2016] UKEAT/0234/15/DA.

[96] See also *R (on the Application of Cornerstone) v Office of Standards in Education* [2020] EWHC 1679 (Admin) [297] and [298].

[97] *Gareddu v London Underground* [2015] Case Number: 2201116/2015.

religious discrimination due to the claimant's religious belief that he was required to return to Sardinia for a period of approximately five weeks around the month of August each year to attend and participate in religious festivals with his family. The Tribunal held that the claim was not made in good faith and that the motive for wanting the time off work related to family arrangements.[98] There would be an intimate link between participating in each individual festival and the claimant's religious beliefs, but there was no such nexus between the five-week period as a whole and his underlying beliefs.[99]

Some decisions have ignored *Eweida*. Perhaps most notably, this was true of the leading UK Supreme Court decision concerning the balancing of the rights of discrimination on the grounds of religion and sexual orientation, *Lee v Ashers Baking Company*,[100] which does not mention *Eweida*. Other decisions have explicitly said that *Eweida* was not relevant.[101] In *Kuteh v Dartford and Gravesham Trust*,[102] concerning an appeal by a nurse sacked for gross misconduct as a result of her initiating inappropriate conversations about religion with patients, counsel submitted the *Eweida* section on general principles, but the Court of Appeal did 'not find anything of assistance in those passages, important though they are in setting out the general principles which apply in Article 9 cases'. Other cases have cited *Eweida*, but to support statements and conclusions that are not compatible with the Strasbourg decision. In *Core Issues Trust v Transport for London*,[103] *Eweida* was cited as summarising the manifestation requirement, but it was then questionably held that Article 9 was not engaged because 'even if the advertisement sought to be placed by the Trust was motivated by a religious belief, it did not actually express that belief. Nor was the Trust required by religious belief to communicate these views by way of advertisement on London buses'. The second sentence, at least, is not compatible with *Eweida*.

The most detailed consideration of the impact of *Eweida* can be found in the Court of Appeal decision in *Mba v Mayor and Burgresses of the London Borough of Merton*,[104] which concerned whether Sunday working constituted indirect discrimination on the grounds of the claimant's Christian beliefs. The Employment Tribunal had dismissed the claim on the basis that in order to be protected, the belief must be a core component of Christianity. The Court of Appeal unanimously dismissed the claimant's appeal because although there had been errors of law in the Employment Tribunal's decision, its ultimate conclusion that the disadvantage had been proportionate was plainly and unarguably right.[105] The judges considered that the requirement that the manifestation be core was an error of law, but did not see *Eweida* as being the catalyst for this conclusion. Maurice Kay LJ held that the claimant's case was not strengthened by *Eweida* because that decision 'was entirely fact sensitive'.[106] Elias J held that the need for a core component could be a relevant factor in the justification discussion for indirect discrimination

[98] ibid [33].
[99] ibid [34].
[100] *Lee v Ashers Baking Company* [2018] UKSC 49, on which see I Leigh, ch 5 in this volume.
[101] *Page v NHS* [2019] UKEAT/0183/18/DA [37].
[102] *Kuteh v Dartford and Gravesham Trust* [2019] EWCA Civ 818 [54].
[103] *Trust v Transport for London* [2013] EWHC 651 (Admin) [162], [165] and [166].
[104] *Mba v Mayor and Burgresses of the London Borough of Merton* [2013] EWCA Civ 1562.
[105] ibid [23]–[24].
[106] ibid [20].

claims that were not against a public body.[107] He noted that although Article 9 did not require group disadvantage to be proved,[108] 'Article 9 cannot be enforced directly in employment tribunals because claims for breaches of Convention rights do not fall within their statutory jurisdiction', a point he said that the Strasbourg Court had not seemed to appreciate.[109] He further held that although domestic law needed to be read in a way that was compatible with Convention rights, it was 'simply not possible to read down the concept of indirect discrimination to ignore the need to establish group disadvantage'. Maurice Kay LJ, though adopting different reasoning, also agreed that although Article 9 does not require group disadvantage, this did not justly reading down the domestic law on indirect discrimination.[110] Subsequent cases have not required manifestations to be core to the religion in order to be protected, but it is unclear whether this is due to the legacy of *Eweida*.[111] However, it is clear that *Eweida* has not led to the abandonment of the group disadvantage requirement in indirect discrimination claims.[112]

VI. Conclusion

Although my initial observation that religious freedom 'died' as a result of *Begum* and was 'reborn' following *Eweida* now seems overstated,[113] it remains undeniable that *Eweida v UK* was a key case and a turning point in the legal regulation of religious freedom in the UK. The decision has not had a dramatic effect: it has not lead to a string of successful cases on religious freedom or the clear articulation of what is and what is not protected by Article 9. However, the position has moved on considerably from the days of *Begum*. The judiciary are slowly but surely becoming more comfortable adjudicating questions of religious liberty. In the cases that do come before the higher courts, it is clear that the battleground is now Article 9(2) rather than Article 9(1): the 'specific situation rule' is now dead and buried. There has not been an avalanche of Article 9 claims, but this is not necessarily a sign that the law is ineffective. And religious discrimination claims continue not only to come regularly before employment tribunals, but also have an unpredictable success rate. That, in sum, is the legacy of the re-articulation found in *Eweida* and of the shock of the UK being found in breach of Article 9 for the first time: now it is no longer expected that religious rights arguments will be quickly dismissed and will lose. Article 9 is worth raising in a domestic court once again.

[107] ibid [33].
[108] He also made the novel point that interference was more likely to be justified in relation to an exceptional belief, in that if the belief was widely shared by the employees, then it may be more difficult for the employer to accommodate those beliefs in a way which is compatible with their business objectives and so non-accommodation would be justified: ibid [34] and [36].
[109] ibid [35].
[110] ibid [21].
[111] *Eweida* was followed in *Sethi v Elements Personnel Services* [2019] Case Number: 2300234/2018.
[112] See *Page v NHS* (n 101) [48].
[113] It was deliberately provocative at the time. *cf* Sandberg (n 10) 1, 217.

5

Lee v Ashers Baking Company

Crumbs of Comfort in the Culture War

IAN LEIGH*

I. Introduction

Many arguments are not what they seem. The context and the history of the disputants has to be taken into account, as well as the ostensible issues in contention. Since the 1980s, the LGBT and conservative Christian communities in the UK have been engaged in a kind of smouldering dispute that periodically bursts into flame: from sex and relationships education in schools, to the extension of equality laws and related exceptions, to the introduction of civil partnerships and same-sex marriage. As legislation has been enacted implementing LGBT equality reforms, the battle has increasingly moved from Parliament to the courts. The remaining questions in contention have grown smaller, but with one side emboldened by success and the other feeling increasingly marginalised and threatened, the heat and shrillness of the discussion have, if anything, intensified. This accounts for how the seemingly trivial refusal by a Christian-owned bakery in Northern Ireland to supply a cake with an iced message in support of same-sex marriage reform came before the UK Supreme Court in 2018 billed as a clash between, on the one side, freedom of conscience and, on the other, gay citizenship. Neither characterisation of the issues is entirely accurate, but at such times symbolism is more potent than technicalities. Therefore, the claim that *Lee v Ashers Baking Company*[1] is a leading case rests in large measure on its value as a weathervane, indicating the shifting air currents in the Culture War.[2]

* I am grateful to Richard Moon for his comments on earlier drafts of this chapter and for fruitful discussion of these questions. In view of our differing positions, the usual disclaimer is more than usually apposite. This work was undertaken with the assistance of the British Academy and the Wolfson Foundation under a British Academy Wolfson Professorship.

[1] *Lee v Ashers Baking Company Ltd and Others (Northern Ireland)* [2018] UKSC 49.

[2] For an overview of the issues, see S Mancini and M Rosenfeld (eds), *The Conscience Wars: Rethinking the Balance between Religion, Identity and Equality* (Cambridge University Press, 2018); J Adenitire (ed), *Religious Beliefs and Conscientious Exemptions in a Liberal State* (Hart Publishing, 2019) and W Eskridge Jr and R Fretwell Wilson (eds), *Religious Freedom, LGBT Rights, and the Prospects for Common Ground* (Cambridge University Press, 2019).

It is useful to begin with a straightforward account of the litigation. In April 2014, the respondent, an LGBT rights activist who was himself homosexual, placed an order for a cake at one of the appellant's shops. The cake was intended for an event by an LGBT advocacy group Queerspace to mark the end of anti-homophobia week. It was to bear the message 'Support Gay Marriage'. Significantly, a proposal to introduce same-sex marriage in Northern Ireland had been defeated in the Northern Ireland Assembly days before. Although the order was initially accepted, the shopowner telephoned days later to cancel it, having reflected on the matter and decided that to fulfil it would be inconsistent with their beliefs. Mr Lee obtained the cake from another supplier, but also approached the Equality Commission for Northern Ireland, which funded his litigation in pursuit of claims of discrimination on the grounds of sexual orientation and political belief.

In May 2015, the County Court found that a bakery had breached equality legislation by its refusal, in accordance with the proprietors' Christian beliefs, to supply a cake for an event with slogan in favour of same-sex marriage.[3] District Judge Brownlie found that the appellants had directly discriminated against the respondent on the grounds of sexual orientation contrary to the *Equality Act (Sexual Orientation) Regulations (NI) 2006* and on the grounds of religious and political belief contrary to the *Fair Employment and Treatment (NI) Order 1998*. The Northern Ireland Court of Appeal rejected an appeal, holding that the bakery had directly discriminated on the grounds of sexual orientation and political opinion.[4] There was in the Court's view an inextricable link between the bakery's opposition to same-sex marriage and sexual orientation, and any interference with freedom of expression was no more than a proportionate means of protecting the rights and freedoms of others. The Supreme Court took a fundamentally different view and held that there was no sexual-orientation discrimination, since the objection was to the message on the cake and not to the customer.[5] It also found that to the extent that there was any discrimination on the basis of political belief, enforcing the anti-discrimination legislation against the bakery would breach the religious freedom (Article 9 of the European Convention on Human Rights (ECHR)) and negative freedom of expression (Article 10) of the owners of the bakery.

II. One Cake, Two Narratives

The 'gay cake' case has sharply divided commentators. In this section, I will argue that this is because the facts and argument can be made to fit two contrasting narratives.

On the one side is the claim that this is straightforwardly about a discriminatory 'refusal to serve'.[6] The discriminatory refusal narrative emphasises Gareth Lee's identification as a gay man and depicts the cancellation of the order as a refusal to treat him with

[3] *Lee v Ashers Baking Co Ltd*, County Court in Northern Ireland, 19 May 2015. For discussion, see R Wintemute, 'Message-Printing Businesses, Non-discrimination and Free Expression: Northern Ireland's "Support Gay Marriage" Cake Case' (2015) 26 *King's Law Journal* 348.

[4] *Lee v McArthur and Others* [2016] NICA 29.

[5] *Lee v Ashers Baking Company* (n 1).

[6] Wintemute (n 3).

equal respect.[7] All he had expected was to be served in the same way as other customers, but, it is argued, that the baker's refusal to do so caused him dignitary harm far in excess of the relatively minor inconvenience involved in obtaining the cake elsewhere.

On this reading, the case assumes a wider significance against the background of resistance to LGBT rights in parts of society in Northern Ireland and by some Christian communities. Northern Ireland is beyond question one of the most morally conservative parts of the UK, due in large measure to the influence of its Christian communities. Consequently, the recognition of LGBT rights has met with considerable resistance and a pattern has emerged of implementing reform only considerably after other parts of the UK in response to external pressure. Homosexual behaviour was decriminalised in Northern Ireland later than in Great Britain and only after a successful application to the European Court of Human Rights.[8] Discrimination on the grounds of sexual orientation was introduced in Northern Ireland by way of a statutory instrument issued by the Westminster government rather than by Stormont.[9] When first civil partnerships and then same-sex marriage were introduced in England and Wales, Northern Ireland was exempt and a long battle ensued in which the unionist majority in the Northern Assembly repeatedly rejected their introduction; the measure was later imposed by Westminster during the Assembly's suspension. Against that pattern of historic discrimination and exclusion, the customer in the 'gay cake' case, Gareth Lee, claimed that the refusal of the cake order made him feel like 'a second-class citizen'.[10]

However, on the other side, this was the latest in a series of legal challenges in recent years in which officials and small businesses have found that questions of conscience based on their religious beliefs put them at odds with legislation protecting LGBT rights. The clear trend (until the Supreme Court ruling) in these 'clashing rights' cases was, on the one hand, for claims of discrimination on the grounds of sexual orientation discrimination to succeed on the basis that accommodation for religious beliefs was not justified or permissible[11] and, on the other hand, for claims of religious discrimination to fail because any difference arising from adherence to sexual orientation equality policies was justified.[12] A similar pattern could be seen in freedom of expression cases of limiting religious speech to protect LGBT sensibilities.[13] More generally, UK courts had repeatedly rejected in various contexts the distinction between same-sex attraction

[7] J Cooper, 'Supreme Court Denied Man His Dignity in Gay Cake Case' *The Times* (19 October 2018), https://www.thetimes.co.uk/article/supreme-court-denied-man-his-dignity-in-gay-cake-case-0q0jt702c; J Adenitire, 'Conscientious Exemptions in a Liberal State' in *A General Right to Conscientious Exemption: Beyond Religious Privilege* (Cambridge University Press, 2020) 281–84. Note, however, that at no stage was the appellant found to have been treated adversely because of his actual or perceived sexual orientation (*Lee v Ashers Baking Company* (n 1) [13] and [22]).

[8] *Dudgeon v UK* (1981) 4 EHRR 149.

[9] *Equality Act (Sexual Orientation) Regulations (Northern Ireland) 2006.*

[10] 'Gareth Lee: It Made Me Feel Like a Second-Class Citizen' *BBC News* (10 October 2018), www.bbc.co.uk/news/av/uk-northern-ireland-45814200/gareth-lee-it-made-me-feel-like-a-second-class-citizen.

[11] *Bull and Another v Hall and Another* [2013] UKSC 73; *Black v Wilkinson* [2013] EWCA Civ 820; see also *Catholic Care (Diocese of Leeds) v Charity Commission for England and Wales* [2013] 2 All ER 1114.

[12] *McClintock v Department of Constitutional Affairs* [2007] UKEAT/0223/07/CEA (31 October 2007), [2008] IRLR 29; *Ladele v Islington LBC* [2010] 1 WLR 955; *McFarlane v Relate Avon Ltd* [2010] EWCA Civ 880, [2010] IRLR 872; *R (on the Application of Johns) v Derby City Council* [2011] EWHC 375 (Admin).

[13] *R (on the Application of Core Issues Trust) v Transport for London* [2014] EWCA Civ 34; *Hammond v DPP* [2004] EWHC 69 (Admin). But contrast *Kirk Session of Sandown Free Presbyterian Church, Re Judicial Review* [2011] NI QB 26.

and behaviour that lies behind much religious teaching on the topic.[14] At the same time, they had repeatedly treated religious adherence as a matter of personal choice and sexual orientation as a status.[15] The impression had taken root that despite the formal equivalence of religious and sexual orientation equality in legislation, the courts were operating their own hierarchy of rights.[16] The pattern was so consistent and striking that it drew the critical attention of a rapporteur to the Parliamentary Assembly of the Council of Europe.[17] Increasingly, some in the Christian community argued that they faced 'Christophobia' or persecution for their beliefs, with a corresponding loss of confidence in the neutrality of courts or the capacity of judges to understand religious language or arguments.[18]

Against this background, the Equality Commission's intervention in the *Ashers* case was therefore seen as partisan and threatening by the tight-knit Protestant community in Northern Ireland of which the bakers were part. Their response was an outpouring of spiritual and practical support for the cause, with large well-attended prayer meetings and donations to fund a lobby group (the Christian Institute) to finance the defence.

The discussion now turns to the sense in which the 'gay cake' case exemplified the escalating arguments in the clash between sexual orientation and religion and belief rights. Just as during the period of the Cold War the logic of confrontation and deterrence produced an escalation in weapons as each side vied for strategic advantage, so a similar trend can be observed in the Culture War. On the one side, discrimination law arguments have grown in terms of their reach and ambition, and, on the other side, new types of freedom of conscience arguments have been deployed in response.

III. Escalation in the Culture War

A. Expanding the Notion of Discrimination

As was noted earlier, the discriminatory 'refusal to serve' narrative emphasises that the baker is merely a provider of goods and that businesses which have entered the marketplace should not seek religious exemptions for their commercial activities.[19] This, however, oversimplifies the discrimination arguments in *Lee v Ashers Baking Company*. There was no evidence that the shopowners knew of or were interested in the customer's sexual orientation.[20] Instead, the controversy revolves around the ideas

[14] See, eg, *R (on the Application of Amicus et al) v Secretary of State for Trade and Industry* [2004] EWHC 860 (Admin) [119] (per Richards J); *Reaney v Herford Diocesan Board of Finance* (2007) ET Case No 1602844/2006 (17 July 2007).

[15] Articulated most clearly by Sedley LJ in *Eweida* v *British Airways* [2010] EWCA 80 [40].

[16] L Vickers, 'Religious Discrimination in the Workplace: An Emerging Hierarchy?' (2012) 12 *Ecclesiastical Law Journal* 280.

[17] Parliamentary Assembly of the Council of Europe, Committee on Equality and Non-Discrimination, *Tackling Intolerance and Discrimination in Europe with a Special Focus on Christians*, Report, Doc 13660, 7 January 2015, http://assembly.coe.int/nw/xml/XRef/Xref-XML2HTML-en.asp?fileid=21340&lang=en.

[18] See the affidavits by George Carey (the former Archbishop of Canterbury) in *McFarlane* (n 12) and *Johns* (n 12).

[19] R Wintemute, 'Accommodating Religious Beliefs: Harm, Clothing or Symbols, and Refusals to Serve Others' (2014) 77 *MLR* 223, 242.

[20] *Lee v Ashers Baking Company* (n 1) [13].

of 'indissociability' and associative discrimination in relation to direct discrimination, which, as employed by the plaintiff and the lower courts, demonstrate the growing reach of discrimination law.[21]

These arguments and the way they were treated show how far the law has travelled from the relatively simple proposition that direct discrimination refers to treating a person differently because of a protected characteristic.[22] Direct discrimination involves treating a person less favourably than other persons 'on grounds of sexual orientation'.[23] No justification can be pleaded for direct discrimination, thus creating a tactical incentive for plaintiffs to bring such claims rather than indirect discrimination ones wherever possible.[24] Moreover, the courts have, to an extent, blurred the distinction between indirect and direct discrimination claims by allowing the latter where the defendant has applied a criterion that is 'indissociable' from the protected characteristic.[25] This has the effect of depriving litigants who might otherwise have been able to plead justification of the benefit of such a defence. While plaintiffs have benefited from not having to demonstrate disparate impact in order to establish prima facie indirect discrimination, defendants have as a consequence, inter alia, been prevented from justifying practices that they have adopted to give effect to their religious beliefs.[26]

In *Lee v Ashers Baking Company*, the County Court judge had found that support for same-sex marriage was indissociable from the protected characteristic of sexual orientation.[27] Therefore, the appropriate comparator was not a heterosexual customer, but rather a heterosexual customer requesting a cake with a message supporting opposite-sex marriage eg, omitting the word 'gay'.[28] Since the bakery would not have objected in those circumstances, this amounted to direct discrimination. This reasoning represents an important shift away from the statutory wording, which simply requires a comparison between two persons. The comparison has become one between customers' behaviour or between the different goods (cakes) they request, in either case more indirectly connected to protected characteristics.[29] The Supreme Court found that the

[21] E Velasco Ibarra, '*Lee v Ashers Baking Company Ltd and Others*: The Inapplicability of Discrimination Law to an Illusory Conflict of Rights' (2020) 83(1) *MLR* 190; C McCrudden, 'The *Gay Cake* Case: What the Supreme Court Did and Didn't Decide in *Ashers*' (2020) 9 *Oxford Journal of Law and Religion* 238, 245.

[22] Confusingly, at first instance the County Court judge appeared to find as a matter of fact that the baker was aware of the customer's sexual orientation, but made no finding that this influenced the cancellation of the order.

[23] *Equality Act (Sexual Orientation) Regulations (Northern Ireland) 2006*, reg 3(1)(a).

[24] Indirect discrimination involves adverse impact that arises from the imposition of a 'provision, criterion or practice' and is subject to a justification defence: ibid reg 3(1)(b).

[25] The concept derives from the European Court of Justice: Case-177/88, *Dekker* [1990] ECR I-3941 (treating less favourable treatment by reason of pregnancy as sex discrimination, since it was based on a characteristic that was indissociable from the complainant's sex).

[26] In *Bull v Hall* (n 11), the Supreme Court treated marriage (the criterion that a bed-and-breakfast proprietor applied to giving double-bedded rooms to couples) as 'indissociable' from sexual orientation, since at that time only heterosexual couples could marry. The owners' consistency in applying the same principle to unmarried heterosexual couples and their religious objections were therefore sidelined, since this refusal to give a room to a same-sex couple amounted to direct discrimination.

[27] *Lee v Ashers Baking Co Ltd* (n 3) [42].

[28] ibid [64] and [66]. For a defence of this reasoning, see Wintemute (n 3) 350–52.

[29] A broader focus of this kind would have been relevant had the case been argued as a matter of indirect discrimination, but that claim was abandoned at an early point (perhaps because it would have allowed the baker to argue justification) and the case proceeded solely as a direct discrimination claim.

District Judge had mistakenly treated support for same-sex marriage as a proxy for sexual orientation, whereas it was to be found in people of all sexual orientations.[30]

A second key question in direct discrimination cases is the meaning to be given to the expression 'on grounds of' in the regulations (referring to less favourable treatment on the grounds of sexual orientation and religion or political belief). The introduction of the concept of associative discrimination dispensed with any requirement that the person be treated less favourably because of a protected characteristic of theirs, so that to deny a person service because of the protected characteristic of those they *associate with* is treated as direct discrimination.[31] So, for example, to refuse to serve a person in a bar because of the race, religion, political opinion or sexual orientation of their companion is unlawful. Thus, if Gareth Lee had been a heterosexual supporter of Queerspace, to refuse to supply him with a cake because of the involvement of LGBT persons in the group would nonetheless have been a clear instance of associative discrimination.

However, the basis on which the lower courts found associative discrimination was altogether different and related to the *message*, which it was argued 'was a statement of association with those of same-sex orientation'.[32] In the Court of Appeal's view, the exact correspondence between those to whom 'benefit' would 'accrue' from the message (ie, if same-sex marriage legislation were enacted in Northern Ireland) and the protected group of homosexual and lesbian persons fulfilled the criteria for associative discrimination.[33]

The Court of Appeal's line of reasoning if anything underlines the appellants' contention that the case was not about discrimination in the supply of a cake, but rather about the message on the cake. Neither the baker nor Queerspace was in a position to confer the benefit of same-sex marriage which lay at the heart of the contested difference in treatment. The Court's reasoning demonstrates the artificiality of extending associative discrimination to messages. This is very different from discriminating against someone because they are in a civil partnership or same-sex marriage recognised by law or because they associate with people who are. Moreover, as Lady Hale explained in the Supreme Court, many heterosexual people support same-sex marriage and to that extent could also be said to benefit from a message in support of it.[34] To depict the objection to the message as either indissociably connected to a protected characteristic or as a form of associative discrimination was misguided.[35] She cautioned against attempts to extend the law beyond its proper scope:[36] the bakery's objection was to the political cause, not to Lee's sexual orientation.[37] Although associative discrimination in

[30] *Lee v Ashers Baking Co Ltd* (n 1) [25].

[31] See Case C-303/06, *Coleman v Attridge Law* [2008] ICR 1128; *English v Thomas Sanderson Blinds Ltd* [2009] ICR 543.

[32] *Lee v McArthur* (n 4) [42].

[33] ibid [58].

[34] *Lee v Ashers Baking Co Ltd* (n 1) [33]. This is also why an indirect discrimination argument would have faced difficulty in establishing disparate impact.

[35] ibid [25], [28]–[34] respectively. The Northern Ireland Court of Appeal had misapplied the relevant tests in the context of the sexual orientation discrimination claim.

[36] ibid [35].

[37] To the extent that there was any discrimination on the basis of political belief, enforcing the anti-discrimination legislation against the bakery would breach the religious freedom (Art 9) and negative freedom of expression (Art 10) of the owners of the bakery: ibid [56].

relation to political belief discrimination was more arguable, to enforce the legislation against the bakery would breach the religious freedom (Article 9) and negative freedom of expression (Article 10) of the owners of the bakery, so that a *Convention*-friendly reading of the legislation should be adopted to prevent this conclusion.[38]

In the binary world of the Culture War, 'homophobia' is frequently taken to mean failure to endorse or approve of same-sex relationships rather than less favourable treatment or exhibiting antipathy towards same-sex-attracted persons. But there are important distinctions that should be made in the interests of moral pluralism.[39] Legislators enacting same-sex marriage in England and Wales carefully preserved the right to dissent by recognising the freedom to express a conflicting opinion critical of the change.[40] A fortiori, the situation in Northern Ireland at the time of *Lee v Ashers Baking Company*: freedom *not* to endorse a *proposed* change in the law. There is a difference between non-endorsement and discrimination, and the Supreme Court judgment respects it. However, had Lee's argument been successful, the effect would have been to grant LGBT rights advocates a special protected status that other political campaigns do not enjoy: of being able to insist that others promote their message, irrespective of the democratic process.

B. Expanding the Reach of Conscience

Critics of the *Lee v Ashers Baking Company* decision have argued that it represents an expansion of freedom of conscience at the cost of the rights of others. The criticism follows lines of argument that have become familiar, particularly in US constitutional jurisprudence and commentary in recent years. Dahlia Lithwick complains of 'conscience creep' – 'a slow but systematic effort to use religious conscience to sidestep laws that should apply to us all'.[41] Critics point to the growth in so-called complicity-based claims[42] and the increasing frequency with which commercial providers are invoking freedom of belief and conscience to claim exemption from non-discrimination norms in particular.[43] Both trends certainly exist, though it can be disputed whether they are,

[38] ibid [48] and [56].

[39] *cf Obergefell* v *Hodges* 135 S Ct 2584, 2602 (2015): 'Many who deem same-sex marriage to be wrong reach that conclusion based on decent and honorable religious or philosophical premises, and neither they nor their beliefs are disparaged here.'

[40] The *Marriage (Same Sex Couples) Act 2013* inserted a defence 'for the avoidance of doubt' preventing 'criticism of marriage which concerns the sex of the parties to marriage' from being taken of itself to be threatening or intended to stir up hatred under the offence of incitement to hatred on the grounds of sexual orientation (*Public Order Act 1986*, s 29JA(2)).

[41] D Lithwick, 'Conscience Creep: What's So Wrong with Conscience Clauses?' *Slate News* (3 October 2013), https://slate.com/news-and-politics/2013/10/is-there-a-principled-way-to-respond-to-the-proliferation-of-conscience-clauses.html.

[42] D NeJaime and R Siegel, 'Conscience Wars: Complicity-Based Conscience Claims in Religion and Politics' (2015) 124 *Yale Law Journal* 2516.

[43] A Sepinwall, 'Conscience in Commerce: Conceptualizing Discrimination in Public Accommodations' (2021) 53 *Connecticut Law Review* 466.

as some have claimed, a kind of rearguard action to resist to progressive legislation,[44] and an imposition of the claimant's beliefs on others,[45] or rather, as proponents would contend, a liberal riposte to attempts to impose a new moral orthodoxy under cover of equality law.[46]

The criticism of complicity-based claims is that they are different in form from classic or standard conscience claims (in particular, conscientious objection to military service). They concern new fields, such as health insurance, marriage registration or wedding services in which the objectors' involvement in the conduct they object to is more indirect, secondary or remote. Typically, the objector seeks to avoid being made *complicit* in an act that they regard as immoral by another person rather than avoiding being required to perform the immoral act themselves.[47]

Although some commentators have seen *Lee v Ashers Baking Company* in this light,[48] that interpretation is a strained one because the contested act (same-sex marriage) was distant not just from the baker's refusal, but, more importantly, also from the customer's order. Being refused a cake with a message in support of same-sex marriage is far removed from being denied the right to marry (which was the effect of legislation in Northern Ireland for which the Assembly was responsible), or being denied a cake to celebrate a marriage. Attempts to somehow link the refusal to these to argue that the baker's action impinged on equality rights are unpersuasive and require a series of leaps over these deep chasms. More is needed than a vague argument that the less favourable treatment 'has something to do with the sexual orientation of some people'.[49]

Moreover, Ashers did not argue that by providing the cake, it would become indirectly complicit or somehow endorse same-sex partnerships, unlike, for example, the claim made by some bed-and-breakfast proprietors refusing rooms or double beds to same-sex couples.[50] The baker's claim was to avert the *direct* harm to them of compelled speech, not an indirect or complicitous one.[51] The argument is narrower and not inherently related to religious belief; it is about political speech.[52] The Supreme Court found as much by treating it as a form of compelled speech that would fall within the ambit of negative freedom of expression.

Whether the refusal impinged on the right to campaign for the introduction of same-sex marriage[53] is more to the point, but presents the obvious difficulty that refusal

[44] NeJaime and Siegel (n 42) argue that their pursuit of complicity claims is part of a political strategy of 'preservation through transformation'; *cf* R Moon, 'Conscientious Objection and the Politics of Cake-Making' (2020) 9 *Oxford Journal of Law and Religion* 329, 345.

[45] T McCarthy, 'Insisting on Complicity' (2018) 18(1) *Contemporary Political Theory* 1: 'a complicity claim entails an insistence that the conduct of a third party should conform to the religious adherent's religious beliefs or face a cost'.

[46] D Laycock, 'Religious Liberty for Politically Active Minority Groups: A Response to NeJaime and Siegel' (2016) 125 *Yale Law Journal Forum* 369, www.yalelawjournal.org/forum/religious-liberty-for-politically-active-minority-groups.

[47] I have argued elsewhere that critics misunderstand the nature of complicity-based claims and exaggerate their novelty: I Leigh, 'Conscience, Complicity and Third Parties: A Fresh Approach' (forthcoming).

[48] See, eg, S Fredman, 'Tolerating the Intolerant: Religious Freedom, Complicity and the Right to Equality' (2020) 9 *Oxford Journal of Law and Religion* 305.

[49] *Lee v Ashers Baking Co Ltd* (n 1) [33], per Baroness Hale.

[50] See, eg, *Bull v Hall* (n 11) [34].

[51] *cf* McCrudden (n 21) 30.

[52] See 75–76 below.

[53] For example, Fredman ((n 48) 326) writes of the owners using Ashers Bakery as 'a vehicle to *deny* the right to others to advocate for an equality value which was central to their identity' (emphasis added).

to be associated with a political message or campaign that one disagrees with is the very life-blood of democracy. In that context, complicity claims are hardly contentious, absent the kind of political discrimination legislation in Northern Ireland, which is virtually unique. In any event, the respondents were keen to bolster their 'refusal to serve' line of argument by stressing that the cake was not for a *campaigning* event. But the message to be iced was undeniably an expression of support for a cause with which the baker disagreed and the respondent was also pursuing a legal claim of political belief discrimination relating to that cause and message.

Turning to the question of conscience claims in the commercial sphere, a number of such claims have been made in recent years by businesses such as cake makers, photographers or florists who decline to provide services to celebrate same-sex weddings.[54] Objections to the relevance of conscience claims in commercial contexts frequently refer to the provider's voluntary participation in the market, the general application of equality laws, and the harm caused by denial of access to goods and services for customers and clients from disadvantaged groups.[55] The underlying assumption is that bona fide conscience claims are limited to unavoidable moral conflicts and that it is reasonable for the objector to bear the cost of their beliefs if there is an escape route by foregoing business opportunities, even if the cost is high[56] and the cost to customers would be low or amount to no more than slight inconvenience.[57] However, broader objections that businesses forgo any claim to conscience by entering the public marketplace are inconsistent with widely applauded forms of ethical business behaviour or corporate social responsibility (investing in the community, subsidising environmental protection, paying a living wage etc).[58] Narrower legal objections to the exercise of freedom of conscience by corporations are mostly about the nature of legal personality and are therefore to the underlying basis for recognition of conscience claims in general (in particular, grounding the right in individual autonomy).[59] Connected to this is the question of whether the owners or directors of incorporated businesses can or should be allowed to lift the corporate veil in specific contexts to claim that the business' legal obligations conflict with their individual consciences.[60]

[54] See, eg, *Masterpiece Cakeshop Ltd v Colorado Civil Rights Commission*, 138 S Ct 1719 (2018) (cake maker); *State v Arlene's Flowers, Inc* (91615-2) 389 P 3d 543 (Supreme Court) (florist); *Elane Photography LLC* v *Willock* 309 P 3d 53 (2013) (Supreme Court of New Mexico) (photographer); and *Telescope Media Group* v *Minnesota* (2019) 936 F 3d 740 (8th Cir) (video maker).

[55] Especially controversial was the ruling of the US Supreme Court in *Burwell v Hobby Lobby Stores, Inc*, 537 US 354 (2014), which allowed a closely held corporation protection under the *Religious Freedom Restoration Act*.

[56] Several small businesses in well-known anti-discrimination cases have closed as a result: J Craddock, 'The Case for Complicity-Based Religious Accommodations' (2018) 12 *Tennessee Journal of Law and Public Policy* 234, 265–66.

[57] Ahdar and Giles point out that in some of these cases, 'it is hard to find much in the way of material or economic harm to the complainants'. See R Ahdar and J Giles, 'The Supreme Courts' Icing on the Trans-Atlantic Cakes' (2020) 9(1) *Oxford Journal of Law and Religion* 212, 221.

[58] B Scharffs, 'Our Fractured Attitude towards Corporate Conscience' in. Robinson and R Williams (eds), *Religious Liberty: Essays on First Amendment Law* (Cambridge University Press, 2016).

[59] A number of counter-objections here relate to the size/impersonality of the business endeavour. In response, see J Iuliano, 'Do Corporations Have Religious Rights?' (2015) 90 *Indiana Law Journal* 47.

[60] R Ahdar, 'Companies as Religious Liberty Claimants' (2016) 5(1) *Oxford Journal of Law and Religion* 1; F Cranmer, 'Can Secular Non-natural Persons be Said to Have a "Conscience"?' in J Adenitire (ed), *Religious Beliefs and Conscientious Exemptions in a Liberal State* (Hart Publishing, 2019).

These general considerations are more narrowly relevant to the plausibility of the business proprietor's claim that in providing the service, they would be personally endorsing or participating in something that goes against their beliefs or enabling or facilitating an activity they believe to be immoral. For example, no doubt mindful of the constitutional protection for expressive conduct, several wedding services businesses in the US have argued that their role is not a mechanical one, but constitutes participatory endorsement that engages their conscience, since it involves a creative contribution to or to presenting the event in its best light.[61] Relevant arguments here cluster around identifying the true nature of the business activity (and, in particular, whether an objective point of view is to be adopted or the business proprietor's own) and the scale of the business (with critics contending that conscience arguments are less tenable in larger enterprises).

In a Northern Ireland context, the difficulties of conscience that sexual orientation legislation could pose for small businesses had been well anticipated. When the *Equality Act 2010* was under parliamentary discussion in England and Wales, unsuccessful attempts were made by religious groups to obtain exemptions both for activities of churches that could be considered to involve supply of goods and services, and to deal with scenarios that small businesses with a religious ethos might encounter.[62] The equivalent opportunity to attempt to amend the legislation had not been available in relation to Northern Ireland because such legislation had been promulgated as statutory instruments as a consequence of the devolution arrangements. Instead, a challenge by way of judicial review was brought to the sexual orientation regulations. However, the Northern Ireland High Court declined to find them incompatible with Articles 9 and 10 of the *Convention* based on hypothetical scenarios, including one which postulated a Christian printer who refused to print material promoting homosexuality. Weatherup J determined that any such challenge was more appropriately brought in defence to discrimination proceedings in the County Court (like those subsequently brought against Ashers) rather than by way of generalised objections brought by judicial review.[63]

Critics argued that since Ashers' business had six shops employing more than 50 employees, the case for treating it is an extension of the religious beliefs of the proprietors was too weak to be credible. The argument is that objectively bakers should not be taken to endorse the messages that they ice on cakes[64] or if there is any such risk of misunderstanding or reputational harm, that it could be avoided by a disclaimer rather than by outright refusal.[65] Fulfilling the order, on the other hand, would be relatively mechanical and would not involve prolonged personal involvement by the proprietor,

[61] See, eg, *Masterpiece Cakeshop* (n 54) 1728, 1738 (Gorsuch and Alito JJ) and 1742–43 (Thomas J). In the end, the US Supreme Court found that the Commission's treatment of a baker who, because of conscientious objections to same-sex marriage, had declined to make a wedding cake for a same-sex couple had violated the First Amendment because of its hostility towards his religious position.

[62] The failure to grant wider exemptions for religious ethos to small businesses certainly influenced the County Court in *Lee v Ashers* (n 3) [32]–[35].

[63] *An Application for Judicial Review Brought by the Christian Institute* [2007] NIQB 66 [85] and [92].

[64] See Wintemute (n 3) 353–55, who argues in favour of the viewpoint of a reasonable onlooker. This argument was explicitly rejected by the Supreme Court (n 1 [54]); *cf Masterpiece Cakeshop* (n 54) 1744, per Thomas J.

[65] Wintemute (n 3) 355. A similar disclaimer argument was rejected in *Masterpiece Cakeshop* (n 54) 1745, per Thomas J.

or could be subcontracted or passed to an employed cake decorator who did not share the same objections of conscience. Alternatively, if certain orders like this one raise questions of conscience, the onus should be on the business to avoid these – for example, by changing their terms of business or excluding certain types of cake or messages. Since it had not done so, it should be required to fulfil the order.[66] Adjusting the range of services offered may indeed allow a business proprietor to avoid conflicts of conscience. For example, a baker like Ashers could cease offering to ice messages on cakes or severely restrict the range (eg, birthday greetings only), a bed and breakfast proprietor could offer single rooms only and so on. However, the cost of lost business may be substantial in some instances, whereas the inconvenience to the potential customer of obtaining the goods or service elsewhere in many cases would be relatively minor.

Cogent as these points may otherwise be, they should be taken in the context of the Supreme Court's rejection of the respondent's claim to have been treated less favourably on the grounds of sexual orientation. If the Court had found that there was discrimination, then the criticism that the baker's claim was an attempt to expand the exceptions in the sexual orientation regulations for religious groups into the realm of commercial services[67] would have carried some weight. However, it did not. The arguments therefore played out in the different context of the political belief discrimination claim and, relatedly, the baker's successful argument that to be required to supply the cake with a message contrary to its proprietor's beliefs would be a form of compelled speech.

C. Compelled Speech

The compelled speech argument can perhaps best be explained by a fictional scenario which more clearly distances it from questions of sexual orientation. Imagine it is July 2016. A hard-fought referendum has just found narrowly in favour of Brexit and popular feelings are running high. A man goes into a print shop and places an order for 'We Love EU' posters. When the proprietor – a keen Brexiteer – reviews the order taken by staff, he cancels it as he refuses to assist in promoting a message contrary to his beliefs. Few people would consider that this scenario raises any legal issues (apart from a potential minor contractual claim). Suppose, however, that the shop was in Northern Ireland, where political belief is a protected characteristic under equality legislation. Many of us would still intuitively reason that the facts concern refusal to promote a message rather than discrimination on the grounds of political belief against the potential customer. The scenario is imaginary of course, but the analogy is appropriate, bearing in mind the contentious vote against same-sex marriage legislation in the Northern Ireland Assembly less than two weeks before Mr Lee ordered his cake and that the person behind the shop counter (Mrs McArthur) had led prayers in her church about this very question.

[66] As McCrudden points out ((n 21) 243–44), there seems to be a misunderstanding of the legal history at work in the background here. In the UK, anti-discrimination law has been laid on top of and is a statutory exception to common law freedom of contract rather than vice versa: A Lester and G Bindman, *Race and Law* (Penguin, 1972) ch 1.

[67] As the District Judge pointed out, the limited exceptions for religious organisations were inapplicable. Lobbying to broaden the exemptions to cover small businesses had failed: *Lee v Ashers Baking Co Ltd* (n 3) [32]–[35].

The claim then was that the baker should not be required to promote a message with which it profoundly disagreed.[68] This is not to be confused with the claim made in some US cases that wedding services (such as cake making or flower arranging) are a form of protected expressive conduct, irrespective of explicit messages If it is accepted that fulfilling the cake order involved the bakery or its directors identifying with the message, then being required to do so in the case of a message that they disagreed with would undoubtedly constitute an interference with their freedom of expression. Equally, approached from the direction of the directors' conscience,[69] the same applies – this is the basis, after all, for the earliest conscience provisions, allowing a person to affirm rather than swearing a religious oath in court or as a condition of public office.[70]

The message was undeniably an expression of support for a cause with which the baker disagreed. The respondent's own legal claim was one of political discrimination relating to that cause and message. In the light of this, the Supreme Court's ruling that political discrimination legislation had to be interpreted subject to the negative freedom of expression and freedom of conscience of the directors is hardly surprising. Where political discrimination is recognised, in a liberal society, as it is in Northern Ireland, inevitably there are limits to that concept to protect the beliefs of third persons.

IV. The Strasbourg Application

Following the rejection of his case by the UK Supreme Court, Gareth Lee has petitioned the European Court of Human Rights.[71] He alleges that his rights under Articles 8, 9, 10 and 14 of the *Convention* have been breached by the Supreme Court's dismissal of his claims. Whether the application succeeds is likely to depend on the Court's choice between the competing narratives outlined above – of discrimination or compelled speech.

The application portrays the case as one of clashing rights,[72] but to characterise it in this way for the purposes of the *Convention* is arguably contentious, especially in view of the *evidential* rejection by the domestic courts of the sexual orientation discrimination

[68] *cf Lexington Fayette Urban County Human Rights Commission v Hands on Originals, Inc* [2017] Court of Appeals 2015-CA-000745-MR (refusal by printer to endorse a gay pride message). And, likewise, with reference to freedom of religion, see *Ontario Human Rights Commission v Brockie* (2002), 222 DLR (4th) 174 (Ontario Divisional Court) [58] for an example of reading in an exemption for a printer being required to print material 'in direct conflict with the core elements of [the business owner's] religious belief'.

[69] For discussion on the approach of the European Court of Human Rights to whether commercial organisations as such have rights under Art 9, see McCrudden (n 21) 257–59; J Calderwood Norton, *Freedom of Religious Organisations* (Oxford University Press, 2016) 179–80.

[70] The European Court of Human Rights has repeatedly found that a requirement to swear a religious oath violates Art 9: *Buscarini v San Marino* (2000) 30 EHRR 208; *Alexandridis v Greece*, Application No 19516/06 (ECHR, 21 February 2008); *Dimitras v Greece*, Application Nos 42837/06, 3269/07, 35793/07 and 6099/08 (ECHR, 3 June 2010).

[71] *Lee v UK*, Application No 18860/19 (communicated by the First Section of the ECtHR on 6 March 2020). At the time of writing, the European Court of Human Rights had not handed down its decision. On 6 January 2022, the Court declared that the case was inadmissible on the basis that the applicants had not exhausted all domestic remedies.

[72] ibid: 'the interference was not proportionate and that the Supreme Court disregarded the democratically chosen resolution to the conflict of rights between religious organisations and persons of same sex orientation, and those supporting the aspirations of such persons'.

claim. According to its settled jurisprudence, the European Court of Human Rights should not re-open evidential questions. Assuming that approach is followed, the narrower question will be whether the Supreme Court's approach to 'associative discrimination' both in relation to sexual orientation and political belief discrimination, first, engages *Convention* rights and, if it does, second, infringes the applicant's rights because the weight given to the baker's rights was disproportionate. These will be difficult arguments to sustain.

On the first point, the *Convention* does not require Member States to grant a domestic remedy for goods and services discrimination (either at all or covering these specific grounds). There is no general *Convention* right to be protected against discrimination by private persons in the provision of goods and services.[73] There are significant variations among European countries over anti-discrimination legislation covering goods and services.[74] Such variations exist even between Great Britain and Northern Ireland: political belief discrimination does not apply in the former.[75] Consequently, it can be argued that the Northern Irish legislation goes considerably further than is required by the *Convention* and raises the danger (which materialised because of the approach of the lower courts in this case) of interfering with rights – of freedom of expression and of religion and belief – that *are* required to be protected under the *Convention*. Conversely, to find that the domestic interpretation of legislation engages the applicant's *Convention* rights would suggest that the Council of Europe states that provide no remedy are in breach of the ECHR, since they have no goods and services discrimination legislation at all – a radical conclusion. The Court appears to be aware of this issue, judging from its questions to the parties, which ask whether Articles 8, 9 and 10 are engaged both alone and in conjunction with Article 14.[76]

As regards the Article 10 claim, the government could contend that there was no interference with Lee's right to freedom of expression or to engage in political advocacy. These rights do not include a liberty to compel other private individuals to assist or endorse his message or belief (at all and, in any event, not contrary to their own beliefs). Arguably, the facts should be understood as raising the question of whether Lee has a *Convention* right to require others (whether or not engaged in commercial services) to assist a political campaign. Same-sex marriage did not apply to Northern Ireland at the relevant time and there can be little doubt that to oppose its introduction falls squarely within the range of political discourse, which is highly protected under Article 10.[77] From this point of view the respondent was free to promote his message for a change in the law, but the appellants, just like anyone else, could not be compelled to assist him.

There is a possibility that, notwithstanding these points, the Strasbourg Court could find that the claim falls within the 'ambit' of a *Convention* right so as to engage Article 14.

[73] Article 14 applies only to discrimination by states in relation to the enjoyment of *Convention* rights. Protocol 12 (which the UK has not signed and therefore could not be pleaded) is wider, but still stops short of requiring states to prohibit discrimination by private parties.

[74] This is why proposals for an EU Directive in that area have made no progress since 2008: European Commission, 'Proposal for a Council Directive on Implementing the Principle of Equal Treatment between Persons irrespective of Religion or Belief, Disability, Age or Sexual Orientation' COM (2008) 0426 final.

[75] Political belief is not a protected characteristic under the *Equality Act 2010*.

[76] *Lee v UK* (n 71). The basis of the applicant's Art 9 claim is unclear; it may be found inadmissible since it was not clearly raised in the domestic proceedings.

[77] *Castells v Spain* (1992) 14 EHRR 445.

However, the text of Article 14 applies to discrimination in the enjoyment of *Convention* rights and where there are such significant variations among Member States, arguably the Court should be reluctant to find that Article 14 is engaged. Admittedly, in its earlier jurisprudence, the Court has sometimes applied the ambit test generously in relation to variations in the recognition of civil partnerships and same-sex marriage among Member States, but, as we have seen, the connection here is considerably more tenuous.[78]

Consequently, it is arguable that there has been no interference with the applicant's *Convention* rights. There is no *Convention* right to be supplied with a cake with a message, still less a political message with which the putative supplier disagrees.

If, however, the Court were to find that the applicant's rights are engaged, it would then consider whether any difference in treatment has an objective and reasonable justification under Article 14. The government would argue that the purpose was to protect the *Convention* rights of the baker. Likewise, if the Court were to find Article 8, 9 or 10 to be engaged standing alone, the question would be whether the Supreme Court's approach amounted to a justified and proportionate limitation to protect the rights and freedoms of others.

If the European Court of Human Rights accepts the compelled speech narrative, then the balance struck by the domestic courts appears to be well within the margin of appreciation. European citizens are expected to tolerate those with differing political, moral and religious opinions according to the vision of pluralism repeatedly articulated by the Court.[79] To attempt to coerce others to endorse or propagate one's views is the antithesis of citizenship in a liberal democracy of the kind presupposed by the *European Convention*.[80]

V. Conclusion

There is perhaps a broader lesson to be drawn from the 'gay cake' case: that religious claims are most likely to succeed when they appeal to other, more generally accepted values or, to put it more contentiously, go incognito. This might appear to support the view advanced by some theorists that the concept of religious liberty could be dispensed with, owing to the protection granted to the underlying interests by freedom of speech, freedom of conscience, the right to privacy and freedom of association.[81] According to the disaggregation thesis of political theorist Cécile Laborde, a liberal state should acknowledge the underlying interests protected by religious freedom, but not because of their 'religious' nature.[82] Freedom of conscience would therefore fall to be protected as an aspect of negative freedom of speech.

[78] Text at 70–72 above.

[79] *Appel-Irrgang v Germany*, Application No 45216/07 (20 October 2009): 'the Court considers that it is not possible to deduce from the Convention a right not to be exposed to convictions contrary to one's own'. See also *Otto-Preminger Institute v Austria*, Application No 13470/87 (20 September 1994) [47]; and *Alekseyev v Russia*, Application Nos 25924/08 and 14599/09 (21 October 2010) [73]: 'Article 11 of the Convention protects a demonstration that may annoy or cause offence to persons opposed to the ideas or claims that it is seeking to promote.'

[80] Contrast Gareth Lee's claim that he felt like 'a second-class citizen' because of Ashers' refusal (n 10).

[81] C Eisengruber and L Sager, *Religious Freedom and the Constitution* (Harvard University Press, 2007).

[82] C Laborde, *Liberalism's Religion* (Harvard University Press, 2019).

Certainly, it could be argued that claimants motivated by religious beliefs are more likely to find a sympathetic hearing from both fellow citizens and judges when they phrase their claims in terms that appeal to common language, concepts and understanding. The normative claim of 'public reason' that there is a duty on citizens to translate religious language into non-comprehensive terms is divisive,[83] but the practical advantage of doing so is clear. It is a common-sense principle of successful advocacy that a case should be presented in a way that commands the widest support and avoids unnecessarily contentious claims. Is it too optimistic to hope that by adhering to such a strategy, we could begin to de-escalate the Culture War?

[83] R Ahdar and I Leigh, *Religious Freedom in the Liberal State*, 2nd edn (Oxford University Press, 2013) 61–69.

6

R v Big M Drug Mart

The Unavoidable Pragmatism of Religious Freedom

RICHARD MOON

I. Introduction

The first freedom of religion case to reach the Supreme Court of Canada, following the enactment of the *Canadian Charter of Rights and Freedom* (hereinafter 'the *Charter*') in 1982, was an appeal from the conviction of a Calgary drug store, Big M Drug Mart, for operating on Sundays contrary to the Federal *Lord's Day Act*.[1] The *Act*, which dated from 1906, prohibited a variety of commercial activities on Sundays, including retail sales. The store argued that the *Act* breached section 2(a) of the *Charter* (freedom of conscience and religion), and that this breach could not be justified under section 1, the *Charter*'s limitations provision.

In *R v Big M Drug Mart* (hereinafter '*Big M*'), the Court took the opportunity to set out what it saw as the purpose or foundation of the *Charter* right. Chief Justice Dickson, writing for the Court, held that section 2(a) protects the liberty of the individual in matters of conscience and religion. It prohibits the state from compelling an individual to engage in a religious practice and from restricting their religious practice without a legitimate public reason. However, within the *Big M* decision were the seeds of another conception of religious freedom. In holding that the *Lord's Day Act* breached section 2(a), Dickson CJ seemed to say not only that the state must refrain from coercion in religious matters, but that it must also refrain from supporting or preferring the beliefs and practices of a particular religious group – that the state should remain neutral in religious matters.

In subsequent cases, the Supreme Court has explicitly adopted a requirement that the state remain neutral in religious matters.[2] However, the neutrality requirement rests on a very different understanding of the freedom's purpose than that set out by the Court in *Big M*. Religious freedom on this account is a form of equality right that treats

[1] *R v Big M Drug Mart* [1985] 1 SCR 295.
[2] *SL v Commission scolaire des Chenes* (2012) SCC 7.

religious practices as the equivalent of individual traits or characteristics (as aspects of the adherent's identity) that should be bracketed off from politics – both excluded and insulated from political decision making.

However, the Court has applied this requirement selectively. The most obvious difficulty with the state neutrality requirement is that religious belief systems often have something to say about the rights and interests of others and the nature of a just society, and that the state must sometimes take a position on these civic issues, either accepting or rejecting different (religious) views. A commitment to state neutrality requires that the courts distinguish between different elements of a religious belief system. The state should not support or privilege the spiritual practices of a particular faith, but it cannot remain neutral towards religiously based values – religious beliefs about civic life. Religious beliefs that address civic concerns can neither be excluded nor insulated from public decision making. This distinction between the civic and spiritual elements is difficult and uncertain, yet unavoidable.

Behind the Court's uneven application of the neutrality requirement lies a complex conception of religious commitment in which religion is viewed as both a cultural identity and a personal commitment to certain beliefs or claims about truth and right. Beginning with *Big M*, the Court has struggled to fit this complex conception of religious commitment into a constitutional framework that relies on a distinction between personal choices or commitments that should be protected as a matter of individual liberty, and shared attributes or cultural practices that should sometimes be respected as a matter of equality. The constitutional framework, and perhaps more deeply our conception of rights and agency, imposes this distinction between judgment and identity on the complex experience of religious commitment.

II. The Historical Context

Canada's early history as a colony and nation was marked by acts of harsh religious suppression and moments of pragmatic religious tolerance.[3] The early efforts of European colonisers, first the French and later the British, to convert Indigenous peoples to a version of Christianity sometimes involved the active suppression of spiritual practices. Cultural suppression became standard practice with the growth of European settlement and the extension of political control by colonial and Canadian authorities over lands occupied by Indigenous communities.[4] Yet the country's early history was also marked by significant acts of religious tolerance. Following the conquest of Quebec by the British in the middle of the eighteenth century, the British Parliament enacted the *Quebec Act, 1774*,[5] which extended to the colony's French Catholic inhabitants the right to maintain the French language, the civil law system and the Roman Catholic faith. The British government's motives were entirely pragmatic: to ensure the stability of the Quebec colony and the loyalty of its inhabitants at a time when the American colonies

[3] See generally R Moon, *Freedom of Conscience and Religion* (Irwin Law, 2014) ch 1.

[4] In the later part of the nineteenth century, spiritual practices, such as spirit dancing in the Prairies and the potlach on the West Coast, were banned by the federal government.

[5] *Quebec Act, 1774* (UK) 14 Geo III, c 83.

were becoming disenchanted with British rule. The political accommodation between Roman Catholic and Protestant communities, while always imperfect and often precarious, shaped the new country's response to the growth of religious plurality in the late nineteenth and early twentieth centuries. This response involved the general protection of individual liberty in religious practice, but also the pragmatic accommodation of certain minority group practices within the context of a general public privileging of Christian or non-denominational Protestant practices.

While much of Canada's early commitment to religious freedom was simply a pragmatic compromise to ensure social peace and political stability, in a succession of judgments in the 1950s concerning the Jehovah's Witness community, the Supreme Court of Canada sought to articulate a principled account of religious freedom. In *Saumur v City of Quebec*, the Court struck down a bylaw that forbade the distribution of literature in the streets of Quebec City without the prior consent of the chief of police – a bylaw that was understood by all as intended to limit the proselytising activities of the Jehovah's Witness community.[6] After setting out some of the history of religious tolerance in Canada, Justice Rand, in the *Saumur* decision, described religious freedom as one of the 'original freedoms which are at once the necessary attributes and modes of self-expression of human beings and the primary conditions of the community life within a legal order'.[7] He went on to hold that the provinces lacked the authority, under the constitutional division of powers, to restrict religious freedom and other fundamental rights – that 'legislation "in relation" to religion and its profession is not a local or private matter … the dimensions of this interest are nationwide … it appertains to a boundless field of ideas, beliefs and faiths with the deepest roots and loyalties; a religious incident reverberates from one end of this country to the other'.[8]

The concern for the protection of rights that emerged in Europe and elsewhere following the atrocities of the Second World War found expression in international human rights treaties such as the *Universal Declaration of Human Rights* (*UNDHR*) and the *International Covenant on Civil and Political Rights* (*ICCPR*), both of which gave protection to freedom of conscience and religion. In Canada, as in other countries, this concern led to the enactment of human rights code restrictions on religious and other forms of discrimination, beginning in the late 1940s, to the introduction of the Canadian Bill of Rights in 1960 and eventually to the constitutional entrenchment of the *Canadian Charter of Rights and Freedom* in 1982.

Section 2(a) of the *Charter*, which protects the individual's 'freedom of conscience and religion', is framed in terms similar to Article 18 *UNDHR* and Article 18 *ICCPR*, as well as Article 9 of the *European Convention on Human Rights*. While the Canadian courts' interpretation of section 2(a) is in many respects similar to the interpretation given to these other provisions, their understanding of the scope and limits of

[6] *Saumur v City of Quebec* [1953] 2 SCR 299 (SCC).

[7] ibid 329.

[8] ibid 32. See also *Chaput v Romain* [1955] SCR 834 (SCC), in which the Quebec provincial police 'broke up' an orderly religious meeting of Jehovah's Witnesses in a private home, seizing Bibles and other religious literature without a warrant. The Supreme Court of Canada found that the police action breached the *Criminal Code* prohibition against obstructing a minister who is conducting a religious meeting. In reaching this conclusion, Taschereau J declared that in Canada, there is no state religion and that all denominations enjoy the same freedom of speech and thought.

the section 2(a) right has been shaped by the particular history and circumstances of Canada – a country in which there has been neither a formal religious establishment, as in the UK, nor a historical resistance to state support for religion, as in the US.

When the *Canadian Charter of Rights and Freedoms* was enacted in 1982, religion in Canada was generally regarded as a private matter, with little visible presence in the country's political life. There were, of course, individuals and groups who were motivated by a religious commitment to take political action, but their objectives were almost always civic – to eradicate poverty, or ban landmines, or prohibit abortion – and not to advance the particular practices of their faith. Indeed, political actors seldom spoke publicly about their faith and did not justify their public actions explicitly on religious grounds. Some of the early support for a charter of rights in Canada had been a reaction to acts of state suppression of religious and cultural practices, such as the 'war without mercy' against the proselytising activities of the Jehovah's Witness community in Quebec in the 1950s.[9] However, by 1982, the state seemed no longer to be engaged in the direct suppression of religious practices.

Yet, at the time of the *Charter*'s enactment, there were also several reasons to think that issues of religious freedom might again become significant. Those who had predicted the ineluctable decline of religious belief had begun to rethink this assumption. Religious commitment seemed not only to be stubbornly persistent, but, indeed, to be experiencing a revival in evangelical, fundamentalist and spiritual forms. Even if most religious adherents accepted that religion and politics should remain separate, they did not always agree about where the line between private spirituality and public secularism should be drawn. In addition, immigration in the later part of the twentieth century had significantly added to the religious diversity of the country. The number of adherents to non-Christian belief systems, including Sikhism, Islam and Hinduism, grew significantly in this period. This growth in diversity raised questions about the historic ordering of public life on the basis of Christian practices. Even if the majority of the country saw the imprint of Christian practice on public life as 'just the way things were' or as cultural rather than religious in character, other religious groups viewed the public traces of Christian practice differently. In the freedom of religion cases that arose in the first decades of the *Charter*, the courts and other state actors were asked to remove the vestiges of Christian practice from the public sphere or to exempt religious minority group members from legal standards that privileged mainstream Christian practice and failed to take account of minority practices.

III. *Big M Drug Mart*: Liberty and Equality

The Court in *Big M Drug Mart* held that section 2(a) protects the liberty of the individual in matters of religion or conscience: the individual must be free 'to hold and to manifest whatever beliefs and opinions his or her conscience dictates, provided inter alia only that such manifestations do not injure his or her neighbours'.[10] According to

[9] Quebec Premier Maurice Duplessis, quoted in W Kaplan, *State and Salvation: The Jehovah's Witnesses and Their Fight for Civil Rights* (University of Toronto Press, 1989) 230.

[10] *Big M* (n 1) [123].

Dickson CJ, the protection of freedom of religion rests on 'the centrality of individual conscience and the inappropriateness of governmental intervention to compel or to constrain its manifestation'.[11] No one should 'be forced to act in a way contrary to his beliefs or his conscience', except when necessary to protect important public interests or individual rights.[12] The freedom precludes the state from compelling an individual to engage in a religious practice and from restricting their religious practice unless necessary to protect the rights and interests of others.

The Chief Justice traced this understanding of religious freedom back to John Locke and other post-Reformation writers, who based their opposition to state coercion in religious matters on the perception that 'belief ... was not amenable to compulsion' and that '[a]ttempts to compel belief or practice denied the reality of individual conscience and dishonoured the God that had planted it in His Creatures'.[13] Locke claimed that spiritual matters lay within the sphere of individual conscience – the individual's divinely endowed capacity to recognise spiritual truth – and were not the business of the state. According to him, the power of the state is exercised exclusively through coercion, which is ineffective in spiritual matters. A government can require its citizens to conform to certain standards of outward behaviour, but it cannot compel them to embrace spiritual truth – to sincerely believe. Religious coercion is at best futile and at worst blasphemous, causing individuals to follow practices in which they do not believe. The state, then, should concern itself only with civil interests, such as life, liberty, health and property.

Locke argued that the protection of religious freedom was necessary for the individual's realisation of spiritual truth and their meaningful commitment to that truth. However, in Dickson CJ's account, freedom of religion is protected not for the religious reasons given by Locke. For Dickson CJ, the protection of freedom of conscience and religion rests instead on secular grounds, such as respect for human dignity and 'our democratic political tradition'.[14] The freedom is protected because it is through the exercise of choice or judgement – the exercise of autonomy – that an individual lives an authentic life, a life that is their own. Dickson CJ was clear that the freedom's protection extends to the individual's most fundamental beliefs, whether these are religious or non-religious in character.

The Court in *Big M* found that the *Lord's Day Act* breached section 2(a) because its 'true purpose' was to compel a religious practice – the observance of the Christian Sabbath.[15] The government had argued that even if the purpose of the law might have once been religious, it could now be understood in more secular terms, as the creation of a common pause day for workers.[16] However, Dickson CJ rejected this attempt to 'shift' the purpose of the law as a way of correcting any constitutional flaws. In his view, the law's purpose 'is a function of the intent of those who drafted and enacted the legislation at the time, and

[11] ibid [121].
[12] ibid [95].
[13] ibid [120].
[14] ibid [122].
[15] ibid [136].
[16] In *R v Edwards Books and Art Ltd* [1986] 2 SCR 713, the Supreme Court upheld a provincial Sunday closing law. Importantly, it held that because the law's purpose was to create a common pause day (which was in the constitutional power of the provinces to do), the law did not compel a religious practice.

not of any shifting variable'.[17] The more serious difficulty with this attempt to reframe the law's purpose was that prior to the enactment of the *Charter*, the federal government had claimed that it had the authority to pass the *Lord's Day Act*, under its power to enact criminal laws, because the law's purpose was to compel Sabbath observance – to enforce 'public morality'. Since the provinces have exclusive jurisdiction under the Constitution to enact laws regulating business and trade activities within their territories, any attempt by the federal government to defend the law under the *Charter* on the basis that it advances a secular purpose, such as the creation of a common pause day for workers, would undermine the law's constitutionality under the federal division of powers. The Chief Justice had little patience for government's argument:

> It seems disingenuous to say that the legislation is valid criminal law and offends section 2 (a) because it compels the observance of a Christian religious duty yet is still a reasonable limit demonstrably justifiable because it achieves the secular objective the legislators did not primarily intend … Parliament cannot rely upon an ultra vires purpose under section 1 of the Charter.[18]

The Chief Justice then found that the law could not be saved under section 1, as a justified limit on the right, because its purpose was to compel a religious practice: 'The characterization of the purpose of the Act as one which compels religious observance renders it unnecessary to decide the questions of whether section 1 could validate such legislation whose purpose was otherwise.'[19] Such a purpose could not be considered pressing and substantial, and so it was unnecessary for the Court to address the other elements of the section 1 proportionality test. It would seem to follow from this that section 1 has no significant role in any section 2(a) cases in which the breach is based on state compulsion of (or support for) religion.

While there could be little doubt that the law's purpose was religious, it was less obvious that its purpose was to coerce a religious practice. After all, the *Lord's Day Act* did not require anyone to honour the Sabbath by attending church or reading the Bible or reflecting upon their spiritual commitments. It prevented individuals from working, but did not require that they worship or even that they rest.[20] However, Dickson CJ adopted a broad view of religious compulsion:

> In my view, the guarantee of freedom of conscience and religion prevents the government from compelling individuals to perform or abstain from performing otherwise harmless acts because of the religious significance of those acts to others. The element of religious compulsion is perhaps somewhat more difficult to perceive (especially for those whose beliefs are being enforced) when, as here, it is non-action rather than action that is being decreed, but in my view compulsion is nevertheless what it amounts to.[21]

[17] *Big M* (n 1) [91].
[18] ibid [141].
[19] ibid [142].
[20] This was the view of the Supreme Court of Canada in an earlier case, *Robertson and Rosetanni v The Queen* [1963] SCR 651, decided in 1963 under the federal Bill of Rights, a statute that limited federal action: 'The practical result of this law on those whose religion requires them to observe a day of rest other than Sunday, is a purely secular and financial one in that they are required to refrain from carrying on or conducting their business on Sunday as well as on their own day of rest. In some cases, this is no doubt a business inconvenience, but it is neither an abrogation nor an abridgment nor an infringement of religious freedom, and the fact that it has been brought about by reason of the existence of a statute enacted for the purpose of preserving the sanctity of Sunday, cannot, in my view, be construed as attaching some religious significance to an effect which is purely secular in so far as non-Christians are concerned' (at 658–59).
[21] *Big M* (n 1) [133].

The Chief Justice recognised that the law did not compel the individual to perform a particular religious act, but, instead, required that they refrain from performing an otherwise lawful activity.

The purpose of the law might then have been simply to support those who wished to keep the Sunday Sabbath by removing the economic costs that would result from not working on Sunday when other people (and, more particularly, other retailers) were prepared to treat it as another business day. Alternatively, its purpose might have been to encourage all individuals to keep the Sunday Sabbath, without actually requiring anyone to do so.

However, the Court seemed prepared to find a breach of religious freedom simply because the law had a purpose that was religious in character. Near the end of his judgment, Dickson CJ stated that it was 'constitutional incompetent for the federal Parliament to provide legislative preference for any one religion at the expense of those of another religious persuasion'.[22] More specifically, on the law at issue in this case, he said:

> To the extent that it binds all to a sectarian Christian ideal, the Lord's Day Act works a form of coercion inimical to the spirit of the Charter and the dignity of all non-Christians. In proclaiming the standards of the Christian faith, the Act creates a climate hostile to, and gives the appearance of discrimination against, non-Christian Canadians. It takes religious values rooted in Christian morality and, using the force of the state, translates them into a positive law binding on believers and non-believers alike. The theological content of the legislation remains as a subtle and constant reminder to religious minorities within the country of their difference with, and alienation from, the dominant religious culture.[23]

Thus, the Court's objection to the *Lord's Day Act* may not have been that it compelled, or was intended to compel, individuals to keep the Sabbath, but was instead that it supported or favoured the practice of the dominant religious group. If so, it rests on a very different understanding of religious freedom – one that is concerned not simply with the protection of individual liberty in spiritual matters, but instead with the equal treatment of different religious belief systems or communities.

Freedom of religion, understood as a liberty, precludes the state from compelling an individual to engage in a religious practice and from restricting their religious practice without a legitimate public reason. However, it does not preclude the state from supporting a religious practice, unless we adopt a very attenuated understanding of coercion, and it does not require the state to compromise its policies in order to accommodate a religious practice.

IV. After *Big M*: Neutrality and Equality

The requirement that the state remain neutral in religious matters was affirmed in later judgments of the Court. Deschamps J, writing for the majority of the Court in *SL v Commission scolaire des Chenes*, accepted that: 'Religious neutrality is now seen by many Western states as a legitimate means of creating a free space in which citizens of

[22] ibid [134].
[23] ibid [97].

various beliefs can exercise their individual rights.'[24] According to the Court, the state is precluded from supporting or preferring the practices of one religious system over another (or religious belief over atheism and vice versa) and from restricting religious practices unless there is a good reason to do so – put more positively, the state has a duty to make some accommodation for religious practices.[25]

To bracket religion off from politics in this way is to treat it as a matter of identity, similar to gender or race. The separation of religion and politics – both the exclusion and the insulation of religion from political decision making or at least political contest – rests on a recognition of the deep connection between the individual and their religious or cultural group and on a concern about the status or vitality of religious groups.[26] Accommodation should be made for the beliefs or practices of different religious groups, because these groups are a source of identity and meaning for their members. Indeed, if the individual's religious beliefs or moral commitments are deeply held or rooted (and should sometimes to be insulated from politics), it is because they are part of a shared tradition or group culture to which their identity (their worldview and sense of place in the world) is tied. More practically, accommodation should sometimes be made to avoid the marginalisation of religious groups within the larger political community. If the law prevents the members of some religious groups from fully participating in society, their identification or connection with that society may be negatively affected and this in turn may result in social conflict. The ties between religious group members, which may be intergenerational and comprehensive, make the group particularly vulnerable to suspicion, discrimination and marginalisation.[27]

The shift in the Court's understanding of the freedom's justification, from liberty to equality, has been accompanied by a narrowing of the freedom's scope. If the requirement that the state accommodate religious practices – that it treat religious practices as a cultural identity that lies outside the scope of politics – is tied to the role of these practices in the life of a religious group, then accommodation may not (often) extend to an individual's non-religious practices. Freedom of conscience, like freedom of religion,

[24] *SL v Commission scolaire des Chenes* (n 2) [17]; and *Mouvement laïque québécois v Saguenay (City)*, 2015 SCC 16. The concurring judgment of LeBel J in *SL* expressed a similar view: 'Moreover, in the modern Canadian political system, the state in principle takes a position of neutrality. And it is barred from enacting private legislation that favours one religion over another' (at [54]). While the courts have sometimes come close to saying that the state should not favour secular (non-religious) over religious beliefs systems, they have generally confined the application of the neutrality requirement to religious belief systems, so that the state is precluded from favouring one religious belief system over another and religious beliefs over non-religious beliefs.

[25] See Moon (n 3).

[26] The reasons for (and the limited/selective application of) state neutrality are discussed in R Moon, 'Freedom of Religion under the Charter of Rights: The Limits of State Neutrality' (2012) 45 *UBC Law Review* 497. See also C Laborde, *Liberalism's Religion* (Harvard University Press, 2017).

[27] The courts have had difficulty acknowledging the group or collective character of religion, and religious freedom, perhaps because within any religious community or tradition, there is an enormous diversity of belief and practice. The followers of a religious tradition may interpret scripture or apply the practices of the tradition in different ways, and yet still understand themselves to be members of that tradition – as Christians or Jews or Buddhists. They may identify with a religious tradition or belief system in different ways, with different levels of commitment and degrees of involvement. This is a reminder of the way in which religion is both a matter of cultural identity and personal commitment – that it is a system or tradition that individual members understand, and identify with, in ways that may be particular or personal.

may only protect practices that can be bracketed off from political contest and treated as part of a personal or communal set of practices. This seems to be what is meant when non-religious practices are described as 'deeply held': that they are part of a distinctive worldview that runs contrary to conventional morality or mainstream practice. As a practical matter, it may be that such practices are seldom sustained outside cultural or religious communities. Despite the apparent breadth of section 2(a) and the Court's formal acknowledgement that freedom of conscience and religion protects both religious and non-religious (fundamental) values and beliefs, the former have been at the centre of the Canadian freedom of religion and conscience cases. The protection of non-religious beliefs and practices (the conscience component of section 2(a)) appears to be limited to practices that resemble in content and structure familiar religious practices.[28]

V. The Limits of Neutrality

A. State Support for Religion

The Court has limited the application of the neutrality requirement in a few ways. First, it has recognised that religious practices have shaped the traditions or customs of the community and cannot simply be erased from the public sphere. In *Mouvement laïque québécois v Saguenay*, the Court said that 'the state's duty of neutrality does not require it to abstain from celebrating and preserving its religious heritage'.[29] The Canadian courts have not demanded that governments (literally or metaphorically) sandblast religious symbols and practices from physical and social structures, some of which were constructed long ago. Yet, it may often be difficult to determine when the use of religious symbols or practices by the state is simply an acknowledgement or preservation of the country's religious history, and when it amounts to a present affirmation of the truth of a particular religious belief system; indeed, it may be that the acknowledgement of history or tradition always involves some form of contemporary affirmation.[30]

Second, the courts have recognised that religion is important in the personal and communal lives of citizens. If a large part of the population is Christian, it is difficult

[28] R Moon, 'Conscience in the Image of Religion' in J Adenitire (ed), *Religious Beliefs and Conscientious Exemptions in a Liberal State* (Hart Publishing, 2019). The only reported Canadian case, in which freedom of conscience under s 2(a) was found to have been breached, involved a refusal by the federal prison authorities to provide an inmate with vegetarian meals; see *Maurice v Canada (AG)* 2002 FCT 69. The inmate's claim in that case was helped by the similarity of his practice (vegetarianism) to a recognised religious practice and indeed by the fact that he had previously been provided with vegetarian meals on religious grounds. The court may also have been willing to protect a belief/practice that in ordinary circumstances is simply a private or personal matter. Outside the prison context, vegetarianism is a practice in which the individual is free to engage and that has no obvious impact on the rights or interests of others. The state ordinarily has no direct involvement in the individual's dietary choices. However, within the prison, all aspects of an inmate's life are controlled by the prison authorities.

[29] *Saguenay* (n 24) [116].

[30] This is the point made in *Saguenay* (ibid [87]): 'the Canadian cultural landscape includes many traditional and heritage practices that are religious in nature. Although it is clear that not all of these cultural expressions are in breach of the state's duty of neutrality, there is also no doubt that the state may not consciously make a profession of faith or act so as to adopt or favour one religious view at the expense of all others'.

to see how the state could not take the practices of this group into account when, for example, selecting statutory holidays or establishing a 'pause day' from work.[31] As long as religion remains part of private life, it will sometimes affect the shape of public action.

The third and most significant exception to the neutrality requirement involves religious beliefs that address civic matters or have public implications. Religious belief systems often say something about the way we should treat others and about the kind of society we should work to create. The courts have sometimes treated religion as a cultural identity towards which the state should remain neutral, and at other times (when it addresses or touches upon civic matters) as a political or moral judgement by the individual that should be subject to the give-and-take of politics.

In *Chamberlain v Surrey School District No 36*, the Supreme Court of Canada held that elected officials may draw on their religious values (or the religious values of their constituents) when making political decisions. Chief Justice McLachlin recognised that: 'Religion is an integral aspect of people's lives, and cannot be left at the boardroom door.'[32]

In deciding that the state is not required to remain neutral towards religious values, the Court relies at least implicitly on a distinction between the spiritual and civic elements of a religious belief system. A religious belief should not play a role in political decision making if the action it calls for is spiritual in character (ie, is concerned with the worshipping or honouring of God). However, if the religious belief relates to a civic matter (individual rights or collective welfare), then it may play a role in political decision making, and the action it calls for will be viewed as public or civic. Religiously grounded beliefs about civic issues may be adopted or rejected by law makers based on a public judgement about their contribution to human good or public welfare.

The courts then must draw a line between the spheres of spiritual and civic life, even if that line is contestable and often seems porous or adjustable. Where the line between the civic and spiritual elements of a religious belief system is drawn will reflect the courts' views about the nature of human welfare and the proper scope of political action. The claim that a religious belief or value may play a role in political decision making when there is a parallel secular argument (when the same or a similar position can be stated in non-religious terms) points to this distinction between spiritual and civic. When a religious value or position (such as supporting the eradication of poverty, or banning drug use or abortion) has a secular analogue, it will be seen as addressing a public or civic concern – as seeking to advance the public interest or to prevent harm to others. Even if these reasons are set out in scripture and valued by adherents on that basis, they can be understood by non-adherents as concerned with public welfare and so as civic values. However, when there is no parallel secular argument, non-adherents are bound to see the religious 'practice' as simply the way in which adherents choose to honour God's will. In other words, a religiously motivated action will be viewed as a spiritual practice (as the worshipping or honouring of God) if non-adherents cannot understand it as relating to human welfare. If the state were to support Sunday Sabbath observance or a particular form of prayer or the wearing of hijab or if it were to ban the consumption of pork, it would be seen as supporting a spiritual practice contrary to

[31] *R v Edwards Books and Art Ltd* [1986] 2 SCR 713.

[32] *Chamberlain v Surrey School District No 36* [2002] SCC 86 [19].

freedom of religion. These actions are viewed as exclusively spiritual, as acts of worship, because they cannot be understood by non-adherents as concerned with the advancement of human good.[33]

If law makers are permitted to draw on particular religious beliefs/values when formulating public policy, they should also be free to reject or repudiate those beliefs/values. In other words, (religiously grounded) civic values should be neither excluded nor insulated from political decision making. The state may remain neutral on spiritual matters, such as when or how to pray or what clothes to wear, but it cannot be neutral on civic issues, such as the recognition of same sex-marriage, the prohibition of gender discrimination or the regulation of abortion.[34]

B. Religious Accommodation: Private Spirituality

Freedom of religion, understood as a liberty, precludes the state from restricting a religious practice because it is the wrong way to worship God. The state must have a public reason to restrict a religious practice, but any public reason will do.[35] However, the Canadian courts have adopted a different approach to the justification of limits on religious practice and have held that any time the state restricts a religious practice in a non-trivial way (even when it is advancing a legitimate public interest), it must justify the restriction under section 1 – the *Charter*'s limitations provision – by balancing the competing civic and religious interests. Yet in practice, the Canadian courts have required very little justification from the state. They have asked the state to make space for religious practices and religious communities only when this can be done without any real impact on state policy. In other words, the courts will only protect a religious practice that can be treated as personal to the individual or internal to the group, even if the boundary between personal/private and civic is subject to contest.[36] While the

[33] In the case of some (religiously based) state actions, such as a ban on public nudity, it may be more controversial whether the action should be viewed as relating to human welfare or as simply a matter of honouring God's will, depending on whether this ban may be supported by other belief systems or may be defended on grounds that are more generally accessible.

[34] In R Moon, 'Conscientious Objection and the Politics of Cake-Baking' (2020) 9 *Oxford Journal of Law and Religion* 329, I argue that: 'the issue in conscientious objection cases is whether the individual's religiously-based objection should be viewed as an expression of personal religious conscience that should be accommodated (if this can be done without noticeable harm to others) or whether it should be viewed as a (religiously-grounded) civic position or action that may be the subject of legal regulation. In determining whether a particular (conscientious) objection should be viewed as a personal/spiritual matter or instead as a civic/political position, two factors may be relevant. The first is whether the individual is being required to perform the particular act (to which they object) because they hold a special position not held by others, notably some form of public appointment. The other factor is the relative remoteness/proximity of the act that the objector is required to perform from the act that they consider to be inherently immoral. The more remote the legally required action the more likely we are to regard the refusal to perform it as a position about how others should behave or about the correctness of the law, rather than as an expression of personal conscience'.

[35] This was John Locke's position. According to Locke, *A Letter Concerning Toleration* (Irvington, 1979 [2689]) 199, the government may prohibit a practice such as animal slaughter provided that the prohibition has a civic purpose and is not enforced exclusively against those who engage in animal slaughter for religious reasons – as a form of worship.

[36] Note the contrast between *Multani v Commission scolaire Marguerite-Bourgeoys* [2006] 1 SCR 256, 2006 SCC 6 and *Alberta v Hutterian Brethren of Wilson Colony*, 2009 SCC 37, [2009] 2 SCR 567.

Court has given section 2(a) the form of an equality right, it has given it the substance of a liberty right.

Religious practices (forms of worship) that are 'personal' in character are sometimes indirectly or incidentally limited by state action. The courts, in seeking to protect religious life, may sometimes carve out 'private' space for a religious practice so that the practice is exempted from the application of an otherwise justified law. A police uniform requirement may have the effect of excluding individuals who wear head coverings for religious reasons, or a school schedule may not take account of the holidays of some religious groups.[37] An exemption to a uniform requirement made for an individual who wears a turban or hijab as an expression of their faith or identity will have an impact on state policy, but only a minor one. Allowing a government employee to take a day off work for a religious holiday that is not included in the list of statutory holidays will not disrupt the unit's operations in any significant way. These practices may be viewed as personal and treated as private since they are not concerned directly with public policy and do not noticeably compromise the state's objectives.[38]

Despite what the courts often say, religious freedom claims are not, and cannot be, resolved through the balancing of civic and religious interests. A court has no way to attach value or weight to a religious belief/practice. From a secular or public perspective, a religious belief/practice has no necessary value; indeed, it is said that a court should take no position concerning its value – that the court should remain neutral on the question of religious truth. To the believer, it is wrong to restrict their ability to engage in certain practices because those practices express or reflect a deeper truth. Secular institutions such as the courts do not – cannot – value the practice for the reason the believer values it: because it is true. The belief/practice is significant, from a civic-secular perspective, only because it matters 'deeply' to the group and its members – because it is part of their cultural identity, and how they understand, and live in, the world – and because its restriction may lead to the marginalisation or alienation of a minority religious group. This harm (and any assessment of it by the courts) rests on a secular concern about the subjective experience of the believer or the community of believers.[39] However, there is no way to balance the subjective value of the practice (and the secular concern about group identity) with the civic purpose or value of the restrictive law.[40]

Thus, the courts' task is not to trade off or balance specific competing values/interests, but to mark out a protected space for religious communities or ways of life – to define the scope of personal or communal religious practice that can be practically insulated (and excluded) from legal regulation. Religious freedom, as a constitutional right in a democratic political system, must be limited in what it protects to matters that can be viewed as private and outside the scope of politics. The protection of religious

[37] *Commission scolaire régionale de Chambly v Bergevin* [1994] 2 SCR 525.

[38] Moreover, we know that police or other uniform requirements or statutory holidays often reflect, or already take account of, the cultural and religious practices of historically dominant groups.

[39] It also means that claimants in these cases must argue before the courts that their practice should be protected not because it is true and right (as they believe), but because it matters deeply to them. In other words, they must also adopt an external, secular, perspective in making their case.

[40] In this way, religious freedom is different from freedom of expression, which is protected because there is value in the activity of expression (its contribution to democracy, knowledge and individual agency).

freedom requires the courts to draw a line between the spheres of spiritual and civic life, even if that line often appears to be pragmatic and moveable.

Sometimes an accommodation claim is made not by an individual, who is seeking exemption for a specific practice, but instead by a religious/cultural organisation or community, which is claiming a degree of autonomy in the governance of its affairs – in the operation of its internal decision-making processes. In these institutional autonomy cases, the key question for the court is whether the exemption from state law will impact the rights and interests of others – of non-members. The right of the Catholic Church, for example, to exclude women from the priesthood (to discriminate against women) is not decided by balancing the religious claim or interest against the claim to gender equality. Because the Catholic Church is viewed as a private religious organisation or institution, it is free to govern its internal affairs according to its own norms and remains insulated from public anti-discrimination requirements. Similarly, a religious school may dismiss a teacher who enters into a same-sex relationship contrary to religious doctrine not because the religious interests of the group or school outweigh the public value of sexual orientation equality, but simply because the school is understood to be a private religious organisation.[41] However, religious organisations operate in the wider world and their actions will almost always have some impact on outsiders. The question is what kind or degree of impact is sufficient to say that the organisation is no longer operating simply as a private religious association?

The courts have generally treated religious organisations as voluntary associations (of individuals pursuing common ends) that should be free to operate as they choose. If the members of a group have voluntarily submitted to the group's rules or decision-making processes, then the state ought not to intervene. An individual's membership in the group may be seen as voluntary as long as they are free to leave the group (and live under ordinary state law) if they disagree with the group's actions. Of course, individuals are often born into a religious community and feel bound to it by ties of kinship and friendship. More significantly, the individual's identity may be tied to the group so that exiting the group is difficult even when there are few material barriers. The state may sometimes intervene in the affairs of a religious community characterised by hierarchy and insularity when the prevailing practices in that community are thought to be harmful to some of its members, even though the members have, at least in a formal sense, chosen to be or to remain part of the community.[42] The deep communal connections that are part of the value of religious life and commitment (a source of meaning and value for adherents) may also be the source of what the courts regard as harm – the lack of meaningful choice or opportunity open to the members of such communities or the oppression of vulnerable group members.[43] However, in most institutional autonomy cases, the issue is simply whether the organisation's actions impact outsiders to the group – a matter of drawing a line between the civil sphere (of government action) and the personal or communal sphere (of religious practice).

[41] See *Caldwell v Stuart* [1984] 2 SCR 603.

[42] See *Bruker v Marcovitz*, 2007 SCR 54.

[43] The protection of the group's autonomy rests on the group being viewed in both these ways – as a voluntary association and as a source of identity – even if these are not entirely compatible perspectives.

VI. Conclusion

In *Big M*, the Supreme Court of Canada's first decision under section 2(a) of the *Charter*, the Court described freedom of religion as a liberty that protects the individual from state coercion in spiritual matters. Yet in this decision were the seeds of a different, competing, conception of the freedom, which required the state to remain neutral in spiritual matters. In subsequent judgments, the Court has stated more clearly that religious freedom is not simply an individual liberty, but also a form of equality right that requires the equal treatment by the state of different religious belief systems or communities. The neutrality requirement rests on a recognition of the deep connection between the individual and their religious or cultural group and on a concern about the standing of such groups and their members in the wider society. The practices of a religious group are treated as part of the cultural identity of the group's members and are excluded and insulated from politics, because experience has taught us that the restriction of these practices may contribute to the marginalisation of the group and the exclusion and alienation of its members from the wider society.

This understanding of the right appears to be based on practical as well as principled concerns and to require the courts to make pragmatic and context-based trade-offs between spiritual claims and civic interests. Thus, the story of religious freedom in Canada may not be simply that of a linear progression from the pragmatic tolerance of religious minorities to the principled protection of the individual's religious freedom. The same concerns about social peace that lay behind the extension of the religious tolerance in Canada's early history continue to be important in the contemporary justification and interpretation of religious freedoms.

However, the courts may be reluctant to openly embrace this pragmatism, since the legitimacy of their role as interpreters of the *Charter* rests on the claim that they are a 'forum of principle', adjudicating rights issues on the basis of principle rather than policy. Thus, it is possible that legitimacy concerns may sometimes lead the court to limit religious freedom to little more than a liberty – a freedom to practise one's faith as long as it does not interfere with legitimate state action, despite its regular references to equality and neutrality.

7

Shalla v State

Is Blasphemy a Religious or Criminal Offence in Nigeria under Islamic Law?

AZIZAT O AMOLOYE-ADEBAYO AND
MUHAMMAD KAMALDEEN IMAM-TAMIM

I. Introduction

A source of tension in the relationship between law and religion generally is in the enforcement of blasphemy laws by some states, notably Nigeria. For instance, on the effect of blasphemy laws on the application of international human rights law, the United Nations Human Rights Committee (UNHRC) had occasion to comment as follows: 'Prohibition of displays of lack of respect for a religion or other belief system, including blasphemy laws, are incompatible with the International Covenant on Civil and Political Rights.'[1] In its consideration, the only exception given by the treaty body, where a blasphemy law may be accommodated, is where the effect is to prohibit incitement to hatred under Article 20 of the *International Covenant on Civil and Political Rights* (*ICCPR*).[2] This point of view has been subject to some criticisms[3] and rightly in our view, as shall be discussed later in this work.[4]

In Nigeria, recent blasphemy cases have also raised debates on the status of blasphemy laws in a multi-religious country. This is especially the case regarding the question of the power of the state to enforce capital punishment for a 'religious' offence or the power of individuals to arrogate to themselves the power to punish for what is considered a 'criminal' act under the banner of religion. This chapter analyses the landmark case of *Shalla v State*[5]

[1] United Nations Human Rights Committee, General Comment No 34, Freedom of Opinion and Expression, CCPR C/GC/34, ¶48 (12 September 2011), www2.ohchr.org/english/bodies/hrc/docs/gc34.pdf.

[2] United Nations Human Rights Committee, Resolution 2200A (XXI); *International Covenant on Civil and Political Rights* (*ICCPR*), art 20 (16 December 1966), https://www.ohchr.org/en/professionalinterest/pages/ccpr.aspx.

[3] See N Cox, 'Justifying Blasphemy Laws: Freedom of Expression, Public Morals, and International Human Rights Law' (2020) 35(1) *Journal of law and Religion* 33.

[4] See section IV below.

[5] *Shalla v State* [2007] 12 SCM (Pt 2) 603, Supreme Court of Nigeria, 5 October 2007, SC.245/2004.

by the Supreme Court, the apex court of Nigeria,[6] in relation to the ways in which it interrogates the status of blasphemy law in Islamic law generally and its application in Nigeria. What is particularly interesting is the careful consideration of the status of blasphemy laws and their objective from the perspective of the religion of Islam on the one hand, while on the other hand viewing with distaste gruesome acts carried out by private individuals in the name of the enforcement of such laws. Refracted from the lenses of the observation of the UNHRC in General Comment 34, as noted above and the attendant criticisms, the Nigerian case of *Shalla v State* appears to lend more credence to the view of the opponents of the position of the UNCHR that it seeks to foster a secular worldview that is contrary to the universality of human rights standards.

II. Nigeria and Religious Diversity

Nigeria presently has a population of close to 250 million divided across over 500 lingual and ethnic groups.[7] It is the most populous African country, ranking seventh in world population size.[8] Within this great diversity, there are a few unifying factors and the most notable are: a national constitution; English language as the lingua franca; and religion. The following statement captures the demographic outlook of Nigeria in relation to religion:

> There seems to be broad agreement that Muslims constitute a slightly larger, if not equal, section of the population than that constituted by Christians, and that there are a substantial number of persons who practise traditional indigenous religions as well as a good number of non-religious believers. It is fair to conclude that Islam and Christianity are the dominant religions in Nigeria.[9]

Thus, the Nigerian legal system has a complex history[10] in terms of the application of religious laws and local customs, the effect of British colonialism and continued influence, as well as Nigeria's obligations under international human rights documents. As a result of this complexity, the Supreme Court, as the apex Nigerian court, has a significant role to determine cases in ways that are responsive to this complexity and Nigeria's great diversity, as exemplified in *Shalla v State*, which is examined below.

[6] In the Nigerian court structure, the Supreme Court as the apex court has original jurisdiction only in cases involving the interpretation of the *Constitution* and on disputes between the federal government and a federating unit or between two federating units. Its appellate jurisdiction is in relation to appeals against the decision of the Court of Appeal, which exists as one court with 16 judicial divisions across the states in Nigeria. All divisions have coordinate jurisdiction subject only to the unifying and final jurisdiction of the Supreme Court. See *Constitution of the Federal Republic of Nigeria*, Act No 24, 5 May 1999 s6, 233 and 239.

[7] See World Bank, 'World Development Indicators' (2019), https://datacatalog.worldbank.org/search/dataset/0038126.

[8] ibid; see also National Population Commission Abuja, *Nigeria Demographic and Health Survey 1999* (Nigeria, December 2000).

[9] ES Nwauche, 'Law, Religion and Human Rights in Nigeria' (2008) 8 *African Human Rights Law Journal* 568, 589–70.

[10] See TO Elias, *Groundwork of Nigerian Law*. (Routledge & Kegan Paul, 1954).

III. The Facts and Background of *Shalla v State*

A rumour went round the villages of Randali and Kardi[11] on 14 July 1999. The story was that one resident of Randali village, Abdullahi Alhaji Umaru (now deceased), insulted the Holy Prophet Muhammad (On Him Be Peace). Abubakar Dan Shalla (the accused and appellant) heard the rumour while he was in front of a mosque somewhere in Kardi. He went home, armed himself with a knife and proceeded to Randali. According to the records, one Shugaban Samari confirmed the rumour to be true. Abdullahi Alhaji Umaru was captured by a mob and a co-accused Musa Yaro reportedly read some quotations from *Risalah*[12] to demonstrate to the mob that whoever abused Prophet Muhammad (On Him Be Peace) should be killed. The mob thereafter beat up Abdullahi Alhaji Umaru, and another co-accused, Muhammadu Sani, allegedly used a machete on the deceased's head, as a result of which he fell to the ground. Thereafter, Dan Shalla slit the deceased's throat with the knife he had with him, killing him. At the trial of the accused for culpable homicide punishable by death at the High Court as the court of first instance, the above facts were not in dispute and the accused did not testify. The High Court found Dan Shalla and Musa Yaro guilty of culpable homicide and sentenced them to death. Being dissatisfied, Dan Shalla appealed to the Court of Appeal, which also affirmed the decision of the High Court. On further appeal to the Supreme Court, culminating in the case under review, the two questions for determination were: (a) whether the learned Justices of the Court of Appeal ought to confirm the conviction and sentence of the appellant by the trial court; and (b) whether the learned Justices of the Court of Appeal were right in raising the issue of defences of justification and provocation without affording the parties the right to be heard on the issue. The Supreme Court resolved both issues against the appellant and upheld the decision of the Court of Appeal confirming the conviction and sentence of the appellant.

IV. Analysis of the Case

Blasphemy-related violence and killings are rife in Nigeria. Since 1999, many people have been attacked and killed for uttering blasphemous statements. In most of the cases, particularly as represented by the case of *Shalla v State*, as shown above, private individuals execute the punishments for blasphemy. The approach of jungle justice cannot be divorced from the long-time informal treatment of the issue of blasphemy by the Nigerian state. Although both the *Penal Code* of northern Nigeria and *Criminal Code Act* of southern Nigeria contain provisions aimed at protecting religions and religious institutions in the country, the rate of enforcement by the masses indicates that blasphemy is more of a religious offence than a criminal offence. Even though the 1999 *Constitution of the Federal Republic of Nigeria* is not expressed to be based on any religious law, in its

[11] These villages are both in the Birnin Kebbi Local Government Area of Kebbi State in the northwestern region of Nigeria.

[12] This text is one of the foremost primers of the Maliki school of law. The Maliki school of law is the official scheme for the interpretation and application of Islamic law in Shariah courts in Nigeria. See s 13 of the *Sharia Court of Appeal Rules*.

preamble, it upholds the aim to unite and harmonise the citizens to live as one indivisible and indissoluble sovereign nation 'under God'. This principle of 'living in unity and harmony under God' is protected by laws in the country. Historically and politically, Nigeria's legal system is a product of various sublegal structures, including customary law, English law, Islamic law and legislation. Both the legislation and case law (as they are known today) were introduced as byproducts of colonial rule in the country. Islamic law is the legal system established by the religion of Islam to govern its subjects, while customary law is a legal structure established by social norms and African Traditional Religions.[13] It is equally historically established that the common law (being the legal foundation for the legislation and case law) metamorphosed from Christian religious norms. This background could account for why the *Nigerian Constitution* established that the unity and harmony of citizens is based on 'God'. Most Nigerians do not believe in atheism.[14] Therefore, it is expected that each of these sublegal systems in the country would have rules for protecting 'God' and institutions ascribed to that God. For example, while describing the status of the African gods, Lainé et al explained that:

> Showing disrespect to the *vodun-si* – and, therefore, to the *vodun* – through insults, beatings, or calling the initiate by his or her former name is an act of sacrilege and desecration. Anyone guilty of such an offence must make up for the insult by paying for and organizing a ceremony of re-consecration.[15]

The facts in *Shalla v State* exemplify this notion and perspective of citizens within the Islamic religious ideology. In Islamic law, the majority of scholars consider blasphemy (otherwise known and referred to as 'sabb Allah' and 'sabb an nabiyy') as a *hadd* (capital) offence.[16] *Hadd* offences are the felonious offences for which punishments have been fixed in the Islamic legal codes, particularly the *Qur'ān* and *Sunnah*, both of which are unanimously accepted as the primary sources of Islamic law.[17] Therefore, the majority view of the Islamic jurists is that the punishment for blasphemy is death.[18] However, this position is not the exclusive stance of Islamic jurists on the criminal status and punishment for blasphemy, as the act constitutes one of the most jurisprudentially debated legal concepts in Islamic law. Though all jurists are unanimous that blasphemers are sinners, they are markedly divided on whether they must be put to death or whether the death penalty could be suspended if the blasphemer repents. The nuances in the discussions and debates underlie the legal basis for their respective conclusions. From the juristic discussions, it is deduced that the punishment for blasphemy had two purposes: achieving political order and punishing criminal liability. Regardless of the positions taken by the jurists, they share a common ground that punishing blasphemy is the prerogative

[13] JO Kayode, *Understanding African Traditional Religion* (University of Ife Press, 1984) 6–7.

[14] EB Idowu, *African Traditional Religion: A Definition*, (SCM Press, 1973) 139; E Udo, *Religion and Cultural Identity* (Hope Publications, 2002) 162; MO Opeloye, 'Evolution of Religious Culture among the Yoruba' in D Ogunremi and B Adediran (eds), *Culture and Society in Yorubaland* (Rex Charles Publications, 1998) 139.

[15] D Lainé, T Nathan, A Stamm and P Saulnier, *African Gods: Contemporary Rituals and Beliefs* (Flammarion, 2007) 26.

[16] TJ Alalwani, *Apostasy in Islam: A Historical and Scriptural Analysis* (International Institute of Islamic Thought, 2012).

[17] ibid.

[18] ibid.

of the state authorities through their judicial apparatuses. As noted earlier, the Maliki school of law is the officially recognised Islamic jurisprudential school of law in Nigeria. This school vehemently asserts that blasphemy is a capital crime which entitles the blasphemers to be killed without the option of repentance. This position repeatedly found in most Maliki treatises on the subject influences the attitude of Nigerian Muslims, particularly in the northern states, towards mobbing any blasphemer, as they consider the act primarily as a religious offence. Hence, they often summarily execute perceived offenders without involving the state's law enforcement agencies, as had occurred in the case of *Shalla v State*.

At this juncture, it is important to emphasise that blasphemy is officially recognised as a criminal offence under the *Penal Code* that operates in the northern states of Nigeria and the *Criminal Code Act* that applies to the southern states. While the *Criminal Code* was an adaptation of the *Queensland Criminal Code 1899*, the *Penal Code* was adapted from the *Indian* and *Sudanese Penal Codes*.[19] The *Sudanese Penal Code* was chosen for the northern Nigerian states because of the strong roots of the Maliki school variant of Islamic law in the region, hence the need for a criminal statute with an Islamic law flavour, which the *Sudanese Penal Code* represented.[20] Both the *Penal Code* and the *Criminal Code Act* contain provisions designed to preserve the dignity of religions in Nigeria.

Sections 204–06 of the *Criminal Code Act* contain provisions outlawing offences relating to religious worship, wherein acts of insult to a religion, harassing ministers of religion and disturbing religious worship are penalised. In section 204, it is provided that:

> Any person who does an act which any class of persons consider as a public insult on their religion, with the intention that they should consider the act such an insult, and any person who does an unlawful act with the knowledge that any class of persons will consider it such an insult, is guilty of a misdemeanour, and is liable to imprisonment for two years.

Further, in section 205, any person who is found to attempt to prevent, actually prevent, obstruct, assault or arrest a minister of religion, thereby disallowing him to lawfully perform his religious duty shall be liable to two years' imprisonment. Section 206 also makes a person subject to two months' imprisonment if he is found guilty of disturbing a lawful religious gathering. Section 210 of the *Penal Code*, which operates in the majority of northern Nigerian states, also contains similar provisions criminalising insults against religion, as similar provisions are manifestly entrenched in the *Shariah Penal Codes* of the 12 states that have re-introduced an Islamic penal system.[21] For instance, the Zamfara, Gombe, Sokoto, Kebbi and Yola Shariah *Penal/Criminal Codes* provide for two years' imprisonment, a fine or both, with one year's imprisonment or a fine of 20,000 naira or both prescribed in Kano, while the *Kaduna State Penal Code* established it as a *ta'azir* offence left at the discretion of the judge.[22] The presence of these provisions

[19] CO Okonkwo, *Okokwo and Naish on Criminal Law in Nigeria* (Spectrum Books Ltd, 2010) 4–11.

[20] ibid 10–11.

[21] R Peters, *Islamic Criminal Law in Nigeria* (Spectrum Law Books, 2003) 41; H Bourbeau, M Sani Umar and P Bauman, *Shari'ah Criminal Law in Northern Nigeria: Implementation of Expanded Shari'ah Penal and Criminal Procedure Codes in Kano, Sokoto, and Zamfara States, 2017–2019* (United States Commission on International Religious Freedom, 2019) 41–42.

[22] ibid.

in the criminal statutes no doubt clearly indicates the perspective of the Nigerian state's criminal policy to regard blasphemy as a criminal offence punishable by the formal criminal justice apparatuses with a view to maintaining peace, law and order in society.

Interestingly, this dichotomy between the private conception of the offence of blasphemy as religious, and thus justifying private action, and its official description as a criminal act punishable by the state is amply illustrated by the facts in *Shalla v State*. As outlined above, the accused person (Shalla) neither testified at his trial nor called evidence. In fact, in his confessional statement to the police following his arrest, he claimed that:

> On Wednesday 14/7/99 at about 20:00 hrs after Isha'I [*sic*] prayers, I sat down at the frontage of the Mosque at Faransi Area of Kardi then one Musa Yaro of Kardi came and met me with an information that, someone abused Prophet Mohammad at Randali Village which he is not sure, but he will try to find out at Randali. On hearing that, I stood up and went inside my house and carried knife along with me, and I moved to Randali. On reaching there, I went straight to one Shugaban Samari for confirmation about the abusing of Prophet Mohammad and he assured me that, the issue is true, and that there were witnesses to testify but he did not tell me the kind of abuse. And from there, I heard someone saying, that Abdullah Alh. Umaru who abused the Prophet had been arrested at Kardi, then I quickly went back to Kardi and met Abdullahi who was together with Adamu Aljani, Kalli Odita and others whom I was not able to know then. Then we later sent the following: Musa Yaro, Usman Kaza and Abdullahi Ada to the Village Head of Kardi to know what is happening in his village. As they returned back from the village head's house, Musa Yaro made some Quotation [*sic*] in Risalah which means that, whoever abused Prophet Mohammad shall be killed, then people started beating Abdullahi Alh. Umaru and Mohammadu Sani macheted him and he fell down, then I removed the knife that was in my possession with my right hand and slaughtered him 'deceased' just along Randali-Kardi Road near burial ground of Kardi. And we all dispersed. When I reached home, I fetched some water and washed the knife and part of my [cloth] that was stained, the cloth is light blue in colour. That's all my statement.[23]

Two facts are apparent from the confessional statement of Shalla. First, he believed himself to be under the religious duty to kill the victim who had abused the Prophet Muhammad (On Him Be Peace), and thus the killing was justified under the law. Oguntade JSC, who read the lead judgment of the court, commented that:

> In the manner the appellant and the other accused persons behaved during their trial by not calling evidence to deny the allegations against them; and by in fact admitting that they killed the deceased, there is no doubt that they laboured under a notion that they had a duty under Islamic injunction to kill the deceased.[24]

In fact, the substance of the appeal against the conviction of Shalla for murder by the trial court at the Court of Appeal and finally at the Supreme Court was that the appellant was entitled to be heard on the defences of justification and provocation as made out by his counsel at the appellate courts. The decision of the Court of Appeal that was

[23] *Shalla v State* (n 5) 611–12.
[24] ibid 612.

copiously affirmed in the same words by the concurring opinion of Muhammad JSC was to the effect that:

> It will be very clear that the appellants with their shallow knowledge of Sharia or Islamic law and calling themselves Muslim Brothers, have in ignorance or deliberate disregard of the rules of judgement and procedure under the said Sharia as contained in the same text of Risala, arrogated to themselves the function and role of a court of law or a khadi and wrongly (without any proof or evidence) or based on rumour or hearsay, convicted, sentenced and inflected [*sic*] or carried out the execution of the supposed punishment. They cannot claim that to be the way of life of their community because they were not supported by the both the Village Head and Ustaz Mamman. Although, the prosecution did not call the Ustaz as a witness it is however clear that he gave them the advise [*sic*] in the presence of some of the witnesses … but they refused to heed and even went to the extent of describing him as an infidel or a non-Muslim for giving them such as advice. There is no legal justification in the action taken by the appellants in killing the deceased for his supposed offence. Islamic religion is not a primitive religion that allows its adherents to take the law into their own hands and to commit jungle justice.[25]

Second, religious sentiments should not and cannot be taken lightly: people will kill in the name of religion in the expectation of rewards in the afterlife. In the case under consideration, and as the judges rightly noted, the accused did not at any point bother to confirm the exact words uttered by the victim and to form an independent opinion (whatever it was worth) regarding the extent of their blasphemous nature. All that mattered was that anyone had the temerity to utter disparaging words about Prophet Muhammad (On Him Be Peace). This is not an isolated incident and available records of similar occurrences elsewhere show a backlash from Muslims anywhere to perceived insults to the *Qur'ān* or the Prophet Muhammad (On Him Be Peace). The reaction to the Danish cartoons in 2005[26] and the attack on the *Charlie Hebdo* offices in January 2015 and more recent killings are cases in point.[27] The extent and level simply vary from one context to another, but the consequences are the same: loss of life. In our opinion, blasphemy laws should thus be viewed rather as careful strategies to achieve a balance between freedom of expression that results in chaos and loss of lives, and protection of religious sentiments within reasonable limits than stifling modalities on freedom of expression. This line of discussion is taken up in the next section.

V. *Shalla v State* in the Light of UNHRC General Comment 34

As noted earlier, the UNHRC published its General Comment 34 in 2011 to purportedly further clarify obligations in relations to freedom of expression and opinion as

[25] ibid 640–41.

[26] R Kahn, 'Flemming Rose, The Danish Cartoon Controversy and the New European Freedom of Speech' (2010) 2 *California Western International Law Journal* 253, 260; see also D Scally, 'Ten Years on Danish Daily Stands by Muhammad Caricatures' *Irish Times* (30 September 2015), https://www.irishtimes.com/news/world/europe/ten-years-on-danish-daily-stands-by-muhammad-caricatures-1.2371640.

[27] See S Parmar, 'Freedom of Expression Narratives after the Charlie Hebdo Attacks' (2018) 18(2) *Human Rights Law Review* 267; see also 'The *Guardian* View on Charlie Hebdo: Those Guns were Trained on Free Speech' *The Guardian* (7 January 2015), www.theguardian.com/commentisfree/2015/jan/07/guardian-view-charlie-hebdo-guns-trained-free-speech.

contained in the ICCPR.[28] The treaty body contended that 'prohibition of displays of lack of respect for a religion or other belief system, including blasphemy laws, are incompatible with the International Covenant on Civil and Political Rights'.[29] In its consideration, the only exception given by the treaty body where a blasphemy law may be accommodated is where the effect is to prohibit incitement to hatred under Article 20 ICCPR.[30] If the case of *Shalla v State* as discussed so far and the events that led up to it are given serious consideration, the view expressed by the UNHRC may appear persuasive, but only to the extent that perhaps blasphemy laws signal bias for a particular religion in multi-religious contexts and validate human rights abuses of perceived offenders. However, this notion appears to have proceeded from an erroneous basis that expressions are considered blasphemous because such expressions have been criminalised as such in order to favour religion. Therefore, the basis of criminalisation is law and not religion itself. So, once the criminalisation is removed, religious people lack the legitimacy to be offended by sentiments that purportedly disparage their religious tenets. What is left is simply to prohibit, as the UNHRC suggests, 'incitement to hatred', which in our view protects religious people against human rights violations based on their belief system, but not their sentiments.

Though somewhat persuasive, the line of argument by the UNHRC not only takes too much for granted, but in our view it is also dangerous. In the first place, evidence of actual events such as the *Charlie Hebdo* case in France, despite the absence of official recognition of a blasphemy law for the religion concerned, suggests that people will attempt to combat disrespect for religious sentiments and idiosyncratic beliefs regardless of the level of recognition or otherwise by law. Validation for such acts is thus not sought from the law, but from the religion itself. As *Shalla v State* also demonstrates, it appears that once people feel religiously outraged to act in response to perceived insulting representations of their religious belief, it may not matter whether such expressions have been criminalised in a blasphemy law or not before heinous reprisal attacks are contemplated and (in some situations) enacted. Within this reasoning, there is much ground to agree with Cox[31] that the view expressed by the UNHRC was too wide and secularist, representing just one of many worldviews contrary to the supposed universality of human rights standards.[32] Moreover, as Cox rightly suggests, even though some blasphemy laws may be draconian and anachronistic, some can still be justified as serving a legitimate purpose and constitute a proportionate interference with rights.[33] This is because the value that is sought to be protected evinces what constitutes public morality in that particular context.

The point to be made is that some blasphemy laws, as in the Nigerian context, must do more than simply prohibit incitement to hatred. As the events in *Shalla v State* indicate, the appellant considered the abuse to Prophet Muhammad (On Him Be Peace)

[28] See M O'Flaherty, 'Freedom of Expression: The International Covenant on Civil and Political Rights and the Human Rights Committee's General Comment No 34' (2012) 14(2) *Human Rights Law Review* 627.
[29] United Nations Human Rights Committee (n 1).
[30] United Nations Human Rights Committee, Resolution 2200A (XXI); *ICCPR*, art 20.
[31] Cox (n 3).
[32] ibid 36.
[33] ibid 35.

as provocative, and this justified the killing of the victim. This mindset was clearly a product not of law, but of religion. The facts are chilling: an act of murder with a lot of preparation and cleaning up afterwards. Even though the court held that the appellant's belief was erroneous that he had the right to kill the deceased under Islamic law, it is still clear that the appellant's sense of duty was based on religion, whether rightly or wrongly conceived. In our considered view, respect for religious sentiments should not be considered lightly where individuals may be at the mercy of a frenzied mob in the name of protecting freedom of expression. At any rate, if expressions such as sexual orientation are protected and acts disparaging a person's sexual orientation are considered homophobic, for instance, why would the same not be the case for religious sentiments, especially where religion is expressed as a way of life, as in the Nigerian situation? It is in this sense that we consider the postulations in General Comment 34 as being too narrow and unrealistic on blasphemy laws for the Nigerian context. The jurisprudence of the Supreme Court in *Shalla v State* appears more workable and is also relevant for similar contexts to Nigeria.

VI. Conclusion

The effect of *Shalla v State* in terms of citizens' perceptions of the nature of blasphemy is that it is both a religious and criminal offence in Nigeria. It is religious insofar as it seeks to protect religious sentiments/worldviews from incitements that can result in violence in the name of religion. It is also criminal because only the state can punish after due process in a court of law with all the available defences to which an accused person would ordinarily be entitled. In a multi-religious context such as Nigeria, this balancing jurisprudence of the Nigerian apex court is not only necessary but also primordial for two reasons. On the one hand, it serves as an acknowledgement that religion is an important constitutive element of the Nigerian identity and sentiments based on it should therefore appropriately qualify as public morals deserving protection, contrary to the indication by the UNHRC. On the other hand, this protection should not be taken as a licence for private individuals or entities to self-enforce through disorganised, frenzied mob actions. Doing so is counter to the raison d'etre of blasphemy laws – the maintenance of peace, order, individual autonomy and the right to religious sentiments within reasonable limits. The affirmation of the death sentence of the accused person, who felt justified in having killed another in the name of religion outside of the state apparatus, is certainly a good signal to deter similar acts. Recent events in Nigeria[34] where similar supposedly blasphemous acts were reported to the police for state action indicate that the Nigerian Supreme Court made a landmark decision in *Shalla v State*.

[34] See, for example, the following media reports: 'Nigerian Singer Sentenced to Death for Blasphemy in Kano State' *BBC News* (10 August 2020), https://www.bbc.co.uk/news/world-africa-53726256; 'Blasphemy: Kano Islamic Cleric, Abduljabbar, Arrested' *Vanguard* (16 July 2021), https://www.vanguardngr.com/2021/07/blasphemy-kano-islamic-cleric-abduljabbar-arrested; 'Kano Singer Arrested for Blasphemy Released on Bail' *The Guardian Nigeria* (22 June 2021), https://guardian.ng/news/kano-singer-arrested-for-blasphemy-released-on-bail; https://kanofocus.com/2021/06/19/dss-arrests-singer-accuse-of-blasphemy (19 June 2021).

8

Adelaide Company of Jehovah's Witnesses v Commonwealth

Balancing Free Exercise and Public Order

PAUL T BABIE

I. Introduction

To an extent unlike all of the other cases in this book, the High Court of Australia decision in *Adelaide Company of Jehovah's Witnesses v Commonwealth*[1] forms part of an extensive body of jurisprudence in many national jurisdictions dealing with the freedom of religion or belief (FoRB) of the Jehovah's Witnesses.[2] In the US alone, between 1938 and 1946, the Jehovah's Witnesses obtained judicial review before the Supreme Court in over 20 cases.[3] Similarly, in Canada, between 1951 and 1959, the Supreme Court reviewed five cases from just one province, Quebec.[4] While a great deal of this jurisprudence deals with FoRB claims concerning the right to refuse medical treatment, usually blood transfusions in emergencies, this body of law also set the parameters of FoRB enjoyed by all religious groups in the relevant national jurisdiction. Of the American cases, Richard Lee Hough suggested that:

> No matter what one's feelings are concerning the extremist views and unorthodox practices of the Witnesses, it must be admitted that they performed a valuable service to our democratic polity when they carried their legal fight to the Supreme Court, and dropped into its lap the thorny task of constitutionally defining the area of religious freedom and the limits which circumscribe it.[5]

Supreme Court Justice Harlan Fiske Stone added that: 'I think the Jehovah's Witnesses ought to have an endowment in view of the aid which they give in solving the legal

[1] *Adelaide Company of Jehovah's Witnesses v Commonwealth* (1943) 67 CLR 116 (hereinafter '*ACJW*').

[2] S Woolley, 'Children of Jehovah's Witnesses and Adolescent Jehovah's Witnesses: What are Their Rights?' (2005) 90 *Archives of Diseases in Childhood* 715; S Woolley, 'Jehovah's Witnesses in the Emergency Department: What are Their Rights?' (2005) 22 *Emergency Medicine Journal* 869.

[3] RL Hough, 'The Jehovah's Witnesses Cases in Retrospect' (1953) 6(1) *Western Political Quarterly* 78. For a list of these cases, see *Niemotko v Maryland*, 340 US 268, 273 (1951) (Frankfurter J).

[4] *R v Boucher* [1951] SCR 265; *Saumur v City of Quebec* [1953] 2 SCR 299; *Chaput v Romain* [1955] SCR 834; *Roncarelli v Duplessis* [1959] SCR 121; *Lamb v Benoit et al* [1959] SCR 321.

[5] Hough (n 3) 78.

problems of civil liberties.'[6] The same is true wherever the Witnesses have initiated FoRB litigation.[7]

In addition to its significance as a part of the body of world jurisprudence dealing with FoRB, *ACJW* comprises one of a trilogy of High Court of Australia cases,[8] spanning almost a century, giving meaning to the FoRB guarantee in section 116 of Australia's *Constitution*. Section 116 relevantly provides that: 'The Commonwealth shall not make any law for prohibiting the free exercise of any religion.' *ACJW* adopts the High Court's reasoning in the first case of the trilogy, the 1912 decision in *Krygger v Williams*, and is itself upheld, on narrow grounds, by the third, the 1997 decision in *Kruger v Commonwealth*. The *Krygger* test limits the application of section 116 to those legislative and executive actions which:

> Prohibit[] the practice of religion – the doing of acts which are done in the practice of religion. To require a man to do a thing which has nothing at all to do with religion is not prohibiting him from a free exercise of religion. It may be that a law requiring a man to do an act which his religion forbids would be objectionable on moral grounds, but it does not come within the prohibition.[9]

Practitioners and scholars take this test specifically, and the trilogy generally, to mean two things: that federal laws of general application which have the effect but not the express purpose of infringing upon FoRB do not violate section 116;[10] and that the words of section 116 do no more than establish a limitation on legislative power, as opposed to protecting a fundamental individual right.[11]

Yet, it was possible in 1901 and remains so today to interpret the words of section 116 as both protecting against laws of general application which have the *effect* – not merely the express purpose – of infringing upon free exercise, meaning that this protection is much more than a mere limitation upon legislative power. The current restrictive understanding of free exercise results from a failure to understand a fundamental point: that no right is absolute. Thus, taking a purposive and large and liberal approach to the FoRB guarantee of section 116, the Australian judiciary might have come to conclusions similar to those reached by the American judiciary with respect to the very similar words of the First Amendment: that assessing claimed violations of free exercise

[6] MI Urofsky, *Religious Freedom: Rights and Liberties under the Law* (ABC-CLIO, 2002) 140, citing SF Peters, *Judging Jehovah's Witnesses: Religious Persecution and the Dawn of the Rights Revolution* (University Press of Kansas, 2002) 186.

[7] Cases involving the Jehovah's Witnesses continue to reach the courts in many jurisdictions; see, eg, W Fautré, 'The Belgian Case against the Jehovah's Witnesses: The Bible in the Dock?' *Bitter Winter* (26 February 2021), https://bitterwinter.org/the-belgian-case-against-the-jehovahs-witnesses-the-bible-in-the-dock.

[8] *Krygger v Williams* (1912) 15 CLR 366; *ACJW* (n 1); *Kruger v Commonwealth* (1997) 190 CLR 1.

[9] *Krygger* (n 8).

[10] *Church of the New Faith v Commissioner of Pay-roll Tax (Vic)* (1983) 154 CLR 120. A vast scholarly literature has developed around the interpretation of s 116: see, eg, P Babie, 'The Ethos of Protection for Freedom of Religion or Belief in Australian Law' (2020) 47(1) *University of Western Australia Law Review* 64; P Babie, 'The Concept of Freedom of Religion in the Australian Constitution: A Study in Legislative-Judicial Cooperative Innovation' (2018) 1(1) *Quaderni di diritto e politica ecclesiastica* 259; P Babie, 'National Security and the Free Exercise Guarantee of Section 116: Time for a Judicial Interpretive Update' (2017) 45(3) *Federal Law Review* 351; P Babie and N Rochow, 'Feels Like Déjà Vu: An Australian Bill of Rights and Religious Freedom' (2010) 3 *Brigham Young University Law Review* 821; R Barker, *State and Religion: The Australian Story* (Routledge, 2020); L Beck, *Religious Freedom and the Australian Constitution: Origins and Future* (Routledge, 2018).

[11] *Attorney-General (Vic) ex rel Black v Commonwealth* ('*DOGS Case*') (1981) 146 CLR 559.

involves a two-step process. The first involves discerning the ambit of the free exercise right and whether it has been infringed, while the second involves determining whether the limitations imposed upon that right are justifiable. Using this approach, the American judiciary allows the right to encompass and so protect against the effects of laws of general application, without necessarily holding such laws to be unconstitutional in every case where an infringement is found to exist. That latter conclusion follows only from a finding, in the second step, that the limitations imposed by the effects of the impugned law are unjustifiable.

This is no mere academic exercise. Rather, the two-step approach commonly used in the US and, indeed, in most other nations which protect FoRB is already found in the approach of the High Court in *ACJW*. Yet, the judgments are confusing, and so finding the two-step approach in them requires a careful reading of the case. But as nations everywhere confront religious extremism, international terrorism, the effects of global pandemics, and environmental crises, the need to do so, and to combine a robust protection of FoRB with strong recognition of the community interest in safety and security, has never been more urgent.

The chapter contains four subsequent sections. Section II provides the background to the faith of the Jehovah's Witnesses and the conflict which brought them to the High Court in *ACJW*. Section III carefully analyses the judgments delivered in *ACJW*, grouping them into four themes that make clear the two-step process: whether the *Constitution* contains a power for the Commonwealth (federal) government to legislate with respect to religion; the meaning of 'religion' as found in section 116; the relationship between conscience and conduct, and the relationship between individual conduct and community social order. Section IV examines what a re-appraisal of the judgments in *ACJW* means for section 116: the recognition that the FoRB guarantee protects both freedom *of* and freedom *from* religion; that *ACJW* itself contains the two-step test for assessing the application of section 116 (the first step encompassing the ambit of the guarantee and the second step the process of assessing infringements of the guarantee); and, finally, and perhaps most controversially, the potential for section 116 to extend to protecting against infringements committed by the states as opposed to the federal government alone. Section V briefly concludes.

II. Background

A. Wartime Defence

Sir John Quick and Sir Robert Garran, in their definitive annotated commentary to the Australian *Constitution*, noted that 'a federation of the naval and military forces … was "one of the strongest arguments ever submitted in favour of the political federation of the Australian colonies"'.[12] And the two World Wars produced extreme tensions

[12] J Quick and RR Garran, *The Annotated Constitution of the Australian Commonwealth*, revised edn (LexisNexis Butterworths, 2015) 656–60, quoting Major General Edwards, as cited in S Kiefel, 'The High Court Justices and the Weight of War', Tenth Sir Harry Gibbs Memorial Oration (30 September 2018) 2.

over the use of this defence power, contained in section 51 of the *Constitution*, with the justices of the High Court feeling 'the weight of war' heavily upon them, both institutionally and personally.[13] Indeed, both wars 'test[ed] the Justices of the … High Court in the approach that they would take to the use of the defence power to legislate for emergency powers'.[14]

During the First World War, the Commonwealth legislatively conferred wide-ranging powers upon the executive government,[15] which the Court largely upheld.[16] That changed, though, with the Second World War,[17] when the Court became much less willing to allow sweeping powers. While it continued to recognise that there may be emergencies which would necessitate use of the defence power,[18] in three cases between 1942 and 1944, the Court required that there be a 'real connection' between that power and regulations enacted thereunder,[19] that there be a 'necessity or justification' for them which might outlive the emergency,[20] and that actions taken thereunder must not be 'arbitrary, capricious and oppressive'.[21] It was against the backdrop of the Second World War that *ACJW* came to the Court.[22]

B. Jehovah's Witnesses

Established as a Protestant Bible study group by Charles Taze Russell in the late 1870s, 'Russell's Millennial Dawnists' or 'Bible Students'[23] taught a millenarian eschatology – the end of the world was near, Christ would destroy all worldly kingdoms, a paradise earth populated by members of the group but open to all who would accept this message, although only a remnant of 144,000, made up of the first faithful since the time of Christ, would go to heaven to rule over the faithful and resurrected dead on earth.[24] It was therefore incumbent on members to preach this message to as many as possible, and because 'the end of the present system was imminent, Russell advised [members] not to vote, hold public office or serve in the military'.[25] By 1931, the group was known as the Jehovah's Witnesses.[26]

Russell predicted 1914 as the Second Coming of Christ, and the First World War was considered a sign that this had happened invisibly and that this 'Battle of Armageddon' had ushered in a time in which Witnesses in a state of grace could await the destruction of secular nations, members of other religions, and anyone who was not a Witness.

[13] Kiefel (n 12) 13.
[14] ibid 2.
[15] ibid.
[16] ibid 2–10.
[17] ibid 10.
[18] *Stenhouse v Coleman* (1944) 69 CLR 457; *Australian Communist Party v Commonwealth* (1951) 83 CLR 1.
[19] *R v Commonwealth Court of Conciliation and Arbitration ex parte Victoria* (1942) 66 CLR 488.
[20] *ACJW* (n 1) 154 (Starke J).
[21] *Stenhouse* (1944) 69 CLR 457. See also *R v Foster ex parte Rural Bank of New South Wales* (1949) 79 CLR 43.
[22] For an assessment of these cases, see Kiefel (n 12).
[23] J Persian, '"A National Nuisance": The Banning of Jehovah's Witnesses in Australia in 1941' (2008) 25 *Flinders Journal of History and Politics* 4, 4, fn ii.
[24] ibid 4, fn iii.
[25] ibid 4.
[26] ibid 4, fn ii.

For Russell, allegiance to any country and membership of this 'theoretical kingdom' were mutually exclusive.[27] By the 1930s, under the leadership of JF Rutherford, the opposition to secular nations and other religions had become a political neutrality, combined with aggressive attacks on big business, politics, and religion, and a vocal opposition to military service.[28] This led to frequent clashes with governments.[29]

By the time of the Second World War, under the leadership of Nathan H Knorr, most nations viewed the Witnesses as nothing less than subversive, and banned the religion and its literature. As a group, Witnesses 'were subject to mob violence, [while] individual Witnesses were persecuted, imprisoned and executed as conscientious objectors'.[30] Still, by that time, the Witnesses had moved 'progressively away from confrontation with the world and towards missionary activity at home and abroad'.[31] By this time, as is true today, 'the most visible hallmarks of Jehovah's Witnesses are their Kingdom Halls, their door-to-door ministry, the public sale of their magazines *The Watchtower* ... and *Awake!* ..., and their vast assemblies held in public stadia'.[32] The Kingdom Hall in Adelaide, South Australia, became the centre of the dispute between the Witnesses and the Commonwealth of Australia.

C. Ban

Following the declaration of war by the UK government in 1939, the Liberal government, led by Robert Menzies, announced that as a consequence, Australia was also at war. The Witnesses continued to promote their worldview, which brought them under the surveillance of the Army, the Navy, Military Intelligence, the Police and the Commonwealth Investigation Branch.[33] The government came under significant public pressure to ban the Witnesses, to which it succumbed between December 1940 and January 1941.[34] To effect the ban, the Governor-General promulgated the *National Security (Subversive Associations) Regulations* (1940) (Cth) pursuant to section 5 of the *National Security Act 1939–1940* (Cth).

On 17 January 1941, acting pursuant to regulation 3, the Governor-in-Council declared by Order in Council the Adelaide Company of Jehovah's Witnesses, being 'prejudicial to the defence of the Commonwealth or the efficient prosecution of the war … to be unlawful'.[35] On the same day, 'the Attorney-General … pursuant to the authority conferred … by the Regulations, directed an officer of the Commonwealth to take possession of, control and occupy, certain premises including the … Kingdom Hall'

[27] ibid 4, citing FL Cross (ed), *Oxford Dictionary of the Christian Church* (Oxford University Press, 1957) 717. See also FL Cross and EA Livingstone (eds), *The Oxford Dictionary of the Christian Church*, 3rd edn (Oxford University Press, 1997), 'Jehovah's Witnesses'.

[28] Persian (n 23) 5.

[29] Cross and Livingstone (n 27) 'Jehovah's Witnesses'.

[30] Persian (n 23) 5, fn v, citing Cross (n 27) 717. See also Cross and Livingstone (n 27) 'Jehovah's Witnesses'.

[31] Cross and Livingstone (n 27) 'Jehovah's Witnesses'.

[32] ibid.

[33] Persian (n 23) 5–6.

[34] ibid 5–11.

[35] Commonwealth of Australia, *Government Gazette*, 17 January 1941, No 8.

in Adelaide.[36] Thereafter, all Jehovah's Witnesses and anyone professing the Jehovah's Witness faith were excluded from the Kingdom Hall.[37] Jayne Persian writes of these events that:

> It seems possible that Menzies was manipulating Cabinet proceedings in order to assert his leadership as Prime Minister over Cabinet. Menzies had become Prime Minister after the sudden death of Joseph Lyons in April 1939, and he inherited a faction-ridden government. His hold on the Prime Ministership was not strong and [the Attorney-General] was a rival, particularly after the outbreak of war when [the Attorney-General] volunteered to lead the country once more in a time of crisis. The banning of the Witnesses, then … may have owed as much, if not more, to political rivalry as it did to any notions of national security.[38]

But whether the ban was brought about by genuine national security concerns or by political rivalry, the outcome was the same: 'Jehovah's Witnesses were no longer permitted to meet for study and worship, and were not allowed to print, circulate or have in their possession, any Witness literature. Their property … [was] to be seized and confiscated, under the National Security (Subversive Associations) Regulations.'[39] This seizure also resulted in the destruction of the property rights of Witnesses' creditors. The Witnesses challenged this ban as an infringement of the FoRB guarantee of section 116 of the Constitution.

III. The High Court Decision

On 4 September 1941, the Witnesses issued a writ in the High Court against the Commonwealth for an injunction to restrain trespass and seeking damages.[40] The Witnesses argued that: (i) the Regulations, the Order in Council and the direction of the Attorney-General were unauthorised by the Constitution; (ii) the Act contravened section 116 of the Constitution; (iii) the Act impinged upon the judicial power of the Commonwealth; and (iv) on their proper interpretation, the Regulations did not extend to the Witnesses.[41] The dispute came directly to the Court following an application before Starke J in which the parties agreed to the facts and stated questions of law for resolution.[42] For present purposes, the relevant questions involved whether the *National Security (Subversive Associations) Regulations*, the Order in Council, and the direction of the Attorney-General were beyond the legislative power of the Commonwealth or contravened the FoRB guarantee of section 116.[43]

[36] *ACJW* (n 1) 118.
[37] ibid.
[38] Persian (n 23) 10–11.
[39] ibid 11–12 (footnote omitted).
[40] *ACJW* (n 1) 118.
[41] ibid 150 (Starke J).
[42] ibid 119. See also G Sawer, *Australian Federalism in the Courts* (Melbourne University Press, 1967) 169. Stated cases arise pursuant to s 16 of the *Judiciary Act 1903* (Cth) and r 27 of the *High Court Rules 2004* (Cth). See also 'Legal Terms' *Opinions on High*, https://blogs.unimelb.edu.au/opinionsonhigh/about-the-high-court/legal-terms.
[43] *ACJW* (n 1) 119–20.

High Court Bench
Adelaide Company of Jehovah's Witnesses v Commonwealth
1943

Sir John Greig Latham GCMG QC
Chief Justice of Australia
11 October 1935 – 7 April 1952

Sir George Edward Rich KCMG QC
Justice
5 April 1913 – 5 May 1950

Sir Hayden Erskine Starke KCMG
Justice
5 February 1920 – 31 January 1950

Sir Edward Aloysius McTiernan KBE
Justice
20 December 1930 – 12 September 1976

Sir Dudley Williams KBE MC QC
Justice
15 October 1940 – 31 July 1958

A High Court bench of Latham CJ and Rich, Starke, McTiernan and Williams JJ heard the stated case. While the Court found no violation of section 116, 'the protection which the Court failed to accord in the name of religious values it did accord in the name of the protection of economic values; the Court held that the destruction of the Witnesses' property rights and of the rights of their creditors was so drastic as to be beyond the scope of the defence power'.[44] Our focus here, though, is FoRB. Each justice wrote a separate opinion which, taken together, provide guidance on four primary issues concerning the scope of section 116 free exercise: Commonwealth power to legislate

[44] Sawer (n 42) 170.

with respect to religion; the meaning of 'religion' as found in section 116; the difference in protection to be afforded freedom of belief and conduct taken in furtherance of that belief; and the means of balancing the individual's interest in free exercise with the community's interest in social order.

A. Power to Legislate

The very existence of section 116 posed a threshold question: does this provision both confer a power to legislate concerning religion and simultaneously limit it where to do so interferes with FoRB? The Court found that the Constitution contained no power to legislate with respect to religion and, as such, section 116 constitutes a general overriding prohibition which, Latham CJ wrote, 'prevails over and limits all provisions which give power to make laws … All the legislative powers of the Commonwealth are subject to the condition which s 116 imposes'.[45] Starke J was clearer: 'The Parliament is given no express power to legislate with respect to religion, but it has many other legislative powers. And those other powers cannot be exercised in contravention of the provision for religious liberty or freedom protected and guaranteed by the Constitution.'[46]

B. 'Religion'

For Latham CJ, 'religion' in section 116 meant all religions[47] because:

> [I]t would be difficult, if not impossible, to devise a definition of religion which would satisfy the adherents of all the many and various religions which exist, or have existed, in the world. There are those who regard religion as consisting principally in a system of beliefs or statement of doctrine. So viewed religion may be either true or false. Others are more inclined to regard religion as prescribing a code of conduct. So viewed a religion may be good or bad. There are others who pay greater attention to religion as involving some prescribed form of ritual or religious observance. Many religious conflicts have been concerned with matters of ritual and observance. Section 116 must be regarded as operating in relation to all these aspects of religion, irrespective of varying opinions in the community as to the truth of particular religious doctrines, as to the goodness of conduct prescribed by a particular religion, or as to the propriety of any particular religious observance.[48]

Latham CJ added two fundamental points in interpreting the meaning of 'religion': first, that 's 116 operates not only to protect the freedom of religion, but also to protect the right of a man to have no religion … [It] proclaims not only the principle of toleration

[45] *ACJW* (n 1) 122–123 (Latham CJ), 156–57 (McTiernan J).
[46] ibid 154 (Starke J).
[47] ibid 123 (Latham CJ).
[48] ibid and see also 156 (McTiernan J). See also J Puls, 'The Wall of Separation: Section 116, The First Amendment and Constitutional Religious Guarantees' (1998) 26 *Federal Law Review* 139, 143, 150–56; *cf* A Deagon and BB Saunders, 'Principles, Pragmatism and Power: Another Look at the Historical Context of Section 116' (2020) 43(3) *Melbourne University Law Review* 1033.

of all religions, but also the principle of toleration of absence of religion';[49] and, second, that section 116 protects not merely the religious belief of the majority, but also, more importantly, that of the minority.[50] Thus, the ambit of the protection in section 116 is very wide, covering both religion in all of its manifestations, majority and minority, as well as freedom from any such belief at all.

C. Conscience versus Conduct

In *Cantwell v Connecticut*, Roberts J wrote for the US Supreme Court that there is a distinction to be drawn between 'freedom to believe and freedom to act. The first is absolute, but, in the nature of things, the second cannot be. Conduct remains subject to regulation for the protection of society'.[51] In other words, what does a protection for free exercise protect: is it restricted to the freedom to believe or does it also cover, subject to justifiable limitations to protect society, the freedom to act upon that belief? This has been a central concern of American First Amendment free exercise jurisprudence. The question arises, too, in respect of section 116, and Latham CJ wrote that:

> The section refers in express terms to the *exercise* of religion, and therefore it is intended to protect from the operation of any Commonwealth laws acts which are done in the exercise of religion. Thus the section goes far beyond protecting liberty of opinion. It protects also acts done in pursuance of religious belief as part of religion.[52]

Section 116 thus protects both the freedom to believe and the freedom to act on those beliefs. But, as Roberts J concluded concerning the First Amendment, while the freedom to believe is absolute, the freedom to act on that belief cannot be absolute. How does a court determine whether the state legitimately interferes with free exercise?

D. Conduct versus Social Order

The reason Roberts J found it necessary to address the difference between belief and conduct stems from the failure of the First Amendment to provide a means of analysing when limitations might be placed around conduct for the preservation of social order. The express words of section 116 seem similarly lacking. The Supreme Court of the United States has developed, over a long period of time, a hierarchy of constitutional standards of scrutiny for use in considering the justifiability of restrictions which might be placed upon conduct in furtherance of belief, or free exercise.[53] Although it has been largely overlooked by subsequent scholarship, *ACJW* did the same for section 116.

[49] *ACJW* (n 1) 123 (Latham CJ) and see also 156 (McTiernan J).
[50] ibid 124 (Latham CJ) and see also 148 (Rich J).
[51] *Cantwell v Connecticut*, 310 US 296, 303–04 (1940) (Roberts J).
[52] *ACJW* (n 1) 124–25 (Latham CJ).
[53] ibid 127–31 (Latham CJ). See also AK Blair, 'Constitutional Equal Protection, Strict Scrutiny, and the Politics of Marriage Law' (1998) 47 *Catholic University Law Review* 1231; RG Spece Jr and D Yokum, 'Scrutinizing Strict Scrutiny' (2015) 40 *Vermont Law Review* 285; E Gerstmann and C Shortell, 'The Many Faces of Strict Scrutiny: How the Supreme Court Changes the Rules in Race Cases' (2010) 72 *University of Pittsburgh Law Review* 1.

For Latham CJ, section 116 is not merely about the exercise of religion, but also the 'free' exercise of religion, and the meaning of the conduct so protected turns on that word, the meaning of which is 'vague and ambiguous'.[54] Latham CJ considered the plain meaning of the terms, concluding that the word may mean both freedom from physical restraint and freedom of thought, expression and physical movement. The obligation to comply with laws which apply generally to the community is not inconsistent with freedom in this sense.[55] The same is true of freedom of speech, which, while 'a highly valued element in our society', does not mean that it is entirely unlimited if doing so is necessary for the maintenance of social order within the community.[56] Some balancing of the competing individual and community interests is necessary, or, put another way, individual free exercise must, in some instances, give way to the community interest in social order.

For Latham CJ, drawing upon John Stuart Mill's harm principle,[57] 'it is consistent with the maintenance of religious liberty for the State to restrain actions and courses of conduct which are inconsistent with the maintenance of civil government or prejudicial to the continued existence of the community'[58] and:

> [I]f the guarantee is to have any real significance it must be left to the courts of justice to determine its meaning and to give effect to it by declaring the invalidity of laws which infringe it and by declining to enforce them. The courts will therefore have the responsibility of determining whether a particular law can fairly be regarded as a law to protect the existence of the community, or whether, on the other hand, it is a law 'for prohibiting the free exercise of any religion'. The word 'for' shows that the purpose of the legislation in question may properly be taken into account in determining whether or not it is a law of the prohibited character.[59]

Thus, context determines when freedom may be constrained in the community interest;[60] indeed, as Rich J said, 'it is … a mistake for the Court to lay down general or abstract propositions as to the effect of s 116. It is typically a provision the interpretation of which should be developed by specific decisions applicable to the particular facts of the given cases'.[61] And for Starke J, 'liberty and freedom in an organized community are relative and not absolute terms',[62] and 'liberty and freedom of religion guaranteed and protected by the Constitution is subject to limitations which it is the function and the duty of the courts of law to expound' for 'the protection of the community and in the interests of social order'.[63] In other words, the liberty of free exercise is subject to limitations in order to protect society.

The Court concluded that the defence power, exercised during wartime, represented one of the most obvious instances in which limitations could be imposed. Latham CJ found that the Commonwealth government had the requisite power pursuant to sections 51(vi)

[54] *ACJW* (n 1) 126 (Latham CJ) and see also 159–60 (Williams J).
[55] ibid 126–27 (Latham CJ).
[56] ibid 127 (Latham CJ).
[57] See JS Mill, *On Liberty* (G Himmelfarb (ed)) (Penguin, 1985 [1859]).
[58] *ACJW* (n 1) 131–32 (Latham CJ) and see also 159–60 (Williams J).
[59] ibid.
[60] ibid 127 (Latham CJ). See also Sawer (n 42) 169–70.
[61] *ACJW* (n 1) 148–49 (Rich J).
[62] ibid 154–55 (Starke J).
[63] ibid 155 (Starke J).

(defence) and 61 (executive power) of the *Constitution* to further the existence of the state by enacting such laws as a matter of defending the people from both external and internal attack.[64] And the *National Security (Subversive Associations) Regulations* (Cth) were a valid means of the executive government carrying into execution the powers conferred by the *National Security Act 1939–1940* (Cth), itself validly enacted pursuant to the defence power of section 51(vi) of the *Constitution*.[65] Based upon the Court's 1912 decision in *Krygger*, Latham CJ found that the impugned laws were not for the purpose of infringing free exercise and so did not contravene section 116.[66] Justice Rich concluded that 'the peace, good government and order of the Commonwealth may be protected at the same time as the freedom of religion is safeguarded. Freedom of religion is not absolute. It is subject to powers and restrictions of government essential to the preservation of the community'.[67] Justice Williams was clear and straightforward: 'A state of war … justifies legislation by the Commonwealth Parliament, in the exercise of the defence power, which makes many inroads on personal freedom, and which places many restrictions on the use of property of an abnormal and temporary nature which would not be legitimate in times of peace.'[68]

In developing this analytical approach, the High Court drew heavily on US free exercise jurisprudence – including *Cantwell v Connecticut*[69] – developed both before and after the coming into force of the Australian *Constitution*. For Latham CJ, the US experience provided significant guidance for the principle 'according to which it is left to the court to determine whether the freedom of religion has been *unduly* infringed by some particular legislative provision. This view makes it possible to accord a real measure of practical protection to religion without involving the community in anarchy'.[70] More importantly, it is decidedly the judiciary, both in the US and in Australia, which is tasked with interpreting the meaning of 'free' to reach this principle.[71] Thus, Latham CJ concluded that 'there is … full legal justification for adopting in Australia an interpretation of s 116 which had, before the enactment of the Commonwealth Constitution, already been given to similar words in the United States'.[72]

IV. Re-appraising the Interpretation of Section 116

The vast majority of contemporary scholarship dealing with *ACJW* adopts the accepted view that it merely serves to confirm the *Krygger* test, which itself was affirmed in *Kruger*. However, upon closer inspection, there is much more in *ACJW* than a mere adoption and application of *Krygger*. Indeed, what *ACJW* actually contains are two significant

[64] ibid 132 (Latham CJ). Starke J (at 150–54) disagreed, finding that 'the Regulations are beyond the power conferred upon the Governor-General in Council by the *National Security Act 1939–1940*'.
[65] *ACJW* (n 1) 133–44 (Latham CJ) and see also 161 (Williams J).
[66] ibid 133 (Latham CJ).
[67] ibid 149–50 (Rich J).
[68] ibid 161 (Williams J).
[69] ibid 127–31 (Latham CJ), 154–55 (Starke J).
[70] ibid 131 (Latham CJ) (emphasis in original).
[71] ibid 126, 128 (Latham CJ).
[72] ibid 131 (Latham CJ).

expansions of what section 116 protects. First, it reveals the proper definition of 'religion' for the purposes of section 116. Second, section 116 protects not only against infringements through the express purpose of a law or executive action, but, more importantly, such infringements may also arise due to the effects of otherwise facially neutral laws. This involves applying a two-step approach to the analysis of section 116 infringements.

In addition to these important expansions of the meaning of section 116, though, I conclude here, quite controversially, with a third expansion of section 116, not so much found in what *ACJW* decided, but in the spirit of the creativity which the High Court used in analysing section 116. I suggest that the courts might extend the protection of section 116 to the states as well as the Commonwealth. This would involve using the text of section 116 as implying, within the democratic framework established by the text as a whole, the protection of FoRB no matter how it may be infringed, by the Commonwealth or by a state. Readers may want to reject this final claim entirely as being far-fetched and fanciful. I make this claim, however, not so much because I think the courts will accept it, but more as a suggestion that that courts can be creative with a written constitution if they had the inclination to do so. For, after all, what are implications but judicial creativity with a text?

A. 'Religion': Freedom *of* and *from*

In 1983, the High Court decided *Church of the New Faith v Commissioner of Pay-roll Tax* (Vic), in which, for the purposes of taxation law, the majority attempted to define, in great detail, what a religion is.[73] Justice Murphy, citing Latham CJ in *ACJW*, rejected this approach, writing that:

> If each purported religion had to show that its doctrines were true, then all might fail. Administrators and judges must resist the temptation to hold that groups or institutions are not religious because claimed religious beliefs or practices seem absurd, fraudulent, evil or novel; or because the group or institution is new, the number of adherents small, the leaders hypocrites, or because they seek to obtain the financial and other privileges which come with religious status. In the eyes of the law, religions are equal. There is no religious club with a monopoly of State privileges for its members. The policy of the law is 'one in, all in'.
>
> …
>
> The better approach is to state what is sufficient, even if not necessary, to bring a body which claims to be religious within the category … On this approach, any body which claims to be religious, whose beliefs or practices are a revival of, or resemble, earlier cults, is religious. Any body which claims to be religious and to believe in a supernatural Being or Beings, whether physical and visible, such as the sun or the stars, or a physical invisible God or spirit, or an abstract God or entity, is religious … Any body which claims to be religious, and offers a way to find meaning and purpose in life, is religious. The Aboriginal religion of Australia and of other countries must be included. The list is not exhaustive; the categories of religion are not closed.[74]

[73] *Church of the New Faith v. Commissioner of Pay-roll Tax* (n 10).
[74] ibid 150–51 (Murphy J).

It is often thought that Murphy J's approach is an outlier, with the majority approach in *Church of the New Faith*, and its detailed definition of religion, providing the correct test not only for tax law, but also for section 116. That is not so. Latham CJ's approach is the correct – indeed, the only – approach to defining religion which applies to the *Constitution* and section 116. And, of course, Latham CJ's approach expands to take in not only the freedom to exercise one's faith, but also the freedom from any religion whatsoever. Indeed, section 116 would be 'worthless unless it gave a fairly wide protection to religious *and* anti-religious beliefs, and protected the odd beliefs of minorities rather than the conventional beliefs of majorities who could look after themselves'.[75]

A re-appraisal of *ACJW* would not so much mean a change in this understanding of the free exercise limb, as an affirmation of Latham CJ's position being the controlling interpretation. The *Constitution* is not taxation law; it is high time we remembered Latham CJ's approach to religion and distinguished the narrow interpretative approach to religion employed in *Church of the New Faith* as being relevant only to taxation law, and not to the *Constitution*. The *Constitution* requires a purposive, liberal reading of religion, which Latham CJ (and Murphy J) provided.

B. Infringement: A Two-Step Test

A broad definition of religion might prove unworkable unless an appropriate method of analysis for assessing purported violations is employed. An absolutist approach to free exercise violations will not do. To put it another way, as we have already seen, no right is absolute. Every right is susceptible to reasonable limitations in order to protect the community. And *ACJW* provides such a test, making clear that section 116 analysis involves *two* separate steps.[76] The first step focuses on the individual – and allows the widest possible scope to what counts as a religion which may be violated – while the second takes account of the community interest.

i. Step One: Ambit

Justice Starke wrote in *ACJW* that 'the Parliament is given no express power to legislate with respect to religion'[77] and that while it has no power to legislate directly in respect of religion: 'Parliament … has many other legislative powers. And those other powers cannot be exercised in contravention of the provision for religious liberty or freedom protected and guaranteed by the Constitution. But liberty and freedom in an organized community are relative and not absolute terms.'[78] This is effectively an admission that the free exercise guarantee allows no circumstances in which the *express* purpose of legislation could be found to violate the free exercise guarantee. Recognising this truth would give a wide ambit to the free exercise guarantee. But doing so is not tantamount to establishing an absolute guarantee, for there will certainly be instances where

[75] Sawer (n 42) 170; Puls (n 48).
[76] See also Babie, 'National Security' (n 10).
[77] *ACJW* (n 1) 154 (Starke J).
[78] ibid.

government intrusion may be justified. In other words, recognising the existence of a wide ambit for the right means also admitting that there will be instances in which the state might, in order to protect the collective or community interest, impose limitations upon that right. Here is where the real work of the courts begins: the assessment of the justifiability of limitations placed upon the guarantee of FoRB.

ii. Step Two: Limitations

Many human rights instruments contain express 'limitations clauses' to assist the courts in doing this work. These include instruments in the international sphere (such as the *Universal Declaration of Human Rights*[79] or the *International Covenant on Civil and Political Rights*),[80] the national domestic constitution of a state (such as the *Canadian Charter of Rights and Freedoms*[81] and the *Constitution of India*),[82] the quasi-constitutional law of a group of states (such as the *European Convention on Human Rights*)[83] or the domestic legislation of a nation or one of its constituent states (such as the Victorian *Charter of Human Rights and Responsibilities Act 2006* (Vic)).[84] Other instruments contain the protection of fundamental rights, such as FoRB, but no express limitations clause; yet, in these cases, the courts have judicially crafted a limitations test. The most notable example of this approach is the standard of review created by the Supreme Court of the United States for use in assessing limitations imposed upon on FoRB as protected by the First Amendment to the *Constitution*.[85]

The High Court itself consistently utilises a limitations test for use in analysing infringements of both express and implied freedoms contained in the *Constitution*. The most notable of the former is found in relation to the free trade and commerce protection in section 92. *Palmer v Western Australia* provides the most recent confirmation and clarification of the appropriate limitations standard:[86] a violation will be impermissible if 'the burden cannot be justified as proportionate to the non-discriminatory, legitimate purpose of the law which is sought to be achieved. Whether it is proportionate is to be determined by [a] test[] of structured proportionality'.[87]

[79] UN General Assembly, *Universal Declaration of Human Rights*, 10 December 1948, 217 A (III), arts 18 and 29(2).

[80] UN General Assembly, *International Covenant on Civil and Political Rights*, 16 December 1966, United Nations, Treaty Series, vol 999, 171, art 18(1)–(3).

[81] *Canadian Charter of Rights and Freedoms*, s 1, pt 1 of the *Constitution Act, 1982*, being sched B to the *Canada Act 1982* (UK), 1982, c 11.

[82] *Constitution of India*, 26 January 1950, art 25(1)–(2).

[83] Council of Europe, *European Convention for the Protection of Human Rights and Fundamental Freedoms*, as amended by Protocols Nos 11 and 14, 4 November 1950, ETS 5, art 9(2).

[84] *Charter of Human Rights and Responsibilities Act 2006* (Vic), s 7(2).

[85] Which began with *United States v Carolene Products Company*, 304 US 144 (1938) fn 4 (Stone J). See also L Lusky, 'Footnote Redux: A "Carolene Products" Reminiscence' (1982) 82(6) *Columbia Law Review* 1093; H Gillman and E Chemerinsky, *The Religion Clauses: The Case for Separating Church and State* (Oxford University Press, 2020) 95–160; CC Wolanek and H Liu, 'Applying Strict Scrutiny: An Empirical Analysis of Free Exercise Cases' (2017) 78 *Montana Law Review* 275.

[86] *Palmer v Western Australia* [2021] HCA 5.

[87] ibid [62] and [52]–[62] (Keifel CJ and Keane J), [217], [261]–[276] (Edelman J). But see [94], [140]–[162] (Gageler J), [198]–[200] (Gordon J), rejecting structured proportionality in favour of reasonable necessity.

Political communication remains the only implied freedom currently recognised by the High Court.[88] Analysis of infringements involves a two-question approach:

> First, does the law effectively burden freedom of communication about government or political matters either in its terms, operation or effect? Second, if the law effectively burdens that freedom, is the law reasonably appropriate and adapted to serve a legitimate end[?][89]

The High Court has since adopted a detailed structured proportionality test for use in analysing the second question[90] – it is this to which the Court referred in *Palmer v Western Australia*. In *McCloy v New South Wales*, the majority wrote:

> The term 'proportionality' in Australian law describes a class of criteria which have been developed by this Court over many years to determine whether legislative or administrative acts are within the constitutional or legislative grant of power under which they purport to be done.[91]

Clearly, then, every jurisdiction, including Australia, with experience in protecting fundamental rights and freedoms provides a means for analysing the justifiability of limitations to be imposed upon those rights. The same is undoubtedly true of section 116, and *ACJW* makes that clear.[92]

Assessing the limitations imposed upon the FoRB guarantee of section 116 involves a balancing of the protection to be afforded the right and the reasons given for justifying its limitation. And it is the judiciary that must, on the one hand, determine the ambit of the right protected by the free exercise guarantee and, on the other hand, determine whether limitations placed upon it can be reconciled with or justified by the requirement for ordered government.[93] Justice Starke put it this way: 'the liberty and freedom of religion guaranteed and protected by the Constitution is subject to limitations which it is the function and the duty of the courts of law to expound'.[94]

C. Reach: Extension to the States

It seems clear that the framers of the *Constitution* at the very least considered extending the reach of section 116 to protect against infringements of both the Commonwealth and the states. Ultimately, though, the draft adopted omitted reference to the states, while leaving section 116 in Chapter V, which deals with the states. Nonetheless, it seems clear today that 'whilst the Constitution forbids the Federal Parliament to interfere with the free exercise of religion, it does not make any provision for protecting the citizens of the States in their religious worship or religious liberties; this is left entirely to the State Constitutions and laws, and there is no inhibition in regard to the

[88] On the place and existence of implied freedoms in the Australian Constitution, see A Stone, 'Australia's Constitutional Rights and the Problem of Interpretive Disagreement' [2005] *University of Melbourne Law Research Series* 3.

[89] *Lange v Australian Broadcasting Corporation* (1997) 189 CLR 520, 567.

[90] *McCloy v New South Wales* (2015) 257 CLR 178; *Brown v Tasmania* (2017) 261 CLR 328.

[91] *McCloy v New South Wales* (n 90) [3]–[5] (French CJ, Kiefel, Bell and Keane JJ) (citations omitted).

[92] *ACJW* (n 1) 131–32 (Latham CJ).

[93] ibid 131 (Latham CJ).

[94] ibid 155 (Starke J).

subject imposed upon the States'.[95] Yet, might we be more creative in our approach to section 116? I want to suggest here, controversially, that we can.

In a seminal piece of scholarship, Michael Detmold argued that while a constitution is the ordering of a community, over time, the power arrangements within that community may change. That is true of Australia since Federation:[96]

> The old constitutional law concerned mainly the political entities, Commonwealth and States, and to a diminishing degree, United Kingdom. Indeed, it was often remarked that the absence of a systematic concern for the rights of citizens made a sharp distinction between our constitution and that, say, of the United States. This has now changed. In a very short time the High Court has created a new constitutional law of individual (citizens') rights that is profound and far-reaching. Moreover, it is not just that there is a new law of individual rights on top of the old – the new is taking over from the old in the sense that old problems of the relations of the political entities (loosely referred to as problems of federalism) are actually being solved in terms of citizens' rights.[97]

Whereas the *Constitution* once dealt with the relationships between one type of political entity – the state – through judicial creativity in the use of implications, it has shifted to one which mediates the relationships between liberal political entities, the individual or individuals. And Detmold advances a novel argument concerning section 92, which provides: 'On the imposition of uniform duties of customs, trade, commerce, and intercourse among the States, whether by means of internal carriage or ocean navigation, shall be absolutely free.' For Detmold, this means that there is not 'a new section 92, but rather, section 92 in the new constitutional law'.[98] In this new constitutional arrangement of powers:

> It is important to emphasise that the movement that section 92 protects is an ordinary thing – not a special thing. Communities are nothing but movement – movement of the thought, word and deed of humans in relation to one another … And the idea of discrimination in the new constitutional law is simply the idea of the invalidity of laws which construct barriers to those communal movements. Laws, that is, which keep people out.[99]

Federation established 'the constitutional unity of the Australian people "in one indissoluble Federal Commonwealth"'.[100] What this means is that the old constitutional law, concerned as it is with the relationships between states or sovereign entities, has moved such that subjects of those states have become citizens and, as such, the relevant relationship has become one between citizens:[101]

> [And with] the movement from sovereign to citizen is also a movement from states to citizens' relations. This shows that the integration of the section 92 cases into the new constitutional law is only one part of the whole movement. The states in Australian constitutional law are (were) cases of (minor) sovereignties. With the movement of that law from sovereignty to the rights of citizens the states become communities of citizens. And there is a virtual infinity of these: there is a virtual infinity of combinations of discriminatory power.[102]

[95] Quick and Garran (n 12) 1162.
[96] MJ Detmold, 'The New Constitutional Law' (1994) 16(2) *Sydney Law Review* 228, 229.
[97] ibid 230.
[98] ibid 232–33.
[99] ibid 233–34.
[100] *Leeth v Commonwealth* (1992) 66 ALJR 529, 537 (Brennan J), citing the First Preamble to the *Constitution*.
[101] Detmold (n 96) 235.
[102] ibid 237–38.

Section 92, then, breaks down borders, thus creating freedoms, subject only to rational grounds for limiting that movement. Detmold develops a lengthy and sophisticated argument surrounding the nature of the Australian states and the borders between them: the states are political entities, to which citizens may be analogised. In other words, citizens are political entities, *states*, too.[103] As such, '[a]ll the freedoms are freedoms against borders. When borders are constitutionally systematic they constitute the equivalent of States'.[104] Here is where Detmold advances a creative argument for extending the rights implied in the *Constitution* to all people, in all states and *against* all states. This is achieved through section 92 and the first implied right, political communication. He argues that '[a]ny restriction at all on human movement creates a border. By human movement [is] mean[t] any of the ways, physical or mental, by which humans relate to each other. Now, the constitutional word for this human movement is "intercourse"',[105] as that word is found in section 92. He concludes that because the self only exists in community, is relational:

> The new constitutional law is the law of the freedom of human movement in body and mind throughout the Australian Commonwealth … Every aspect of our lives that involves a relation to another is a movement of thought, word or deed.
>
> …
>
> We in Australia are in the fortunate position of not having our freedom constricted by a word or set of words such as is found in a Bill of Rights. Instead, the matter being one of implication in the Constitution (more precisely, we have shown, implication in the having of a constitution), it is consigned to the common law; and the argument about the limits of the constitutional guarantee will go where it will in the case by case way of the common law. So any human movement at all in thought, word and deed is the broad issue, and any distinctions within that category or limitations of it will arise by virtue of principled common law argument from the new cases.[106]

Detmold is speaking here of the implied freedom of political communication, but he is using this as his example of a right implied by the having of a constitution, and those rights are not limited to political communication alone. Instead, he means that all human rights are capable of implication from the having of a constitution, and that the judiciary is free in this regard to act creatively to imply those rights, not constrained by the written text of a Bill of Rights as is the judiciary of the United States or Canada, or any of the Western democracies which have such a text. For Detmold, the *lack* of a text is an advantage, as it allows maximal creativity to the judges.

In the case of FoRB, the existence of section 116 might provide guidance for that creativity, in the sense that the rights found in section 116 can be extended to prohibit interferences with FoRB as against the states as well, because to allow otherwise would be to create a distinction in the way in which citizens were treated by the Commonwealth as opposed to the states, and would interfere with and create borders to the ways – physical or mental, which surely must include religion – in which citizens may relate to

[103] ibid 238–43.
[104] ibid 243.
[105] ibid 246.
[106] ibid 247–48.

one another. Of course, Detmold's analysis, as is mine, is controversial. But its appeal lies in its creativity, a creativity exercised by the High Court in its approach to section 116.

V. Conclusion

ACJW remains the most important of the High Court's decisions dealing with FoRB in section 116, not because it is one of only three such cases or because it is the controlling law as concerns free exercise – which it is – but for its promise. It offers the promise of a purposive, large, liberal approach to FoRB in section 116. That approach would expansively define religion, in turn recognising that infringements of free exercise may follow not merely from laws or executive action which takes as its express purpose the infringement of religion, but, and much more realistically, the effects of laws of general application too. Above all, because it would recognise creativity in the judicial approach to this important right, it might even allow for the expansion of section 116's protection to encompass both Commonwealth and state legislative and executive activity.

PART III

Religion and State Relations Around the Commonwealth

9

Iki Putra Mubarrak v Kerajaan Negeri Selangor and Others

Re-defining Religious Federalism in Malaysia?

DIAN AH SHAH

I. Introduction

One of the perennial struggles in Malaysia's constitutional development has revolved around the issue of religion. As a Muslim-majority, yet multi-ethnic and multi-religious polity, the constitutional contests on religion have often implicated the position of Islam as the religion of the Federation and, by extension, the evolving boundaries of Islamic law within what is intended to be a secular constitutional order.[1] The *Federal Constitution* deals with Malaysia's sociolegal pluralism by establishing a legal system that allows for the operation of Islamic institutions and laws. In other words, while the general law in Malaysia is secular (and enacted by secular institutions such as the Parliament), there exists a separate *Syariah* jurisdiction that governs 'offences against the precepts of Islam', as well as personal and family matters for 'persons professing the religion of Islam'. This is spelled out the Ninth Schedule, List II of the *Federal Constitution*, which specifies a list of matters in which state legislatures (as opposed to the Federal Parliament, except with regard to the federal territories) are authorised to regulate, including issues that would fall under the *Syariah* jurisdiction. Thus, individual states across Malaysia have enacted laws dealing with – among other issues – divorce, custody, inheritance, maintenance and alimony, as well as specific 'Islamic' criminal offences such as consumption of alcohol, preaching without state authorisation, *khalwat* (suspicious close proximity between unmarried couples in a private setting) and *liwat* (sodomy).

This system of laws is buttressed – through a constitutional amendment in 1988 – by Article 121(1A), which provides that civil courts shall have no jurisdiction in matters that are exclusively within the *Syariah* jurisdiction. This creates an autonomous sphere of authority and legal development for *Syariah* courts, as civil (secular) courts are precluded

[1] The constitutional position of Islam as the 'religion of the Federation' is cemented in art 3(1) of the *Federal Constitution*. See generally DAH Shah, *Constitutions, Religion and Politics in Asia: Indonesia, Malaysia and Sri Lanka* (Cambridge University Press, 2017); JM Fernando, *The Making of the Malayan Constitution* (Malaysian Branch of the Royal Asiatic Society, 2006).

from reviewing *Syariah* court decisions in certain matters that are *exclusively* – as mandated by the Ninth Schedule, List II – within the *Syariah* jurisdiction.[2] The intention behind this scheme was straightforward. First, it was originally thought that questions involving *Syariah* law (in the limited areas where the law applies) required the expertise of those trained in Islamic jurisprudence.[3] Second, there were concerns that the two courts were issuing conflicting decisions, as evinced in a number of cases at the time.[4]

In any case, all this brings to light a crucial aspect of state–religion relations and religious regulation in Malaysia: the federalised system of managing Muslim legal affairs. Although the *Constitution* stipulates an autonomous sphere of authority for state legislatures with regard to specific Islamic law matters, federal law may supersede state laws where there is a conflict. Yet, in practice, state Islamic laws have sought to regulate matters that are explicitly dealt with by federal laws. This was the core issue confronting the Federal Court in *Iki Putra Mubarrak v Kerajaan Negeri Selangor and Others.*[5]

In what follows, this chapter examines the boundaries of federal–state dynamics in matters implicating 'Islamic' matters – specifically, the Court was confronted with the question of the constitutionality of state-level (Islamic) statutes that regulate matters that are already regulated by federal-level laws. This case takes on an even greater significance because the Federal Court has been reluctant to declare a state *Syariah* law to be unconstitutional whether for offending fundamental liberty guarantees or for regulating a matter that clearly falls under the list of federal legislative authority. This has to be considered and understood in light of three further issues. The first is the view that if a piece of legislation 'in pith and substance' deals with an Islamic matter, then it is a law that only the state legislatures are empowered to enact.[6] The second revolves around judicial attitudes towards reviewing any matter or exercises of power implicating Islam – for many years, the courts – have been quick to avoid deciding on matters implicating Islam, even where fundamental constitutional questions arise. In relation to this is a third issue, that is, the ways in which the constitutional position of Islam as the religion of the Federation has been interpreted, conceived and practised in the Malaysian legal and political discourse.

Against this background, this chapter begins – in section II – by elaborating on the facts and legal questions from *Iki Putra Mubarrak*. It will also contextualise this case and several other cases in Malaysia's constitutional jurisprudence on law and religion by explaining the key legal and constitutional structures associated with Islam as the 'religion of the Federation'. Section III delves into the legal and political dimensions of Malaysia's religious federalism, illustrating the ways in which the *Iki Putra Mubarrak* decision recalibrates the federal–state division of powers on religion. Finally, section IV addresses the boundaries of regulating 'offences against the precepts of Islam' in Malaysia's constitutional order.

[2] DL Horowitz, 'Islam and the Common Law: Islamic Law Reform and the Theory of Legal Change' (1994) 42(2) *American Journal of Comparative Law* 293, 237.

[3] SS Faruqi, 'Freedom of Religion under the Constitution' *The Sun* (18 May 2006), www.sun2surf.com/article.cfm?id=14147.

[4] A Ibrahim, 'The Amendment of Article 121 of the Federal Constitution: Its Effect on the Administration of Islamic Law' (1989) 2 *Malayan Law Journal* xvii.

[5] *Iki Putra Mubarrak v Kerajaan Negeri Selangor and Others* [2021] 1 LNS 47 (Federal Court).

[6] The 'pith and substance test' was adopted in *Mamat bin Daud v Government of Malaysia* [1988] 1 MLJ 119, 120 (Supreme Court).

II. Facts and Background

Malaysia's *Penal Code* is a remnant of British colonial legacy, modelled on and transplanted – almost in its entirety – from the *Indian Penal Code* of 1860.[7] Among the provisions that were adopted, word for word, from the *Indian Code* are a range of sexual offences, notably, the clause on 'carnal intercourse against the order of nature'.[8] Under section 377A, a person is deemed to have committed such offence where he has 'sexual connection with another person by the introduction of the penis into the anus or mouth of the other person'. However, on the pretext of regulating 'offences against the precepts of Islam', states across the Federation of Malaysia have also enacted *Syariah* criminal enactments that criminalise homosexual relations and conduct of Muslims. These are typically found in chapters dealing with 'offences relating to decency', which also covers other offences such as incest, prostitution and adultery (the former two offences are also covered by the *Penal Code*), but the enactments contain different kinds of offences, including under 'offences relating to *aqidah*' (Islamic creed)[9] and 'offences relating to the sanctity of the religion of Islam and its institutions'.[10]

In *Iki Putra Mubarrak*, what was at stake was the constitutionality of section 28 of the *Syariah Criminal Offences (Selangor) Enactment 1995* (*SCOE*), which provides that:

> Any person who performs sexual intercourse against the order of nature with any man, woman or animal is guilty of an offence and shall be liable on conviction to a fine not exceeding five thousand ringgit or to imprisonment for a term not exceeding three years or to whipping not exceeding six strokes or to any combination thereof.

On 21 August 2019, Iki Putra Mubarrak was charged (in the Selangor *Syariah* High Court) by the state *Syariah* prosecutor for attempting to commit sexual intercourse against the order of nature with certain other (non-Muslim) male persons. He pleaded not guilty to the charge and proceeded to file a petition to the Federal Court – invoking the Court's original jurisdiction – for a declaration that section 28 *SCOE* is invalid as against the *Constitution*.

In particular, he argued that section 377A of the *Penal Code* already criminalises the offence covered by section 28, and therefore the Selangor state legislature lacked competence to legislate. This is because the Ninth Schedule, List II of the *Constitution* empowers states to pass laws pertaining to offences against the precepts of Islam 'except in regard to matters included in the Federal List'. The Federal list of legislative authority, embodied in the Ninth Schedule, List I of the *Constitution*, explicitly includes criminal law and procedure, and these areas of law are governed by the *Penal Code* and the *Criminal Procedure Code*. In short, the core focus of the case was on the interpretation of the words 'except in regard to matters included in the Federal List' (which the Federal Court termed as the 'preclusion clause') within the broader context of Malaysia's federalised system of

[7] See generally A Ibrahim, 'Towards a History of Law in Malaysia and Singapore' (Inaugural Braddell Memorial Lecture 1970).

[8] Section 377A of the *Penal Code*.

[9] See, eg, s 7 of the *Syariah Criminal Offences (Selangor) Enactment 1995* (Enactment No 9 of 1995) and s 4 of the *Syariah Criminal Offences (Federal Territories) Act 1997*. Both provisions deal with the propagation of 'false doctrine'.

[10] See, eg, ss 13 and 16 of the *Syariah Criminal Offences (Selangor) Enactment 1995*; and ss 12 and 13 of the *1997 Federal Territories Act*.

regulating and managing Islamic affairs. In this respect alone, the *Iki Putra Mubarrak* case was groundbreaking because there had never been a challenge to state *Syariah* laws on the basis that such laws had encroached into the federal legislative competence, even though – as mentioned above – such laws have existed for decades.

Previously, cases that raised questions about the constitutionality of executive action or legislations relating to Islamic law were – by and large – grounded in violations of constitutional fundamental liberties guarantees. For example, in 2014, three men, who were prosecuted by religious authorities in the state of Negeri Sembilan for cross-dressing, challenged the constitutionality of section 66 of the *Syariah Criminal Enactment (Negeri Sembilan) 1992* on the grounds that it infringed the right to life and personal liberty and the right to equality.[11] In a religious conversion case, the petitioner, a Christian convert who was prevented from removing the word 'Islam' on her national identity card as she had not sought permission from the *Syariah* courts to formalise her conversion, argued that her right to religious freedom was violated.[12] In a case that was perhaps most relevant to *Iki Putra Mubarrak*, a Muslim man was charged under section 377D of the Penal Code for acts of 'gross indecency' (he had confessed to committing sodomy with Anwar Ibrahim, the former Deputy Prime Minister).[13] However, he argued that the civil courts had no jurisdiction to try the offence because such an offence was within the exclusive jurisdiction of the *Syariah* courts.

In any case, in *Iki Putra Mubarrak*, the Selangor state argued that the state legislature had jurisdiction to enact section 28 because the subject matter concerned 'offences against the precepts of Islam' (as mandated by the Ninth Schedule, List II) and that because section 28 is worded differently from the Penal Code, both regimes governing the same offence can co-exist.[14] With regard to the former point, the respondents posited that item 4(h) in the Federal List (List I) only refers to the 'creation of offences in respect of any of the matters included in the Federal List or dealt with by federal law', without any mention of 'offences against the precepts of Islam'.[15]

Both these arguments were unanimously rejected by a full, nine-member bench of the Federal Court. The Court declared that section 28 *SCOE* was inconsistent with the *Constitution* and therefore void.[16] The Court's reasoning was grounded in the core principles and mechanics underpinning Malaysia's religious federalism, that is, state legislatures – though empowered to enact laws in specific matters relating to Islam as stipulated in the Ninth Schedule, List II – do not have the authority to legislate on matters included in the Federal List. This is read together with Articles 74(3), 75 and 77 of the *Constitution*, all of which underline the role of the federal legislature (Parliament) as the primary law-making authority with regard to criminal law. Article 74 addresses the boundaries (in terms of subject matter) of legislative power, while Articles 75 and 77 deal with situations of inconsistencies between federal and state laws and the states' residual legislative power, respectively.

[11] *Muhammad Juzaili bin Mohd Khamis and Others v State Government of Negeri Sembilan and Others* [2014] MLJ Unreported 1063 (Court of Appeal).

[12] *Lina Joy v Majlis Agama Islam Wilayah and Another* [2007] 4 MLJ 585 (Court of Appeal).

[13] *Sukma Darmawan Sasmitaat Madja v Ketua Pengarah Penjara Malaysia and Another* [1999] 2 MLJ 241 (Court of Appeal).

[14] *Iki Putra Mubarrak* (n 5) [14].

[15] ibid [34].

[16] ibid [84].

Based on a textual, contextual and originalist approach to construing Article 74(3), which provides that legislative power (of both federal and state legislatures) is subject to restrictions in the *Constitution*, the Federal Court took the position that state legislative power is clearly restricted by the preclusion clause of the Ninth Schedule, List II. This was buttressed by several considerations. First, the constitution drafters – conscious of the possibility of a divergence between federal and state policies – had explicitly envisaged Parliament as the sole law-making authority in matters enumerated in the Federal List and, while in general states retain exclusive power to legislate in matters that fall within their exclusive jurisdiction, in certain circumstances the Federation has overriding powers.[17] This scheme of overriding powers is found in Article 76, which spells out three situations where the Federal Parliament can legislate on the matters provided in the State List: (1) to implement international agreements; (2) to promote legal uniformity between two or more states; and (3) where Parliament is explicitly requested to legislate by state legislatures. Second, where there is a conflict between federal laws and state laws, the former will prevail and, finally, the residual power of state legislatures to make laws beyond what is explicitly stated in the Ninth Schedule is limited, in that such laws cannot address matters that fall within the federal legislative authority.[18] As the following sections will demonstrate, although this decision is skilfully and convincingly grounded in the complexities of Malaysia's federal–state division of powers, there are potentially broader implications with respect to questions on religion.

III. Malaysia's Religious Federalism: Legal and Political Dimensions

The arrangements in the *Federal Constitution* institutionalise a limited scheme of religious federalism in Malaysia. In spite of Article 3(1) (ie, the provision stating that Islam is the 'religion of the *Federation*'), it is a 'federalised' system in the sense that matters implicating Islam are under the purview of the states, and for those states with a traditional royal household (these are the nine Malay states), the *sultan* is the head of Islam. This arrangement on Islam is closely tied to the traditional role and constitutional function of the *sultans* in their respective states. The *Malay State Constitutions* of the nineteenth and early twentieth centuries stipulated that the Ruler of the State (the *sultan*) must be a Muslim and serves as the head of Islam in his state. During the British colonial period, some aspects of the traditional political arrangements were retained: the British Residential System provided a British Resident whose advice 'must be asked and acted upon' by the *sultan* on all questions, but the *sultan* retained control over matters pertaining to Islam and Malay customs.[19] Therefore, the *Constitution* (through Article 74(2) and the Ninth Schedule, List II) devolves autonomy on *certain* Islamic matters to individual states because historically, matters relating to Islam were under

[17] ibid [68]; and art 75 of the *Constitution*.

[18] Article 77 of the *Constitution*.

[19] KYL Tan, 'The Creation of Greater Malaysia: Law, Politics, Ethnicity, and Religion' in A Harding and DAH Shah (eds), *Law and Society in Malaysia: Pluralism, Ethnicity and Religion* (Routledge, 2018) 3. See also A Harding, *Law, Government and the Constitution in Malaysia* (Kluwer Law International, 1996) 13.

the prerogative of the *sultans* in their respective states. *Sultans*, as the *Khalifahs* (God's Regent on Earth), maintained a spiritual role for their Malay subjects.

Although these arrangements may seem clear on paper, one of the recurrent debates in Malaysia's constitutional discourse has revolved around the position of Islam (and Islamic laws) within this religious federalism scheme. The *Iki Putra Mubarrak* decision brings this to light, but does so by framing the debate in terms of the *legal* question of the federal–state division of power rather than by addressing politically-charged questions about religion or religious regulation. Legally, the states' authority and autonomy over Islam is limited. While federalism paved the way for retaining the *sultan*'s prerogatives in matters relating to Islam in his state, and while the traditional monarchies and the existing state constitutions are retained in the nine Malay states,[20] the adoption of the constitutional monarchy and Westminster model of government meant that state constitutions had to conform to the *Federal Constitution* and Westminster principles.[21] The *Constitution* was deliberately designed to create a strong central government with limited autonomy for the states. Indeed, the *Iki Putra Mubarrak* decision recognised that 'the terms of our [*Federal Constitution*] and the history of its founding make it abundantly clear that the primary legislative powers of the Federation shall lie ultimately with Parliament save and except for specific matters over which the States shall have legislative powers'.[22] In addition, as explained above, the sphere of *syariah* or Islamic matters on which states could legislate is limited, and its contours are explicitly spelled out in the State List (Paragraph 1, List II of the Ninth Schedule).[23] On this point, the Federal Court's decision in *Iki Putra Mubarrak* also reinforced the principles underpinning federal–state law-making dynamics by emphasising that the constitutionality of state laws would be assessed as against the subject matter included in the *Federal List*, not against any existing federal *law*.[24] This is important because one could imagine a situation (or an argument in a future case) where, for instance, state legislatures might attempt to justify regulating a criminal offence on the basis that federal laws have not yet regulated such a matter. In such a case, we are left with the possibility that the determination of whether states have the competence to enact a law on a particular matter would depend on whether federal law has addressed that matter.[25] As the Federal Court recognised in *Iki Putra Mubarrak*, such a situation would render the Federal List nugatory.[26]

[20] There were only nine Malay states that had traditional monarchies: Selangor, Pahang, Perak, Negeri Sembilan, Johor, Kedah, Kelantan, Terengganu and Perlis. The first four states formed the Federated Malay States, and the remaining five were known as the Unfederated Malay States.

[21] A Harding, *The Constitution of Malaysia: A Contextual Analysis* (Hart Publishing, 2012) 54.

[22] *Iki Putra Mubarrak* (n 5) [68].

[23] Ninth Schedule, List II (para 1) describes the jurisdiction of states, which covers, '[e]xcept with respect to the Federal Territories of Kuala Lumpur, Labuan, and Putrajaya, [the] Islamic law and personal and family law of persons professing the religion of Islam, including the … creation and punishment of offences by persons professing the religion of Islam against precepts of that religion, except in regard to matters included in the Federal List; [as well as] the constitution, organisation and procedure of Syariah courts, which shall have jurisdiction only over persons professing the religion of Islam and in respect only of any of the matters included in this paragraph, but shall not have jurisdiction in respect of offences except in so far as conferred by federal law'.

[24] *Iki Putra Mubarrak* (n 5) [51]–[52].

[25] In fact, this was the argument made by Abdul Hamid Mohamad CJ in *Latifah bte Mat Zin v Rosmawati bte Sharibun and Another* [2007] 5 MLJ 101 (Federal Court).

[26] *Iki Putra Mubarrak* (n 5) [51].

At this juncture, it is also worth noting that theoretically, each individual state could enact different *Syariah* laws (in terms of content and substance) as long as the subject matter of those laws falls within the scope in paragraph 1. To promulgate, administer and enforce Islamic laws and policies, as well as advise the Heads of Islam (be they hereditary monarchs or appointed Heads of State) at the state level, each state has its own religious council, religious department and a system of *syariah* courts. However, state powers and authority are further demarcated *politically*. At the federal level, the Department of Islamic Development (JAKIM), which is set up under and overseen by the Prime Minister's Department, has played the crucial role of carrying out the federal government's policies and agenda on Islam across state lines. Aside from its interstate coordinating role, JAKIM has led efforts to standardise Islamic laws nationwide. This 'standardisation' imperative was crucial to the federal government's desire to ensure a degree of mainstreaming and control over the kinds of Islamic doctrines and teachings that are developed and practised in the Muslim community.

In the past, when the Barisan Nasional (BN) government was dominant at both the federal and state levels, achieving this was virtually uncomplicated. As a result, *syariah* enactments are largely similar in form and content across state lines. But there are divergences, for instance, between the *syariah* criminal codes in Kelantan and Terengganu on the one hand, and *syariah* criminal enactments in the remaining states (including the Federal Territories) on the other. More specifically, in Kelantan and Terengganu, the state *Syariah* criminal codes provide punishments for *hudud* offences. These offences include theft, robbery, adultery (including sodomy, which is defined as male-to-male carnal intercourse or male-to-female anal intercourse), alcohol consumption and apostasy, and the punishments include amputation for theft offences and stoning for adultery or same-sex sexual conduct. Yet even in this case, we see federal arrangements limiting state laws – these aspects of the Kelantan and Terengganu codes could not be implemented because of the limitations set by the 1965 *Syariah Courts (Criminal Jurisdiction) Act*. This federal-level law only authorises *Syariah* courts to impose a maximum sentence of three years' imprisonment, a fine not exceeding 5,000 Malaysian ringgits and/or six strokes of the cane.

Be that as it may, the *Iki Putra Mubarrak* decision is clear in reinforcing Malaysia's scheme of religious federalism – state laws cannot encroach on the authority of the Parliament to enact laws in matters explicitly provided in the Federal List. And if there is any conflict or inconsistency between state and federal laws, the latter will prevail. This means that existing provisions in other state *Syariah* criminal enactments that regulate the kind of offences enumerated in section 28 *SCOE* (male-to-male homosexual conduct) are unconstitutional, simply because such offences have already been regulated by federal law. At the same time, this decision does not alter the fact that state legislatures could continue to enact laws (criminal or otherwise) regulating Islam, as long as they do not go beyond the limits spelled out in the State List.

IV. Regulating Offences against the Precepts of Islam

Iki Putra Mubarrak is not the first case where the courts had to tackle federal–state law-making dynamics in matters implicating Islam. In *Mamat bin Daud*, for instance, what happened was the opposite – the petitioners challenged the validity of section 298A of the *Penal Code* (federal law) on the grounds that the provision concerned a matter (ie, causing religious disunity) that ought to be regulated by the state as opposed to the federal legislature. The provision in question criminalises speech or actions that may be prejudicial to harmony and unity in the context of religion and religious relations, but there are subsections that deal with more specific offences, including defying or undermining actions of (state-endorsed) religious officials (section 298A(2)) and the prohibition of unappointed religious officials performing functions 'of a religious character' (section 298A(5)).[27] It is beyond the scope of this chapter to explain the political motives behind the enactment of these provisions,[28] but suffice it to note that this is yet another manifestation of federal mechanisms to control and enforce the state's 'brand' of Islam.

The petitioners in *Mamat bin Daud* were charged under section 298A for acting as an unauthorised *Bilal* (a person who gives the Muslim call to prayer), *Khatib* (a person who delivers the sermon at Friday prayers) and *Imam* (a person who leads congregational prayers) at a Friday prayer[29] – they were deemed to have engaged in an 'act which is likely to prejudice unity among persons professing the Islamic religion'. For the petitioners, the crux of the issues governed by section 298A fell within the purview of state legislative power because they fundamentally concerned the Islamic religion – they were offences against the precepts of Islam. The Supreme Court held in favour of the petitioners, holding that section 298A was 'in pith and substance' a law relating to the Islamic religion which should be under the exclusive purview of state legislatures, and thus it was unconstitutional. In particular, the majority opinion thought that section 298A aimed to ensure that practices relating to the Islamic religion must conform to the tenets, precepts and practices of Islam spelled out by the states.[30]

An issue that *Mamat bin Daud* did not explicitly address, but that was nonetheless an undercurrent of the *Iki Putra Mubarrak* decision, concerns the boundaries of regulating 'offences against the precepts of Islam'. There are two further questions surrounding this issue, parts of which have animated the discussions in other contentious cases such as *Lina Joy*[31] and *Indira Gandhi*.[32] The first concerns the scope of 'offences against the precepts of Islam' and the second involves the relationship between regulations governing such offences and the fundamental rights provisions of the *Federal Constitution*.

With regard to the question on scope, the Federal Court in *Iki Putra Mubarrak* affirmed its earlier decisions that 'the definition of "precepts of Islam" is wide and is

[27] Even though they do not specifically address Islam, these provisions appeared to be motivated by concerns over the activities of unauthorised religious individuals or preachers who may be using their influence and position in anti-government propaganda. In addition, in a context where religion – particularly Islam – is highly regulated by the state, there has always been some disquiet about the spread of doctrines or practices that 'diverge' from the 'official' Islamic denomination (ie, Sunni) endorsed by the state.

[28] For an explanation of this, see DAH Shah, 'Offences against Religion in Malaysia: Navigating the "Secular" Federal Constitution and the Salience of Islam in the Constitutional Order' in L-A Thio and J Neo (eds), *Religious Offences in Common Law Asia: Colonial Legacies, Constitutional Rights and Contemporary Practice* (Hart Publishing, 2021).

[29] *Mamat bin Daud v Government of Malaysia* [1988] 1 MLJ 119 (Supreme Court).

[30] ibid 122.

[31] *Lina Joy* (n 12).

[32] *Indira Gandhi a/p Mutho v Pengarah Jabatan Agama Islam Perak* [2018] 1 MLJ 545 (Federal Court).

not merely limited to the five pillars of Islam',[33] and it would 'include every single rule, conduct, principle, commandment, and teaching of Islam prescribed in the Syariah'.[34] But what was particularly significant was Zabariah Mohd Yusof J's concurring opinion, which sought to shed further light on the parameters of 'offences against the precepts of Islam'. Here, Zabariah J identified three categories of *Syariah* criminal offences across states in Malaysia that are applicable to persons professing the religion of Islam: offences relating to *aqidah* (for instance, teaching false or deviating doctrines); offences relating to sanctity of religion and its institution (for example, failure to perform Friday prayer); and offences against morality (for instance, alcohol consumption and sexual intercourse out of wedlock). These offences are deemed 'purely religious in nature' and are 'directly concerned with religious matters or religious affairs'.[35] For Zabariah J, these are the kinds of offences that fall under the exclusive jurisdiction of state legislatures. In addition, the Court acknowledged – in obiter – that a range of offences including corruption, theft, robbery and rape could be said to be against the 'precepts of Islam'. However, notwithstanding the fact that the *nature* of the offence is against the precepts of Islam, the Court took the position – as explained above – that state legislatures are precluded from regulating a subject matter that falls within the purview of the federal legislative competence. This is crucial as it renders certain provisions in the *Syariah* criminal codes in the states of Kelantan and Terengganu that regulate offences such as theft and robbery unconstitutional.

In any case, we are still left with the question of whether regulations on offences against the precepts of Islam could be unconstitutional for violating the *Constitution*'s fundamental liberties guarantees. This is where constitutional debates surrounding the role of Islam (and Islamic laws) become especially thorny. In *Lina Joy*, for example, a Muslim-born woman who converted to Christianity was prevented from changing her religious status on her national identity card as she had not formalised her conversion through the *Syariah* court. Even though the Federal Court's decision did not uphold Lina Joy's freedom to change her religion, and even though the net effect of the decision was to make one's exercise of religious freedom *conditional* upon the satisfaction of procedures to renounce Islam, it is worth noting that the majority did not categorically reject the *possibility* of renunciation of Islam.[36] Instead, the judgment emphasised that a would-be apostate must follow the relevant procedures to do (even in the absence of specific provisions in the relevant state laws specifying the procedures to be followed), and the matter – being an 'offence against the precepts of Islam' – fell outside the jurisdiction of the civil courts.[37] Herein lies the complexities of Malaysia's dual civil-*Syariah* system: the jurisdictional conflict between civil and *Syariah* courts and, more specifically, the inability or unwillingness hitherto to resolve crucial constitutional questions where a subject matter implicates *both* constitutional rights (such as freedom of religion) and the exclusive *Syariah* jurisdiction in certain Islamic matters. In other words,

[33] *Iki Putra Mubarrak* (n 5) [86].

[34] ibid 98.

[35] *Iki Putra Mubarrak* (n 5) [121]–[122].

[36] *Lina Joy* (n 12) 618. See MJ Nelson and DA H Shah, 'Operationalizing and Regulating Religious Freedom: Apostasy and Administrative "Reasonableness" in Malaysia and Beyond' (2018) 16(4) *International Journal of Constitutional Law* 1293, 1299.

[37] ibid 1303–04.

Lina Joy demonstrates that civil courts – invoking Article 121(1A) of the *Constitution*[38] – have had the tendency to abrogate judicial power in favour of the *Syariah* branch when a matter implicates Islam, even if constitutional rights and interpretation questions are at stake.

There are several ways in which this position is untenable. First, the principles of constitutionalism and constitutional supremacy mandate that all laws, actions and state institutions are not without limits and they ought to conform to constitutional injunctions. Second, despite Article 121(1A), which protects the jurisdiction of the *Syariah* courts, such courts are creatures of (state-level) statutes tasked to interpret and apply Islamic laws enacted by state legislatures, and the provision does not (and should not) affect the powers of the civil courts in interpreting the *Constitution*. Indeed, the intent behind the introduction of Article 121(1A) was to resolve conflicting decisions in civil and *Syariah* courts, and to ensure that matters concerning Islamic law were dealt with by experts and judges trained in the field. Third, if time and again the civil courts surrender jurisdiction whenever a matter implicates Islam or *Syariah*, even when constitutional rights are at stake, this would render the fundamental liberties protection meaningless.

Some of these considerations were at the heart of the Federal Court's decision in *Indira Gandhi*, which involved the case of a non-Muslim mother who challenged the unilateral conversion (ie, conversion without her consent) of her children to Islam. As in *Lina Joy* and many other cases involving state religious authorities, what lurked beneath the case was also the concern about 'protecting' the authority and exclusivity of Islamic institutions. Yet, stressing the role of the judiciary in upholding the rule of law, the Federal Court held that judicial review is an 'essential feature of the basic structure of the Constitution'. As such, Article 121(1A) does not affect the inherent judicial powers of the civil courts to interpret and enforce the *Federal Constitution* and to review the legality of the state's exercises of power. In short, notwithstanding the religious implications of the case, the Court remains empowered to review the legality and constitutionality of a public authority's administrative action (in this case, the religious authority's decision to issue the Certificates of Conversion for Indira's children).

Against this background, the *Iki Putra Mubarrak* decision is significant in at least two respects. The concurring opinion in the *Iki Putra Mubarrak* decision sought to delineate the boundaries of regulations on 'offences against the precepts of Islam', first, by stating that both federal and state legislatures 'cannot … promulgate laws, which are contrary to the constitution'.[39] Then, the concurring opinion argued that if both state and federal laws regulating the same subject matter (in this case, homosexual conduct) were allowed to co-exist, this would violate the equal protection guarantee in Article 8 of the *Constitution*. This is because, in a factual matrix where there are multiple parties in the same offence (male-to-male sexual intercourse) with different religious identities, the non-Muslim offender would be subjected to more severe punishment than the Muslim offender. A charge under section 377A of the *Penal Code* carries an imprisonment term of up to 20 years and a fine or corporal punishment (whipping). By contrast, an offender found guilty under the *Syariah* criminal enactment would only face a maximum jail

[38] This provision provides that the High Courts 'shall have no jurisdiction in respect of any matter within the jurisdiction of the Syariah Courts'.

[39] *Iki Putra Mubarrak* (n 5) [94].

term of three years, a fine not exceeding 5,000 Malaysian ringgit or a maximum of six strokes of the cane. This, for the Court, discriminates against a non-Muslim offender and violates Article 8(1)'s guarantee that all persons are equal before the law and entitled to equal protection under the law. Although this is at best obiter, a generous reading of this suggests that the Court is open to examine (and challenge) the validity of *Syariah* laws as against the fundamental liberties protection in the *Constitution*.

V. Conclusion

Despite the pattern of judicial abrogation in matters involving Islam, more recent decisions – including *Iki Putra Mubarrak* – demonstrate that there is some willingness on the part of the civil courts to assert their power to interpret the *Constitution* and to adjudicate issues of constitutional importance. While the decision appears ground-breaking at the Federal Court level, it is pertinent to note that previously, the Court of Appeal had, in the 2014 cross-dressing case (*Juzaili*), declared a provision of the *Syariah* criminal enactment in the state of Negeri Sembilan to be unconstitutional. The provision, which imposes criminal sanctions on males who dress and pose as women in public, was held to have violated the right to life and the constitution's anti-discrimination clause (Article 8(2)).[40] In particular, the Court opined that discrimination on the basis of gender is rooted in the fact that section 66 only prohibits male Muslims from cross-dressing; there were no comparable provisions prohibiting or criminalising females who dress or pose as males.[41] Unfortunately, the significance of the cross-dressing decision was short-lived: just under a year later, the Federal Court overturned the decision on technical (procedural) grounds. According to the Federal Court, the three men should have challenged the constitutionality of section 66 through the specific procedure in Articles 4(3) and 4(4) of the *Constitution*, which required them to file an application for leave to a Federal Court judge, instead of seeking judicial review through the High Court.[42] The Federal Court's approach in the cross-dressing case (*Juzaili*) could thus be seen as another manifestation of the long-standing avoidance of civil courts when they are confronted with cases implicating Islam. In other words, by invoking technical issues, the Court avoided reviewing and determining – conclusively – the key, legal question of whether section 66 was unconstitutional.

Therefore, all this accentuates the significance of *Iki Putra Mubarrak*. Even if the Federal Court's ratio decidendi focused on the issue of federal–state legislative competence, several other aspects of the decision – read as a whole – mark a major step in recalibrating state–religion relations in Malaysia.

[40] *Muhammad Juzaili bin Mohd Khamis* (n 11) [35]–[43].

[41] ibid [50]–[51].

[42] *Government of Negeri Sembilan and Others v Muhammad Juzaili bin Mohd Khamis and Others*, Civil Appeal No 01(f)-8-02-2015(N) and 01-7-02/2015(N), 8 October 2015 (Federal Court of Malaysia).

10

Aston Cantlow v Wallbank

Defining the Public and Private Functions of the Established Church of England

MARK HILL QC

I. Introduction

From before the sealing of Magna Carta in 1215, *ecclesia anglicana* has connoted a particular understanding of the English Church,[1] a matter which was accentuated in the sixteenth century when the Henrician Reformation saw a break with papal authority and the clear association of the Christian Church in England with the monarch and the state.[2] Whilst in the intervening period the UK has become more pluralistic and more secular, the Church of England has continued to enjoy a unique position in civil and political society, which is both a privilege and a burden.[3]

Accordingly, in 2004 the Law Lords[4] were provided with an opportunity to consider the constitutional status of the Church of England when determining the appeal in *Aston Cantlow v Wallbank*.[5] Although the presenting issue was the enforceability of a landowner's obligation to fund costly works to the fabric of a parish church under the archaic provisions of the Chancel Repairs Act 1932, codifying principles of property law dating back to the Middle Ages, the importance of the case derives from its treatment of the groundbreaking Human Rights Act 1998. This was one of the first cases to reach England's highest appellate court to address the provisions of the Human Rights Act. At issue – although this was perhaps not immediately apparent from the papers filed by the parties – was whether the Church of England might be uniquely disadvantaged

[1] Note the reflections of Lord Williams of Oystermouth in R Williams, 'Saving Our Order: Becket and the Law' (2021) 23 *Ecclesiastical Law Journal* 127.

[2] See generally R Griffith-Jones and M Hill, *Magna Carta, Religion and the Law of Law* (Cambridge University Press, 2015); and RH Helmholz, *The Canon Law and Ecclesiastical Jurisdiction from 597 to the 1640s* (Oxford University Press, 2004).

[3] Discussed more fully in M Hill, *Ecclesiastical Law*, 4th edn (Oxford University Press, 2018) 1.19–1.21.

[4] Who were to mutate into the UK's Supreme Court with effect from 1 October 2009.

[5] *Aston Cantlow and Wilmcote with Billesley Parochial Church Council v Wallbank* [2004] 1 AC 546, [2003] 3 WLR 283, [2003] 3 All ER 1213, HL.

in enjoying the right to freedom of religion, guaranteed by Article 9 of the European Convention on Human Rights. As Lord Hope observed:

> But the questions about the scope and effect of the Human Rights Act 1998 which your Lordships have been asked to decide in this appeal, and on which I wish to concentrate, are of current interest and very considerable public importance. They raise issues whose significance extends far beyond the boundaries of the Parish of Aston Cantlow.[6]

II. A Tale from Shakespeare

In England, from medieval times, the Church had the benefit of the institution of tithes, which constitutes money raised from local landowners for the work of the Church. However, in many instances, in lieu of the payment of tithes, a parcel of land was allotted to a landowner, often the lord of the manor. In return, this landowner, known as a lay rector or lay impropriator, became responsible for the cost of the upkeep of the chancel of the parish church. The Chancel Repairs Act 1932 provided a system for enforcing this obligation, medieval in origin, through the secular courts.[7]

The Saxon church of Aston Cantlow, dedicated to St John the Baptist, lies three miles from Stratford-upon-Avon. It was here that William Shakespeare's parents, John Shakespeare and Mary Arden, were married in 1557. Mr and Mrs Wallbank owned Glebe Farm. Like their predecessors in title, they were lay rectors, a status which ran with the land.[8] The Wallbanks did not dispute that their property carried with it the obligation to repair the chancel of the parish church. However, they set out to argue that the obligation was unenforceable as a consequence of the Human Rights Act 1998. Their argument was that the obligation was akin to an unlawful tax levied by the church,[9] and therefore in violation of Article 1 of the First Protocol to the European Convention on Human Rights.[10]

The Wallbanks' concession may have been generously made. It was widely believed that chancel repair liability had almost fallen into desuetude.[11] Lord Nicholls of Birkenhead was scathing about it:

> The anachronistic, even capricious, nature of this ancient liability was recognised some years ago by the Law Commission: *Property Law: Liability for Chancel Repairs* (1985) Law Com No 152. The Commission said 'this relic of the past' is 'no longer acceptable'. The Commission recommended its phased abolition.[12]

[6] ibid [23].

[7] The secular courts, as opposed to the ecclesiastical courts.

[8] This was converted into a civil obligation in 1743 as a result of an enclosure award made under a Private Act of Parliament of 1742 entitled *An Act for Dividing and Inclosing, Setting out and Allotting, certain Common Fields and Inclosures within the Manor and Parish of Aston Cantlow, in the County of Warwick.*

[9] The liability was not for a trivial sum. At the start of the proceedings, the estimated cost for the repair of the chancel exceeded £95,000.

[10] 'Every natural or legal person is entitled to the peaceful enjoyment of his possessions. No one shall be deprived of his possessions except in the public interest and subject to the conditions provided for by law and by the general principles of international law': European Convention on Human Rights, First Protocol, art 1.

[11] When the land came into the possession of Mrs Wallbanks' parents in 1970, the conveyance stated it was 'subject to the liability to repair the chancel of Aston Cantlow … so far as the same still affects the property conveyed and is still subsisting and capable of being enforced'.

[12] *Aston Cantlow v Wallbank* (HL) (n 5) [2].

The distinguished legal historian, Professor Sir John Baker QC, described the liability as:

> One of the more unsightly blots on the history of English jurisprudence.[13]

However, this chapter is not concerned with the hangover of an ancient property right, but with the far-reaching issues concerning the nature and status of the Church of England which emerged as this recondite matter made its way through the legal process.[14]

III. The Course of the Litigation

In February 2000, the case came before Ferris J at first instance in the Chancery Division of the High Court.[15] The judge determined that the law on chancel repair liability was clear and unambiguous. It did not amount to a deprivation of the Wallbanks' possessions because it was not in the nature of a levy or tax, but an incumbrance[16] and one of the 'incidents of ownership' on the land in question. Article 1 of the First Protocol was not engaged. Ferris J also rejected the argument that the liability infringed the Wallbanks' freedom of religion (Article 9) or discriminated against them (Article 14).

The Wallbanks appealed to the Court of Appeal[17] and the case came on for hearing on 29 March 2001. Significantly, during the intervening period, on 1 October 2000, the Human Rights Act 1998 had come into force. As a consequence, the shape and scope of the argument changed significantly compared to when it was before the lower court.[18] The architecture of this novel piece of legislation needs to be fully understood. It was designed to make the provisions of the European Convention on Human Rights directly enforceable in the UK's domestic courts, without recourse to the European Court of Human Rights in Strasbourg. However, the Act did not create an unfettered freestanding cause of action for breach of the Convention. Instead, under section 6, it was made unlawful for a public authority to act in a manner incompatible with a Convention right.[19] Section 7 of the Act provided that a person who claims that a public authority has so acted may bring proceedings against the authority if he or she is (or would be) a victim of the unlawful act.[20]

Accordingly, the Court of Appeal had to grapple with an issue that had not been in play before the High Court, namely whether a Parochial Church Council (PCC)[21] is a

[13] 'Lay Rectors and Chancel Repairs' (1984) 100 *Law Quarterly Review* 181.

[14] For ease of reference, after the first full citation hereinafter, the separate judgments will be designated (HC) for the High Court, (CA) for the Court of Appeal and (HL) for the House of Lords (now Supreme Court).

[15] *Aston Cantlow Parochial Church Council v Wallbank* (2001) 81 P & CR 14, [2000] 2 EGLR 149 (Ferris J) (HC).

[16] Akin to a mortgage, restrictive covenant or other incumbrance. The land had always been subject to the liability, so the Wallbanks were not being deprived of anything.

[17] *Wallbank v Aston Cantlow and Wilmcote with Billesley Parochial Church Council* [2001] EWCA Civ 713 (CA), where it came before Sir Andrew Morritt Vice-Chancellor, sitting with Robert Walker and Sedley LJJ.

[18] As the judgment stated, 'the scene has shifted radically, and with it the locus of the argument' (ibid [25]).

[19] Human Rights Act 1998, s 6(1).

[20] ibid s 7(1).

[21] PCCs are the elected bodies responsible for parish churches (akin to vestries in the Episcopalian Church) and are not to be confused with parish councils, which, although also elected bodies, are the lowest tier of local civil government.

public authority for these purposes. And it dealt with that question swiftly and somewhat superficially.[22] Crucially, it relied on the fact that the PCC is created and empowered by law,[23] and 'forms part of the church by law established'.[24] The Court of Appeal went on to hold that the PCC's enforcement of chancel repair liability was incompatible with Article 1 of the First Protocol, being in the nature of a tax whose operation was arbitrary, and that it was discriminatory, which was contrary to Article 14.

Leave to appeal to the Judicial Committee of the House of Lords was granted on 11 February 2002[25] and the matter proceeded to a hearing on 3–5 March 2003. Judgment was delivered on 26 June 2003. The appeal was allowed. A 3:0 unanimous defeat for the PCC in the Court of Appeal was converted into a 5:0 victory in the House of Lords. Unusually, even though all five Law Lords were in agreement as to the outcome of the appeal, each delivered a separate judgment setting out their reasoning. Front and centre was the legal status of the Church of England.

IV. The Legal Status of the Church of England

It was affirmed by Lord Hope of Craighead, perhaps to the surprise of some, that 'the Church of England as a whole has no legal status or personality'.[26] Instead, legal personality is dispersed amongst various office-holders and bodies which exist within its overall structure.[27]

But as Lord Nicholls of Birkenhead observed:

> Historically the Church of England has discharged an important and influential role in the life of this country. As the established church it still has special links with central government. But the Church of England remains essentially a religious organisation. This is so even though some of the emanations of the church discharge functions which may qualify as governmental. Church schools and the conduct of marriage services are two instances.[28] The legislative powers of the General Synod of the Church of England are another. This should not be regarded as infecting the Church of England as a whole, or its emanations in general, with the character of a governmental organisation.[29]

22 CA [28]–[35].

23 Parochial Church Councils (Powers) Measure 1956.

24 CA [35].

25 The Law Lords had provisionally indicated that permission to appeal would be granted on condition that irrespective of the outcome of the appeal, the PCC would bear the legal costs of both parties at first instance, in the Court of Appeal and in the House of Lords. The reasoning of the Appeal Committee (Lord Hutton, Lord Hobhouse of Woodborough and Lord Millett) was that the Church Commissioners were wealthy and the Wallbanks were not. It was emphasised by counsel at the permission hearing on 11 February 2002 that the PCC was a separate legal entity from the Church Commissioners. It was further pointed out that the Church Commissioners are themselves lay rectors for many parishes, and may have a financial interest in the appeal failing. Leave to appeal was granted unconditionally, upon the PCC undertaking not to pursue its costs in the House of Lords.

26 HL [61] per Lord Hope of Craighead.

27 ibid [84] per Lord Hobhouse of Woodborough.

28 Interestingly, at the time of writing, the role of the Church of England as both a provider of education and marriage officiant is subject to increasing criticism.

29 HL [13].

Lord Hope was critical of the Court of Appeal's reasoning that the fact that a PCC forms part of the church 'by law established' showed that it was a public authority:[30]

> The implication of these observations is that other bodies such as diocesan and deanery synods and the General Synod itself fall into the same category. In my opinion however the legal framework of the Church of England as a church by law established does not lead to this conclusion.[31]

He continued:

> There is no Act of Parliament that purports to establish it as the Church of England: *Sir Lewis Dibden, Establishment in England: Essays on Church and State* (1932), p111. What establishment in law means is that the state has incorporated its law into the law of the realm as a branch of its general law. In *Marshall v Graham* [1907] 2 KB 112, 126 Phillimore J said:
>
> > A Church which is established is not thereby made a department of the State. The process of establishment means that the State has accepted the Church as the religious body in its opinion truly teaching the Christian faith, and given to it a certain legal position, and to its decrees, if rendered under certain legal conditions, certain civil sanctions.
>
> The Church of England is identified with the state in other ways, the monarch being head of each … It has regulatory functions within its own sphere, but it cannot be said to be part of government. The state has not surrendered or delegated any of its functions or powers to the Church. None of the functions that the Church of England performs would have to be performed in its place by the state if the Church were to abdicate its responsibility … The relationship which the state has with the Church of England is one of recognition, not of the devolution to it of any of the powers or functions of government.

Lord Rodger of Earlsferry put the matter as follows:

> The juridical nature of the Church is, notoriously, somewhat amorphous. The Church has been described as 'an organised operative institution' or as 'the quasi corporate institution which carries on the work' of the Church of England: *In re Barnes Simpson v Barnes* [1930] 2 Ch 80, 81 note.[32]

V. What is a Public Authority?

Lord Nicholls recognised that the expression 'public authority' is not defined in the Human Rights Act,[33] nor is it a recognised term of art in English law.[34] In essence, the reach of the concept of public authority is intended to extend to those bodies for whose acts the state is answerable to the European Court of Human Rights, who are now subject to a domestic law obligation not to act incompatibly with Convention rights.[35]

[30] CA [32].

[31] HL [60].

[32] ibid [154].

[33] Lord Hope noted (at ibid [36]) that the Court of Appeal 'had been invited to enter into largely uncharted territory' and that in revisiting the matter, the Law Lords had the benefit of criticisms which had been made of its decision, notably D Oliver, 'Chancel Repairs and the Human Rights Act' [2001] *Public Law* 651.

[34] HL [6]. The Court of Appeal declined to look to Hansard for assistance in construing the term and Lord Hope considered it correct to do so (at [37]). There was no ambiguity so as to bring the issue of statutory interpretation within the limited exception described in *Pepper v Hart* [1993] AC 593.

[35] HL [6]. See D Oliver, 'The Frontiers of the State: Public Authorities and Public Functions under the Human Rights Act 1998' [2000] *Public Law* 476.

Lord Nicholls sought a touchstone for deciding whether a function is public and found there to be no single test of universal application.[36] He remarked:

> Factors to be taken into account include the extent to which in carrying out the relevant function the body is publicly funded, or is exercising statutory powers, or is taking the place of central government or local authorities, or is providing a public service.[37]

Lord Hope noted that the Court of Appeal had left out of account the jurisprudence of the European Court of Human Rights as to the meaning to be given to non-governmental organisations.[38]

The foregoing discussion related to what commentators generally refer to as 'core' public authorities.[39] The Human Rights Act created another category, to which the label 'hybrid' public authority is generally applied,[40] although it does not appear in the legislation. The expansive definition of 'public authority' in section 6 of the Act is stated to include 'any person, certain of whose functions are functions of a public nature'.[41] Here again, the test is one of function. In a somewhat circular fashion, the Act states that: 'In relation to a particular act, a person is not a public authority by virtue only of subsection (3)(b) if the nature of the act is private.'[42]

VI. The PCC as a Core Public Authority

Lord Nicholls did not think that PCCs were 'core' public authorities, observing that 'the Church of England remains essentially a religious organisation'.[43] He considered that there was nothing in their constitution and functions to lend support to the view that they should be characterised as governmental organisations. He continued, with greater specificity:

> Parochial church councils are established as corporate bodies under a church measure, now the Parochial Church Councils (Powers) Measure 1956. For historical reasons this unique form of legislation, having the same force as a statute, is the way the Church of England governs its affairs. But the essential role of a parochial church council is to provide a formal

[36] Lord Nicholls noted the victim paradox (discussed below) and observed that the fact that a core public authority is incapable of having Convention rights of its own is a matter to be borne in mind when considering whether or not a particular body is a core public authority. It must always be relevant to consider whether Parliament can have intended that the body in question should have no Convention rights (HL [8]).

[37] ibid [12].

[38] ibid [48]–[51]: in particular, *Holy Monasteries v Greece* (1995) 20 EHRR 1; and *Hautanemi v Sweden* (1996) 22 EHRR CD 156. Lord Hope also noted that while the two main churches in Germany (Roman Catholic and Lutheran) have public legal personality and are public authorities bound by the provisions of art 19(4) of the German Constitution (*Grundgesetz*) or Basic Law which guarantees recourse to the court should any person's basic rights be violated by a public authority, they are in general considered to be 'non-governmental organisations' within the meaning of art 34 of the *Convention*. As such, they are entitled to avail themselves of, for example, the right to protection of property under art 1 of the First Protocol: JA Frowein and W Peukert, *Kommentar zur Europäische Menschenrechtskonvention*, 2nd edn (Engel Verlag, 1996), art 25, para 16.

[39] Lord Hope (HL [35]) adopted the alternative term 'standard' public authority, borrowing from R Clayton and H Tomlinson, *The Law of Human Rights*, vol 1 (Oxford University Press, 2000) para 5.08.

[40] Or 'functional' as used by Lord Hope, again borrowing from Clayton and Tomlinson.

[41] Human Rights Act 1998, s 6(3)(b).

[42] ibid s 6(5). The distinction between public and private acts has a bearing on whether a hybrid public authority may be a victim entitled to bring proceedings under the Act: see below.

[43] HL [13].

> means, prescribed by the Church of England, whereby *ex officio* and elected members of the local church promote the mission of the Church and discharge financial responsibilities in respect of their own parish church, including responsibilities regarding maintenance of the fabric of the building. This smacks of a church body engaged in self-governance and promotion of its affairs. This is far removed from the type of body whose acts engage the responsibility of the state under the European Convention.[44]

Lord Hope noted in clear terms that: 'There is no doubt that parochial church councils are an essential part of the administration … of the affairs of the Church of England.'[45] He stated:

> The parish itself has been described as the basic building block of the Church and the PCC as the central forum for decision-making and discussion in relation to parish affairs.[46]

He noted that a PCC is constituted by statute,[47] as a body corporate, and that they had statutory powers which they might exercise against any person liable to repair the chancel.[48] But he continued with equal clarity:

> But none of these characteristics indicate that it is a governmental organisation, as that phrase is understood in the context of article 34 of the Convention. It plainly has nothing whatever to do with the process of either central or local government. It is not accountable to the general public for what it does. It receives no public funding, apart from occasional grants from English Heritage for the preservation of its historic buildings. In that respect it is in a position which is no different from that of any private individual. The statutory powers which it has been given by the Chancel Repairs Act 1932 are not exercisable against the public generally or any class or group of persons which forms part of it.[49]

Lord Hope's firm conclusion was that a PCC is not a core public authority.[50] Lord Hobhouse was equally forthright: 'clearly not'.[51] He observed that the functions of a PCC:

> [C]learly include matters which are concerned only with the pastoral and organisational concerns of the diocese, and the congregation of believers in the parish. It acts in the sectional not the public interest.[52]

[44] ibid [14].

[45] ibid [58].

[46] ibid, citing M Hill, *Ecclesiastical Law*, 2nd edn (Oxford University Press, 2001) 48 and 74, paras 3.11 and 3.74.

[47] Parochial Church Councils (Powers) Measure 1956, s 3. PCCs were introduced by its statutory forerunner, the Parochial Church Councils (Powers) Measure 1921. Strictly this Measure conferred powers onto PCCs already constituted under the Schedule to the Church of England (Powers) Act 1919. Lord Rodger considered this important: PCCs were created by the Church to carry out functions to be determined by the Church (HL [151]–[152]).

[48] HL [58], citing Chancel Repairs Act 1932, s 2.

[49] HL [59].

[50] ibid [63]. Lord Scott of Foscote agreed with him, and with Lord Rodger of Earlsferry (at [129]).

[51] ibid [86].

[52] ibid: 'The fact that the Church of England is the established church of England may mean that various bodies within that Church may as a result perform public functions. But it does not follow that PCCs themselves perform any such functions.'

Lord Rodger's examination of the status of the PCC was the fullest of all the five judges in the House of Lords. He stated:

> The origins of PCCs can be traced back to the movement that began in the nineteenth century for greater self-government and better representation of the laity in the Church of England. Part of the problem was that, while the Convocations of Canterbury and York could pass canons which were binding on the clergy, any wider legislation had to be by Act of Parliament and Parliament passed only relatively few of the Acts for which the Church asked. In 1916 a special committee set up to look into the question recommended the formation of a Church Council with power to legislate on ecclesiastical matters. Eventually, after further work by another committee, the necessary scheme was approved by the Convocations of Canterbury and York.[53]

The scheme included the constitution of what is now the General Synod of the Church of England. Paragraph 17 of the Constitution provided that, before entering on any other legislative business, further provision should be made for the self-government of the Church by passing two measures, the second being to confer 'upon the Parochial Church Councils constituted under the Schedule to this Constitution' such powers as the National Assembly may determine.[54]

Lord Rodger continued:

> The key to the role of the PCC lies in the first of its general functions: co-operation with the minister in promoting in the parish the whole mission of the Church. Its other more particular functions are to be seen as ways of carrying out this general function. The mission of the Church is a *religious* mission, distinct from the secular mission of government, whether central or local. Founding on scriptural and other recognised authority, the Church seeks to serve the purposes of God, not those of the government carried on by the modern equivalents of Caesar and his proconsuls. This is true even though the Church of England has certain important links with the state. Those links, which do not include any funding of the Church by the government, give the Church a unique position but they do not mean that it is a department of state: *Marshall v Graham* [1907] 2 KB 112, 126 per Phillimore LJ. In so far as the ties are intended to assist the Church, it is to accomplish the Church's own mission, not the aims and objectives of the government of the United Kingdom. The PCC exists to carry forward the Church's mission at the local level.[55]

VII. The PCC as a Hybrid Public Authority

The question of whether a PCC is a hybrid public authority turns on whether the enforcement of chancel repair liability is a private act as opposed to the discharge of a public function. Lord Nicholls was able to deal with this matter very shortly:

> [W]hen a parochial church council enforces, in accordance with the provisions of the Chancel Repairs Act 1932, a burdensome incident attached to the ownership of certain pieces of land: there is nothing particularly 'public' about this. This is no more a public act than is the enforcement of a restrictive covenant of which church land has the benefit.[56]

[53] ibid [149].
[54] ibid.
[55] ibid [156].
[56] ibid [16].

Lord Hope similarly identified the relevant act as the enforcement of a civil liability and noted that the liability is one which arises under private law, enforceable by the PCC as a civil debt by virtue of the 1932 Act.[57] The 1932 Act did not alter the pre-existing law: in return for financial and proprietorial advantages then conferred upon them, the impropriators accepted the obligation to repair the chancel as and when the need arose. This is a private law obligation arising from the ownership of glebe land:[58] the enforcement of a civil debt.[59] Lord Hobhouse was of the same opinion:

> From the point of view of both the PCC and the Wallbanks, the transaction and its incident were private law, non-governmental, non-public activities and not of a public nature. Again, this conclusion is adverse to the Wallbanks' defence.[60]

Lord Rodger was in agreement:

> There is nothing in the nature of the obligation itself, or in the means or purpose of its enforcement, that would lead to the conclusion that the PCC of Aston Cantlow is exercising a governmental function, however broadly defined, when it enforces the lay rectors' obligation to pay for chancel repairs. Therefore, even when it is enforcing that obligation, the PCC is not to be regarded as a public authority for the purposes of section 6 of the 1998 Act.[61]

On the hybrid public authority point, Lord Scott of Foscote disagreed with the other four Law Lords. He considered, on balance, that the following factors pointed towards a PCC carrying out functions of a public nature:

> 1. The parish church is a church of the Church of England, a church by law established.
> 2. It is a church to which the Anglican public are entitled to have recourse, regardless of whether they are practising members of the church, for marriage, for baptism of their children, for weddings, for funerals and burial, and perhaps for other purposes as well.
> 3. Members of other denominations, or even other religions, are, if parishioners, entitled to burial in the parish churchyard.
> 4. The church is, therefore, a public building. It is not a private building from which the public can lawfully be excluded at the whim of the owner.
> 5. The PCC is corporate and its functions are charitable. Its members have the status of charity trustees. Charitable trusts are public trusts, not private ones.
> 6. A decision by a PCC to enforce a chancel repairing liability is a decision taken in the interests of the parishioners as a whole. It is not taken in pursuit of any private interests. If it were so taken, it would I think be impeachable by judicial review.[62]

Notwithstanding being an outlier on the issue of the public nature of the function, Lord Scott was in full agreement with the other Law Lords that the obligation was enforceable, notwithstanding the Wallbanks' arguments under the Human Rights Act.[63]

[57] ibid [63].

[58] ibid [64]. As Lord Hope stated: 'The responsibility for repairing the chancel was since 1743 an incident of the ownership of certain particular parcels of land. When Mr and Mrs Wallbank acquired the title to that land they assumed that responsibility to repair and the consequent liability in default if they should fail to discharge it. This was not a responsibility and liability which they shared with the public in general; it was something which they had personally assumed voluntarily by a voluntary act of acquisition which at the time they apparently thought was advantageous to them.'

[59] ibid.

[60] ibid [90].

[61] ibid [171].

[62] ibid [130].

[63] ibid [133]–[135].

VIII. The Victim Paradox

As Lord Nicholls pointed out, one consequence of being a 'core' public authority is that the body in question does not itself enjoy Convention rights. It is difficult to see how a core public authority could ever claim to be a victim of an infringement of a Convention right, being 'inherently incapable' of satisfying the Convention description of a victim.[64] Only victims of an unlawful act may bring proceedings under section 7 of the Human Rights Act.[65]

One ironic consequence of the Court of Appeal's determination would have been that a PCC, being a core public authority, would not enjoy Convention rights. Thus, a PCC would not be able to claim the right to freedom of religion under Article 9.[66] As Lord Nicholls stated:

> The conclusion that the church authorities in general and parochial church councils in particular are 'core' public authorities, would mean these bodies are not capable of being victims within the meaning of the Human Rights Act. Accordingly they are not able to complain of infringements of Convention rights. That would be an extraordinary conclusion. The Human Rights Act goes out of its way, in section 13,[67] to single out for express mention the exercise by religious organisations of the Convention right of freedom of thought, conscience and religion. One would expect that these and other Convention rights would be enjoyed by the Church of England as much as other religious bodies.

IX. The Lasting Effects of the House of Lords' Judgment

The decision of the House of Lords had a range of consequences. The Land Registration Act 2003 had passed through Parliament on the assumption that the Court of Appeal decision was correct. When the Law Lords took a different view, corrective legislation needed to be brought into effect.[68] The decision shone a light into the dark corners of the overriding interests under ancient property law. It caused thousands of parishes to register chancel repair liability and sent a shock wave though conveyancing practitioners and mortgage providers.[69]

[64] ibid [8]. Under art 34 of the European Convention on Human Rights, the status of victim (a prerequisite for bringing a claim for relief in Strasbourg) is defined as: 'any person, *non-governmental organisation* or group of individuals' (emphasis added). Lord Hope deals with the matter at [45]–[48], emphasising at [52] the significance of the jurisprudence of Strasbourg as to 'those bodies which engage the responsibility of the State for the purposes of the Convention'.

[65] HL [8]. The Convention description of a victim (above) is incorporated into the Human Rights Act by s 7(7).

[66] The associational nature of the right is clear from the fact it is to be enjoyed 'either alone or in community with others'.

[67] For a trenchant discussion of judicial disregard of s 13, see S Lee, 'The Cardinal Rule of Religion and the Rule of Law: A Musing on Magna Carta' in R Griffith-Jones and M Hill (eds), *Magna Carta, Religion and the Rule of Law* (Cambridge University Press, 2015) 314–33.

[68] Land Registration Act 2002 (Transitional Provisions) (No 2) Order 2003, SI 2003/2431; see Hill (n 3) para 3.46.

[69] See E Nugee, 'The Consequences of *Aston Cantlow*' (2004) 7 *Ecclesiastical Law Journal* 452.

More importantly, this landmark case makes clear that the Church of England is, essentially, a religious organisation and not a limb of government. It marks the conclusion of a journey which began when Henry VIII sought an annulment of his marriage, and in doing so claimed ultimate authority over the Church in England. Nearly 20 years on from the decision of the House of Lords, defining and describing the cleavage between the public and private functions of the Church of England remains problematic and foreshadows some degree of constitutional re-establishment upon the death of Her Majesty Queen Elizabeth II and the accession to the throne of Prince Charles.[70] The decision marks a trajectory towards, if not the disestablishment of the Church of England, then at least its re-establishment: the re-drawing of the bonds between the Church and the State.[71] The Church of England is judicially recognised as essentially a religious organisation, not an organ of government. Whilst there may be some enduring symbolism in the retention of vestiges of establishment, the judgment seems to reinforce the prevalent mood of modern secularism, sidelining religion into the status of little more than a hobby or leisure pursuit.[72]

Several times in the judgment, reference is made to the function of parochial clergy in the solemnisation of marriage. This is repeatedly – and correctly – identified as a public function of priests of the Church of England. In the two decades which have followed the judgment, the nature of marriage has changed almost beyond recognition. They have witnessed the introduction of civil partnerships[73] and subsequently same-sex marriage.[74] Neither of the Acts setting up these new legal relationships permitted the clergy of the Church of England to solemnise such unions. Further, a document issued by the House of Bishops indicated that it would not be appropriate to authorise a public liturgy to follow the solemnising of a same-sex marriage, or for clergy to provide a service of blessing.[75] The mood of the nation, and perhaps also the Church of England,[76] seems to be changing. History will come to see the House of Lords' decision in *Aston Cantlow* as a pivotal moment in the slow evolution of the relationship between the Church and the State in England.

[70] The deference owed to the Queen following her 70 years of devoted service as monarch and Supreme Governor has been a powerful restraint on disestablishment. Her words, on her twenty-first birthday in 1947, speak volumes: 'I declare before you all that my whole life whether it be long or short shall be devoted to your service and the service of our great imperial family to which we all belong'. The deference and restraint will die with her. The death of HRH Prince Philip, Duke of Edinburgh in 2021 has served to accentuate the fragility of the constitutional settlement of Church and State in the twilight years of the current monarch.

[71] See the papers delivered at the Ecclesiastical Law Society Conference, March 2018, *Church and State in the Post-Elizabethan Age*.

[72] See J Rivers, 'The Secularisation of the British Constitution' (2012) 14 *Ecclesiastical Law Journal* 371.

[73] The Civil Partnership Act 2004, creating a legal union for same-sex couples, subsequently extended to opposite-sex couples as a consequence of a decision of the Supreme Court: *R (on the Application of Steinfeld and Keidan) v Secretary of State for International Development* [2017] UKSC 32.

[74] Marriage (Same Sex Couples) Act 2013.

[75] The *House of Bishops' Pastoral Guidance on Same Sex Marriage* (15 February 2014).

[76] See the Living in Love and Faith project, https://www.churchofengland.org/resources/living-love-and-faith.

11

Attorney-General (Victoria) ex rel Black v Commonwealth

The High Court's Attempt to Make the Establishment Clause of the Australian Constitution *Mean Very Little*

LUKE BECK

I. Introduction

The High Court of Australia's decision in *Attorney-General (Victoria) ex rel Black v Commonwealth*[1] is not the High Court's finest piece of constitutional jurisprudence. The decision purports to the give the *Australian Constitution*'s command that 'The Commonwealth shall not make any law for establishing any religion' an extremely narrow meaning; so narrow, in fact, that the Church of England in the UK would not count as being established. The *DOGS Case* – as it is often called – is to date the only occasion on which the meaning of the establishment clause of section 116 of the *Australian Constitution* has been the issue for the decision in the High Court.

The popular name of the case comes from the name of the organisation that was behind the litigation: the Association for the Defence of Government Schools. DOGS was formed in Melbourne in 1966 as an advocacy organisation and political party focused on public education.[2] During the 1970s, DOGS organised a constitutional challenge to the federal government's policy of providing federal funding to Catholic schools. The case was argued before the full bench of the High Court in 1980. The central argument was that the legislation providing for federal funding of Catholic schools contravened the establishment clause.

The challenge failed, with the result that federal funding of religious schools (at least when that funding is distributed in a non-discriminatory manner) is not unconstitutional. This practical result may be defensible, but the constitutional reasoning the High

[1] *Attorney-General (Victoria) ex rel Black v Commonwealth* (1981) 146 CLR 559 (hereinafter '*DOGS Case*').

[2] WJ Byrt and F Crean, *Government and Politics in Australia: Democracy in Transition* (McGraw-Hill, 1982) 253.

Court gave for reaching this outcome is deeply flawed. This chapter outlines the *DOGS Case*, its historical context and its implications.

The chapter begins by explaining the context of controversies over government funding of religious schools in both colonial and modern Australia. It then outlines the decades-long political and logistical planning for a constitutional challenge to federal government funding of religious schools. It then turns to the *DOGS Case* itself, examining what the case actually decided, the deep flaws in the interpretation given to the constitutional concept 'establishing any religion', and the serious problems in the High Court's approach to constitutional reasoning leading to the flawed interpretation. The final sections of the chapter examine the implications of the case and look at the short-term political response to the decision, what the case might mean for the contemporary so-called 'special deal' for federal funding of Catholic schools, and the future of establishment clause jurisprudence.

II. Controversies Over Government Funding of Religious Schools

Government funding of religious schools in Australia has long been contentious. Contemporary controversy has a number of dimensions. Perhaps the broadest dimension of contemporary controversy concerns the apparent overfunding of non-government schools (both religious and non-religious) in comparison to the underfunding of government schools responsible for educating the overwhelming majority of Australian children.[3] A more specific dimension of contemporary controversy, to which this chapter will return, concerns what Malcolm Turnbull, Prime Minister from 2015 to 2018, described as the 'special deal'[4] that sees federal funding for Catholic schools organised on seemingly more favourable terms than for other non-government schools (both religious and non-religious).

There was controversy too in colonial times. In the second half of the nineteenth century, each of the Australian colonies (now states) enacted legislation making public education compulsory, secular and free: all children regardless of religion or wealth were entitled to a good education. At the same time, the colonies withdrew public funding (sometimes referred to as 'state aid') from the non-government, usually church-run, schools which had been largely responsible for providing education to Australia's children.[5] Unsurprisingly, given the withdrawal of public subsidies, religious schools began to wane, although they did not completely disappear.[6]

[3] See, eg, 'Public Schools Face $19b Shortfall But Private Schools Over-funded' *9 News* (2 October 2020), www.9news.com.au/national/education-funding-public-school-shortfall-private-schools-over-funded/25239624-f071-4fe5-bd46-21fa9ecbdc57; 'Private School Funding Grows 15 Times Faster Than State School Funding' *The Age* (29 June 2020), www.theage.com.au/politics/victoria/private-school-funding-grows-15-times-faster-than-state-school-funding-20200629-p557cy.html; 'Education Minister Simon Birmingham Says Some Private Schools Over-funded' *ABC News Online* (27 September 2016), www.abc.net.au/news/2016-09-27/education-minister-acknowledges-some-private-schools-over-funded/7880058.

[4] M Turnbull, *A Bigger Picture* (Hardie Grant Publishing, 2020) 529.

[5] See *Public Instruction Act 1880* (NSW); *Education Act 1872* (Vic); *Education Act 1875* (SA); *Education Act 1885* (Tas); *Education Act 1875* (Qld); *Elementary Education Act 1871* (WA); *Assisted Schools Abolition Act 1885* (WA).

[6] For overviews of public funding of religious schools in this period, see, eg, D Mayrl, *Secular Conversions: Political Institutions and Religious Education in the United States and Australia, 1800–2000* (Cambridge

Federal funding of religious schools seems to have begun in 1956 when the federal government provided funding to religious schools in the Australian Capital Territory in the form of paying the interest on their loans.[7] Newspapers reported a degree of consternation within the governing political party over this policy. Ministers announced the policy publicly to church leaders before government backbenchers knew about the policy.[8]

Funding to religious schools went nationwide in 1964 when federal legislation was enacted to authorise funding of the construction of science classrooms in religious schools throughout the country.[9] The proximate cause of this initiative was the so-called Goulburn School Strike, a political manoeuvre organised by the Catholic Church.[10] The National Museum of Australia's 'Defining Moments' website explains that 'about 2,000 Catholic children descended on the town's six government schools, which could only take 640 of them'.[11] The episode was a warning shot, intended to demonstrate the Catholic Church's willingness to overwhelm the public school system with a flood of new enrolments if its demands for public funding of Catholic schools were not met.[12]

In 1968, federal capital grants to religious schools were extended to pay for school libraries.[13] Federal funding of religious schools was broadened significantly in 1970 when legislation came into effect authorising recurrent funding to religious schools for their general operations.[14] The federal government continues to provide capital and recurrent funding to non-government schools.

III. Challenging Government Funding of Religious Schools

At the same time as federal funding of religious schools began in 1956, activists opposed to public funding of non-government schools generally, and of religious schools especially, began contemplating a constitutional challenge in the High Court.[15] The argument would be that the legislation authorising the funding was invalid for contravening the

University Press, 2016) ch 1; A Austin, *Australian Education, 1788–1900: Church, State, and Public Education in Colonial Australia*, 3rd edn (Pitman Pacific Books, 1971).

[7] See 'Payment of Interest Offered as Aid to Church Schools' *Canberra Times* (10 July 1956) 1. There does not appear to have been any specific statutory authorisation for this policy, presumably in reliance on the now-rejected theory that appropriation acts authorise the expenditure of funds. The contemporary position is that funds appropriated from the Consolidated Revenue Fund may be expended only if some other law authorises the expenditure: see *Pape v Commissioner of Taxation* (2009) 238 CLR 1; *Williams v Commonwealth (No 2)* (2014) 252 CLR 416.

[8] 'Liberals Criticise Aid to Church Schools' *Canberra Times* (1 November 1956) 3.

[9] *States Grants (Science Laboratories and Technical Training) Act 1964* (Cth).

[10] Mayrl (n 6) 221.

[11] National Museum of Australia, 'Aid for Non-government Schools', www.nma.gov.au/defining-moments/resources/aid-for-non-government-schools.

[12] See M Hogan, *The Catholic Campaign for State Aid: A Study of A Pressure Group Campaign in New South Wales and the Australian Capital Territory, 1950–1972* (Catholic Theological Faculty, 1978).

[13] *States Grants (Secondary Schools Libraries) Act 1968* (Cth).

[14] *States Grants (Independent Schools) Act 1969* (Cth).

[15] See, eg, 'Church School Aid to Be Challenged' *The Argus* (10 October 1956) 1.

establishment clause of section 116 of the *Australian Constitution*. This clause provides: 'The Commonwealth shall not make any law for establishing any religion.'

Constitutional concerns were raised in Parliament, but were not given much attention. During parliamentary debate in 1971 on revised legislation for authorising federal funding of religious schools, Senator John Wheeldon of the centre-left Labor Party complained that proper consideration had not been given to the constitutionality of the arrangements:

> The question is whether section 116 of the *Constitution* which provides for the separation of Church and State is being infringed by allocations of this kind. This seems to me to warrant some sort of discussion because if section 116 is not being infringed by a Bill of this nature one can only wonder what one would have to do in order to breach section 116 of the *Constitution*. Certainly an almost identical provision in the *United States Constitution* was held by the United States Supreme Court to prohibit grants of this kind being made in that country and one would have thought that at least when this rather unique proposition was presented to the Senate the Minister, if only in passing, would have touched on this very important matter relating to our *Constitution*.[16]

The establishment clause argument had some plausibility. During the 1970s, the US Supreme Court had held on multiple occasions that a similar clause in the *US Constitution* – the First Amendment's command that 'Congress shall make no law respecting an establishment of religion' – had the effect of prohibiting public funding of religious schools.[17] Furthermore, the framers of the *Australian Constitution* had explained that the federal government they were creating would have no power to give funds to churches. '[Y]ou have only two powers of spending money, and a church could not receive the funds of the Commonwealth under either of them',[18] delegates to the Convention drafting the *Australian Constitution* were told by Edmund Barton, Leader of the Convention and later Prime Minister and High Court justice.

Testing the establishment clause argument would require bringing a case to court, and getting a case into court is not easy. The financial cost of doing so is one hurdle. The rules around standing are another. A person has standing to challenge the validity of legislation only if they are specially and directly affected by it. On the other hand, each of the Federal and State Attorneys-General has general standing to commence proceedings in order to ensure that constitutional limits are respected.[19] Each Attorney-General can also grant a fiat to another person permitting that other person to bring an action using the Attorney-General's name and standing.

[16] Commonwealth, Parliamentary Debates, Senate, 1 December 1971, 2241.

[17] *Lemon v Kurtzman*, 403 US 602 (1971) (public funding for teachers' salaries and instructional materials at religious schools contravenes the establishment clause); *Committee for Public Education and Religious Liberty v Nyquist*, 413 US 756 (1973) (public funding for facilities maintenance and repair at religious schools and school fees reimbursement to parents of students at religious schools contravene the establishment clause); *Meek v Pittenger*, 421 US 349 (1975) (public funding for instructional materials at religious schools contravenes the establishment clause).

[18] Official Record of the Debates of the Australasian Federal Convention, Melbourne, 2 March 1898, 1772.

[19] See Westlaw AU, Thomson Reuters, *The Laws of Australia* (at 1 May 2020) 5 Civil Procedure, '5.4. Parties and Joinder' [5.4.600]: 'In an action to compel the performance of a public duty or restrain a public mischief, the Attorney-General is the only plaintiff recognised by law'; LexisNexis, *Halsbury's Laws of Australia*, 'Practice and Procedure, I Preliminary Matters, (5) Parties, (E) Relator Actions' [325–1415].

As early as 1957, activists had sought the fiat of an Attorney-General. The Victorian Protestant Federation sought the Federal Attorney-General's fiat in 1957.[20] Perhaps unsurprisingly, they did not get it. The grant of a fiat is at an Attorney-General's discretion and therefore political considerations inevitably come into play. Why would the Federal Attorney-General help a challenge to his own government's new legislation which he personally supports?

The Association for the Defence of Government Schools eventually obtained the fiat of the Victorian Attorney-General in 1973 on behalf of a group of individuals recruited by DOGS to 'represent a cross-section of Australian society (symbolically representing the widespread opposition to state-aid)'.[21] DOGS itself was not one of the relators. As an unincorporated association, it was not a legal person with capacity to engage in legal action. Among the relators were teachers, parents, union officials, the Chairman of the Labor Party's education committee, and office-holders of the Australian Council of State School Organisations such as Joan Kirner (who later served as Premier of Victoria from 1990 to 1992).[22]

Obtaining a fiat was not easy. DOGS had approached the Attorney-General of every state as well as the Federal Attorney-General over the course of 1972 and 1973. The *Canberra Times* newspaper reported that: 'Some [Attorneys-General] admitted [their refusal to grant a fiat] was for political reasons. They thought that to give open support for action against state aid would cost a lot of Roman Catholic votes.'[23]

The *Australian Financial Review* newspaper reported that the need for a technical amendment to the fiat was seized upon by the Catholic Church as 'a second chance to quash the challenge', its earlier efforts to pressure the Victorian Attorney-General to refuse to grant the fiat in the first place having failed.[24] The newspaper reported that 'Catholic education groups have planned coordinated action at the national level if [the Victorian Attorney-General] consents to the amendment'.[25] In the event, the Victorian Attorney-General consented to the amendment to the fiat allowing the case to proceed, but, along with the other states, intervened in the case, arguing that federal funding of religious schools was valid.

Real movement in the case itself came some years later when it was formally filed in the High Court in 1978.[26] Chief Justice Garfield Barwick (who had previously been Attorney-General in Robert Menzies' centre-right Liberal Government) ordered that the matter be referred to a single justice to determine the facts.[27] Evidence was taken by Lionel Murphy J (who had previously been Attorney-General in Gough Whitlam's centre-left Labor Government) over the course of 1979, and in early 1980 he ordered

[20] IKF Birch, 'State-Aid at the Bar: The Dogs Case' (1984) 26(1) *Critical Studies in Education* 31, 35; MJ Ely, *Erosion of the Judicial Process: An Aspect of Church-State Entanglement in Australia, 1956–1980* (Defence of Government Schools, 1981) 4.

[21] Birch (n 20) 36, quoting a letter from DOGS to the Australian Council of State School Organisations, 16 March 1972.

[22] ibid 36. Kirner was removed as a relator following her appointment to the Commonwealth's Schools Commission: see ibid 39.

[23] 'Judges Fail to Rule on "Standing" Requirement' *Canberra Times* (11 February 1981) 15.

[24] 'Catholic Time-Bomb Set to Explode' *Australian Financial Review* (10 May 1974) 1.

[25] ibid.

[26] Birch (n 20) 40.

[27] 'School-Aid Action before High Court' *Canberra Times* (21 November 1978) 3.

that the matter be determined by the full bench of the High Court. In the event, Barwick CJ considered the factual material to be 'in truth for the most part irrelevant to the resolution of the question whether the nominated statutes, individually, collectively or in any combination, are or contain a law for establishing a religion'.[28]

IV. What Did the *DOGS Case* Decide?

The collection of statutes under challenge in the *DOGS Case* did not empower the Federal Government to fund religious schools directly. The *Australian Constitution* permits the Federal Parliament to make laws in respect of only a defined list of subject matters and there is simply no head of federal legislative power that would support a federal law authorising direct federal funding of religious schools (or, indeed, any schools).[29] But section 96 of the *Australian Constitution* supports laws granting funds to states on such terms and conditions as the Federal Parliament thinks fit. This mechanism is used by the Commonwealth to engage in an enormous variety of spending programmes: funds are given to the states on condition that they pass the funds on to the intended final recipients subject to whatever conditions the Federal Government stipulates. The states, in effect, are 'acting as the Commonwealth's conduit pipe'.[30]

In simple terms, the legislation under challenge provided a mechanism for calculating the amount of money per student in a non-government school or non-government school system that should be funnelled via the states to that student's school or school system.[31] While most of the federal money for non-government education found its way to Catholic schools and school systems, the dollar amount per student did not vary based on the religious affiliation of either the student or the student's school or school system. It was irrelevant whether the school, school system or student was affiliated with one religion or denomination or another or was not religious at all. The legislation also provided a mechanism for calculating funding to be funnelled via the states to non-government schools and school systems for capital works projects. Again, religious affiliation was not a factor impacting the calculations.

That most of the federal money for non-government education went to Catholic schools was simply a consequence of Catholic schools outnumbering other non-government schools. As Ronald Wilson J summarised in his judgment:

> In 1976 … there were a total of 2,002 non-government schools which received financial assistance from the Commonwealth under the legislation in question, of which 1,965 were schools which acknowledged some religious character either by way of affiliation with a religious body or simply as Christian schools. Of these, 1,657 schools were conducted by the Roman Catholic Church.[32]

[28] *DOGS Case* (n 1) 576.

[29] The exception is that the 'territories power' in s 122 would support a federal law authorising federal funds being paid directly to schools located in territories.

[30] *Deputy Federal Commissioner of Taxation v WR Moran Pty Ltd* (1939) 61 CLR 735.

[31] Some non-government schools are standalone entities, while others belong to non-government school systems that operate multiple non-government schools. Most, but not all, systems of non-government schools are Catholic.

[32] *DOGS Case* (n 1) 645.

The legislation had the purpose of assisting the primary and secondary education provided by non-government schools rather than assisting in any religious activities in which those schools might also engage. The legislation also expressly prohibited funding for facilities for use, wholly or principally, for religious worship.

Whether or not in practice there was actually (and in a manner not authorised by the statute) some favourable treatment of Catholic schools, each of the majority justices in the *DOGS Case* based their decision on the premise that the legislation under challenge did not permit discrimination between non-government schools, school systems or students based on religious affiliation.[33]

In the result, six of the seven High Court justices held that this federal legislative scheme for funding non-government school education in a manner that did not discriminate on the basis of religion did not contravene the establishment clause of section 116. While this result may be defensible, the reasoning that led the High Court to it is fundamentally flawed.

V. Flawed Interpretations

While there is some variation and differences of emphasis among the majority justices – as well as some internal inconsistencies in individual judgments – in the *DOGS Case*, two key propositions inform the majority's interpretation of the establishment clause. The first is that the establishment clause prohibits only national establishments of religion. The second is that the establishment clause prohibits only single establishments of religion. Each of these propositions is deeply flawed.[34]

The first key proposition informing the majority's interpretation of the establishment clause is that the establishment clause prohibits only national establishments of religion. Chief Justice Barwick explained that the establishment clause prohibits 'set[ting] up the religion as an institution of the Commonwealth'.[35] Justice Ninian Stephen explained that the prohibition is against 'the setting up of a national church'.[36] Justice Anthony Mason said that he agreed with Wilson J that the establishment clause prohibits the recognition of a religion as a 'national institution'.[37]

This proposition is deeply flawed. If the proposition were true, then, for example, a federal law proclaiming that 'Roman Catholicism is the established religion of the Northern Territory' would not contravene the establishment clause. Justice Harry Gibbs was the only majority justice who seemed to recognise that federal laws creating non-national establishments of religion would contravene the establishment clause. He explained that a grant of federal funds under section 96 to a state on condition that the state establishes a religion (which would necessarily be a non-national establishment of religion) would be

[33] ibid 585 (Barwick CJ), 604 (Gibbs J), 604, 610 (Stephen J); 612, 617–18 (Mason J), 635 (Aickin J), 643–44 (Wilson J).

[34] This section draws upon ideas in L Beck, 'Dead DOGS? Towards a Less Restrictive Interpretation of the Establishment Clause: *Hoxton Park Residents Action Group Inc v Liverpool City Council (No 2)*' (2014) 37(2) *University of Western Australia Law Review* 59.

[35] *DOGS Case* (n 1) 583; see also 581–82.

[36] ibid 610; see also 609.

[37] ibid 612, 616 (Mason J), 653 (Wilson J).

invalid for contravening section 116.[38] Justice Keith Aickin – who, before his appointment to the High Court, had twice rejected DOGS's approaches for him to be its lead counsel in the case[39] – did not deliver a full judgment, instead saying that he agreed with both Gibbs J and Mason J.[40] Confusingly, this judge therefore adopted the contradictory propositions that only national establishments of religion are prohibited and that both national and non-national establishments of religion are prohibited.

Although he did not seem to recognise it, Mason J's judgment points to compelling evidence as to why non-national establishments of religion brought about by federal laws are prohibited by section 116. Immediately after asserting that the establishment clause is concerned only with national establishments of religion, Mason J's judgment goes on to remark that the framers of the *Australian Constitution* 'were acutely familiar with the relationship between church and state in England and Wales, Scotland and Ireland. They were aware that the Church of England, the Church of Scotland and the Church of Ireland respectively were referred to as "the Established Church"'.[41]

The Church of England has been a non-national established church ever since the union of the Kingdoms of England and Scotland. The same is true of the Church of Scotland. The separate establishment of the (Anglican) Church of England following the union was preserved by *An Act for securing the Church of England as by Law Established 1706* (Eng). The separate establishment of the (Presbyterian) Church of Scotland following the union was preserved by the *Protestant Religion and Presbyterian Church Act 1707* (Scot).[42] The territorial extent of the establishment of the Church of England has also diminished over time. The *Irish Church Act 1869* (which came into effect in 1871) dissolved the union between the Irish and English Churches and provided that 'the Church of Ireland, as so separated, should cease to be established by law'.[43] Similarly, the *Welsh Church Act 1914* operated to 'terminate the establishment of the Church of England in Wales and Monmouthshire'.[44] Therefore, the UK experience demonstrates that non-national establishments of religion are possible.

There is nothing in the text or background historical context to section 116 to support the *DOGS Case* notion that the establishment clause should be understood as if it said: 'The Commonwealth shall not make any law for establishing any national religion.'

The second key proposition informing the majority's interpretation of the establishment clause is that the establishment clause prohibits only single establishments of religion. Justice Gibbs held that the establishment clause prohibits 'conferring on *a particular* religion or religious body [the status of being established]' (emphasis added).[45] For Stephen J, the focus of the prohibition is against only 'the elevation of

[38] ibid 592.

[39] MJ Ely, *Erosion of the Judicial Process: An Aspect of Church-State Entanglement in Australia, 1956–1980* (Defence of Government Schools, 1981) 6.

[40] *DOGS Case* (n 1) 635.

[41] ibid 616–17.

[42] See also *Union with England Act 1707* (Scot) Anne c 7; *Union with Scotland Act 1706* (Eng) 6 Anne c 11.

[43] 32 & 33 Vict, c 42 preamble. See further J Lucas and RM Morris, 'Disestablishment in Ireland and Wales' in RM Williams (ed), *Church and State in 21st Century Britain* (Palgrave Macmillan, 2009).

[44] 4 & 5 Geo 5, c 91 preamble. The *Suspensory Act 1914* 4 & 5 Geo 5, c 88 delayed the coming into effect of the *Welsh Church Act* 4 & 5 Geo 5, c 91. For a discussion, see, eg, Roger L Brown, 'The Disestablishment of the Church in Wales' (1999) 5 *Ecclesiastical Law Journal* 252.

[45] *DOGS Case* (n 1); see also 597–98.

one church above all others' (emphasis added).[46] Similarly, for Mason J, section 116 'reflects a concern with the establishment of *one* religion as against others' (emphasis added).[47] Wilson J concurred, saying that 'establishment involves the deliberate selection of *one* to be preferred from among others' (emphasis added).[48] As noted above, Aickin J expressed his agreement with both Gibbs J and Mason J.

Justice Murphy's dissent complained that the 'one religion' interpretation trivialised the constitutional provision:

> To read s 116 as prohibiting only laws for establishing one religion or church, but permitting laws for establishing a number of religions or churches is inconsistent with the comprehensive terms of the prohibition. There is no warrant for reading 'any religion' as 'any one religion'; yet this is necessary if 'establishing' refers only to the recognition or setting up of one national church or religion. Such a reading trivializes the section.[49]

The proposition that the establishment clause prohibits only single establishments of religion is also deeply flawed. If the proposition were true, then, for example, a federal law proclaiming that 'Roman Catholicism and Sunni Islam are the established religions of Australia' would not contravene the establishment clause.

At the time of Federation, as the justices in the *DOGS Case* knew, 'in the United Kingdom there were two established churches'.[50] Those two churches – the (Anglican) Church of England and the (Presbyterian) Church of Scotland – remain established. Multiple establishments of religion are not just confined to the UK. For example, 'Finland has *two* established churches'.[51] As these examples show, multiple religious establishments in a country might take the form of religious establishments confined to different regions within the country or might take the form of territorially overlapping establishments. Equally, the nature of the establishment of the various preferred religions need not be of the same kind or in the same form.

Australia's own history provides examples both of multiple establishments of religion in practice and of recognition of the concept of multiple establishments. As Renae Barker has summarised:[52]

> The state-religion relationship in Australia from the mid 1830s to the mid 1860s is often described as 'plural' or 'multiple establishment' as a result of the operation of the Church Acts in the colonies of New South Wales and Van Diemen's Land (VDL), which provided for direct funding of religion by the state.[53] Gascoigne, for example, in referring to funding of religion under the Church Acts, claims that '[Governor] Bourke, in effect, instituted a system of multiple establishment'. Gascoigne further recognised the uniqueness of the institution of plural or multiple establishment, claiming that it was 'a bold and largely unprecedented move'.[54]

[46] ibid 610.
[47] ibid 615.
[48] ibid 653.
[49] ibid 623–24.
[50] HM Carey, 'An Historical Outline of Religion in Australia' in J Jupp (ed), *The Encyclopedia of Religion in Australia* (Cambridge University Press, 2009) 5, 7.
[51] F Cranmer, 'Church-State Relations in Scandinavia' in F Cranmer, J Lucas and B Morris, *Church and State: A Mapping Exercise* (The Constitution Unit, 2006) 78, 85.
[52] R Barker, 'Under Most Peculiar Circumstances: The Church Acts in the Australian Colonies as a Study of Plural Establishment' (2016) 3 *Law & History* 28, 30.
[53] SV Monsma and JC Soper, *The Challenge of Pluralism: Church and State in Five Democracies* (Rowman & Littlefield, 2009) 93; J Gascoigne, *The Enlightenment and the Origins of European Australia* (Cambridge University Press, 2002) 28–29.
[54] Gascoigne (n 53) 29.

> Hogan describes the Church Acts as having 'four established churches instead of one'.[55] Monsma and Soper also describe the period of the Church Acts in this way. Like Gascoigne, they emphasise the boldness of the Church Acts and their egalitarian nature, commenting that 'the act revised the established church model by allocating colonial funds on a more equal basis'.[56]

There is nothing in the text or background historical context to section 116 to support the notion adopted by the majority in the *DOGS Case* that the establishment clause should be understood as if it said: 'The Commonwealth shall not make any law for establishing any one religion only.'

VI. Flawed Approaches to Constitutional Reasoning

It is not surprising that the substantive propositions of constitutional doctrine arrived at by the majority justices are deeply flawed. The approach to constitutional reasoning seen in the *DOGS Case* is also fundamentally flawed.[57]

Some constitutional provisions – such as the rule that each original state shall have the same number of senators[58] – do not require the development of much constitutional doctrine to explain what they mean and how they apply. Others – like the establishment clause of section 116[59] – require the development of 'doctrine to articulate what a constitutional provision means and guide the evaluative reasoning necessary to apply it'.[60]

The approach to the development of constitutional doctrine employed by the majority justices in the *DOGS Case* is now considered by the High Court to be fundamentally flawed and wrong. The justices employed a number of flawed approaches to the development of doctrine.

The first flawed approach adopted by the *DOGS* majority is in giving the establishment clause a narrow meaning. Many constitutional concepts, including 'establishing any religion', are capable of a range of possible meanings, some narrow and some broad. The New South Wales Court of Appeal has observed that 'the term "establishing" in s 116 was given a restrictive meaning' in the *DOGS Case*.[61] One scholar has even described the approach in the *DOGS Case* as being 'uniquely narrow'.[62]

As the discussion above shows, all of the majority justices adopted a narrow interpretation of the concept of 'establishing any religion', and all of them except Barwick CJ[63] explained that they were doing so deliberately as an interpretative approach. Justice Gibbs said that: 'There is no reason to give such a provision [ie, s 116] a liberal interpretation.'[64]

[55] M Hogan, *The Sectarian Strand: Religion in Australian History* (Penguin, 1987) 56.
[56] Monsma and Soper (n 53) 97.
[57] This section draws upon ideas in Beck (n 34).
[58] *Australian Constitution*, s 7.
[59] See L Beck, *Religious Freedom and the Australian Constitution: Origins and Future* (Routledge, 2018) 156–58.
[60] L Beck, *Australian Constitutional Law: Concepts and Cases* (Cambridge University Press, 2020) 55.
[61] *Hoxton Park Residents Action Group Inc v Liverpool City Council (No 2)* (2011) 256 FLR 156, 165 [28].
[62] R Mortensen, 'The Establishment Clause: A Search for Meaning' (2014) 33 *University of Queensland Law Journal* 109, 110.
[63] See *DOGS Case* (n 1) 577.
[64] ibid 603.

Justice Stephen said that the establishment clause set out a '*specific* restriction [on legislative power]' (emphasis added).[65] Justice Mason agreed[66] with Wilson J, who explained that while grants of power 'should be construed with all the generality which the words used will admit … the same is not true of a provision which proscribes power'.[67]

The idea that restrictions on legislative power should be given narrow meanings has since been rejected by the High Court.[68] Indeed, in a case considering the religious tests clause of section 116, the High Court has now even expressly rejected the idea that section 116 should be interpreted narrowly.[69] The contemporary orthodoxy is that constitutional provisions should be construed with all the generality with which the words used will admit.

Strangely, only a few weeks before the High Court said that section 116 should not be interpreted narrowly, *obiter* remarks in a criminal case express another very narrow and deeply flawed understanding of the concept of established religion. In the 2012 case of *PGA v The Queen*,[70] the joint judgment of French CJ and Gummow, Hayne, Crennan and Kiefel JJ commented:

> Further, unlike the situation in England, in the Australian colonies there was to be no established religion. The Anglican Church was expressly enjoined from exercising any authority or jurisdiction in matrimonial causes.[71]

The strangeness and wrongness of the passage in *PGA* has been described elsewhere in these terms:

> The High Court appears to be saying that the fact that the Anglican Church had no legal authority over divorce is sufficient proof that that Church was not established [in colonial Australia]. That appears to be an incredibly narrow view of the meaning of established religion and one that appears to be narrower than the views expressed in the *DOGS case*. It might also be observed that the established Church of England exercises no authority or jurisdiction in matrimonial causes in the United Kingdom today.[72]

It is also worth adding that the Federal Parliament could not empower a church to exercise authority or jurisdiction over divorce even if section 116 did not exist. Chapter III of the *Australian Constitution* has the effect that only 'courts' may exercise federal judicial power.[73] On the *PGA* view of establishment, the establishment clause of section 116 has no potential effect at all and means effectively nothing.

[65] ibid 609.

[66] ibid 612.

[67] ibid 653.

[68] See, eg, *Street v Queensland Bar Association* (1989) 168 CLR 461 (overruling older case law that gave s 117 a narrow interpretation); *JT International SA v Commonwealth* ('*Plain Packaging Case*') (2000) 202 CLR 479 (re-affirming that the prohibition on laws acquiring property otherwise than on just terms should not be interpreted narrowly).

[69] *Williams v Commonwealth* (2012) 248 CLR 156 [110]. The religious tests clause provides that 'no religious test shall be required as a qualification for any office or public trust under the Commonwealth'.

[70] The case concerned a historical rape accusation by a woman against her former husband. The question for the High Court was whether the common law as it existed in the 1960s presumed a wife's consent to sexual intercourse with her husband.

[71] *Williams v Commonwealth* (n 69) [26].

[72] Beck (n 34) 67–68.

[73] *Australian Constitution*, s 71. See, eg, *Lane v Morrison* (2009) 239 CLR 230 (federal legislation creating a body that did not possess all of the defining characteristics of a federal court to exercise federal judicial power

The second flawed approach adopted by the *DOGS* majority is fairly basic: a failure to consider and engage with existing High Court thinking on the issue. The New South Wales Court of Appeal has observed that at least one earlier High Court case seems to express a broad understanding of the concept of established religion. The earlier case is the 1948 charitable trusts case of *Wylde v Attorney-General (NSW) (ex rel Ashelford)*.[74] The judgments of Latham CJ and Dixon J in *Wylde* had some relevance to the *DOGS Case*. *Wylde* is not cited, let alone discussed, by the majority in the *DOGS Case*.

Justice Dixon's judgment in *Wylde*, while not stating any definition, describes the collection of features of the Anglican Church in colonial New South Wales, which he says made it possess the status of an established church for some decades.[75] In the *DOGS Case*, a number of majority justices assert that the legal situation of religion and the arrangements by which the government funded and was otherwise involved in religion in colonial Australia provide no useful analogy by which to understand the mischief with which the establishment clause is concerned.[76] They give no full explanation for this assertion. Justice Dixon's analysis was plainly relevant to this issue.

Rather strangely, the passage in which Dixon J's analysis is found was cited by the High Court in *PGA* in the passage extracted above. Justice Dixon's analysis with its broad understanding of the concept of established religion provides no support for the idea contained in the quoted passage from *PGA*.

Chief Justice Latham's judgment in *Wylde* also contained thinking relevant to the reasoning in the *DOGS Case*. In *Wylde*, Latham CJ describes as established any 'religious body teaching a religion which is supported and encouraged by the State'.[77] On this view, a federal law that operates to support and encourage a religion would contravene the establishment clause. This is plainly a much broader understanding of the concept of established religion than that adopted in the *DOGS Case*.

The third flawed approach to reasoning adopted by the *DOGS* majority is refusing to have recourse to the Convention Debates – the Hansard transcripts of the Australasian Federal Convention that drafted the *Australian Constitution* – to assist the process of constitutional interpretation. This approach was prevailing orthodoxy at the time. As Barwick CJ noted in his judgment, 'the settled doctrine of the Court is that [the Convention Debates] are not available in the construction of the Constitution'. He added that looking at looking at the Convention Debates 'might well distract the mind from the proper meaning of unambiguous words in the text'.[78] Justice Mason similarly commented that any attempt to understand 'why it was considered necessary to include in the Constitution s 116 or its first clause … is speculative and it does not assist in the resolution of the problems which now arise'.[79]

Despite the insistence that the drafting history of section 116 cannot be relevant to its interpretation, these justices relied upon their own speculations about section 116's

was invalid); *Burns v Corbett* (2018) 265 CLR 304 (the purported exercise of federal judicial power by an entity that did not possess all of the defining characteristics of a court was invalid).

[74] *Wylde v Attorney-General (NSW) (ex rel Ashelford)* (1948) 78 CLR 224.

[75] ibid 284–86.

[76] *DOGS Case* (n 1) 608 (Stephen J), 167 (Mason J) and 651 (Wilson J).

[77] *Wylde* (n 74) 262.

[78] *DOGS Case* (n 1) 577–78.

[79] ibid 612.

drafting history in their interpretation of the provision. Without looking at the Convention Debates, Barwick CJ was able to divine 'an intention' on the part of the framers of the *Australian Constitution* that the Australian establishment clause should operate differently from the American establishment clause.[80] Justice Mason, without looking at the Convention Debates, was able to convince himself that the framers of the *Australian Constitution* 'would have had in mind' a particular understanding of the American establishment clause as they were drafting the *Australian Constitution*.[81] Given the shunning of any primary sources such as the records of the Convention Debates, these judges did not rely on the *actual* drafting history of section 116 in their reasoning; instead, they relied on *imagined* drafting histories of section 116 in their reasoning.

The High Court's contemporary approach is that the process of constitutional interpretation may have regard to the Convention Debates 'for the purpose of identifying the contemporary meaning of language used, the subject to which that language was directed and the nature and objectives of the movement towards federation from which the compact of the Constitution finally emerged'.[82] The New South Wales Court of Appeal has observed that reference to the Convention Debates might 'allow submissions to be made supporting a more a flexible approach to the constraints on legislative power expressed in s 116'.[83]

VII. Political Response to the *DOGS Case*

Even before the High Court had handed down its decision, politicians were thinking about how they would react. While the *DOGS Case* was before the High Court and before any judgment had been delivered, the then Liberal Prime Minister Malcolm Fraser indicated that he would be prepared to hold a referendum to amend the *Constitution* if the High Court were to rule that the federal funding of religious schools was unconstitutional.[84]

Given the outcome of the case, such a referendum was not needed. But the impact of the *DOGS Case* was felt in a referendum a few years later. In 1988, the so-called 'Rights and Freedoms Referendum' was held. The Constitution Alteration (Rights and Freedoms) Bill 1988 proposed by Bob Hawke's Labor government would have extended section 80's guarantee of jury trials for federal indictable offences to state offences, section 51(xxxi)'s guarantee of compensation for acquisitions of property under federal law to acquisitions of property under state law, and section 116's various limitations on federal power respecting religion to the states. The proposal would have seen the establishment clause of section 116 read: 'The Commonwealth, a State or Territory shall not establish any religion.'

The Bill's explanatory memorandum stated that there was 'no change that would render the decision in [the *DOGS Case*] inapplicable to the new section'.[85] Nevertheless,

[80] ibid 579.

[81] ibid 614.

[82] *Cole v Whitfield* (1988) 165 CLR 360. The High Court was insistent that this is quite different from seeking to discover the subjective intentions of the framers.

[83] *Hoxton Park Residents Action Group Inc v Liverpool City Council (No 2)* (2011) 256 FLR 156, 166 [34].

[84] See eg, Commonwealth, Parliamentary Debates, House of Representatives, 13 May 1980.

[85] Explanatory Memorandum, Constitution Alteration (Rights and Freedoms) Bill 1988, 6.

Opposition politicians raised concern that the proposed amendment would change the constitutional rules about public funding of religious schools.[86] The same concern prompted the Australian Catholic Bishops Conference to issue a public statement urging people to vote 'no' at the referendum.[87] Some Catholic schools also wrote letters to the parents of their students urging them to vote 'no'.[88] The referendum failed, with the proposed amendments suffering the highest ever 'no' vote of any referendum to amend the *Australian Constitution*.[89]

Starting on the day that the High Court handed down its decision, there were warnings about where the decision might lead. Ray Nilsen, the Chairman of the Association for the Defence of Government Schools, was quoted in the media describing the High Court's decision as marking a 'black day' and suggesting that the decision 'will be an invitation for the churches to plunder the taxpayers' money'.[90] Nilsen also predicted an increase in the number of religious schools in Australia in the following years. This prediction was right. In the late 1970s, approximately one-fifth of Australian students attended non-government schools.[91] By 2019, approximately one-third of Australian students attended non-government schools, with enrolments at Catholic schools forming the majority of enrolments at non-government schools.[92]

The day after the High Court's decision, John Dawkins, Labor's Shadow Minister for Education, commented that: 'The fact that the High Court has ruled that assistance can be provided to non-government schools provides no justification for putting those schools in a privileged position compared to government schools'. He added that: 'The needs of the poorest and resource-starved schools must be put ahead of the wealthiest private schools.'[93] His comments were prescient. The contemporary arrangement for federal funding of non-government schools includes what is often referred to as a 'special deal' for Catholic schools, which in practice advantages wealthy Catholic schools (to the disadvantage of poor Catholic schools).

VIII. The Future of Federal Funding for Catholic schools

Despite the flaws of its reasoning, the *DOGS Case* reached a sensible holding that federal funding of non-government school education in a manner that does not discriminate

[86] Beck (n 59) 152–55.

[87] C Sharman, 'The 1988 Referendums and Their Context' in B Galligan and JR Nethercote (eds), *The Constitutional Commission and the 1988 Referendums* (Centre for Research on Federal Financial Relations, 1989) 105, 113.

[88] ibid.

[89] A constitutional amendment requires the support of a majority of voters nationally plus the support of a majority of voters in a majority of States: *Australian Constitution*, s 128. The results were: nationally: 31% in favour; New South Wales: 30% in favour; Victoria: 33% in favour; Queensland: 33% in favour; South Australia: 26% in favour; Western Australia: 28% in favour; Tasmania: 25% in favour.

[90] '"Black Day" for Court' *Canberra Times* (11 February 1981) 1.

[91] C Ryan and L Watson, *The Drift to Private Schools in Australia: Understanding its Features*, Discussion Paper No 479 (Centre for Economic Policy Research, 2004) 1, https://rse.anu.edu.au/researchpapers/CEPR/DP479.pdf.

[92] Australian Bureau of Statistics, 'Schools – 2019', https://www.abs.gov.au/statistics/people/education/schools/2019.

[93] 'Labor Seeking Reassurance on School-Funding' *Canberra Times* (12 February 1981) 8.

on the basis of religion does not contravene the establishment clause of section 116. It is unlikely that if the High Court were to reconsider the meaning of the establishment clause and adopt a more sensible interpretation, the practical result in the *DOGS Case* would be undermined.

However, there remains an open question as to whether the so-called 'special deal' for Catholic schools that exists in the current federal funding arrangements for non-government schools contravenes the establishment clause. The reason for this is that the 'special deal' appears to involve discrimination between non-government schools based on their religious affiliation, and the existence of that discrimination allows the situation to be distinguished from the situation considered in the *DOGS Case*.

The contemporary 'special deal' works in this way.[94] The legislative scheme requires that federal funding for non-government schools be paid, via the states, to the individual schools unless the school is part of a non-government school system. Where a school is part of a non-government school system, federal funding for that school is paid, via the states, to the agency controlling the school system and not to the individual school. It is then a matter for the agency to determine how to distribute the money among the various schools within the school system. The legislative scheme in its terms does not differentiate between school systems on the basis of religion or on the basis of any other attribute.

This scheme has the fulsome support of the Catholic Church's leadership. The scheme exists specifically at their behest. Most Catholic schools are part of a school system, and most school systems are Catholic. It is often the case that a portion of the federal funds calculated for Catholic schools serving low- and middle-income families are diverted to prestigious Catholic schools serving wealthy families. When Liberal Prime Minister Malcolm Turnbull proposed in 2017 that each school's individual entitlement be published online for the purposes of transparency, but to nevertheless permit the redistribution of funds within school systems to continue, he was lobbied personally by Anthony Fisher, the Catholic Archbishop of Sydney. In his autobiography, Turnbull writes:

> Over the years Catholic bishops … had always insisted that the virtue of funding Catholic schools in one lump sum, as a system, was so that they could cross-subsidise the poorer schools at the expense of those in wealthier suburbs. And this claim seemed so plausible, given the Church's mission, that none of us gullible politicians questioned it.
>
> As it turned out, quite the reverse was the case. Anthony Fisher, the archbishop of Sydney, was the one tasked to speak to me and explained that 'the problem' with our needs-based model was that more funding would go to schools in 'the poorer outer suburbs of Sydney and country New South Wales'.
>
> I was astonished. 'But don't you do that now?' …
>
> The archbishop sighed. 'I am afraid to say, on this occasion, the politician has a more idealised view of human nature than the archbishop.'
>
> I pressed my case and explained that while the funding was assessed on a school-by-school basis, and transparently so, it would still all come to the Church in one cheque and they could then distribute it as they saw fit. If they wanted to subsidise fees in posh areas at the expense of schools in poor areas, they were free to do that.

[94] See *Australian Education Act 2013* (Cth), s 71.

> 'Oh, come on, Malcolm,' said Fisher. 'You know, once you tell people how the government has assessed need and show much each school would get, we could never get away with it. People would say we were short-changing poor schools to benefit rich ones.'
>
> This was the fundamental issue: he was objecting to transparency and accountability and wasn't prepared publicly to defend how they moved government money around their school system …
>
> We'd been misled, perhaps by our own naiveté, into thinking the Church would allocate funding strictly according to need.
>
> … [W]e faced continued resistance from the Catholic school system in Victoria, where a particularly vicious campaign … tried to mobilise Catholic school parents in Liberal seats to protest and, when the time came, vote against us.[95]

This legislative scheme involves no direct discrimination on the basis of religion. The calculation of funding entitlement does not depend on the religion of a student, school or school system. Equally, the ability of a school system to distribute funds between schools within its system does not depend on the religion of the school system.

However, Australian constitutional law recognises that discrimination may also be indirect.[96] Indirect discrimination exists where a rule that is neutral on its face has a disparate or disproportionate impact on a group sharing a particular characteristic and is not reasonably appropriate and adapted to a legitimate purpose. For example, a rule requiring all shop assistants not to wear headwear has a disproportionate impact on Sikh men because wearing a turban is a religious observance and is unlikely to be appropriate and adapted to achieving a non-discriminatory purpose. The rule is a form of indirect discrimination on the ground of religion.[97] By contrast, a rule requiring all mining site workers to wear protective hardhats might also have a disproportionate impact on Sikh men, but is likely to be appropriate and adapted to achieving a non-discriminatory purpose (in this case, safety).

Do the twin facts that most non-government school systems are Catholic and that most Catholic schools are part of Catholic school systems mean that the legislative scheme involves indirect discrimination on the ground of religion? There are two related possible avenues for suggesting that the answer is yes. The first avenue focuses on the disproportionate detriment experienced by non-Catholic non-government schools. The education authorities of one religious group exercise a decision-making function with important real-world consequences that in practice is not exercisable by the education authorities of other religious groups. Catholic school authorities are, in practice and by intent, vested with power to determine how much federal funding will go to particular schools. Catholic authorities can in effect veto a school's statutory entitlement and substitute a different amount.[98] The same is not true, in practice, of the school

[95] M Turnbull, *A Bigger Picture* (Hardie Grant Publishing, 2020) 529–31.

[96] For overviews of the case law on this point, see L Zines and G Lindell, 'Form and Substance: "Discrimination" in Modern Constitutional Law' (1992) 21 *Federal Law Review* 136, 142–43; A Simpson, 'The High Court's Conception of Discrimination: Origins, Applications, and Implications' (2007) 29 *Sydney Law Review* 263, 277; L Beck, 'The Australian Constitution's Religious Test Clause as an Anti-discrimination Provision' (2016) 42(3) *Monash University Law Review* 454, 568–70.

[97] Whether discrimination is unlawful depends on the legal regime governing the situation.

[98] In the context of the American establishment clause, see *Larkin v Grendel's Den Inc*, 459 US 116 (1982) (statutory power vested in churches to veto for no reason or any reason the grant of a liquor licence

authorities of other religions. Those groups do not get to exercise any similar power. There is differential treatment in practice and that differential treatment appears to serve the purpose of assuaging political demands made by the Catholic Church.

The second avenue for suggesting that there is indirect discrimination on the ground of religion is a corollary of the first and focuses on the disproportionate detriment experienced by Catholic non-government schools. The 'special deal' exposes Catholic schools to the prospect that they will not receive the full 'amount of financial assistance that a school attracts for a year ... worked out using the formula in [the statute]'.[99] The non-government schools associated with other religious groups are much less likely to receive less than the full amount of federal funding to which the statutory formula entitles them. It is not clear how either aspect of 'special deal' can be seen as pursuing the statute's stated object of providing a 'needs-based funding model' for non-government schools.[100]

The claim here is not that the 'special deal' necessarily contravenes the establishment clause; it is only that there is an argument to be had about its constitutionality validity. Further, the claim here is not that discrimination between religions or between religion and non-religion is the only way in which a federal law might contravene the establishment clause; it is only that it is likely that discrimination between religions or between religion and non-religion is one way in which a federal law might contravene the establishment clause. That claim is arguable, even if the *DOGS Case* is considered authoritative. The claim is even more arguable once it is recognised that the reasoning in the *DOGS Case* is not authoritative.

IX. Conclusion: The Future of the Establishment Clause

The *DOGS Case* was an attempt by the High Court to make the establishment clause of the *Australian Constitution* mean very little. While the majority judgments are cast in the dry tones of constitutional law, it is difficult not to wonder whether one motivation for the very narrow and odd approach taken in this case was a desire on the part of the majority justices to prevent the High Court becoming a participant in political and cultural debates of the kind seen in the US. Justice Gibbs almost said as much: his judgment notes in passing the 'emotional' and 'continuing' controversies in the US involving the US Supreme Court over public funding of religious schools and the relationship of government with religion.[101]

Such concern is misplaced. Most of the subject matters of the politically interesting American establishment clause case law – such as religious displays on government property, prayer in public schools and creationism in public school curriculums – are

contravenes the establishment clause). See also *Board of Education of Kiryas Joel Village v Grumet*, 512 US 687 (1994) (delegation of discretionary governmental powers in respect of schools to a group defined by religion contravenes the establishment clause).

[99] *Australian Education Act 2013* (Cth), s 4.

[100] ibid s 3(a).

[101] *DOGS Case* (n 1) 601, 603.

a product of both a very different political culture and the result of state laws. The American establishment clause binds both federal and state governments in the US,[102] whereas the Australian establishment clause binds only the federal government.

The Association for the Defence of Government Schools still exists.[103] It maintains a website, issues media releases, and produces a weekly radio show focusing on issues relating to public education and separation of religion and state on a community radio station.[104] It may be that DOGS or another group like it will organise another establishment clause challenge to federal funding of religious schools or to particular elements of federal funding of religious schools.

Of course, the constitutional prohibition on federal laws for establishing religion applies generally and not just in the context of funding schemes. For example, it has been suggested that the federal statute proclaiming that the Queen of Australia holds her position 'by the grace of God' – a form of words included in the statute at the Queen's personal request[105] – might contravene the establishment clause.[106]

Until the High Court is presented with another opportunity to rule directly on the meaning of the establishment clause, Australian constitutional jurisprudence is left with a case that seems to reach a defensible outcome by means of fundamentally flawed reasoning.

[102] *Everson v Board of Education*, 330 US 1 (1947) (the requirements of the First Amendment establishment clause are incorporated by the Fourteenth Amendment to bind the states).

[103] See www.adogs.info.

[104] See www.3cr.org.au/dogs.

[105] A Twomey, *The Chameleon Crown: The Queen and Her Australian Governors* (Federation Press, 2006) 108.

[106] L Beck, 'Clear and Emphatic: The Separation of Church and State under the Australian Constitution' (2008) 27(2) *University of Tasmania Law Review* 161, 176–79, referring to the *Royal Style and Titles Act 1973* (Cth).

12

M Siddiq (D) Thr Lrs v Mahant Suresh Das and Others

Inconsistencies in the Law and Politics of Indian History in the Ayodhya Case

SAWINDER SINGH

I. Introduction

On a fine morning in one of the courtrooms of the Punjab and Haryana High Court, an old woman was standing near the elevated podium of the judge. The courtroom was filled with the low hum of the usual chatter of the lawyers and the court staff. On the arrival of the judge, people stood up and there was silence. When everybody got settled, the old lady was still standing facing the bench with folded hands. The judge asked in Punjabi: 'Yes *mata ji* what do you want?' She answered: 'I want justice, please do justice in my case.' The judge promptly replied with a chuckle: 'There is no justice here, there are only decisions.'[1] The judgment of the Supreme Court of India in *M Siddiq (D) Thr Lrs vs Mahant Suresh Das and Others* (hereinafter 'the *Ayodhya Case*')[2] is one such judgment where a definitive decision was made on a very long-standing religious controversy. But it can hardly be said that the Court delivered justice.

The *Ayodhya Case* dealt with a property dispute broadly between Hindu religious organisations and Muslim religious organisations.[3] The dispute involved a piece of land in the city of Ayodhya (now district Faizabad in the state of Uttar Pradesh) in northern India, on which stood the Babri Mosque until it was destroyed by a well-coordinated far-right Hindu mob[4] on 6 December 1992. Hindu organisations claim that Babri Mosque

[1] Ronald Dworkin narrates a similar story which includes Justice Oliver Wendell Holmes and a young lawyer, Learned Hand, who later became a highly respected judge. See R Dworkin, *Justice in Robes* (Harvard University Press, 2008) 1.

[2] *M Siddiq (D) Thr Lrs* v *Mahant Suresh Das and Others*, AIR (2019) SC 1420, https://www.sci.gov.in/pdf/JUD_2.pdf.

[3] The Supreme Court of India loosely used the terms 'Hindus' and 'Muslims' in its judgment to refer to the two parties. But this is not accurate. 'Hindus' in the judgment certainly do not represent all citizens of India following the Hindu religion and the same is true of the usage of the term 'Muslims'.

[4] A political movement, known as Rath Yatra, to build Ram Temple in the place of the Babri Mosque was led by Lal Krishna Advani, the then-leader of a major Indian political party, the Bhartiya Janata Party, in

was built in 1528 by an Irani-Uzbeki invader, Babur, the first Mughal emperor, after destroying a Temple dedicated to the Hindu deity Lord Ram. The Sunni Waqf Board[5] denied this and claimed that the Mosque was built by Mir Baqi, a General of Babur and later Subedar (Governor) of Awadh, on vacant land. The origins of the Ayodhya litigation thus reach back not only into the British colonial era, but also much earlier into the ancient and medieval history of India.

This chapter, which contains four subsequent sections, critiques the final judgment of the Supreme Court of India in the *Ayodhya Case*. Section II briefly sets out the long historical background of the litigation beginning in the British colonial era and concluding in the independent India era. Section III examines some significant inconsistencies in the Supreme Court's logic specifically pertaining to the law of evidence, property and the application of the burden of proof. Section IV highlights the political misuse of history by the Hindu and Muslim organisations according to their communal agendas throughout the period of this litigation. To fulfil these communal agendas, the Hindu organisations have distorted and exaggerated the wrongs committed against them in the medieval era, and the Muslim organisations have blatantly denied historical atrocities perpetually committed by the Muslim rulers on the communities practising other religions during the same period in history. This section also highlights the fact that the judgment is inconsistent with the established legal and constitutional principles of India to the extent that its use of the concepts of 'Justice, Equity and Good Conscience' fails to reflect the *Constitution*'s secular values. It concludes that the Supreme Court's decision concerning the title of the disputed land violated the basic common law principle that no person should benefit from their own wrong. Section V offers brief concluding reflections.

II. Chronology of the Litigation

The violent and passionate background of this dispute demonstrates the importance ascribed to the Babri Mosque in Ayodhya by both the Hindus and Muslims of the Indian subcontinent. Both the communities in this struggle derived their sentiments from history. The majority of the Hindu community believed that a foreign Islamic invasion not only led to the razing of the Temple of their major deity, but that it also replaced it with an Islamic mosque. On the other hand, India's modern Muslims had difficulty comprehending this fact, and they have denied that their ancestors had been responsible

1990. A number of extremist Hindu organisations such as the Rashtriya Swayamsevak Sangh (RSS), Hindu Mahasabha, Shiv Sena and Bajrang Dal were involved. On 6 December 1992, this movement culminated in the destruction of the Babri Mosque. Later on, this matter was handed over to the Central Bureau of Investigation, which imposed criminal charges on the leaders of these extremist Hindu organisations. Eventually, on 30 September, 2020, all the accused were acquitted. See https://www.thehindu.com/news/national/babri-masjid-demolition-case-a-timeline/article32732622.ece.

[5] The Waqf Board is a statutory body in India formed in 1954 in order to manage historical, religious and heritage Islamic buildings. In 1964, a Central Waqf Council was established by the Central Government of India to coordinate and manage state Waqf Boards. The Waqf Council and Boards come under the purview of the Central Government's Ministry of Minority Affairs. In this litigation, the Sunni Central Waqf Board was the main Muslim party which represented the Muslim community and claimed, on the grounds of continued possession, that the title of the entire disputed property should be in favour of Muslims.

for this destruction. This section recounts the events of this struggle, bloody and legal, between the two communities. It will help to contextualise the political and moral pressures under which the communities and the state institutions handled this dispute.

A. Communal Incidents and Litigation during the Colonial Period (1857–1947)

On 11 February 1856, the British East India Company annexed the princely state of Awadh.[6] In that year, riots broke out between the Hindus and Muslims over the right to worship in the Babri Mosque. The Hindu *bairaagis* (ascetics) claimed that they had the right to worship their deity, Lord Ram. To maintain the status quo, the British administration constructed a brick grill wall effectively bifurcating the mosque between an inner and an outer courtyard.[7] The inner courtyard contained the main structure of the Mosque managed by a *Muazzim* (manager of the Mosque). The outer courtyard of the Mosque was given to the Hindu devotees, who built a *chabutra* (a concrete platform) to worship their deity in this area.[8]

Subsequently, the Hindus and Sikhs tried to usurp the inner courtyard in various violent incidents. In November 1858, a group of 25 Sikhs (*Nihangs*)[9] captured the inner courtyard of the Mosque. They erected another *chabutra* in the three-domed structure main building of the Mosque. They installed an image of the Hindu deity Lord Ram, performed a Hindu ritual involving lighting of a fire (*Hawan*), erected a Sikh religious flag (*Nishan Sahib*) and wrote 'Ram' in charcoal on the Mosque walls.[10] When a complaint was filed by the *Muazzim* of the Mosque with the police against this incident, these Sikhs were evicted by force only after the magistrate's orders. Similarly, an application was filed by Mir Rajjib Ali on 5 November 1860 against another *Nihang* who built a *chabutra* and a *Kutir* (hut) inside an adjoining graveyard. The application stated that some *bairaagis* along with this *Nihang Singh* were creating a nuisance: that whenever *aazan* (Muslim prayer) was recited in the Mosque, the other party started blowing (*shankh*) conch shells.[11] Another complaint was filed by the Mosque authorities on 25 September 1866 against a person named Tulsidas, a Hindu *bairaagi*. He, along with other *bairaagis*, according to this complaint, built a *kothri* (small room) within the compound of the Mosque and the perception was that it would lead to a fresh round of violence between the devotees of both religions. Orders were made against Tulsidas by the Deputy Commissioner of Faizabad.[12]

These communal tussles also often led to frequent civil litigation. In August 1868, the Commissioner of Faizabad dismissed an appeal titled *Niyamat Ali and*

[6] Before the Mughals, Awadh had been part of many Hindu kingdoms and Muslim Sultanates. It was made part of the Mughal Empire by Humayun in 1555. Awadh formally became a princely state in 1818 until it was annexed by the British in 1856.

[7] *M Siddiq* (n 2) [46].

[8] ibid [683].

[9] Nihangs are the traditional Sikh warriors.

[10] *M Siddiq* (n 2) [46], [683].

[11] ibid [46], [684]–[685].

[12] ibid [686].

Mohd Shah v Gangadhar Shastri. The matter first appeared before the officiating Deputy Commissioner, where it was dismissed, followed by the same result before the Commissioner. It was alleged by the Mosque caretakers that one Gangadhar had encroached on the northwestern wall of the Mosque and that this was a deliberate encroachment by the Hindus.[13] In November 1873, some Hindu devotees installed an image of the deity on the *chabutra* in the outer courtyard of the Babri Mosque. Regarding this, an order was made by the office of the Deputy Commissioner in the case of *Mohd Asghar v Mahant Baldo Das*, which directed the removal of the installed image, but this was never complied with by the defendants.[14]

In April 1877, the Deputy Commissioner granted permission to the Hindu parties to open a new door in the outer northern wall of the disputed building for the devotees to use. An appeal was filed against this order by the caretaker of the Mosque. This appeal argued that matters relating to the Mosque must be handed over only to the Muslims. It referred to the orders in the previous dispute whereby the Deputy Commissioner ordered the Hindu parties to remove the image of the deity from the *chabutra* in the outer courtyard. And it argued that since Hindus legally did not have the right to install any image in the Mosque premises, therefore they also did not have any right to alter the wall of the Mosque. But this appeal was turned down by the Commissioner, who said that the decision to open a new door (*Singh Diwar*) was taken by the Deputy Commissioner himself in order to avoid any untoward incidents, especially during the Hindu holy days when there was a huge rush of devotees entering and exiting the outer courtyard.[15]

In November 1882, the caretaker of the Mosque instituted a new suit entitled *Mohd Asghar v Raghubir Das Mahant and Nirmohi Akhara* against the Hindu parties, claiming that the defendants should pay them rent as the *chabutra* was situated near the door of the Mosque and it was used daily by the defendants. This suit was dismissed by the Sub-judge of Faizabad.[16] Another complaint was brought up by the caretaker of the Mosque in November 1883 before the Assistant Commissioner. This time it was stated that the right to take care of the Mosque's entire building, including its repairs and paint, fell squarely on the Muslims. The complainant claimed that previously all these repairs to the Mosque had been performed by the Muslim party, but this time during the white-wash, it was obstructed by the Hindus, ie, Mahant Raghubar Dass. Consequently, the caretakers of the Mosque were allowed to carry on their own repairs and painting, and the Hindu party was restrained from carrying out any repairs on its own.[17]

Importantly, in 1885, Mahant Raghubar Das instituted a suit against the Secretary of the State for India seeking permission that he be allowed to build a temple covering the *chabutra* situated in the outer courtyard of the Babri Mosque. The sought relief was not allowed by the Sub-judge, who refused any construction of the Temple in order to maintain the status quo and to avoid any further communal incident. There were two appeals by the appellant; both were dismissed on the ground that maintaining the status

[13] ibid [687]–[688].
[14] ibid [689].
[15] ibid [46], [690].
[16] ibid [46], [693].
[17] ibid [694].

quo was important for the continuation of peace.[18] The decision in this particular suit was discussed later by the Supreme Court in some length. The next major communal riot took place in 1934during which the building of the Mosque itself was damaged. The Deputy Commissioner fined the Hindu *bairagis* in order to recover the cost of the damage done to the Mosque.[19]

B. Executive Bias in Independent India

On the night of 22–23 December 1949, a large group of Hindu devotees desecrated the Babri Mosque by installing idols of the Hindu deity Lord Ram in the main building of the Mosque.[20] This incident was said to show blatant executive bias as well as judicial 'bad faith'.[21] Kirpal Singh, the Superintendent of Police for the district of Faizabad, assessed the situation in Ayodhya. According to his estimation, there was an imminent danger to the Babri Mosque which could well lead to fresh communal clashes. He noted the presence of many Hindu devotees and *bairagis* preparing many *Hawan kunds* (a small ceremonial hole dug in the ground to light sacred fire) around the Mosque with the intention to surround the whole area and deny Muslims passage to the Mosque. He addressed a letter to KK Nayyar, the Deputy Commissioner of Faizabad, on 29 November 1949, which stated;

> I visited the premises of Babri mosque and the Janam Sthan in Ayodhya this evening … They have a proposal to construct a very big Havan Kund … Several thousand Hindus, Bairagis and Sadhus from outside will participate … The plan appears to be to surround the mosque in such a way that entry for the Muslims will be very difficult and ultimately they be forced to abandon the mosque. There is a strong rumour, that on puranmasi the Hindus will try to force entry into the mosque with object of installing a deity.[22]

Signalling the same on 10 December 1949, Waqf Inspector Mohammad Ibrahim submitted a report to the secretary of the Mosque stating that Hindus and Sikhs were preventing Muslims from performing *namaz* (Islamic prayer) in the Mosque.[23] But in response, KK Nayyar wrote back to the Home Secretary of the state of Uttar Pradesh downplaying the seriousness of the situation, in which he said:

> Muslims, mostly of the Faizabad have been exaggerating these happenings … This is an entirely false canard inspired apparently by a desire to prevent Hindus from securing in this area possession or rights of a larger character than have so far been enjoyed … As far as I have been able to understand the situation the Muslims of Ayodhya proper are far from agitated over this issue[24]

[18] ibid [46], [695]–[698].
[19] ibid [47], [699]–[701].
[20] Details of the events leading up to this incident are described in K Jha and D Jha, *Ayodhya: The Dark Night* (HarperCollins, 2012).
[21] A Bindal, 'Complete Justice'? Silences and Erasures in the Ayodhya Judgment' (2020) 11(1) *Journal of Indian Law and Society* 48.
[22] *M Siddiq* (n 2) [49].
[23] ibid [49].
[24] ibid [49].

After the idols were placed in the Mosque on 22–23 December 1949, the state government ordered their removal. But the Deputy Commissioner refused to execute these instructions, claiming that to do so would lead to loss of life. He also later claimed in a written reply to the Chief Secretary of the state of Uttar Pradesh that the incident of placing idols in the Mosque was 'unpredictable and irreversible'.[25] A police complaint was lodged by the Mosque authorities which mentioned that 50–60 people had broken the locks of the Mosque building and entered the main building in order to place the idols. Once the idols were placed, around 5,000 Hindu devotees gathered around the Mosque to worship their deity.[26] Thereafter, Additional City Magistrate Faizabad-cum-Ayodhya under section 145 of the *Indian Civil Procedure Code*[27] attached the disputed property via orders dated 29 December 1949. A receiver was appointed, who took charge of the management of the attached property.

After this incident of placing the idols in the Mosque and the disputed property being attached in 1949, subsequent decades saw many suits by both parties. On 16 January 1950, a suit was instituted (referred to as Suit 1 by the Supreme Court) by a Hindu devotee seeking a declaration that he be allowed to worship inside according to the rituals of his religion within the inner courtyard.[28] More importantly, even though the building was evidently a mosque and previous British administrations always took action to remove non-Islamic installations from the Mosque, an interim injunction was allowed by the Court in independent India that the idols should not be removed from the Mosque.

In December 1959, another Hindu party called Nirmohi Akhara, a sect of Hindu *bairaagis*, filed a suit (Suit 3) claiming the management of the disputed property.[29] Its claim was different from the previous Hindu claims and at times it clashed with the claims of other Hindu parties. Then on 18 December 1961, the Sunni Central Waqf Board and nine Muslim residents of Ayodhya filed a suit before the Civil Judge in Faizabad (Suit 4). They sought a declaration that the entire disputed property was a mosque, that it should be delivered back to the Muslims and that all the non-Islamic features erected within the Mosque, especially the idols, should be removed.[30] In July 1989, another important suit (Suit 5) was brought before the Civil Judge in Faizabad. This suit aimed to include the Deity (ie, Lord Ram himself) as the party to the dispute. And it also sought to include the 'Birth Place' of this deity as a party to this suit, which the Hindu parties now specifically claimed to be under the central dome of the Mosque. This claim had never been made before in any litigation instituted by the Hindu parties.[31] The Supreme Court discussed the jurisprudence of the juristic personality in detail in order to satisfy the claims made in this suit. The Court agreed that a deity is a juristic personality and thus can be a party to this legal dispute. It refused to accept 'Birth Place' as a juristic personality. For the Hindu parties, this was a particularly clever legal move as it allowed them to

[25] ibid.
[26] ibid [12], [49], [719]–[722].
[27] https://indiankanoon.org/doc/1405190.
[28] *M Siddiq* (n 2) [13].
[29] ibid [16], [217]–[307]. Suit 2, which had been filed in the interim, was later withdrawn: see [309].
[30] ibid [17], [599]–[787].
[31] ibid [20].

shift the claim towards the title of the entire property from previous limited claims on the outer courtyard and merely management rights.

Then, on 6 December 1992, after a long communal and divisive campaign led by a Hindu nationalist party, the Bhartiya Janata Party, a well-organised and coordinated mob destroyed the Babri Mosque. This led to widespread communal riots and thousands of deaths across the nation. In October 1994, the Allahabad High Court caused these disputes to start again after it struck down a provision of the *Ayodhya Acquisition Act 1993* in the case of *Dr M Ismail Faruqui v Union of India*.[32] The Constitution bench of the Allahabad High Court delivered its final verdict on this issue on 30 September 2010, which distributed the entire property equally to all the three parties. Against this decision, an appeal was heard before the Supreme Court of India, which delivered a final verdict on 9 November 2019.

III. Inconsistencies in Applying the Legal Concepts

In its final verdict, the Supreme Court of India quashed the Allahabad High Court's decision to divide the property between the three parties, ie, the Hindus, Muslims and Nirmohi Akhara. In May 2011, the Supreme Court of India issued a stay on the Allahabad High Court's orders. Justice RM Lodha clearly stated that: 'The decree of partition was not sought by the parties … How can a decree for partition be passed when none of the parties prayed for it?'[33] This judgment, which was also critiqued for being biased,[34] was overturned by the Supreme Court. The Supreme Court further critiqued the Allahabad High Court's logic in its final decree by saying: 'In assessing the correctness of the decree of the High Court, it must be noted at the outset that the High Court was not seized of a suit for partition.'[35] It also stated that 'the High Court has completely erred in granting relief which lay outside the ambit of pleadings and the cases set up by the plaintiffs in Suits 3, 4 and 5'.[36]

Consequently, after almost two decades of arguments, the Supreme Court of India delivered its final judgment in November 2019. It reversed the High Court's ruling and gave the entire disputed property to the Hindu party ie, the plaintiff in Suit 5. Before handing down its final decision, the Supreme Court of India tried to justify that this decision had nothing to do with faith, but was a product of the pure application of positive law, emphasising that;

> The court does not decide title on the basis of faith or belief but on the basis of evidence. The law provides us with parameters as clear and profound as ownership and possession. In deciding title to the disputed property, the court applies settled principles of evidence to adjudicate upon which party has established a claim to the immovable property.[37]

[32] *Dr M Ismail Faruqui v Union of India* (1994) 6 SCC 360.
[33] N Menon, 'The Ayodhya Judgment: What Next?' (2011) *Economic and Political Weekly* 81.
[34] 'The Verdict on Ayodhya' (2010) 45 (50) *Economic and Political Weekly*, various articles.
[35] *M Siddiq* (n 2) [791].
[36] ibid [793].
[37] ibid [796].

In the judgment, the Supreme Court made a focused attempt to convince the reader that faith and belief had nothing to do with this decision. But the Supreme Court's assertion that faith had not influenced this judgment becomes doubtful after observing the manner in which an Addenda was added to this judgment.[38] In spite of these blatant signs, the Supreme Court announced:

> On the balance of probabilities, there is a clear evidence to indicate that the worship by the Hindus in the outer courtyard continued unimpeded in spite of the setting up of a grill brick wall in 1857. Their possession of the outer courtyard stands established together with the incidents attaching to their control over it.
>
> As regards the inner courtyard, there is evidence on a preponderance of probabilities to establish worship by the Hindus prior to the annexation of Oudh by the British in 1857. The Muslims have offered no evidence to indicate that they were in exclusive possession of the inner structure prior to 1857 since the date of the construction in the sixteenth century.[39]

It must be noted that the disputed property's title was impossible to prove, given the unique circumstances of this case. Muslim parties argued that the Mosque was built in 1528 AD by Babur. The Hindu parties argued that there was a temple dedicated to Lord Ram built by the great king of the Gupta dynasty, Chandragupta II Vikramaditya,[40] who reigned from 375 to 414 AD[41] and is known to have ruled the area bordering Afghanistan to the Bay of Bengal.[42] This temple, the Hindu parties claimed, was razed by Babur and the Islamic mosque was erected using the material of the destroyed temple. In the absence of any possible 'title deed' from these previous ancient and medieval regimes, the title of this disputed property, according to the Supreme Court of India, was solely decided in accordance with the various concepts and doctrines of possession of immovable property developed within the common law legal system. In this regard, the Supreme Court opined: 'The claim to title will have to be judged from the perspective of long and continued possession.'[43]

A. The Physical Structure of the Mosque and Proof of *Namaz*

As far as the question of exclusive possession by the Muslims, recitation of the *namaz* (Islamic prayer) and the existence of the physical structure of the Mosque is concerned, the Supreme Court's reasoning seems questionable. In an interview, Faizal Mustafa, Vice Chancellor of NALSAR University of Law, said that the Supreme Court's finding that there was no proof of *namaz* in the Babri Mosque before the annexation of Oudh was 'laughable'.[44] The parties were supposed to prove their ownership by demonstrating

[38] J Sebastian and F Rahman, 'The Babri Masjid Judgment and the Sound of Silence' *The Wire* (6 December 2019), https://thewire.in/law/the-babri-masjid-judgment-and-the-sound-of-silence.

[39] *M Siddiq* (n 2) [797]–[798].

[40] ibid [39], [40], [67], [272].

[41] See R Mookerji, *The Gupta Empire* (Motilal Banarsidas, 2007).

[42] G Dwivedi, 'The Western Limits of Gupta Empire' (1973) 34 *Proceedings of the Indian History Congress* 76; see also A Lal, 'Chandragupta-II', https://www.ancient.eu/Chandragupta_II.

[43] *M Siddiq* (n 2) [772].

[44] https://thewire.in/law/watch-parts-of-ayodhya-judgment-laughable-different-standards-of-proof-unfair.

that they had uncontested exclusive possession of the premises. Given that there was a historic mosque on the site, it is arguable that this issue should have been decided in favour of the Muslim party.

The Supreme Court rejected the argument made by Nirmohi Akhara in Suit 3 that there was never a mosque. In fact, the Court agreed that there was a mosque. While discussing the pleadings in the suit initiated by the Sunni Waqf Board, it categorically stated: 'In assessing the title of the Muslims, the physical structure of the mosque is one fact to be taken into consideration.'[45] Moreover in a separate section – ie, 'Judicial review and characteristics of a mosque in Islamic law'[46] – the Supreme Court dealt with the submissions made by the Hindu party in Suit 5, whereby it dismissed the arguments that the structure of the Babri Mosque 'lacked the essential features of a valid mosque under Islamic jurisprudence'.[47] There were many averments made by the Hindu party in order to deny the Babri Mosque the status of being a mosque. Some of the arguments were that the building was surrounded by a graveyard from three sides, the building did not have *minerettes* (towers), there was no tomb, the architectural structure did not resemble the Turkish style, there were engravings of a non-Islamic nature in the building and there was no place for storage of water for *vazoo* (an Islamic tradition of washing the hands, face and feet before entering the mosque).[48] After listening to all these arguments, the Supreme Court refused to take part in any exegesis of Islamic religious texts and while categorically rejecting this argument, it opined: 'The true test is whether those who believe and worship have faith in the religious efficacy of the place where they pray. The belief and faith of the worshipper in offering *namaz* at a place which is for the worshipper a mosque cannot be challenged.'[49]

Now in this scenario, if the Supreme Court agreed that the building was a mosque, then ordinarily this means that it is a place where *namaz* is performed, just as a Hindu temple presupposes the practice of *pooja* (a form of Hindu prayer) and Hindu rituals. But, on the contrary, the Supreme Court asked for further proof of *namaz*. It is a very strange situation where the Court agrees that there is a mosque, but then goes on to demand the proof of *namaz* recital in the mosque from the time of its construction to 1857. The Court could have taken judicial notice of the self-evident fact that *namaz* is always offered in the mosque. A mosque is a mosque because primarily it is a place where *namaz* is performed. All of the books, gazettes and relevant literature mention it as a mosque. If the existence of the physical structure of the mosque cannot be denied, then it must lead to the logical conclusion that *namaz* was being offered there. It would have been a different issue if any party had averred that there was a derelict physical structure of some sort and that it stood abandoned. In this scenario, it would have been logical to demand proof of *namaz*. But none of the parties argued that the structure known as the Babri Mosque was ever dilapidated. Hence, if that building was not dilapidated and it had been colloquially known and referred as a functional mosque throughout its existence, then this means that *namaz* was being performed.

[45] *M Siddiq* (n 2) [772].
[46] ibid [69]–[77].
[47] ibid [69].
[48] ibid [71].
[49] ibid [77].

Therefore, the Supreme Court should have taken note of this self-evident fact of *namaz* being performed in a functional mosque. This is supported by the relevant literature under section 57(13) of the *Indian Evidence Act 1872*. The Supreme Court did not take note of this. Though it discussed section 57 of the *Evidence Act 1872*, this was only in the context of the evidentiary value of the travelogues and gazetteers. It concluded that it read them with caution as these documents were not conclusive as far as the question of the title of the disputed property was concerned.[50]

This technique of demanding the proof of the facts which can be logically deduced or are self-evident or are already proven or accepted is not new for the Supreme Court of India. For example, in another major case[51] involving reservation (quotas) for the weaker section of society, the Supreme Court demanded proof from the state to show that Scheduled Castes and Scheduled Tribes (formerly known as untouchable castes) are actually socioeconomically disadvantaged. The fact that this was a self-evident fact and had already been accepted by a much larger bench of the Supreme Court of India[52] and by the Parliament[53] did not concern the judges. This technique of denying the very fundamental empirical facts imposes an unreasonable burden on the party at the receiving end of this demand. In the case of *M Nagraj*,[54] it was the Scheduled Castes and Scheduled Tribes – in this judgment, the Muslim party – that were at the receiving end.

In yet another subsection of the judgment entitled 'Proof of *Namaz*',[55] the Supreme Court entertained the statements of the witnesses who deposed on the behalf of the Sunni Waqf Board in Suit 4. After discussing the statements of some 12 witnesses, the Court concluded: 'Assessing the statements it cannot be concluded that *namaz* was not being offered at all at the disputed property … There is evidence on record to hold that Muslims offered Friday *namaz* at the Mosque and had not completely lost access to or abandoned the disputed property.'[56] This begs another question – if in colonial times there were *Muazzims* appointed and there had been recitation of *namaz* until the property was attached in 1949, then should not the burden of proof be imposed on the Hindu parties to prove that there was no *namaz* before 1857?

As far as the standard of proof was concerned, the Supreme Court wrote: 'The court in a civil trial applies a standard of proof governed by a preponderance of probabilities. This standard is also described sometimes as a balance of probability.'[57] Then in a brief discussion, the Court explained the different steps taken in order to systematically apply this doctrine. First, the Court explained, there can be 'different degrees of probabilities'[58] and 'the degree depends on that subject matter'.[59] Quoting from *NG Dastane v S Dastane*,[60]

[50] ibid [594].
[51] *M Nagraj v Union of India*, AIR (2007) SC 71.
[52] *Indra Sawhney v Union of India*, AIR (1991) SC 477.
[53] These facts were presented to the Parliament of India in the Mandal Commission Report, which was accepted.
[54] This judgment was challenged before the Supreme Court. But the condition to produce quantifiable data to prove backwardness of the Scheduled Castes and Scheduled Tribes remains. See *Jarnail Singh v Lacchmi Narayain* (2018) 10 SCC 396.
[55] *M Siddiq* (n 2) [704]–[718].
[56] ibid [718].
[57] ibid [506].
[58] ibid [506].
[59] ibid.
[60] *NG Dastane v S Dastane* (1975) 2 SCC 326.

it explained that in applying this balance of probabilities in civil matters, the initial step is to ascertain the potential probabilities and then to weigh them according to the facts and circumstances of the given case. It is important to discard the impossible probabilities at once and then to discard those which are less likely to be true. In the end, we are left with the probability which is most likely to be true. Through this process, the preponderance of a particular probability is decided.

Now if this process is applied on the issue discussed above – ie, to demonstrate the proof of *namaz* in the Mosque – then it is submitted that the balance of probabilities falls in favour of the Muslim party. If there was a mosque before 1857, which was not abandoned, then there was most *probably* the recital of *namaz* as well. It can reasonably be argued, after balancing the probabilities in the given circumstances, that it is much more *probable* than not that *namaz* was recited in the Babri Mosque because it was identified as a mosque and not as an abandoned building. More importantly, following this logic, the burden of proof should have been imposed on the Hindu parties to prove that there was no recitation of *namaz* in the Babri Mosque before 1857 rather than demanding the Muslim party to prove whether there was recitation of *namaz*.

B. The Burden of Proof and Possessory Title

One of the most glaring inconsistencies in this judgment was the inconsistent application of the burden of proof between the parties. Regarding this, Amit Bindal noted: 'The Muslim community was asked to furnish proof of "exclusive possession" … However, one cannot find a similar requirement expected from the other side.'[61] In many scholarly works and especially editorials, this aspect of the burden of proof is amply critiqued. But what was the Supreme Court's logic for not shifting the burden of proof on to the Hindu parties? The Supreme Court discussed its reasoning for not doing so in a section entitled 'Analysis of evidence in Suit 4'.[62] It summarised the Waqf Board's argument, stating that Muslim parties built their argument on the basis of their claim to possession of the entire property. The Muslim party's argument was that Muslims have always been in possession of the inner and outer courtyards and, hence, this possession created title in the favour of the Muslims. If the Hindu parties wanted to challenge the title of the Muslim parties, then the burden of proof should have been on the Hindu parties, as is provided in the section 110 of the *Evidence Act 1872*, which says:

> *Section 110 Burden of proof as to ownership* When the question is whether any person is owner of anything of which he is shown to be in possession, the burden of proving that he is not the owner is on the person who affirms that he is not the owner.

Clearly, according to this provision, if the Hindu parties are claiming that title should not be given to the Muslim parties, then the burden is on them. The Supreme Court first agreed that if there is continuous possession, then it will create a presumption that title belongs to the party which is in possession and that 'Section 110 is based on the

[61] Bindal (n 21).
[62] *M Siddiq* (n 2) [774]–[781].

principle that title follows possession'.[63] But then the Supreme Court observed a problem in this argument. In this particular scenario, it opined that:

> In assessing this limb of the submission on the applicability of Section 110 the crucial test is whether the disputed site represents 'anything of which' the Muslim parties are 'shown to be in possession'. Unless the 'shown to be in possession' requirement is fulfilled, the presumption would not arise and there would be no question of placing the burden of establishing that the plaintiffs in Suit 4 are not the owners on the contesting Hindu parties.[64]

This means that the precondition of substituting the burden of proof on Hindu parties was for the Muslims to show that they were in possession of the whole property, which, according to the Supreme Court, they were not. Therefore, the burden could not be shifted onto the Hindu parties. And before discussing the application of burden of proof, the Court had already held that 'it cannot be said that Muslims have been able to establish their possessory title to the disputed site as a composite whole'.[65]

But how did the Supreme Court reach the conclusion that Muslims were not in the possession of a historic mosque? If they were not, then who was? Especially when the Supreme Court agreed that the building had never been abandoned? Unfortunately, the answer to these questions lies in the fact that the Supreme Court throughout the judgment discussed the incidents concerning this disputed property in a very selective and a narrow way. This helped it to build a sequence of logic from which it ultimately derived the conclusion that Muslims were not in possession of a historic mosque.

To illustrate this, the Supreme Court on multiple occasions mentioned the trespasses of Sikhs and Hindus as evidence of the contested possession of the inner courtyard. The Court used these incidents to strike down the Muslim argument of having a continuous possession of not only the whole property, but even of the inner courtyard, ie, main building of the Mosque. According to the Court, there was a 'contest' for possession of the inner courtyard, but 'insofar as the outer courtyard is concerned, the Hindus were in settled possession',[66] and they were in settled possession of the outer courtyard because their right 'was not merely in the nature of a prescriptive right to enter for the purpose of worship'.[67] Rather, according to the Court, the Hindus were exclusively present there, the administration allowed them to open a new door in 1877 and, most importantly, there was an 'absence of any evidence to indicate that the Muslims had asserted any right of possession or occupation over the area of the disputed property beyond the railing'.[68] This claim made by the Court that the Hindus were in settled possession of the outer courtyard is a misrepresentation of the facts and the Court's logic is simply not correct. This is the best example of a selective picking of the facts.

First, the Supreme Court condoned the trespasses of the Sikhs and Hindus in the inner courtyard of the Mosque as a legitimate assertion of legal right, then it took note of the fact that a new door was allowed by the administration in the outer courtyard. This was done in 1877, but that in itself was no assertion of any substantial legal right in

[63] ibid [784].
[64] ibid [785].
[65] ibid [781].
[66] ibid [786].
[67] ibid [720].
[68] ibid.

favour of the Hindus, as it was merely an administrative decision to create ease of access for the Hindu devotees. On the other hand, the Court ignored the fact that against this decision, the Muslim party filed an appeal on the ground that the Mosque basically belonged to the Muslims, even the outer courtyard. Is this appeal not a legitimate expression of the Muslims in contesting that they owned even the outer courtyard? Similarly, in 1873, the Muslims filed an appeal because the Hindus installed an image of the deity on the *chabutra* in the outer courtyard, which was decided in favour of the Muslims. This was a clear assertion of Muslim rights over the outer courtyard. Then in 1882, Muslims instituted another suit demanding rent from the Hindu parties as the *chabutra* was situated in the outer courtyard. One only asks for rent if one considers the property one's own. Hence, this is another example of the Muslims' contest for the entire Babri Mosque premises, including the outer courtyard. But the Supreme Court ignored this too and held that there was no assertion of rights over the outer courtyard by the Muslims; it seems that only trespass and violence by the Sikhs and Hindus were considered to be assertions of rights by the Court.

IV. Interpretation of History and the Constitution

Misrepresenting historical facts to fulfil political aims is an ancient technique. This has been perfected over the past few centuries by political groups in order to establish a basis for their ideologies and justify their political aims. Evidently, from the Confederacy's propaganda in the American Civil War to Nazi ideology's usage of 'historical facts' of its 'racial superiority', these historical misrepresentations have proved themselves to be a very effective tool in polarising society. For India, this is very evident in the case of the Ayodhya dispute. The one-sided interpretation of history by both the Hindus and the Muslims resulted in cultural and religious violence spanning three centuries. Moreover, the tragedy here is that along with right-wing historians, even the majority of the much-respected progressive historians of the country professing professional neutrality have played a role of intellectual partisans. And with this judgment the Supreme Court has now joined their ranks.

A. The Archaeological Report

An Archaeological Report concerning whether there was a Hindu temple below the Babri Mosque was submitted before the Allahabad High Court by the Archaeological Survey of India (ASI). The High Court discussed and accepted its conclusions. Then in its judgment, the Supreme Court discussed the Archaeological Report in detail along with the objections to its conclusions and the oral evidence.[69] Interestingly, the Hindu parties claim that one of the findings of the ASI corroborates their historical claim: that Muslim invaders destroyed the Hindu Ram Temple and then used the temple's material to construct the Mosque over it. And sure enough, in the process of this survey, the

[69] ibid [447]–[505].

report classified the layers of the dig into successive historical epochs and found that the existing structure of the Mosque does not stand on its own foundations, but on the foundation of a previously existing structure:

> Subsequently, during the early medieval period (eleventh–twelfth century AD) … a huge structure … was constructed which seems to have been short lived … On the remains of the above structure was constructed a massive structure with at least three structural phases and three successive floors attached with it … providing sufficient evidence of a construction of public usage which remained under existence for a long time during period VII (medieval-Sultanate level-twelfth to sixteenth century A.D.) It was over the top of this construction during the early sixteenth century [that] the disputed structure was constructed directly resting over it. There is sufficient proof of existence of a massive and monumental structure … Just below the disputed structure.[70]

On the objection that the structure below the Mosque may not necessarily be a Hindu temple, the ASI gave its final clarification:

> Now, viewing in totality and taking into account the archaeological evidence of a massive structure just below the disputed structure and evidence of continuity in structural phases from the tenth century onwards up to the construction of the disputed structure along with the yield of stone and decorated bricks as well as mutilated sculpture of divine couple and carved architectural members including foliage patters, *amalaka, kapotapali* doorjamb with [a] semi-circular pilaster, broken octagonal shaft of black schist pillar, lotus motif, circular shrine having *pranala* (waterchute) in the north, fifty pillar bases in association of the huge structure, are indicative of remains which are distinctive features found associated with the temples of north India.[71]

This passage makes clear that the structure under the Mosque was a Hindu temple. The ASI made sure to give its opinion and amply discuss the various factors in reaching this conclusion. In spite of this clear opinion, there were various objections to this report which the Supreme Court dealt with and, while agreeing with the conclusions of the Allahabad High Court, dismissed them one by one, like the objection to the stratigraphy and periodisation in the report.[72] The ASI based its argument on the existence of no fewer than 50 pillar bases, giving rise to its opinion that there was a massive structure that had been in public use below the disputed Mosque structure. This was also challenged[73] and, after some discussion, the Supreme Court accepted the conclusion of the ASI.[74] In the face of a major objection that the ASI's report 'is not direct evidence of a fact and is inherently speculative and inconclusive',[75] the Court opined: 'The report constitutes the opinion of an expert. Expert opinion has to be sieved and evaluated by the court and cannot be conclusive in and of itself.'[76]

It is pertinent to mention here a costly mistake committed by the Sunni Waqf Board. The Supreme Court noted that in the original pleadings filed by the Board, it denied

[70] ibid [455].
[71] ibid [455].
[72] ibid [463]–[465].
[73] ibid [466].
[74] ibid [500].
[75] ibid [486].
[76] ibid [487].

that there was any structure present beneath the Mosque and categorically stated that the Mosque was built on a vacant piece of land. But in the light of the findings of the ASI, especially when a *pranala* (waterchute) was found, which according to the ASI indicates the existence of a Shiva shrine,[77] the Board took a u-turn in its pleadings and argued that there was an *Idgah* (an open space used for prayer on special occasions) or a *kanati Masjid* (a 'canopy' mosque, an informal structure). Against this, the Supreme Court, after discussing the measurements of this structure and the possibility of it being an Islamic structure, concluded: 'The *Idgah* defence was hence an afterthought, quite contrary to the pleadings of the Sunni Central Waqf Board. The defence was an attempt to gloss over the initial case that the Mosque was built over vacant land. The underlying structure was not of an Islamic origin.'[78] In a civil dispute, if and when a party makes an absolutely contradictory claim against its original argument without any reasonable evidence, there is a presumption of *malafide* intention against that party. This was a wrong decision by the Waqf Board. Property trials are notorious in India for the reason that one cannot go beyond the written pleadings and cannot make an opposite claim without giving credible reasons for doing so.

There was another important objection raised by the Waqf Board, which was that even if there is a temple beneath the Mosque, there is no proof that such a temple was demolished by Babur or anyone else.[79] In fact, the ASI was silent on the issue of whether the temple was destroyed by natural forces or by any human agency. Both Courts – ie, the Allahabad High Court and the Supreme Court of India – agreed that the ASI had not directly commented on this point. Yet, the High Court derived its conclusion based on the historical circumstances, which was later on endorsed by the Supreme Court:

> Sufficient indication has been given by ASI that the building did not have its own foundations but it was raised on the existing walls. If a building would not have been existing before [the] construction of the subsequent building, the builder might not have been able to use [the] foundation of the erstwhile building without knowing its strength and capacity of bearing the load of [the[new structure.[80]

This implies that the existing structure of Babri Mosque was standing on the foundation of some previous structure that was not its own, and that the previous structure, in the opinion of the ASI, was a North Indian Hindu temple. According to the Allahabad High Court's conclusion, the person who built the Babri Mosque on the foundations of the previously existing structure knew what kind of weight this foundation could support. Observing the conclusions of the ASI objectively, there should be no reason for any academic or expert to disagree with them, unless there is another equally credible report that reaches different conclusions. Such a report was never presented to any court and the Sunni Waqf Board also did not press any argument of *malafide* intention on the part of the ASI.[81]

In the end, after a full discussion of the report, the Supreme Court specifically put forward the question of 'whether a determination of title can rest on the basis of the ASI

[77] ibid [454].
[78] ibid [499].
[79] ibid [510]–[512].
[80] ibid [510].
[81] ibid [505].

findings as they stand'.[82] Later on, it declared that the decision about the title was made completely in accordance with positive law, not history or politics: 'The mere existence of a structure underneath the disputed property cannot lead to a legally enforceable claim to title today'.[83] Therefore: 'The law must stand apart from political contestations over history and religion … In deciding title to the disputed property, the court applies settled principles of evidence'.[84]

So if the title of this disputed property was not decided on the basis of this report, then what is its importance? In fact, this report and the various politically and communally motivated narratives of history relating to the Ayodhya dispute played a powerful role in polarising modern Indian society along religious lines. This report gripped the imagination of the general population who have been emotionally invested in this dispute for decades. People have not only misunderstood and misinterpreted this report, but they have also certainly misused it by spinning the historical facts in accordance with their communal loyalty or political opinion.

B. Politics Through History

Exaggeration and denial are two aspects in the interpretation of historical facts that are used as tools in order to form the basis of an ideology or a worldview by a community. In plural societies, every community builds its own worldview of how well it has done in history, whether it has been a victim of oppression, external aggression or systematic exclusion from power and privilege. Such communities might also take pride, nostalgically, in the fact that their community was very successful in the past: that they were great warriors or conquerors etc. In any case, it is highly likely that the communities build a very linear and simplistic view of history about themselves, often building an exaggerated historical narrative of the greatness of their past and even exaggerating the oppressions they suffered at the hands of their fellow communities or external forces. The partisan role that the Indian historians played in the Ayodhya dispute is a classic example of the exaggeration of historical facts by one party and the blatant denial by the other. It is because of this narrow-minded and parochial attitude of the people, political parties and even academics that for far too long, modern Indian society has remained polarised and hence was not able to resolve this conflict through dialogue.

The categorical denials by the Muslims of countless religious massacres of the Hindus and Sikhs over centuries of Muslim rule helped Hindu extremist elements to build a grand narrative of oppression, which in turn is often exaggerated. The sad part is that the progressive and left-leaning historians, who should have followed an approach based on facts, indirectly allowed themselves to be guided by their ideological convictions in these historical debates.[85] This helped the extremist groups (especially Hindu

[82] ibid [512].

[83] ibid [648].

[84] ibid [795]–[796].

[85] Another instance of an academic conflict with powerful cultural repercussions in India is the debate around the Aryan invasion theory, where historians have taken sides in accordance with their political inclinations. The dispute concerns whether the ancient Vedic culture was introduced to India by 'Aryan' people who invaded or migrated to India from Central Asia, or whether the Vedic culture originated in India and there was no Aryan invasion.

right-wing groups) to propagate the idea that the majority of progressive historians and academics are biased, and that they are determined only to glorify Muslim rule while hiding and justifying their terrible oppressive religious persecutions. One of the recent examples that seems to justify this Hindu claim is the work of the American historian Audrey Truschke on the Mughal Emperor Aurangzeb,[86] in which she has tried to absolve the emperor of his religious bigotry and extreme tyranny towards the Hindus and Sikhs. The overall result of such intellectual attitudes towards history is that it has helped Hindu and Muslim extremists to weave a very complex web of false historical and cultural narratives that only serves their communal agendas.

This politics of history is further reflected in the so-called 'Historian's Report'[87] during the proceedings of the Ayodhya dispute before the Allahabad High Court. This report was submitted by four prominent historians of India as a reply against the claims made by one of the Hindu parties in the litigation. It categorically denied all the claims made by the Hindu party, including that there never was any temple in place before the Mosque. The Supreme Court dismissed the claims made by this report, citing the fact that it was submitted before the final result of the Archaeological Report. In a separate part of the judgment called the Addenda, one member of the Supreme Court discussed the Historian's Report in some detail. The last 34 pages of the *Ayodhya* judgment are termed as Addenda. It is not clear in what capacity this so-called Addenda is part of the judgment. The numbering of paragraphs restarts and yet it is attached to the main judgment. It is also not known who the author of this part of the judgment is. It is basically an exegesis of the Hindu scriptures.

The Addenda asserted that, while this report is submitted by the most prominent historians of the country, its arguments are based on conspicuously false historical facts. For example, a very well-known early medieval (eighth-century) Hindu text called *Sakanda Purana* was claimed by these historians to be a product of the eighteenth century.[88] Yet, in fact, historian VA Smith says that the existence of *Sakanda Purana* can be easily situated 'as early a date as the middle of the seventh century … on palaeographical grounds'.[89] This was clearly a politically motivated claim, since the Hindu party was relying on this text to prove the existence of an ancient temple where the Mosque now stood. So instead of engaging in a fact-based academic debate, the historians' report flat out denied the 1,000 years of existence of a major Hindu religious text. Such blatant denials can easily be interpreted as an attack on religious and cultural identity by the concerned community. The Supreme Court noted that this report is also a reply in a property dispute and it is expected that a party submitting a reply will deny the arguments of the opposite party. But this was neither any common property dispute, nor were the party submitting reply laymen – they were academics of the highest reputation. And it was reasonable to believe that this Historian's Report would potentially create political and cultural reverberations across society as this 'expert opinion' would be used by all the religious groups involved in the dispute.

[86] A Truschke, *Aurangzeb* (Stanford University Press, 2017).
[87] *M Siddiq* (n 2) [595]–[598].
[88] ibid Addenda [54].
[89] VA Smith, *Early History of India* (Oxford University Press, 1908) 20.

Similarly, when one reads the Addenda attached to the judgment, one cannot but marvel at the eagerness of the judicial author to discuss the Hindu religious texts. The Addenda uses the Sanskrit verses written in religious texts like *Ayodhya Mahatmya* to identify the *ashrams* (Hindu monasteries) of great Sages of ancient India, like *Lomasa* and *Vashishtha*. And through those verses, it tries to identify the location of Lord Ram's birthplace.[90] With all its mammoth effort in producing an exegesis of many Hindu religious texts and proving that the Babri Mosque was the birthplace of Lord Ram, the Addenda inadvertently gave us the clue of its selective interpretation of the history. It relies upon and uses at least three verses of another medieval Hindu text called *Ramcharitmanas* in order to support its claim of proving the birthplace of the deity. The author presented this text as an authority which is 'revered, read and respected by Hindus, which has acquired the status of an Epic in Hindu faith'.[91] But, apparently, the same text also makes extreme casteist claims: 'Venerate a Brahmin even if he is devoid of all virtue, but not a Shudra even if he is packed with virtue and knowledge'[92] ('Shudra' is the term used for the formerly untouchable castes). This in itself, among many other things, questions the efficacy of any such religious text to be used for legal purposes in the Supreme Court. And that is why the Court as a secular institution must be careful in terms of the sources it relies upon, especially when interpreting complex religious texts. The rhyme and reason of the entire Addenda is not explained, and, even worse, it is not known who wrote this part of the judgment. Is it to be interpreted as just an 'extra something' attached to the judgment? Or perhaps it is an insight into the deep religious convictions of the bench who seemed to be quite convinced, on the basis of religious texts, not law, that the birthplace of Lord Ram was directly under the Mosque!

So in popular culture and politics, especially concerning the Ayodhya controversy, the historical facts have always been spun. On the one hand, Muslim groups have tried to deny or at least gloss over the historical atrocities and religious persecutions committed during centuries of Muslim rule over people of other faiths. Similarly, Hindu groups never acknowledge the countless murders of Bodhhi monks and the destruction of Buddhist temples by the Hindu kings after the disintegration of the Maurya Empire.[93] However, they are quick to deny so many cultural, religious, literary, artistic and economic contributions made by Turkic, Persian and Arabic rule to Indian culture. Both parties deny or exaggerate the historical facts in accordance with their agenda to support their communal narratives. And unfortunately among Indian intellectuals, there is a sharp divide on these issues of history. Apparently, external aggression or internal oppression is not taken as a universal principle to critique a historical era or a particular regime. Rather, according to a given political loyalty or ideological leaning, historians choose their favourite oppressors to defend or critique. The politics of history relating to the Ayodhya dispute clearly reflects the lack of maturity in society at large and the lack of civilisational character in the middle class, and it has exposed some politically motivated stands taken by academics.

[90] *M Siddiq* (n 2) Addenda [46]–[50].

[91] ibid Addenda [73].

[92] *Mandal Commission Report*, 1980, vols 1 and 2, ch IV, 16.

[93] Smith (n 89) 321–22; DN Jha, *Against the Grain: Notes on Identity, Intolerance and History* (Manohar Publishers & Distributors, 2019); U Singh, *Political Violence in Ancient India* (Harvard University Press, 2017).

C. The Absence of Secularism from 'Justice, Equity and Good Conscience'

In giving relief, the Supreme Court of India granted the entire disputed property to the Hindus on the basis that 'on [the] balance of probabilities, the evidence in respect of the possessory claim of the Hindus to the composite whole of the disputed property stands on the better footing than the evidence adduced by the Muslims'.[94] Also for the Muslims, it announced: 'Suit 4 must also be partly decreed by directing the allotment of alternate land to the Muslims.'[95] Using the wide discretionary powers granted to the Supreme Court in Article 142 of the *Constitution of India*, it declared: 'Muslims were dispossessed upon the desecration of the mosque … which was ultimately destroyed … There was no abandonment of the mosque by the Muslims.'[96] Therefore, as partial relief to the Sunni Waqf Board, it said that 'we direct that land admeasuring 5 acres be allotted to the Sunni Central Waqf Board'.[97]

But the main constitutional issue, in spite of all the history, civil procedure and property law discussed, is whether this decision amounts to justice. In particular, when it has been pointed out that if the physical structure of the Mosque was not illegally destroyed, could the Supreme Court have directed the razing of the Babri Mosque in order to grant the land to the Hindus? And on what basis did the Supreme Court grant the compensation of alternate land to the Muslims? Why did it not order the restoration of the Mosque on the same land and grant alternate land to the Hindus?

We will not find any explanation for these questions in the text of the judgment. The Supreme Court dealt with some issues of justice and secularism, but merely as a formality. In a subsection entitled 'Justice, Equity and Good Conscience',[98] the Supreme Court discussed the evolution of the concept of equity, its applicability in India, and the inherent requirement of equity in interpreting Article 142 of the *Constitution of India*. This subsection of the judgment is basically a discussion of how to interpret statutes. There were some obvious conclusions; the Supreme Court at one point even cited Ronald Dworkin's concept of 'Fit & Justification'.[99] But the Court did not go into any analysis of what secularism means in the context of Indian society and history. It also never discussed how the principle of secularism should be manifested in this decision, whose proceedings were presented as a property dispute. The fact is that this was one of the most defining moments for Indian secularism culturally, politically and constitutionally. It is argued in this chapter that this case inherently dealt with the constitutional interpretation of secularism, yet the Supreme Court never entered into any meaningful discussion to define or apply the principle of secularism in the circumstances of the case. We must acknowledge that the Court did enlighten us with many statements affirming the plurality of Indian society and the secular character of the *Constitution*.

[94] *M Siddiq* (n 2) [800].
[95] ibid [800].
[96] ibid.
[97] ibid [801].
[98] ibid [653]–[676].
[99] ibid [676].

However, it never applied secularism as a principle in exercising its discretion under Article 142 of the *Constitution*.

In Indian constitutional jurisprudence, all the notions of justice and equity are to be interpreted through the prism of the preambular values.[100] The *Indian Constitution* is much more explicit in asserting its fundamental political values through a constitutional doctrine called the Basic Structure Doctrine.[101] This doctrine, along with Part IV of the *Constitution* (*Directive Principles of State Policy*),[102] very clearly provides political and moral objectives for every interpretative exercise to be conducted by any court of law in India. In the case of *Keshavnanda Bharti*, the Supreme Court decreed that the values enshrined in the Preamble to the *Constitution* cannot be amended because these values are key to the very identity of the modern Republic of India, and secularism, as a value, is embedded in the Preamble. Therefore, in the circumstances of the present case, justice, equity and good conscience could not have been anything other than an expression of the principle of secularism, which the Court left undefined in the first place. The result was that the Court was able to maintain the narrative of secularism, yet in the end, with the help of legal technicalities like demanding the proof of *namaz*, the land on which a historical mosque was situated was given to the Hindu parties even though the Court agreed that Muslims had been deprived of their fundamental right to possession of property. The party which organised the destruction of the Mosque was rewarded with the fruits of its illegal and unconstitutional actions. This is not secularism, but surely it is a violation of the basic principles of common law, for how can a wrongdoer be awarded for their wrong actions?

V. Conclusion: Justice or Peace?

Reflected in folklore, the legendary Indian King Vikramaditya imposes such a colossal impression on the Indian psyche that many kings took his name as a title. A king from the Gupta Dynasty, Chandragupta II, who allegedly built the Ram Temple at Ayodhya, also took this title for himself. Though legends tell us the story of the successful military conquests of Vikramaditya, his fame does not depend on that story. The fame and veneration commanded by Vikramaditya is because of his compassion and absolute impartial justice in every situation. The notion of an impartial, compassionate monarch who always imparts justice, even to the extent of putting his own kingdom or life at risk, has been a more acceptable notion in India than the murdering conquests of kings like Taimur or Henry V. The interpretation of the law, the *Constitution* and history by the Supreme Court of India has led to disappointment. It is submitted that the Supreme Court with its lofty praise for Indian civilisation itself fell short of the standards of justice said to be espoused by Indian civilisation through the agency of personalities

[100] This term denotes all the values embedded in the preamble to the *Constitution*. See A Singh Rathore, *Ambedkar's Preamble* (Penguin, 2020).

[101] *Keshavnanda Bharti v State of Kerela* (1973) 4 SCC 225.

[102] These are non-justiciable socioeconomic rights enshrined as principles to follow while enacting any policy or interpreting a law. See arts 36–51 of the *Constitution of India*.

like Vikramaditya. Ironically, it abandoned the magnanimity, tolerance and wisdom of that same civilisation.

This critique of this judgment is based on the view that the Supreme Court of India failed to follow India's civilisational ethos and, more importantly, its constitutional values. Having said that, it is important to note that one view advocates that this decision may not be legally perfect, but it will mean communal peace in India. It is true that insofar as this particular Supreme Court decision is concerned, there has been no subsequent communal violence in the country – yet. It is hard to tell whether the Muslim population will accept this decision and forgive the fact that the Babri Mosque was destroyed by force and then not restored by the apex court of the land. Another possibility is that this decision will encourage Hindu extremist groups to demand and act in term of destroying more historic mosques which it is claimed are built on Hindu temples. The Supreme Court of India, it seems, bought peace at the cost of justice. Only time will tell that whether this decision will establish peace in the long run or not.

13

Benazir Bhutto v Federation of Pakistan

Using Islamic Principles to Expand Judicial Powers

UMAR RASHID

I. Introduction

Over the last three decades, the Supreme Court of Pakistan (SC) has developed powerful original jurisdiction under Article 184(3) of the 1973 *Constitution*. This chapter analyses the landmark judgment in *Benazir Bhutto v Federation of Pakistan* (1988),[1] which laid the foundation for the development of the activist jurisprudence of the Court under Article 184(3). The Court relied on the centrality of Islam to the constitutional structure, utilising vague and imprecise principles to interpret Article 184(3) and fundamental rights contained in the *Constitution*. Over the years, this practice of using vague concepts without providing precise definition, justified through reference to Islamic principles and protection of fundamental rights, has allowed the Court to expand its judicial review and *suo motu* powers. This has also allowed the Court to interpret fundamental rights quite broadly and protect the rights of individuals in situations where they would have no other practical means of protection. At the same time, this continued expansion of power has seen the Court interfering in virtually all areas of state policy reminiscent of an institution engaged in social reform, though not always successfully.

The chapter is divided into five sections. Section II briefly outlines early attempts at the Islamisation of laws in Pakistan. Section III analyses the judgment in *Benazir Bhutto* and discusses how the use of Islamic principles and vague concepts foreshadowed the development of the Supreme Court's expansive powers. Section IV discusses the extent of the Court's powers. Section V concludes. This chapter shows how Islamic principles have been used by the Court to expand its judicial powers to protect fundamental rights, although not without controversy and interference in the work of other state institutions.

[1] *Benazir Bhutto v Federation of Pakistan* [1988] PLD 416 (SC).

II. History of Islamisation Efforts in Pakistan

Since the creation of Pakistan, continuous efforts have been made to Islamise the legal system and create mechanisms for the invalidation of laws repugnant to Islamic principles.[2] In an unfortunate irony, immediately following independence, Islamic religious parties, which had opposed Muhammad Ali Jinnah's struggle for a separate state for Muslims of India, started to clamour and agitate for the creation of an Islamic legal system based on Sharia.[3] During the first three decades of Pakistan's existence, the effect of these attempts on the legal system remained largely symbolic and theoretical. The use of Islamic principles by the superior courts remained limited, except in family matters.[4]

The first major political success for Islamisation was the adoption of the Objectives Resolution by the Constituent Assembly on 12 March 1949.[5] The Resolution declared that sovereignty 'over the entire universe belongs to Allah' and He has delegated authority to the state through its people as a 'sacred trust' to be 'exercised within the limits proscribed by Him'. The Objectives Resolution attempted to circumscribe the British principles of parliamentary and popular sovereignty inherited by the new state and to introduce the principle of 'Divine Sovereignty'.[6] The Resolution declared that the new *Constitution* would be subject to the ideals of democracy, human rights and social justice as understood by Islam. It imposed an obligation on the state to ensure that Muslims are 'enabled to order their lives … in accordance with the teachings and requirements of Islam as set out in the Holy Quran and the Sunnah'. The Resolution was not legally binding, but carried significant symbolic value, influencing subsequent constitutional development in Pakistan. It was adopted despite strong opposition by minority representatives, none of whom voted for it.[7]

Despite continuous efforts by religious parties when the first *Constitution of Pakistan* was enacted in 1956, it contained no enforceable mechanism for the Islamisation of the legal system. To appease various religious parties, the Objectives Resolution was adopted as the Preamble to the *Constitution*. Similarly, Islamic provisions were added to the *Constitution* as part of the non-justiciable 'Directives of State Policy'.[8] Article 25 imposed an unenforceable obligation on the state to provide facilities for the learning of the Quran and Sunnah, make the teaching of the Quran compulsory for Muslims and promote the observance of Islamic moral principles. The state was also required to ensure that Muslims were able to order their lives according to the Quran and Sunnah.

[2] See, eg, M Lau, *The Role of Islam in the Legal System of Pakistan* (Brill, 2005) 6–8; MH Cheema, 'Beyond Beliefs: Deconstructing the Dominant Narratives of the Islamization of Pakistan's Law' (2012) 60 *American Journal of Comparative Law* 875, 878.

[3] Maulana Maududi, the founder of Jamaat-e-Islami, opposed the creation of Pakistan and Jinnah's efforts as un-Islamic and contrary to the ideals of Muslim pan-Islamism; see H Alavi, 'Pakistan and Islam: Ethnicity and Ideology' in F Halliday and H Alavi (eds), *State and Ideology in the Middle East and Pakistan* (Macmillan Education UK, 1988) 64.

[4] Lau (n 2) 10–12.

[5] For debate, see *The Constituent Assembly of Pakistan Official Report, Volume V, 1949* (7–12 March 1949), Fifth Session of the Constituent Assembly of Pakistan, www.na.gov.pk/en/debates.php.

[6] For a discussion of 'Divine Sovereignty', see M Ahmed, 'Sovereignty of God in the Constitution of Pakistan: A Study in the Conflict of Traditionalism and Modernism' (1965) 4 *Islamic Studies* 201.

[7] ibid.

[8] Article 23(2) made these provisions explicitly non-justiciable.

Article 198(1) imposed obligations on the legislature not to create laws repugnant to the injunctions of Islam and to bring existing laws into conformity with Islamic principles. It provided no enforcement mechanism, except the creation of an advisory body that only had the power to make recommendations to the Parliament.

A mere two years after its promulgation, the 1956 *Constitution* was abrogated by martial law in 1958.[9] The military regime of General Ayub enacted a new *Constitution* in 1962. The 1962 *Constitution* changed the state from an Islamic Republic to a Republic, echoing Ayub's secular outlook,[10] though the Islamic provisions remained similar to the 1956 *Constitution*.[11] The Objectives Resolution became the Preamble to the *Constitution*. While it recognised that the authority exercised by people is a sacred trust from Allah, it removed any mention of delegation and limits proscribed by God. This reflected Ayub's aim of creating a constitutional structure that remained under his control and imposed no limits on the legislature controlled by him.[12] Thus, in Part II of the *Constitution*, human rights and Islamic provisions were enacted as non-justiciable 'Principles of Law-Making', and laws incompatible with them remained valid. The *Constitution* created an Advisory Council of Islamic Ideology to provide recommendations about current and proposed laws regarding their repugnancy to the Injunctions of Islam.[13] As before, the body had no power to supervise or enforce the implementation of its recommendations.[14] However, mounting political pressure forced the introduction of the First Amendment to the *Constitution* in 1964, which reverted the country's name to the Islamic Republic of Pakistan and made human rights justiciable.[15]

The 1973 *Constitution of Pakistan* adopted this same approach of non-justiciability for incompatibility with the Injunctions of Islam.[16] Like its predecessors, the *Constitution* created an advisory body, the Council of Islamic Ideology, without giving any enforcement mechanisms to deal with laws that were contrary to the Injunctions of Islam.[17]

General Zia-ul-Haq initiated wide-ranging Islamisation reforms to provide legitimacy for his 1977 military coup and subsequent rule.[18] These changes provided the constitutional basis for the amalgamation of Islamic principles with fundamental human rights, and the opportunity for the Supreme Court to expand its jurisdiction and review powers. Zia made two significant changes to the *Constitution* to achieve his

[9] For a brief introduction to the 1962 *Constitution*, see DP Singhal, 'The New Constitution of Pakistan' (1962) 2 *Asian Survey* 15; S Kaushik, 'Constitution of Pakistan at Work' (1963) 3 *Asian Survey* 384.

[10] Lau (n 2) 7.

[11] For a detailed discussion, see M Ahmed and SM Sharif, 'Islamic Aspects of the New Constitution of Pakistan' (1963) 2 *Islamic Studies* 249.

[12] See eg, S Kaushik, 'Constitution of Pakistan at Work' (1963) 3(8) *Asian Survey* 384, 384–85; F Rahman, 'Islam and the Constitutional Problem of Pakistan' (1970) 32 *Studia Islamica* 275; Ahmed and Sharif (n 11).

[13] Articles 199–206.

[14] See arts 5 and 6. This was confirmed by the Supreme Court in *Tanbir Ahmad Siddiky v Province of East Pakistan*, [1968] PLD 185 (SC).

[15] See, eg, YY Pardesi, 'An Analysis of the Constitutional Crisis in Pakistan (1958–1969)' (2012) 7(4) *Dialogue (Pakistan)* 375; R Braibanti, 'Pakistan: Constitutional Issues in 1964' (1965) 5(2) *Asian Survey* 79; Rahman (n 12).

[16] Article 8 of the 1973 *Constitution* states that any law incompatible with fundamental rights is void.

[17] Article 230 of the 1973 *Constitution*.

[18] See, eg, S Qureshi, 'Islam and Development: The Zia Regime in Pakistan' (1980) 8 *World Development* 563.

objectives, which have endured. First, the Federal Shariat Court was created in 1980 and was given powers to invalidate any law repugnant to the Injunctions of Islam.[19] Appeals from the Federal Shariat Court are to the Shariat Appellate Bench of the Supreme Court, which is made up of three Muslim judges of the Supreme Court and a maximum of two Ulema appointed as ad hoc members of the Court.[20] Second, the Objectives Resolution was made a substantive part of the *Constitution* under Article 2A in 1985.[21]

Zia, as the President, retained absolute powers in relation to the appointment of judges to the Federal Shariat Court under Article 203C(2). Under Article 203C(4), the maximum tenure of the Shariat Court judges was only three years and only one year if the appointed judge was elevated from the High Court. This tenure was extendable at the discretion of the President. A High Court judge who refused appointment to the Shariat Court would be forcibly retired under Article 203C(5). Under Article 203D, the Federal Shariat Court had the power to examine and strike down any law for its incompatibility with the Injunctions of Islam, whether on its own motion, or on a petition by a citizen, or by the Federal or Provincial Government.

Despite this control by Zia, there remained one area where the Shariat Court could exert its power, especially since it aligned with the Islamisation project of Zia. The Court embarked upon an ambitious project to examine the compatibility of the laws of Pakistan with the Injunctions of Islam. It used its *suo motu* powers to examine virtually all statutory provisions.[22] The successful use of *suo motu* powers without extensive political backlash demonstrated to the superior judges the potential scope of their power, especially if that power was exercised to uphold Islamic principles. This activist phase of Federal Shariat Court coincided with the landmark judgment of the Supreme Court in *Benazir Bhutto v Federation of Pakistan* (1988). By the time the Supreme Court came to deliver its decision, General Zia had died in a plane crash, which provided the perfect opportunity for the Court to assert its independence.

Repeated imposition of martial law in Pakistan had made the courts very aware of their limitations. While judicial independence had been severely curtailed over the years, decisions based on Islamic provisions provided one safe avenue for the judiciary to assert its power and engage in relatively safe judicial activism. This can be observed in

[19] The *Constitution (Amendment) Order, 1980 (President's Order No 1 of 1980)* inserted a new chapter into the *Constitution* entitled 'Federal Shariat Court' and promulgated 11 new articles – arts 203A–J. Zia continued to make changes to these new articles through various subsequent Orders, all of which were given constitutional validity through art 270A enacted by the *Constitution (Eighth Amendment) Act, 1985*.

[20] Under art 203F, the ad hoc members are appointed by the President after consultation with the Chief Justice. The changes are still in effect.

[21] Inserted in the *Constitution by the Revival of Constitution of 1973 Order, 1985 (President's Order No 14 of 1985)*. The constitutional validity of this Order was ensured through art 270A enacted by the *Constitution (Eighth Amendment) Act, 1985*.

[22] For details on the cases decided by the Shariat Court and the use of its *suo motu* powers, see Lau (n 2) 127–30, 143–88. In Pakistan, *suo motu* powers initially developed in the Federal Shariat Court and are now exclusively used by the Supreme Court under its art 184(3) original jurisdiction. Under this power, the Supreme Court can take cognisance of any issue that the Justices are aware of, without the matter being formally brought before the Court. The Court can order any relevant parties (both public and private) to make submission to the Court on any point that it raises and can issue legally binding orders/judgments creating new rights and obligations. The only limitation is that the Court justifies its use of *suo motu* powers under art 184(3), which requires the matter to raise a question of public importance with reference to the enforcement of any of the fundamental rights. In recent years, the Court usually exercises its *suo motu* powers without actually justifying the use of power under art 184(3).

the activists' role of the Federal Shariat Court during its first decade, despite Zia's strong control over the Court.[23] This showed the superior judiciary that they were unlikely to face a strong backlash and severe political opposition as long as they used Islamic principles in their reasoning. The following section discusses how the Supreme Court in the *Benazir Bhutto* case laid the foundation for its powerful original jurisdiction under Article 184 of the Constitution. The Court did this by combining the interpretation of fundamental rights with Islamic principles and relying on very general and vague concepts, developing judicial review powers under which virtually all matters of government policy are reviewable.

III. *Benazir Bhutto v Federation of Pakistan*

The case of *Benazir Bhutto v Federation of Pakistan* arose out of the constitutional petition filed by Benazir Bhutto, the Chairperson of the Pakistan Peoples Party under Article 184(3) of the Constitution. She was the daughter of former Prime Minister Zulfiqar Ali Bhutto, who was sentenced to death for conspiracy to commit murder after General Zia overthrew his government.[24] The petition challenged various amendments made to the *Political Parties Act 1962* (*PPA*) by Zia's military regime, which imposed unreasonable restraints on political parties and made it impossible for the Pakistan Peoples Party to contest the upcoming general elections. The petition argued that various sections of the *Act* violated Article 17 of the *Constitution*, the right to freedom of association, and thus were void. The case raised several critical constitutional questions, which the Supreme Court answered in the light of Islamic principles and their relationship to the constitutional structure of Pakistan. Eleven Justices of the Supreme Court heard the case. Chief Justice Muhammad Haleem authored the unanimous decision. Although five justices also wrote concurring opinions, there was no significant difference of reasoning amongst the justices.

Though the main issue before the Court was the validity of the various sections of the *PPA*, it looked at both Article 184(3) and Article 270A before dealing with it. It first looked at the maintainability of the petition under the Article 184 original jurisdiction of the Supreme Court. The Court's decision relied on the importance of Islamic principles to lay the foundations for the future development of public interest litigation (PIL) in Pakistan and the expansion of the Court's *suo motu* powers.[25] The Court then looked

[23] Lau (n 2) 130, 143–88.

[24] The death sentence of Zulfiqar Ali Bhutto, the first democratically elected Prime Minister of the country, for conspiracy to commit murder was upheld by a split 4:3 decision of the Supreme in *Zulfiqar Ali Bhutto v State* [1979] PLD 53 (SC). After his retirement as the Chief Justice of Pakistan, Dr Nasim Hassan Shah, who was one of the Justices who voted in favour of upholding the conviction, stated in two separate media interviews that their decision was wrong and Bhutto should never have been subjected to the death penalty. See I Hanif, 'Former CJ Nasim Shah Passes Away' *Dawn News* (4 February 2015), www.dawn.com/news/1161394.

[25] See, eg, P Hassan and A Azfar, 'Securing Environmental Rights through Public Interest Litigation in South Asia' (2004) 22 *Virginia Environmental Law Journal* 215, 232; F Hussain, 'Public Interest Litigation in Pakistan' (1993) 12 *Journal of Law and Society (University of Peshawar)* 11; MS Khan, 'Genesis and Evolution of Public Interest Litigation in the Supreme Court of Pakistan: Toward a Dynamic Theory of Judicialization' (2014) 28 *Temple International & Comparative Law Journal* 285, 293–94.

at the validity and scope of Article 270A, since it granted validity to the amendments made to the *PPA*. Only then did the Court look at the compatibility of multiple sections of the *PPA* with the fundamental rights protected under Chapter 1 of Part II of the Constitution. The Court used Islamic principles and their effect on various constitutional provisions to reach its decision.

A. Original Jurisdiction of the Supreme Court

Article 184 provides two bases for the original jurisdiction of the Supreme Court. Sub-article (1) grants original jurisdiction in disputes between two or more governments of the Federation. Sub-article (3), which was relevant in the *Benazir Bhutto* case, grants original jurisdiction for enforcement of fundamental rights:

> Without prejudice to the provisions of Article 199, the Supreme Court shall, if it considers that a question of public importance with reference to the enforcement of any of the Fundamental Rights conferred by Chapter I of Part II is involved have the power to make an order of the nature mentioned in the said Article.

Article 199 grants original jurisdiction to the High Courts in Pakistan; however, unlike the wording of Article 184(3), Article 199(1)(c) explicitly requires a petition to be brought by an 'aggrieved party' for the enforcement of fundamental rights.[26] The Court dealt with two main questions regarding the interpretation of Article 184(3): first, whether only an aggrieved party could lodge petitions under Article 184(3); and, second, whether the Supreme Court could exercise its original jurisdiction even where the High Court has jurisdiction under Article 199.

The Attorney-General, representing the Federation of Pakistan, first argued that the mention of Article 199 in Article 184(3) meant that the sub-article limited locus standi to an aggrieved party as Article 199(1)(c) did.[27] The Supreme Court had briefly examined Article 184(3) in *Begum Nusrat Bhutto v Chief of Army Staff and Federation of Pakistan* (1977).[28] In this case, Mrs Bhutto had lodged a constitutional petition under Article 184(3) challenging the arrest of her husband Zulfiqar Ali Bhutto and several members of the Pakistan Peoples Party following General Zia's military coup. The Court held that since the petitioner was the Acting Chairman of Pakistan Peoples Party to which all those arrested belonged and was the wife of one of the detained individuals, she was an aggrieved party within the meaning of Article 184(3) read with Article 199. It was possible to infer from the wording of the judgment that the Court in *Nusrat Bhutto* believed that a petitioner needed to be an 'aggrieved party' for petitions under Article 184(3). The Court in *Benazir Bhutto* held that since there was no independent consideration of Article 184(3) and an aggrieved party initiated proceedings in the *Nusrat Bhutto* case, it did not provide an authoritative answer to the first question.[29]

[26] Article 199(1)(c). Unlike art 199(1)(a) and 199(1)(c), art 199(1)(b) does not limit itself to application by aggrieved party, instead allowing 'application of any person' for habeas corpus petitions and petitions asking that those holding public office show under what authority of law they claim to hold office.

[27] *Benazir Bhutto* (n 1) 477.

[28] *Begum Nusrat Bhutto v Chief of Army Staff and Federation of Pakistan* [1977] PLD 657 (SC).

[29] *Benazir Bhutto* (n 1) 492–93.

Therefore, the Court would look at the article afresh.[30] It held that Article 184(3) does not require a petition to be brought by an aggrieved party and, as long as its requirements are fulfilled, the petition can be lodged at the Supreme Court despite the availability of the option to initiate proceedings in the relevant High Court under Article 199.[31]

The proceeding paragraphs will discuss the reasoning of the Court in its interpretation of sub-article (3) in greater detail. The judgment of the Court on Article 184(3) started with a discussion on how to interpret constitutional provisions.

i. *How to Interpret the Constitution*

The Court held that the interpretation of constitutional provisions should not be based on narrow and 'ceremonious observance of the rules or usages of interpretation', but should be based on the principles that 'saturate and invigorate the Constitution'.[32] These principles can be found in the Objectives Resolution,[33] fundamental rights[34] and directives of state policy,[35] which impose a greater demand on judicial functions.[36] The purpose behind including these provisions in the *Constitution* was 'to uphold the ideals of democracy, tolerance, equality and social justice according to Islam' as stated in the Preamble to the *Constitution*.[37] Therefore, Article 184(3)'s interpretation should take into account the purpose and objective behind the provision, which could be gleaned from the principles mentioned above.[38]

The Court held that the interpretation of a constitutional provision should start with teleology, the purpose that the provision is intended to serve, and whether the interpretation chosen achieves this purpose. While deciding whether an interpretation achieves the particular purpose, the Court would need to keep in mind the social context in which the legal system operates.[39] In the case of Pakistan, the purpose that successive constitutions wanted to achieve could be gleaned from their preambles, which were similar to the Objectives Resolution.[40] As far as the 1973 *Constitution* is concerned, the Objectives Resolution has been made a substantive part of the *Constitution* under Article 2A.[41] The Court highlighted that these preambles are 'an eloquent testimony of the affirmation of Pakistan Ideology', which is based on Islamic ideology and Muslim nationhood, which formed the basis for the two-nation theory[42] and the creation of Pakistan.[43]

[30] ibid.
[31] ibid 493, 496–97.
[32] ibid 489.
[33] Article 2A of the *Constitution*.
[34] ibid ch 1 of pt II.
[35] ibid ch 2 of pt II. Unlike ch 1, ch 2 provisions are non-justiciable, although the Directive Principles require that state organs should, as far as possible, act in accordance with these Principles; see art 29.
[36] *Benazir Bhutto* (n 1) 489.
[37] ibid.
[38] ibid.
[39] ibid.
[40] See discussion at ibid 489–91, 521–22.
[41] ibid 490.
[42] For a brief discussion of the two-nation theory, see C Bennett, 'Two-Nation Theory' in ZR Kassam, Y Kornberg Greenberg and J Bagli (eds), *Islam, Judaism, and Zoroastrianism* (Springer Netherlands, 2018).
[43] *Benazir Bhutto* (n 1) 522.

This approach of the Court requiring judicial function to have regard to these central principles is similar to Dworkin's view on 'law as integrity', insofar as Haleem J was stating that the interpretation of laws take into account the 'coherent conception of justice and fairness'[44] contained in the *Constitution*. The Court's reasoning in *Benazir Bhutto* makes it clear that for the Court, the coherent conception of justice and fairness would be found in Islamic provisions that permeate the *Constitution* in the form of Article 2A, Part IX of the *Constitution* and through mention of Islamic provisions in various other articles.[45] Thus, the Court explicitly introduced the touchstone of Islamic provisions in the interpretation of the *Constitution*, while failing to define these general and vague terms and concepts.[46] Since Islamic principles contained in the Quran and Sunnah and those mentioned in the *Constitution* are open to a wide range of interpretations, the Court effectively gave itself very broad discretion to interpret constitutional provisions, especially in relation to fundamental rights.

ii. The Role of the Supreme Court in the Constitutional Structure

While doing so, the Court also explained the importance of its role in the constitutional structure. It held that since the *Constitution* declares that 'all authority exercisable by the people is a sacred trust from Almighty Allah', justice in Pakistan is of Divine origin.[47] Through their oaths, judges submit to the *Constitution* and undertake a duty to ensure that justice and equality required by the *Constitution* prevails.[48] Thus, the Court was enunciating what Article 184(3) requires from it. It grants original jurisdiction to the Supreme Court to enforce fundamental rights to ensure the discharge of this duty.

This would also require the Court to consider the social context in which it is supposed to discharge this duty. It held that it needs to be kept in mind the fact that not every person in the country has the capacity to approach the courts, especially the poor and disadvantaged sections of society.[49] In this regard, the Court highlighted the importance of public interest litigation, which can be initiated by any person acting bona fide on behalf of those who cannot access the courts themselves.[50] It held that if Article 184(3) was limited to an aggrieved party, it would defeat the advancement of

[44] R Dworkin, *Law's Empire* (Harvard University Press, 1986) 225; see also ch 7 for discussion on Dworkin's third conception of law: 'Law as integrity'.

[45] Part IX of the *Constitution* deals with Islamic provisions and require that all laws be compatible with the Injunctions of Islam; see arts 227–29. In addition, Islamic principles inform provisions on fundamental rights, principles of policy, and eligibility requirements for Members of Parliament. They also require the President, the Prime Minister and the Chief Justice to be Muslim.

[46] To give an idea of how general and vague some of the words and phrases that incorporate Islamic provisions in the *Constitution* are and the wide discretion they can thus provide to the courts, an incomplete list is provided: 'glory of Islam', 'public order', 'decency', 'morality', 'principles of democracy, freedom, equality, tolerance and social justice, as enunciated by Islam', 'Islamic teachings and practices', 'good moral reputation', 'sagacious', 'righteous', 'honest', '*ameen*' and 'ideology of Pakistan'.

[47] *Benazir Bhutto* (n 1) 545 (Muhammad Afzal Zullah J).

[48] ibid (Muhammad Afzal Zullah J).

[49] ibid 490–491 (Haleem CJ).

[50] ibid. The Chief Justice referred to the Indian Supreme Court case of *SP Gupta and Others v President of India and Others* [1982] AIR 149 (SC), which expanded the scope of art 32 of the *Indian Constitution* by relaxing the locus standi requirements and defined the term 'public interest litigation' in the Indian context. He termed the approach of the Indian Supreme Court 'creative and beneficial' for the enforcement of fundamental rights and for securing social and economic justice as intended by the *Indian Constitution*.

'national hopes and aspirations of people permeating the Constitution' and the promise of 'access to justice to all'.[51] Such an approach would be contrary to Article 4, which guarantees equal protection of the law and incorporates the concept of the rule of law into the *Constitution*.[52]

Thus, the Court saw a central role for itself in the fulfilment of the nation's hope and aspirations. The Court's views about itself and its role can be gleaned from what the justices stated when discussing the validity of the provision of the *PPA*. While discussing the vagueness of the test that would determine whether a political party should be dissolved, Haleem CJ stated that there is no danger of abuse, since the Supreme Court would be interpreting the concepts contained in the test.[53] Justice Abdul Kadir Shaikh put this more explicitly when he stated that because the Supreme Court is the final arbitrator for these concepts, there is sufficient safeguard against their vagueness and potential misuse. Since the Supreme Court is the 'repository of the nation's faith and confidence', it will 'discharge [these] duties and perform functions in accordance with the Constitution and the law'.[54] The same approach was taken by Muhammad Afzal Zullah J when he wrote that '[o]ne high mark of this institution is an immense devotion to the cause of national progress, fitness and survival'[55] – all without explaining what these concepts actually mean and their ambit.

iii. Adversarial System, Locus Standi, Abuse of Process and Purely Theoretical Questions

In reaching this conclusion, the Supreme Court rejected several other arguments. First, while accepting that the rules relating to the aggrieved party are central to the adversarial system found in Anglo-Saxon legal systems such as Pakistan, the Court rejected it. It held that these rules could not inform the working of Article 184(3) since it is silent on this issue, and such an interpretation would fail to consider the purpose of the sub-article and the social context. For various reasons, many people in Pakistan cannot approach the courts to redress their grievances. Therefore, relaxing the locus standi rules would allow person(s) acting bona fide to initiate public interest litigation in case of violation of the fundamental right of those people 'whose grievances go unnoticed and unredressed'.[56]

Second, the Attorney-General argued that allowing a party to initiate proceedings under Article 184(3) at the Supreme Court when there is an aggrieved party who should approach the relevant High Court under Article 199 could lead to abuse of process in the form of individuals or groups filing petitions indiscriminately in both the relevant High Court and the Supreme Court under Article 199 and Article 184(3) respectively.[57]

[51] ibid 489 (Haleem CJ).

[52] ibid.

[53] For more details on this, see the discussion in section III.C below.

[54] *Benazir Bhutto* (n 1) 574 (Abdul Kadir Shaikh J).

[55] ibid 544 (Muhammad Afzal Zullah J). The Objectives Resolution that is now a substantive part of the *Constitution* imposes this limitation on the power of the people and the state, requiring that power be 'exercised within the limits prescribed by Him', which is held as sacred trust by the state through its people.

[56] ibid 490–91 (Haleem CJ).

[57] ibid 493, 496.

The Court rejected this argument, stating that such potential cannot justify the curtailment of remedy provided by the *Constitution*.[58] Each case would be judged on its particular facts to determine if petitioners are abusing the process. Thus, the Court was able to ensure that its jurisdiction would not be curtailed by the possibility that an individual could go to the High Court and need not have petitioned the Supreme Court.[59]

Third, the Attorney-General argued that discarding the requirement for an aggrieved party would lead to petitions that raise purely theoretical or abstract questions.[60] The Court distinguished legislation that is *ex facie* violative of fundamental rights from legislation that is capable of being administered in a way that violates fundamental rights, but is not *ex facie* violative. The Court relied on *Jibendra Kishore v Province of East Pakistan*[61] and *Waris Meah v State*[62] to hold that where legislation is *ex facie* violative of fundamental rights, there is no need to prove actual violation in order to engage the Court's jurisdiction under Article 184(3). Where the legislation is not *ex facie* violative, the Court would have jurisdiction under Article 184(3) only in cases where legislation has been proven to have been administered in a violative manner.[63] In the Court's opinion, there was already a mechanism to prevent decisions on purely abstract or theoretical questions; therefore, there was no need to add the requirement of an aggrieved party.[64]

iv. Requirements for Exercise of Jurisdiction under Article 184(3) and Future Developments

Compared to how it operates today, the Supreme Court's original jurisdiction could have remained relatively narrow if it had strictly construed the condition that either a

[58] See ibid 493–97.

[59] The Court in this case relied on a previous case, *Begum Zeb-un-Nisa v Pakistan* [1958] PLD 35 (SC), where the Supreme Court had held that art 22 of the 1956 *Constitution*, which guaranteed the right to petition the Supreme Court for enforcement of fundamental rights, could not be curtailed simply because petitioning the Supreme Court is assumed to be a use of 'an extraordinary power which should be used with circumspection'. On the same issue, the Court also relied on the Indian case *KK Koochunni v State of Madras* [1969] AIR 725 (SC), where the Indian Supreme Court had held that the existence of an adequate alternative legal remedy was not sufficient to deny relief under art 32 of the *Indian Constitution*, which provides the right to petition the Indian Supreme Court for enforcement of fundamental rights, in a similar fashion to art 184(3). See ibid.

[60] ibid 477.

[61] *Jibendra Kishore v Province of East Pakistan* [1957] PLD 9 (SC). In *Jibendra Kishore*, the *East Bengal State Acquisition and Tenancy Act, 1950* was challenged. Under the *Act*, the Provincial Government had the power to acquire interest of rent-receivers by notification and on payment of compensation. It was argued that the *Act* gave arbitrary power to the government to pick and choose which rent-receivers it would choose for acquisition, and thus the *Act* could be applied in a discriminatory manner. The Court held that the *Act* was capable of being administered in a non-discriminatory manner and that in order to succeed, the petitioner had to prove that the *Act* had been administered in a discriminatory manner, ie, 'has actually been administered to the detriment of a particular class and in a partial, unjust and oppressive manner'.

[62] *Waris Meah v State* [1957] PLD 157 (SC). In *Waris Meah*, the Supreme Court judged the compatibility and validity of the amendments made under the *Foreign Exchange Regulation (Amendment) Act*. The *Act* created three distinct authorities, each with different procedures and punishments for the same category of offences, while giving the Central Government the power to determine where the offender would be tried. It was held that the existence of discretion in the use of three different modes for the same class of offences was *ex facie* violative of the right to equal protection before the law under art 5 of the *Constitution*, and there was no need to prove an actual violation.

[63] *Benazir Bhutto* (n 1) 483 (Haleem CJ).

[64] ibid 477–86.

statute is *ex facie* violative or an actual violation of fundamental rights has occurred. Similarly, if in the future the Court strictly construed the two requirements listed in Article 184(3) – that the matter before the Court raises a question of (a) 'public importance' and (b) with reference to the 'enforcement of any of the fundamental rights' – the ambit of Court's original jurisdiction could have remained relatively small.

However, it will be seen below that later developments ignored any such limitations.[65] The seeds for this were contained in the *Benazir Bhutto* judgment. On the issue of the definition of public importance, the Court simply stated that public importance 'should not be understood in a limited sense'.[66] Without explaining the concept in any detail, the Court held that public importance would cover 'the constitutional rights of freedoms and liberties, their protection and invasion of such freedoms in a manner which raises a serious question regarding their enforcement'.[67] This was immediately followed by a discussion on the benefits of PIL and the important duty of the judges in fulfilling Divine justice, foreshadowing the extensive development of PIL and the Court's vast *suo motu* powers.

In a constitutional structure where courts have the power to invalidate any law that is incompatible with fundamental rights,[68] the superior judiciary would invariably end up engaging in an analysis of the purpose behind constitutional provisions when interpreting statutes and judging their compatibility with fundamental rights. However, the presence of such a structure does not automatically turn courts into social reformers. In Pakistan, the Supreme Court did start acting like a social reformer.[69] In the *Benazir Bhutto* case, the Court opened the door for this when it emphasised the vague ideals expressed in the Objectives Resolution, on the vague and contested concepts of Islamic Ideology, the Ideology of Pakistan, and non-justiciable Directives Principles. The Court stated that it derives its duty from a Divine mandate and highlighted the sacred trust on it to create an Islamic society that upholds 'principles of democracy, freedom, equality, tolerance and social justice as enunciated by Islam'. It highlighted the importance of these concepts, but did not discuss the appropriateness of using such vague concepts. Nor did the Court provide any definition or clarification for these concepts. Instead, the Justices simply pointed towards their own fitness to judge these issues and their devotion to the national cause. This expansion is discussed in greater detail in section IV below.

B. Article 270A

The next issue raised in the *Benazir Bhutto* case was the validity, scope and meaning of Article 270A. Article 270A was added to the *Constitution* through the *Constitution (Eighth Amendment) Act 1985*. It affirmed and validated the *Martial Law Proclamation* of 5 July 1977 and various laws promulgated between 5 July 1977 and 11 November

[65] See section IV below.
[66] *Benazir Bhutto* (n 1) 491.
[67] ibid.
[68] Per art 8(1) and 8(2).
[69] For details, see section IV below.

1985 by General Zia during his military dictatorship.[70] Article 270A states that any laws created during this period are considered to have been made by the competent authority and are valid 'notwithstanding any judgment of any court and, notwithstanding anything contained in the Constitution' and that their validity could 'not be called in question in any court on any ground whatsoever'. The Attorney-General argued that the wording of Article 270A validated the laws enacted during the relevant period, cured any constitutional defects in those laws and prevented the courts from judging the validity of such laws.[71]

Rejecting this argument, the Supreme Court held that, though valid, Article 270A could not oust the jurisdiction of the Court to review laws under Article 8 for their compatibility with fundamental rights. The aim of Article 270A was only to ensure that laws created during the relevant period were not challenged for how they were enacted. It could not cure constitutional defects in those laws.[72]

Interestingly, without the point being raised by any of the parties, Haleem CJ wondered whether the validity of such an article and the laws it deals with could be assumed if they were incompatible with the injunctions of the Holy Quran and Sunnah.[73] It seemed as if the Chief Justice was wondering about the validity of a constitutional amendment and the Court's power to review them for their repugnancy with Injunctions of Islam. However, the Chief Justice did not clarify what he meant, simply stating that the Court 'would leave [this issue] open for consideration in some other appropriate case'.[74] By emphasising the centrality of Islamic principles, fundamental rights and parliamentary democracy, the Chief Justice was flirting with the 'basic structure doctrine' or the 'salient feature doctrine', which would even allow the Court to examine the validity of Constitutional amendments.[75]

This was not the first time Pakistani courts had flirted with the basic structure doctrine and the existence of a power to invalidate constitutional amendment. The Court had previously accepted that Islamic principles provided the basic structure to the *Constitution*, but had left the question of whether they had the jurisdiction to strike down a constitutional amendment contrary to the basic structure open.[76] *Asma Jilani v Government of Punjab* was the first major case to recognise that Islamic principles formed part of the basic structure.[77] In *Asma Jilani*, the Court looked at martial

[70] President Zia-ul-Haq finally allowed general elections to be conducted in February 1985. Following the elections, Muhammad Khan Junejo was elected as the Prime Minister of Pakistan. Despite the elections, General Zia, as the President, continued to rule the country for all practical purposes until his death in a plane crash on 17 August 1988. The Eighth Amendment to the *Constitution* was passed under Zia's direction to provide retroactive validity to laws made during his military rule and grant him powers as President to dissolve the National Assembly unilaterally.

[71] *Benazir Bhutto* (n 1) 498, 508 (Haleem CJ).

[72] ibid 509; for detailed discussion of this point, see Haleem CJ at 498–515.

[73] ibid 515.

[74] ibid.

[75] The basic structure doctrine was adopted by the Indian Supreme Court in *Kesavananda Bharati v State of Kerala* [1973] AIR 1641 (SC). In Pakistan, it was formally adopted as the salient feature doctrine by the Supreme Court in 2015 in *District Bar Association, Rawalpindi and Others v Federation of Pakistan* [2015] PLD 401 (SC).

[76] For an analysis of the use of basic structure by the courts in Pakistan before the Supreme Court explicitly stated that it had the power to review constitutional amendments in 2015, see Lau (n 2) 5–29.

[77] In this case, the Supreme Court overruled the infamous *State v Dosso* [1958] PLD 533 (SC), which had validated the imposition of martial law by using Kelsen's Pure Theory of Law to hold that 'A victorious revolution

law regulations enacted by General Yahya Khan after his ouster. The Court held that a martial law could not overthrow the *Constitution* and that the basic structure of the *Constitution*, based as it is on Islamic norms, cannot be altered. The Court held that such alteration is only possible if the 'body politic of Pakistan as a whole, God forbid, is re-constituted on an un-Islamic pattern, which will, of course, mean total destruction of its original concept'.[78]

The Lahore High Court adopted a similar approach in its 1977 decision in *Darvesh M Arbey v Federation of Pakistan*.[79] In contrast to the *Asma Jilani* case, which dealt with the validity of martial law after the ouster of the martial law administrator, the Lahore High Court held the imposition of martial law by Zulfiqar Ali Bhutto to be invalid while he was still in power.[80] Unlike previous martial law administrators, Bhutto was a democratically elected Prime Minister. The majority in the case did not discuss the basic structure doctrine. However, two judges of the High Court, Shameen Hussain Kadri and Zakiuddin Patel JJ, held that Islamic principles provided the basic structure of the *Constitution* and the legislature is not free to enact constitutional amendments that would violate it.[81]

In the *Nusrat Bhutto* case, the Supreme Court also highlighted the centrality of Islamic principles, stating that Islam provided the basic structure for the legal system, in which morality could not be divorced from the law.[82] The Court upheld the validity of Zia's martial law in *Nusrat Bhutto*, for it had no other choice if it did not want to suffer the embarrassment of giving a decision that would never be followed.[83] However, the Court relied upon the basic structure of the *Constitution* to hold that its judicial review powers would continue to exist, despite what the martial law regulations may state. It further held that the imposition of martial law was for a limited duration, where the Chief Martial Law Administrator had 'stepped in to save the country at a time of grave national crisis and constitutional break-down' and had pledged to uphold elections as soon as possible.[84]

or a successful Coup d'état is an internationally recognised legal method of changing a Constitution' and 'the essential condition to determine whether a Constitution has been annulled is the efficacy of the change' (per Muhammad Munir CJ).

[78] *Asma Jilani v Government of Punjab* [1972] PLD 139 (SC) (Sajjad Ahmad J). Chief Justice Hamoodur Rahaman and Sajjad Ahmad, in their separate, but concurring opinions, explicitly recognised the immutability and inalterability of Islamic principles on which the state of Pakistan is constituted. Justice Waheeduddin Ahmad did not pen his own opinion, but agreed with the Chief Justice.

[79] *Darvesh M Arbey v Federation of Pakistan* [1980] PLD 206 (LHC).

[80] Bhutto had imposed martial law in three cities, Lahore, Karachi and Hyderabad; see, eg, LM Simons, 'Bhutto, under Pressure, Imposes Martial Law in Three Cities' *Washington Post* (22 April 1977), https://www.washingtonpost.com/archive/politics/1977/04/22/bhutto-under-pressure-imposes-martial-law-in-three-cities/82563958-4cb5-4fc7-96d9-37c022f8086f. By the time the detailed judgment of the High Court was delivered, Bhutto's government had been overthrown and General Zia had imposed martial law throughout Pakistan.

[81] For a detailed discussion of this, see Lau (n 2) 22–24.

[82] *Nusrat Bhutto* (n 28).

[83] Justice Qaisar Khan's opinion is quite illuminating in this regard, when he bluntly stated that martial law 'cannot be prevented by judgements' and pledges made by the Chief Martial Law Administrator cannot be enforced by the courts; ibid 747.

[84] *Nusrat Bhutto* (n 28) (Anwaral Haq CJ). While the Court may have avoided the embarrassment of giving an unenforceable decision, its belief in the sanctity of Zia's pledge to hold elections turned out to be incorrect. The elections were indefinitely postponed, and Zia undertook far-reaching social and legal programmes for the Islamisation of Pakistani society. Zia finally allowed general elections to take place eight years later, but on

The Supreme Court's use of Islamic principles in *Nusrat Bhutto* to safeguard its jurisdiction is similar to the approach adopted in the *Asma Jilani* case. Justice Sajjad Ahmad in *Asma Jilani* stated this most explicitly when he wrote that 'judicial power as a trust from the Almighty Allah, is lodged in the society as a whole, which, in turn, is irrevocably committed to the Courts as trustees of the society' and does not derive from any executive power.[85] The approach continued in *Benazir Bhutto* case and the subsequent development of jurisprudence under Article 184(3). This culminated in *District Bar Association, Rawalpindi and Others v Federation of Pakistan*,[86] when the Court formally accepted the salient feature doctrine and declared its competence to review constitutional amendments.

C. The *Political Parties Act 1962*

The main issue before the Court was the compatibility of various sections of the *PPA* with the right to freedom of association under Article 17 of the *Constitution*.

Article 17 of the *Constitution* states that:

> (1) Every citizen shall have the right to form associations or unions, subject to any reasonable restrictions imposed by law in the *interest of sovereignty or integrity of Pakistan, public order or morality*.
> (2) Every citizen, not being in the service of Pakistan, shall have the right to form or be a member of a political party, subject to any reasonable restrictions imposed by law in the *interest of the sovereignty or integrity of Pakistan* and such law shall provide that where the Federal Government declare that any political party has been formed or is operating in a manner *prejudicial to the sovereignty or integrity of Pakistan*, the Federal Government shall, within fifteen days of such declaration, refer the matter to the Supreme Court whose decision on such reference shall be final.
> (3) Every political party shall account for the source of its funds in accordance with law.

The case revolved around the compatibility of sections 3, 3A, 3B, 3C, 6, 7 and 8 *PPA* with Articles 17(2) and 17(3). The only limitations that Article 17 entertained for the right to freedom of association appear in italics in the text above and are different for sub-articles (1) and (2).

Section 3(1) *PPA* prohibited the formation of a party 'with the object of propagating any opinion or acting in a manner prejudicial to the Islamic Ideology, or the integrity or security of Pakistan, or morality, or the maintenance of public order'. Section 3(2) prohibited any 'foreign-aided party' and people from joining, associating or forming such parties. Section 3A required political parties to disclose the sources of their funding to the government and have their finances audited by those authorised by the Election Commission. Section 3B(1) required registration of political parties and section 3B(6) prevented any party not registered from contesting elections. Section 3B(3) provided certain conditions that the Election Commission had to be satisfied with before

a non-partisan basis, forming a puppet government, while retaining all powers of governance until his death in 1988.

[85] *Asma Jilani* (n 78) 258 (Sajjad Ahmad J).

[86] *District Bar Association* (n 75).

registering a political party. The petition highlighted section 3B(3)(c) and 3B(3)(d) as being especially problematic. These required the Commission to be satisfied that the political party 'believes in the ideology of Pakistan and the integrity and sovereignty of Pakistan' and provides accounts as required by section 3A. Section 3B(4) provided for the cancellation of registration if a political party propagated any opinion or engaged in any act 'prejudicial to the Ideology of Pakistan, or the sovereignty, integrity or security of Pakistan, or morality, or the maintenance of public order, or the integrity or independence of the judiciary of Pakistan, or which defames or brings into ridicule the judiciary or the Armed Forces of Pakistan' or received any aid, financial or otherwise, from foreign sources. Section 3C gave the Election Commission the discretion to allow any party to contest the upcoming 1988 general elections even if it had not been registered under section 3B.

Section 6(1) provided for the immediate dissolution of a party on publication of a declaration in the Official Gazette by the Federal Government when it was satisfied that the party was foreign-aided or was formed or 'operating in a manner prejudicial to the Islamic Ideology, or the sovereignty, integrity or security of Pakistan, or morality, or maintenance of public order' or contravened section 3A and the Federal Government had referred the matter to the Supreme Court to judge under section 6(2). Section 6(2) required that in the event that such a declaration has been made, the government would need to refer this matter to the Supreme Court within 15 days, and the Court's decision would be final.

Section 7 prevented an office-bearer of a dissolved party from taking part in any political activity for seven years and imposed a maximum sentence of three years for the contravention of the section. Section 8 prevented anyone from being a member of a provincial or federal legislature if they had been members of a party dissolved under section 6 or been convicted under section 7. Section 8(5) gave the President the power to remove the disqualification of any party under the Act.

The final version of the Act was designed to ensure General Zia's control over political parties and general elections by granting wide-ranging discretion to the Federal Government and Election Commission controlled by him. It went through multiple amendments, imposing conditions based on vague terms such as 'Islamic Ideology', 'Ideology of Pakistan', 'security of Pakistan', 'morality', 'maintenance of public order', 'integrity or independence of the judiciary', and defamation or ridicule of the judiciary and the armed forces.

The Supreme Court made clear that restrictions to fundamental rights are only allowed to the extent expressly provided in the relevant parts of the *Constitutions*. Such rights are of a higher stature than ordinary laws and cannot be limited through legislation.[87] Therefore, restrictions on the right to freedom of association beyond those based on 'sovereignty or integrity of Pakistan' were ultra vires the *Constitution* and void. The limitations based on the 'security of Pakistan' in sections 3(1) and 6(1) were held to be void, while those relating to 'Islamic Ideology', 'morality' and 'maintenance of public order' were held to be valid only to the extent that these concepts form part of the 'sovereignty and integrity of Pakistan' as interpreted by the Court in its judgment.

[87] *Benazir Bhutto* (n 1) (Haleem CJ).

The immediate dissolution of a political party by simple publication in the Gazette under section 6 was held to be contrary to Article 17(2), since the Court held that this power has only been granted to the Supreme Court.

The Court upheld section 3A, stating that the requirement of rendering accounts fell within the ambit of Article 17(2) and 17(3). Such conditions were reasonable and could be found in democracies around the world, including the UK, the US and Germany.

Section 3B was held to be void in its entirety. The Court held that since section 3C only dealt with the 1988 general elections and was no longer relevant, there was no need to examine it. It directed the Federal Government to amend sections 7 and 8 in line with the decision in this case.

The vagueness of the phrase 'sovereignty or integrity of Pakistan' provided the Court with the opportunity to discuss the place of Islamic principles in the interpretation of the fundamental rights and to reiterate its special position in the constitutional structure and the powers provided to it. The Court held that fundamental rights, the principles of democracy, freedom, equality and justice are guaranteed in the *Constitution* as enunciated by Islam.[88] It stated that since these rights are provided in different articles with different restrictions, the exercise of each a right is intended to be in the public interest and to promote social solidarity.[89] The Court did not directly explain what 'public interest' and 'social solidarity' might mean. Still, their discussion of the role of Islam in the *Constitution* and the society using vague concepts, and the subsequent practice of the Court, discussed briefly in section IV would lead one to conclude that it means whatever the Court thinks it means.

The Chief Justice's opinion and the concurring opinions simply asserted a link between Islamic Ideology, the Ideology of Pakistan, the sovereignty and integrity of Pakistan, the and security and solidarity of the state. The Court stated that Islamic Ideology and Ideology of Pakistan are closely intertwined concepts, Islamic Ideology informing Ideology of Pakistan, and are essential for interpreting fundamental rights and their limits. It stated that the reason for Pakistan's creation is contained in the Ideology of Pakistan. Any attempts to create doubts about the Ideology of Pakistan, either through force or expression, would therefore challenge the solidarity and security of the state by destroying the legal order, which would be an 'invasion of the sovereignty and integrity of Pakistan'.[90]

The Supreme Court was quite brusque about the effect of such an understanding of the Ideology of Pakistan on religious minorities in Pakistan. It rejected the petitioner's argument that the Partition Agreement,[91] guaranteeing safeguards of minorities in Pakistan, should also be regarded as part of the concept of the Ideology of Pakistan.[92] It reasoned that minorities were protected through fundamental rights guaranteed in the

[88] ibid.

[89] ibid (Haleem CJ).

[90] ibid (Haleem CJ).

[91] The judgment does not clarify what the 'Partition Agreement' being referred to here is. Most likely the petitioner and the Court were referring to the 1950 Liaquat–Nehru Pact, which dealt with the protection of minorities, refugee property and return of abducted women as a result of the horrific violence during the partition of India. For a discussion of the Pact and its success, see P Raghavan, 'Partition: An International History' (2020) 42 *International History Review* 1029.

[92] *Benazir Bhutto* (n 1) (Haleem CJ).

Constitution and through the principles of policy, not through the Ideology of Pakistan, which 'was a special creed' responsible for creating the state, which protects the sovereignty and integrity of Pakistan.

For the Court, the Ideology of Pakistan was a unique concept based on Islamic Ideology and two-nation theory.[93] The Court then went into a discussion of the history of the two-nation theory, terming it the raison d'etre for the creation of Pakistan and claiming that at no time in the history of the Indian subcontinent had Hindus and Muslims or people of different faiths been united as one nation. That history is replete with failed attempts to achieve such unity, including attempts by Emperor Ashoka, Emperor Akbar and the British government.[94] The Court argued that this failure provides the story of the creation of Pakistan – a desire to create a separate homeland for the Muslims of India, where Islam plays a central and pervasive role in the daily lives of the people and the *Constitution*.[95]

After linking the sovereignty and integrity of Pakistan with Islamic Ideology and Ideology of Pakistan, the Court examined the conditions and constraints contained in the *PPA* that went beyond Article 17. It held that since these conditions – morality, Islamic Ideology, security, public order and foreign-aided party – are not mentioned in Article 17(2), they are ultra vires the *Constitution*. Thus, as independent concepts, these conditions were invalid. However, and more significantly, the Supreme Court also held that these conditions formed part of the concept of 'sovereignty and integrity of Pakistan' in Article 17(2).[96] To that extent, these conditions were valid; since then, they fell within the ambit of the limitation of the right to freedom of association contained in Article 17(2).

However, the Supreme Court did not provide precise definitions for these concepts, simply stating that they formed part of the concept of 'sovereignty and integrity of Pakistan'. It accepted that these concepts, especially morality, may be vague, but in Pakistan these concepts are based on Islamic principles and are interpreted in light of and derived from the Holy Quran and Sunnah.[97] The Court reasoned that since Quran requires Muslims to live a moral life individually and collectively, Islamic morality underpins the ideals of democracy, namely freedom, equality, tolerance and social justice. Therefore, political parties are supposed to protect public morals in the same way that 'other legal institutions protect public truthfulness and public symbols of authority'.[98] This imposes certain constraints of morality and obligations of high ethical standards on political parties so that they do not undermine the ability of the state to maintain law and order and damage the 'fabric of the state'.[99] So the Court was reasoning that in certain circumstances, actions against morality, Islamic Ideology, Ideology of Pakistan and public order could be serious enough to affect the security of the state

[93] ibid (Haleem CJ). For a brief introduction to the two-nation theory, see Bennett (n 42).

[94] *Benazir Bhutto* (n 1) (Haleem CJ). The Court not only disregarded the centuries of co-existence of Hindus and Muslims in the Subcontinent, but also the fact that in the neighbouring state of India, the constitutional structure was designed to ensure that people belonging to multiple religions could live as a united nation.

[95] ibid (Haleem CJ).

[96] ibid.

[97] ibid.

[98] ibid.

[99] ibid.

and thus harm the 'sovereignty or integrity of Pakistan'. Without actual clarification, the Court held that to this extent, these concepts limit the Article 17(2) right to freedom of association.

Since political parties are essential for democracy to exist, the Supreme Court held that the abuse of these concepts, which impose restraints on the formation and operation of the political parties, can have very serious consequences for a state. Despite being vague, the Court held that there was no danger of abuse or misuse of these restraints, because a penalty against a political party could only be imposed by the highest judicial forum in Pakistan, ie, the Supreme Court.[100] This was also why the Election Commission could not give such an important function, as sections 3B of PPA tried to do. Such powers can only reside in the Supreme Court as designed by the Constitution.[101]

The Court read Article 17(2) and 17(3) together to uphold the validity of restrictions imposed on foreign-aided political parties and requirements to provide a financial audit.[102] It stated that the phrase 'account for the source of its funds' in Article 17(3) was intended to act as a check on a political party that was supported by foreign actors and whose activities could adversely affect the sovereignty and integrity of Pakistan.[103] Furthermore, the requirement to give accounts of both the sources and expenditure of funds ensures that a political party's activities are not contrary to the 'sovereignty or integrity of Pakistan'. It does not amount to an unreasonable restriction contrary to Article 17.[104]

Finally, the Court held that absolute power given to the President to remove the disqualification of any party under section 8(5) was akin to prerogative powers that a president enjoys in relation to the pardoning of offenders, and thus does not contravene any constitutional provisions.

IV. The Supreme Court's Extensive Powers

By highlighting the importance of very general aims to create an Islamic society in the Objectives Resolution and using vague Islamic principles in the interpretation of fundamental rights without clarifying their definition, scope or extent, the Court in *Benazir Bhutto* laid the foundations for the future expansion of its powers, and its ability to interfere in virtually all areas of state policy, without careful and clear legal analysis.

It was only two years later that the Supreme Court, using its duty to achieve constitutional purpose while keeping the social context in mind, took its first *suo motu* action on a telegram received by the Chief Justice during summer vacations on the plight of brick kiln workers suffering as bonded labourers in *Darshan Masih v State*.[105] Since then, the Court has accepted jurisdiction under Article 184(3) in a wide range of circumstances,

[100] ibid.

[101] The Court held that although registration and cancellation of registration are not the same as dissolution of a political party, since the consequence of being unregistered was ineligibility to contest elections, it would have the same practical effect as dissolution: ibid (Haleem CJ).

[102] Sections 3(2), 3A and 3B(4) *PPA*.

[103] *Benazir Bhutto* (n 1) (Haleem CJ).

[104] ibid (Haleem CJ).

[105] *Darshan Masih v State* [1990] PLD 513 (SC).

ranging from formal public interest litigation initiated by civil society to Justices taking cognisance of issues reported in the media, which has included the Court asking for reports on how the issue is being addressed by the relevant government authorities and even how it should be addressed.[106]

Since the *Benazir Bhutto* case, the Supreme Court has at times stated the importance of upholding the separation of powers. For example, in the case of *Imtiaz Ahmad v Government of Pakistan*, the Court held that judges need to ensure that judicial review, which is a 'great weapon in the hands of judges', should remain strictly judicial and should not unduly encroach in the domain of the other branches of the state.[107] Despite such occasional statements, the Court has continuously expanded its review powers under Article 184(3).

The Supreme Court has used Article 184(3) to annul the President's use of his power to dismiss the Prime Minister and his cabinet under Article 58(2)(b), as being contrary to Article 17.[108] Even purely economic matters have been reviewed by the Court to ensure that national assets are managed for the benefit of the people of Pakistan and not wasted,[109] and in this context, the Court has reviewed the awarding of government contracts[110] and the sale of national assets.[111] The courts have stated that no state decision 'including the most political of decisions' is exempt from judicial review.[112] As long as the Court can make an argument that the action by any state institution (whether executive or legislative) has gone beyond the scope of power granted to it, or was taken under considerations that are perverse, or that no reasonable body of persons properly informed would take, or has been affected by irrelevant and extraneous considerations, or are arbitrary, or are taken *mala fide*, it has struck down the exercise of such power.[113] These have included matters pertaining to the independence and appointment of the judiciary,[114] the appointments, promotions, dismissals, disciplining and accountability

[106] For example, in the famous case of Mukhtar Mai, a victim of gang rape, the Court took several *suo moto* notices on the issue, starting in 2002 when the story became headline news in Pakistan. The *suo motu* orders included the Court monitoring the progress of the investigation and directing that the case be tried in the Anti-Terrorism Court and providing a timeframe for the decision; see *State and Others v Abdul Khaliq and Others* [2011] PSC (Crl) 545 (SC) [3], [7], [10] (Mian Saqib Nisar J).

[107] Justice Fazal Karim, quoting Lord Scarman in *Nottinghamshire County Council v Secretary of State* [1986] All ER 199, 204, in *Imtiaz Ahamd v Government of Pakistan* [1994] SCMR 2142 [12]. In this case, the Court was referring to judicial review under art 199 and did not refer to art 184(3), though the principle of separation of powers remains relevant.

[108] *Mian Muhammad Nawaz Sharif v President of Pakistan* [1993] PLD 473 (SC). In 1997, it upheld the dissolution of Benazir Bhutto's government under the same article: *Benazir Bhutto v President of Pakistan* [1998] PLD 388 (SC).

[109] *Khawaja Muhammad Asif v Federation of Pakistan* [2014] PLD 206 (SC).

[110] *Airport Support Services v Airport Manager, Quaid-e-Azam International Airport, Karachi* [1998] SCMR 2268 (SC).

[111] *Wattan Party v Federation of Pakistan* [2006] PLD 697 (SC).

[112] *Hudabiya Paper Mills Ltd. v National Accountability Bureau* [2012] PLD 515 (LHC) [15].

[113] *In the Matter of Corruption in Hajj Arrangements in 2010* [2011] PLD 963 (SC) (*Suo Motu* Case No 24 of 2010); *Muhammad Azhar Siddiqui v Federation of Pakistan* [2012] PLD 774 (SC); *Asaf Fasihuddin Khan v Government of Pakistan* [2014] SCMR 676 (SC); *Maulana Abdul Haque Baloch v Government of Balochistan* [2013] PLD 641 (SC). That is where the decision-making process is held void on account of arbitrariness, illegality, irrationality and procedural impropriety, or affected by *mala fides*.

[114] *Munir Hussain Bhatti v Federation of Pakistan* [2011] PLD 407 (SC); *Al-Jehad Trust v Federation of Pakistan* [1996] PLD 324 (SC).

of key executive officials,[115] and even holding the Prime Minister in contempt of court and disqualifying him from holding office,[116] and reviewing the government's failure in the form of the deteriorating law-and-order situation in a particular territory.[117]

As mentioned above, after years of confusion as to whether the basic structure doctrine forms part of the constitutional structure of Pakistan, the Supreme Court finally settled the matter in 2015 in *District Bar Association*.[118] Highlighting Islamic provisions as one of the salient features of the *Constitution*, the Court, by a majority of 13 judges to four, held that there are limitations on the powers of the Parliament to amend the *Constitution* and that it can strike down such unconstitutional amendments.[119]

The Supreme Court's use of *suo motu* powers has been far wider. It may have started with the Court using it to protect the fundamental rights of those unable to approach courts, as was the case with the first *suo motu*, but has devolved into the Court using it to interfere in every facet of government policy. For example, this has included *suo motu* action taken on the failure to protect a particular lake from pollution[120] and action taken to prevent the commercial use of land earmarked as a playground/park.[121] *Suo motu* actions have also been taken to order the government to produce missing persons,[122] against government departments on corruption,[123] in the face of the government's failure to protect human life and the deteriorating law-and-order situation in a particular part of Pakistan, and appointing a commission to investigate the issue.[124] The Court has taken *suo motu* action on economic matters, going so far as to provide advice

[115] *Muhammad Yasin v Federation of Pakistan* [2012] PLD 132 (SC).

[116] *Syed Yousaf Raza Gillani, Prime Minister of Pakistan v Assistant Registrar, Supreme Court of Pakistan* [2012] PLD 466 (SC), *Muhammad Azhar Siddiqui v Federation of Pakistan* [2012] PLD 774 (SC). These cases dealt with the conviction for contempt and disqualification of the eighteenth Prime Minister of Pakistan, Syed Yousaf Raza Gillani. In 2017, the then Prime Minister Nawaz Sharif was also dismissed and disqualified from holding any public office; see *Imran Ahmed Khan v Mian Muhammad Nawaz Sharif, Prime Minister of Pakistan* [2017] PLD 692 (SC).

[117] The Court exercised jurisdiction on the question of law and order in the Province of Balochistan in the case of *President Balochistan High Court Bar Association v Federation of Pakistan* [2012] SCMR 1958 (SC).

[118] *District Bar Association, Rawalpindi and Others v Federation of Pakistan* (n 75).

[119] For more detail, see MJ Nelson, 'Indian Basic Structure Jurisprudence in the Islamic Republic of Pakistan: Reconfiguring the Constitutional Politics of Religion' (2018) 13 *Asian Journal of Comparative Law* 333; W Mir, 'Saying Not What the Constitution is … But What It Should Be: Comment on the Judgment on the 18th and 21st Amendments to the Constitution' (2015) 2 *LUMS Law Journal* 64.

[120] *Suo Motu Case No 10 of 2010* [2011] SCMR 73 (SC); however, in this case the Court concluded that the response of the appropriate governmental authority to the population was sufficient to deal with environmental damage and prevent the violation of art 9.

[121] *Suo Motu Case No 10 of 2009* [2010] SCMR 885 (SC).

[122] Amnesty International, 'Pakistan: Denying the Undeniable: Enforced Disappearances in Pakistan' (2008) ASA 33/018/2008 6, https://www.amnesty.org/download/Documents/ASA330182008ENGLISH.pdf. In 2018, Saqib Nisar CJ again directed the authorities to produce the missing persons; see 'CJP Sets up Special Cell to Facilitate Missing Persons' Case' *The Nation* (24 June 2018), https://nation.com.pk/24-Jun-2018/cjp-to-hear-missing-persons-case-in-karachi-today.

[123] For example, *Suo Motu Case No 11 of 2011* [2014] PLD 389 (SC); *Suo Motu Case No 15 of 2009* [2012] PLD 610 (SC); *Suo Motu Case No 18 of 2010, Violation of Public Procurement Rules, 2004* [2011] PLD 821 (SC); *Suo Motu Case No 18 of 2010* [2011] PLD 927 (SC).

[124] *Suo Motu Case No 16 of 2011* [2013] PLD 443 (SC). In this case, the *suo motu* notice was taken on the deteriorating law and order situation in Karachi as a violation of rights under arts 9 (security of person) and 24 (protection of property) of the Constitution. Similarly, in *Suo Motu Case No 16 of 2016 (Quetta Lawyers' Carnage Case)*, a commission was appointed to investigate the attack at a hospital which resulted in the death of more than 50 lawyers; see Qazi Faez Isa J, 'Quetta Inquiry Commission Report' (2016), https://www.supremecourt.gov.pk/downloads_judgements/press_release/QuettaInquiryCommissionReport.pdf.

to the Federal Board of Revenue and the State Bank on taxation, foreign exchange regulation, how to retrieve money held abroad and bilateral tax treaties.[125] It has even tried to fix prices for essential commodities.[126] In addition to the review of services provided by government institutions, the Court has also used *suo motu* powers to target private institutions. It has also ordered private hospitals and schools to appear before it to provide a description of their services and justify their high fees.[127]

Another unique use of its original jurisdiction has been the creation of the Human Rights Cell at the Supreme Court. The breath of its operation can be judged from the fact that from June 2018 to May 2019, the Cell dealt with 105,617 petitions.[128] On the Cell's webpage, the Court mentions the importance and significance of public interest litigation, and gives examples of legislation that has been enacted as a result, such as the *Transgender Persons (Protection of Rights) Act 2018* and the *Human Organ Transplantation Ordinance 2007*.[129]

V. Conclusion

In a society where many people do not understand the law or know their rights[130] and have insufficient resources to approach the courts,[131] public interest litigation and *suo motu* action can provide an important avenue for justice. The *Benazir Bhutto* case laid the foundations for this development. However, over the years, Article 184(3) has become a blunt instrument in the hands of the Supreme Court to maintain its power and interfere in the work of other organs of the state. It cannot be denied that individual applicants in these cases had their rights protected, but the Court's attempts at social reform have failed to create a successful system of governance where rights are protected.[132] The

[125] *Suo Motu Action Taken up in Court* [2018] SCMR 574 (SC); *Suo Motu Action Regarding Maintaining of Foreign Currency Accounts by Pakistani Citizens without Disclosing the Same/Paying Taxes* [2018] PLD 686 (SC). It has even started a campaign to collect funds for the building of the Diamer-Bhasha and Mohmand Dams; see Supreme Court of Pakistan, 'Dam Fund Statistics', https://www.supremecourt.gov.pk/dam-fund-statistics.

[126] *Suo Motu Case No 10 of 2007* [2008] PLD 673 (SC).

[127] For example, 'Constitution Gives Me Right to Visit Hospitals, Says CJP' *Geo News* (11 January 2018), https://www.geo.tv/latest/176347-constitution-gives-me-right-to-visit-hospitals-says-cjp; 'CJP Takes *Suo Motu* Notice of Expensive Healthcare Facilities in Private Hospitals' *The Nation* (15 September 2018), https://nation.com.pk/15-Sep-2018/cjp-takes-suo-motu-notice-of-expensive-healthcare-facilities-in-private-hospitals; 'CJP Takes Suo Motu Notice against Private Universities' *Daily Times* (29 September 2018), https://dailytimes.com.pk/304199/cjp-takes-suo-motu-notice-against-private-universities.

[128] Supreme Court of Pakistan, 'Annual Report June 2018–May 2019' (2019) 76, https://www.supremecourt.gov.pk/downloads_judgements/all_downloads/annual_reports/SCP_Annual_Report_2018_2019.pdf.

[129] Supreme Court of Pakistan, 'Human Rights Cell', https://www.supremecourt.gov.pk/human-rights-cell. So, for example, the *Transgender Persons (Protection of Rights) Act, 2018* and the *Human Organ Transplantation Ordinance 2007* were a direct result of cases decided by the courts.

[130] The laws of Pakistan are in English, which the vast majority of people do not understand. In 1981, the literacy rate of Pakistan was 25.7 per cent; see UNESCO Institute for Statistics, 'Pakistan' (27 November 2016), http://uis.unesco.org/en/country/pk#slideoutmenu.

[131] In the *Benazir Bhutto* case, Haleem CJ explicitly mentioned how there are people who are unable to seek relief from the courts for violations of their rights and 'whose grievances go unnoticed and unredressed'; *Benazir Bhutto* (n 1) 490–91 (Haleem CJ).

[132] So, for example, in its report, the independent Human Rights Commission states that 'Pakistan continued to bear a dismal human rights record in terms of complying with the constitutional guarantees'; see Human Rights Commission of Pakistan, 'State of Human Rights in 2019' (Human Rights Commission of Pakistan,

practice has also generated an unmanageable caseload for the Supreme Court, with more than 48,000 cases pending before it.[133] At the same time, the Court has failed to adequately protect certain rights, especially minority rights based on religion and ethnicity, and the rights of women.[134]

Judicial activism by the Supreme Court continues to enjoy popular support as an effective means to hold the executive accountable and because other state organs have been unable to fulfil their constitutional obligations regarding good governance and human rights.[135] Despite this support, the expansion of its original jurisdiction has been constitutionally problematic and the Court often fails to properly justify how the particular facts before it satisfy the requirements contained in Article 184(3). The current practice of the Court has even dispensed with the need to mention that the Court is taking a *suo motu* notice under Article 184(3) on the particular issue because it raises 'a question of public importance with reference to the enforcement of fundamental rights', let alone justify its use of *suo motu* powers.[136] Continued expansion and inadequately justified use of its original jurisdiction has led to sustained criticism and has brought the Court into repeated conflict with other state institutions – that it is interfering in matters outside its ambit and expertise, that it is becoming a hindrance for other state institutions, and that the Supreme Court justices are engaged in self-aggrandisement.[137] The Court has successfully used Islamic principles and vague concepts to expand its judicial powers and protect human rights. But moving forward, if it wants to avoid constitutional conflicts, it will need to keep these criticisms in mind, justify the use of its powers and realise that it alone cannot enact successful social reform.

2020) 4–5, http://hrcp-web.org/hrcpweb/wp-content/uploads/2020/04/REPORT_State-of-Human-Rights-in-2019-20190503.pdf.

[133] These statistics are valid up to March 2021; see Supreme Court of Pakistan, *Fortnightly Disposal Report* (11 March 2021), https://www.supremecourt.gov.pk/downloads_judgements/all_downloads/Fortnightly_Disposal_Report.pdf.

[134] See, eg, Khan (n 25) 345–50. Ms Asma Jahangir, the Chairperson of HRCP, has highlighted bias against women and minorities in superior courts: see Human Rights Commission of Pakistan, 'Public Interest Litigation Scope and Problems – Report of an HRCP Seminar' (2010) 8, http://hrcp-web.org/hrcpweb/wp-content/pdf/ff/26.pdf; International Commission of Jurists (ICJ), 'Authority without Accountability: The Search for Justice in Pakistan' (2013) 11–15, https://www.refworld.org/pdfid/530f088d4.pdf.

[135] See, eg, I Niaz, 'Judicial Activism and the Evolution of Pakistan's Culture of Power' (2020) 109(1) *Commonwealth Journal of International Affairs* 23; O Siddique, 'The Judicialization of Politics in Pakistan: The Supreme Court after the Lawyers' Movement' in M Tushnet and M Khosla (eds), *Unstable Constitutionalism: law and Politics in South Asia* (Cambridge University Press, 2015) 159.

[136] So, for example, in the recent *suo motu* notice taken on COVID-19, there is no mention of art 184(3) or its requirements in the order; see *Suo Moto Action Regarding Combating the Pandemic of Corona Virus (COVID-19)* SMC 01/2020, https://www.supremecourt.gov.pk/downloads_judgements/s.m.c._01_2020.pdf.

[137] See, eg, M Waseem, 'Judging Democracy in Pakistan: Conflict between the Executive and Judiciary' (2012) 20(1) *Contemporary South Asia* 19; Niaz (n 135); Siddique (n 135).

14

Lakeside Colony of Hutterian Brethren v Hofer

Jurisdiction, Justiciability and Religious Law

KATHRYN CHAN*

I. Introduction

Canadian contributions to the law and religion literature tend to focus on the scope and meaning of section 2(a) of the *Canadian Charter of Rights and Freedoms*. There are good reasons for this focus. The 1982 enactment of the *Canadian Charter*, with its declaration that everyone enjoys freedom of conscience and religion, marked a new era in the protection of religious freedom in Canada. The Supreme Court of Canada has adjudicated a series of increasingly complex disputes involving the application of section 2(a), producing a unique case law that reflects Canada's status as a country with 'neither a formal religious establishment, as in the United Kingdom, nor a historical resistance to state support for religion, as in the United States'.[1] Several of these cases are the subject of extensive commentary.

While section 2(a) cases dominate Canada's law and religion literature, the Supreme Court of Canada has also decided questions of religion–state relations with little or no reference to the constitutional guarantee of religious freedom. The existence of this 'other' case law is partly attributable to section 32 of the *Canadian Charter*, which limits the *Charter*'s application to the Parliament and government of Canada and the legislature and government of each province. Judicial interpretations of section 32 have confirmed that, in the absence of government action, the *Charter* is not applicable to disputes between private parties like a religious community and its members.[2] It remains open to a litigant who is involved in an internal religious dispute to argue that the court should bring the common law into step with *Charter* values.[3] However, unlike in the

* The author would like to thank Frances Miltimore and Gemma Walsh for their excellent research assistance, and Renae Barker, Donna Greschner, Howard Kislowicz and Janna Promislow for their helpful feedback on this chapter.

[1] See R Moon, ch 6 in this volume.

[2] *Dolphin Delivery Ltd v RWDSU, Local 580* [1986] 2 SCR 573.

[3] *Hill v Church of Scientology of Toronto* [1995] 2 SCR 1130 [195].

US, the enforcement of court orders does not generally qualify as government action in Canada. The result, as Alvin Esau has noted, is that religious membership disputes are less easily 'constitutionalized' in Canada than in the US.[4] Because the *Charter* does not apply directly to disputes between private parties, Canadian courts adjudicate (or decide not to adjudicate) internal religious disputes based on statutory, common law and, sometimes, religious legal norms. Some of these disputes concern the ownership of religious community property, while others concern the ejection of members from religious communities.

Lakeside Colony v Hofer[5] is a case that bridges both of these categories of disputes. It began when the majority of members of a Hutterite Colony sought judicial assistance from the Manitoba Court of Queen's Bench to remove a minority group from the Colony's communal property, and culminated in a split decision by the Supreme Court of Canada. Despite having been decided 10 years after the coming into force of section 2(a) of the *Charter*, *Lakeside Colony* contains no mention of religious freedom. However, it engages with several enduring themes of religion–state relations in Canada, including the relationship between justiciability and jurisdiction, and the status of non-state legal norms.

This chapter summarises the Supreme Court of Canada's 1992 decision in *Lakeside Colony* and reflects upon its legacy. In section II, I briefly describe the background to the litigation and the religious community at its heart. In section III, I outline the judgments of the lower courts and the Supreme Court of Canada, and comment on the jurisprudence that has followed *Lakeside Colony*. In section IV, I consider what *Lakeside Colony* has to say about the relationship between justiciability and jurisdiction, and the status of religious law as law. I conclude by reflecting on the relationship between the *Lakeside* line of cases and the constitutional protection of religious freedom.

II. Facts and Background

A. The Hutterian Community in Canada

The Hutterites are an Anabaptist group that migrated from Russia to North America in 1874, founding three small colonies in South Dakota. Since then, the group's population has greatly increased. Currently, about 45,000 Hutterites live on 462 Hutterite colonies in the Great Plains region of Western Canada and the US.[6] Hutterites share religious beliefs and practices with the Amish and other Anabaptist groups, such as adult voluntary baptism, a commitment to separating the church from the broader society and a refusal to bear arms.[7] Unlike many Anabaptist groups, Hutterites embrace modern

[4] AJ Esau, 'The Judicial Resolution of Church Property Disputes: Canadian and American Models' (2002) 40 *Alberta Law Review* 767, 774, citing *New York Times v Sullivan*, 376 US 254 (1963).

[5] *Lakeside Colony of Hutterian Brethren v Hofer* [1992] 3 SCR 165 (hereinafter '*Lakeside*').

[6] See www.hutterites.org/the-leut/distribution.

[7] A Esau, 'Communal Property and Freedom of Religion: *Lakeside Colony of Hutterian Brethren v Hofer*' in J McLaren and H Coward (eds), *Religious Conscience, the State and the Law* (State University of New York Press, 1999) 97.

technology in their economic enterprises. However, the Hutterite view of the separated church includes the notion of 'community of property'. All property in a Hutterite colony, including the land, the housing units, the common facilities and the machinery, belongs to the Hutterian Brethren Church.[8] Individual Hutterites do not own anything, though many have 'a rich bundle of usufructuary rights to colony property that makes them in reality much wealthier than many people in the host society'.[9]

The Hutterian Brethren Church has three levels of governance: the colony level, the conference (Leut) level, and a constitutional level of the conferences.[10] Each colony is headed by a minister and by an executive committee made up of a number of male colony members.[11] While the colonies have a substantial amount of economic independence, they are organised for various temporal and spiritual purposes into three different conferences (or Leut): the Darius-Leut, the Lehrer-Leut and the Schmied-Leut. The conferences are traceable back to the original South Dakota colonies. They share many beliefs and practices, but differ in terms of some of their rules of conduct.[12] A senior elder heads each conference along with a conference-level council, comprising representatives from each colony.[13] Finally, at the constitutional level, a nine-member Board of Managers, comprising three members from each conference, governs the three conferences. Most of these governance structures are set out in the Constitution of the Hutterian Brethren Church and Rules as to Community of Property, which colony representatives executed in 1950. In 1951, a corporation named 'The Hutterian Brethren Church' was also incorporated by a private Act of the Canadian Parliament. The purpose of the statutory incorporation, as found by the Supreme Court of Canada in *Lakeside Colony v Hofer*, was 'to deal with external threats that affected each Hutterite conference equally'.[14]

B. The Dispute

The trigger for the Lakeside Colony litigation was a dispute over patent rights to a hog-feeder. Daniel Hofer Sr, a voting member of Lakeside Colony who worked in the Colony's machine shop, developed a new form of hog-feeder with an innovative 'wet and dry' feeding mechanism. Hofer Sr applied to patent his hog-feeder, but discovered that a neighbouring Hutterite colony had already obtained a patent on the design. Hofer Sr maintained that he was entitled to the patent and continued manufacturing the hog-feeders even when the overseers of Lakeside Colony requested that he cease.[15] The neighbouring colony, which happened to be led by the Senior Elder for the Schmied-Leut Conference, responding by filing a demand for patent infringement.

[8] Esau (n 4) 100–01.
[9] ibid 101.
[10] ibid 99.
[11] ibid 100. Esau notes that women are expected to join the colony as members, but do not have a vote in formal colony decisions.
[12] ibid 99.
[13] ibid.
[14] *Lakeside* (n 5) [58].
[15] ibid [90]–[98].

The dispute came to a head on 20 January 1987, when Hofer Sr put a stop order on a cheque that Lakeside Colony had written to settle the patent infringement claim.[16] On 21 January, the overseers of Lakeside Colony called a meeting of the Colony's voting members to be held later on the same day.[17] Everyone had notice of the 21 January meeting, but there was no explicit notice of the agenda.[18] The meeting focused on the hog-feeder conflict and the placing of the stop order on the cheque. Hofer Sr became angry and disruptive during the discussion, and the chairperson asked him to leave. After he left, the remaining voting members agreed to discipline Hofer Sr with a mild form of shunning. When Hofer Sr rejoined the meeting, he refused to repent. He was told that he was 'expelling himself' from the Colony by refusing to accept the punishment. No formal vote was held, but the members endorsed the Chairman's ruling that Hofer Sr was 'no member, he is out of the church'.[19]

Ten days later, the overseers called another meeting to see if Hofer Sr would repent and seek re-admission to Lakeside Colony. Hofer Sr received no notice of the specific agenda for the 31 January meeting, though the Supreme Court of Canada majority accepted he would have known that his conduct was the meeting's 'major item'.[20] Hofer Sr refused to attend the meeting, requesting instead that a 'higher court' of the church be convened to hear the dispute. The members consulted the Senior Elder of the Schmied-Leut Conference, who declined Hofer Sr's request and advised the Colony that Hofer Sr 'and all those who follow him should be separated from Lakeside'.[21] At a second meeting on the same day, the attending members agreed that Hofer and his two sons who sided with him were no longer Colony members.

Following the 31 January meeting, the members of Lakeside Colony effectively split into two competing groups. Hofer Sr and his followers remained on Colony property despite the expulsions, opening their own bank account, eating in the main dining hall and operating a number of Colony enterprises.[22] The Hutterite doctrine of non-resistance limited the Colony's ability to respond to this conduct, as it ruled out any form of violence or physical ejection.[23] In February, lawyers for Lakeside Colony wrote to Hofer Sr and his followers, asking them to leave Colony property. When they did not leave, the Colony filed a statement of claim, asking the court to order the defendants to vacate the colony land permanently and to return all Colony property in their possession. It also asked the court to declare that the adult defendants were no longer members of the Colony.[24]

[16] *Lakeside* [102].

[17] The Lakeside Colony dispute was complicated by the fact that, due to a series of events in the 1970s, outside overseers had been managing Lakeside Colony on behalf of the Schmied-Leut conference. The overseers were under the supervision of the conference's Senior Elder.

[18] *Lakeside* (n 5) para 103.

[19] ibid [109].

[20] ibid [120].

[21] Ibid [120]–[121].

[22] ibid [126].

[23] ibid [146].

[24] ibid [4].

III. The Judgments

A. The Lower Court Judgments

Lakeside Colony succeeded at trial.[25] The trial judge found that Hofer Sr had effectively expelled himself from Colony membership at the January meetings by refusing to accept the punishment meted out by the majority.[26] The judge declined to review the merits of the Colony's decision and found that the expulsion conformed to the procedural norms of the Hutterian Brethren Church. He ordered the expelled members to leave the Colony without any Colony property, in accordance with Hutterian practice.

At the Manitoba Court of Appeal, a majority upheld the trial judgment.[27] It applied a more robust form of judicial review than had the trial judge, holding that, as the Colony's expulsion implicated property rights, the expulsion had to conform to the rules of natural justice. The majority found that the Colony had dealt fairly with Hofer Sr in the circumstances. It expressed sympathy for the position of the expelled members, but concluded that the court had no basis for intervention. In dissent, O'Sullivan JA held that the Colony had denied natural justice to Hofer Sr and his followers, and had illegally expelled them from membership.

B. The Supreme Court of Canada Judgment

A majority of the Supreme Court of Canada, in an opinion written by Gonthier J, overruled the trial judge and the Court of Appeal majority. It agreed with O'Sullivan JA's dissenting conclusion that the Colony had not carried out its expulsion of the defendants according to the applicable rules and the principles of natural justice.[28] The majority dismissed the Colony's action for enforcement of the expulsion and declared that Hofer Sr and his sons had remained members of the colony throughout.[29] The sole dissent, written by McLachlin J (as she then was), would have upheld the lower court decisions.

The majority opinion in *Lakeside Colony* is a relatively long appellate judgment that is notable for its unusually detailed consideration of testimonial and documentary evidence. The majority divided its analysis into four main parts. First, it addressed and confirmed the court's authority to hear the dispute before it. Gonthier J began with a general statement of principle about judicial intervention in religious disputes:

> The courts are slow to exercise jurisdiction over membership in a voluntary association, especially a religious one. However, the courts have exercised jurisdiction where a property or civil right turns on the question of membership.[30]

[25] *Lakeside Colony of Hutterian Brethren v Hofer* (1989) 63 DLR (4th) 473 (Man QB).
[26] *Lakeside Colony* (SCC) (n 5) [152].
[27] *Lakeside Colony of Hutterian Brethren et al v Hofer et al* (1991) 70 Man R (2d) 191 (Man CA).
[28] *Lakeside* (SCC) (n 5) [1].
[29] ibid [171].
[30] ibid [6].

The majority found that civil rights were engaged in this matter. From the perspective of the Colony, the right at stake was proprietary, while from the perspective of the expelled members, the rights at stake were contractual. Either way, the majority held, the rights were enforceable by the courts:

> [A] contractual right which permits a person to earn his livelihood is on the same footing as a property right in the context of jurisdiction over voluntary associations … If the appellants have a right to stay, the question is not so much whether this is a property right or a contractual right, but whether it is of 'sufficient importance' to deserve the intervention of the court and whether the remedy sought is susceptible of enforcement by the court.[31]

In the case before it, the majority found that the rights in question were of 'utmost importance'. Therefore, the court had to determine whether the defendants had been validly expelled. It was not for the court to review the merits of the decision to expel, the majority held, but it was 'called upon to determine whether the purported expulsion was carried out according to the applicable rules, with regard to the principles of natural justice, and without *mala fides*'.[32]

Second, the majority turned to the institutional framework within which the Lakeside Colony operated. It identified four sources of rules for this framework: (a) the tradition and custom of Hutterites; (b) the Articles of Association entered into by the colony members; (c) the Constitution of the Hutterian Brethren Church and Rules as to Community of Property; and (d) *An Act to Incorporate the Hutterian Brethren Church*, SC 1951, c 77.[33] The majority reviewed each of these sources in some detail, highlighting the provisions in the Constitution and Articles of Association that addressed the expulsion of members. It also addressed the relationship between these sources of authority, a matter to which we will return in the next section.

Third, the majority identified the requirements for expulsion that arose from the Colony's institutional framework and from the requirements of natural justice. The majority interpreted both the Articles and the Constitution as requiring a vote in order for a colony to expel a member. However, it found that the vote did not need to be formal. Given the Hutterian preference for operating by consensus rather than formal votes, it would be 'a question of fact in any given situation whether a consensus has been reached that is sufficiently unambiguous to qualify as a vote'.[34] The majority then laid out the requirements of natural justice, emphasising that the content of natural justice is flexible and dependent on the circumstances in which the question arises.[35] Focusing on the proper content of the notice requirement, the majority held that it was insufficient to give a Colony member notice that their conduct would be considered at a meeting; in addition, the member must be given notice of the cause for which they were to be expelled. Adequate and timely notice provided the person facing expulsion with the opportunity to consider their position and helped to ensure that the decision makers would be able to attend the meeting and contribute to the discussion.[36]

[31] ibid [8].
[32] ibid [10].
[33] *An Act to Incorporate the Hutterian Brethren Church*, SC 1951, c 77.
[34] ibid [74].
[35] ibid [80].
[36] ibid [82].

Finally, the majority considered the sequence of events surrounding the dispute over the hog-feeder in light of the requirements it had identified, and concluded that the expulsions of both Hofer Sr and his sons must be set aside for lack of sufficient notice. The Colony had given Hofer Sr's sons no notice that the Colony would consider their expulsion. The expulsion of Hofer Sr was also procedurally defective. The majority acknowledged that there was a sense in which Hofer Sr had notice of the charge made against him at the 21 January meeting and an opportunity to make representations as to whether he ought to be expelled or not. However, there were only a 'few moments of notice that expulsion was being considered before the issue was actually decided'.[37] A number of factors contributed to the majority's conclusion that the short notice was inadequate: the decision was of great magnitude; there was little urgency with respect to the expulsion; and two voting members of the colony were absent and unable to participate.[38] As the result, the majority allowed the appeal, set aside the judgments of the lower courts and dismissed the Colony's action. Effectively this result meant that Hofer Sr and his followers remained Colony members and maintained a right to remain on the property.

Justice McLachlin dissented. She agreed with much of the majority's reasoning, but concluded that the requirements of natural justice had been met on the facts of the case.[39] She emphasised that advance notice of a decision is not required where the *purpose* of the notice requirement – to protect the right of persons to present their defence against decisions affecting their rights and interests – is fulfilled.[40] Here, formal notice was unnecessary because the expulsion of Hofer Sr and his followers 'was essentially a self-expulsion, freely chosen by them with full knowledge of the consequences'.[41] Even if the Colony had made some sort of choice to expel, the appellants were fully aware of what was to be decided and had the opportunity to defend themselves or seek reconciliation.[42] 'Like Luther with Rome', McLachlin J concluded, 'the problem lay not in unfair procedures or lack of opportunities for hearing; the problem lay rather in the fundamental divergence between the parties, a divergence which doomed any proceedings, no matter how just, to failure.'[43]

Justice McLachlin's diagnosis of the fundamental divergence between the parties appears to have been borne out in the aftermath of the case. Following the Supreme Court decision, the majority of the Colony members continued to shun the dissenters. They also asserted that since the dissenters remained members, all the assets they had accumulated by running enterprises during the litigation period belonged to the Colony.[44] In December 1992, a little more than a month after the Supreme Court released its decision, the Colony voted again to expel Hofer Sr and his sons, this time with proper notice. Hofer Sr again contested the decision, but the Manitoba Queen's Bench upheld the expulsion.[45]

[37] ibid [163].
[38] ibid [166]–[167].
[39] ibid [174].
[40] ibid [177].
[41] ibid [181].
[42] ibid [178], [187].
[43] ibid [189].
[44] Esau (n 4) 106.
[45] *Lakeside Colony of Hutterian Brethren v Hofer* (1994) 93 Man R (2d) 161 (QB). For a detailed account of this second round of litigation, see Esau (n 4) 107–10.

C. The Post-*Lakeside Colony* Jurisprudence

In the years following *Lakeside Colony*, Canadian courts relied extensively on the decision in determining whether and how to proceed with the adjudication of disputes arising in voluntary associations. All levels of court applied the decision to various associations, which ran the gamut from sports clubs to search and rescue organisations to Indigenous political bodies. For instance, in *Métis Nation – Saskatchewan v Morin*, a provincial superior court cited *Lakeside* in ordering a meeting of the executive council of the Métis Nation Legislative Assembly.[46] In *Garcha v Kharsa*, a provincial appellate court invoked *Lakeside* in affirming a trial judge's decision to cancel an election in a Sikh temple because of a defective enrolment process.[47] In *Bruker v Marcovitz*, the Supreme Court applied *Lakeside* to a contract dispute over the enforceability of a *get* (a Jewish religious divorce).[48] And in *Surrey Knights Junior Hockey*, a provincial superior court relied on *Lakeside* in deciding to review an ice hockey team's expulsion from a junior hockey league.[49]

While courts cited *Lakeside Colony* widely in the years following the decision, the precise parameters of the Supreme Court's holding on judicial intervention were the subject of debate. In an early case comment on *Lakeside Colony*, Margaret Ogilvie, a leading law and religion scholar, asserted that the ratio decidendi of the decision was that 'ecclesiastical procedures are subject to the rules of natural justice'.[50] Ogilvie also suggested that because the common law had long regarded religious associations 'to be voluntary associations and the relationships among members to be a multilateral contract', this contract provided a legal nexus for the intervention of civil courts.[51] Subsequent scholarship took issue with the breadth of Ogilvie's interpretation.[52] However, courts continued to interpret *Lakeside Colony* expansively. In 2011, one of Canada's most prominent appellate courts cited *Lakeside Colony* for the proposition that that a court will interfere in a voluntary association dispute 'where the organization's internal processes are unfair … or where the aggrieved party has exhausted the organization's internal processes'.[53]

In 2018, the Supreme Court of Canada took steps to clarify the scope of *Lakeside Colony* in its decision in *Highwood Congregation of Jehovah's Witnesses (Judicial Committee) v Wall*.[54] Randy Wall was a long-standing member of the Highwood Congregation, an unincorporated association of about 100 Jehovah's Witnesses living in Calgary, Alberta. The Congregation's Judicial Committee disfellowshipped Wall after he engaged in alleged wrongdoing related to drunkenness and was found to be

[46] *Métis Nation – Saskatchewan v Morin* [2014] SKQB 421.

[47] *Garcha v Khalsa Diwan Society – New Westminster* [2006] BCCA 140.

[48] *Bruker v Marcovitz*, 2007 SCC 54.

[49] *Surrey Knights Junior Hockey v Pacific Junior Hockey League* [2018] BCSC 1748.

[50] MH Ogilvie, 'Ecclesiastical Law – Jurisdiction of Civil Courts – Governing Documents of Religious Organizations – Natural Justice: *Lakeside Colony of Hutterian Brethren v Hofer*' (1993) 72 *Canadian Bar Review* 224, 245.

[51] ibid 247.

[52] P Hart, 'Justice for (W)all: Judicial Review and Religion' (2017) 43 *Queen's Law Journal* 1, 14.

[53] *Hart v Roman Catholic Episcopal Corporation of the Diocese* [2011] ONCA 728, [2011] CarswellOnt 12820 [19].

[54] *Highwood Congregation of Jehovah's Witnesses (Judicial Committee) v Wall*, 2018 SCC 26.

insufficiently repentant. Wall filed an application for judicial review on the basis that the decision was procedurally unfair and that it negatively affected his work as a realtor with clients who were mostly Jehovah's Witnesses.[55] The chambers judge and a majority of the Court of Appeal concluded that the courts had jurisdiction to consider the merits of the application. On appeal, the Supreme Court of Canada disagreed. In a unanimous and short opinion, it held that the courts had no basis to intervene in the Congregation's decision-making process.

Wall affects the legacy of *Lakeside Colony* in a number of ways. First, the decision establishes a clearer boundary than existed previously in Canadian law between the 'public law' and 'private law' forms of (judicial) review for procedural fairness. The Court in *Wall* applied the term 'judicial review' exclusively to exercises of the superior court's supervisory jurisdiction over the decisions of state authorities.[56] The purpose of judicial review, the Court held, is to 'ensure the legality of state decision making' and it is available only 'where there is an exercise of state authority and where that exercise is of a sufficiently public character'.[57] The Court also discussed the ability of the courts to review decisions of voluntary associations for procedural fairness. The purpose of such review is to protect 'a legal right which a party seeks to have vindicated' and it is available where a claimant can establish they have a distinct legal right sounding in contract, property or tort.[58]

Wall arguably also increased the significance of *Lakeside Colony* by limiting the range of associations that are subject to (public law) judicial review in Canada. The Court adopted a narrow conception of state action in *Wall*, declining to apply the type of multifactoral test that Anglo-Commonwealth courts have used to determine whether a decision has a sufficient public element or character to make it amenable to judicial review.[59] The full implications of the Court's narrow conception of state action, which have already attracted criticism,[60] go beyond the scope of this chapter. However, one practical implication of *Wall* is that some associations that were previously subject to judicial review are no longer subject to it, so that more parties will have to rely on private law review and remedies to challenge membership decisions in court.[61]

With regard to these private law remedies, *Wall* clarified a point that remained murky after *Lakeside Colony*: there is no 'free-standing right to procedural fairness as regards the decisions of religious or other voluntary organizations'.[62] Justice Rowe specifically rejected the argument that *Lakeside* could be read as permitting courts to review the decisions of voluntary organisations for procedural fairness concerns where the issues raised were 'sufficiently important' in some abstract sense. A *legal right* of

[55] ibid [7].
[56] ibid [14].
[57] ibid.
[58] ibid [24], [27].
[59] ibid [12].
[60] P Daly, 'Right and Wrong on the Scope of Judicial Review: *Highwood Congregation of Jehovah's Witnesses (Judicial Committee) v Wall*' (2018) 31(3) *Canadian Journal of Administrative Law & Practice* 339; M Chowdury, 'A Wall between the "Public" and the "Private": A Comment on *Highwood Congregation of Jehovah's Witnesses (Judicial Committee) v Wall*' (2019) 9 *Western Journal of Legal Studies*, https://ojs.lib.uwo.ca/index.php/uwojls/issue/view/941.
[61] Chowdury (n 60) para 9.
[62] *Wall* (n 54) [25].

sufficient importance – such as a property or contractual right – must be at stake before the court has a basis to intervene.[63] Since the Congregation did not have any written governance documents and the parties had not otherwise established that Mr Wall and the Congregation intended to create legal relations, the matters at issue fell outside the jurisdiction of the Court.[64]

While *Wall* clarified several questions arising out of *Lakeside Colony*, it left other questions unanswered. One question was whether the written constitution and bylaws of a voluntary association constituted a contract grounding the intervention of the courts. In *Ethiopian Orthodox Tewahedo Church of Canada St Mary Cathedral v Aga*, the Supreme Court answered 'not necessarily'. An association's rules – whether written or not – do not always constitute a contract. What a complainant must show is an objective intention to enter into legal relations.[65] *Aga* further reduces the availability of the type of 'private law' review that occurred in *Lakeside Colony*, distancing the Canadian position from that of the English courts.[66] However, other questions about religious membership disputes remain. What is the relationship between justiciability and jurisdiction? What is the juridical status of religious customs and laws? Finally, what is the relationship between religious membership disputes and the constitutional protection of religious freedom? The following sections consider what insights *Lakeside Colony* offers on each of these themes.

IV. *Lakeside Colony:* Enduring Themes

A. Justiciability and Jurisdiction

The first prominent theme that emerges from *Lakeside Colony* concerns the relationship between justiciability and jurisdiction. Canadian courts have consistently expressed a reluctance to adjudicate disputes engaging contentious matters of religious doctrine.[67] However, it is often unclear whether this reluctance represents a voluntary 'abstinence' from interfering in religious matters or an acknowledgement of constitutional limits on the authority of the civil courts.[68] In this chapter, I argue that non-justiciability connotes voluntary abstinence, while jurisdiction connotes a lack of authority to decide.

[63] ibid [27].

[64] ibid [28]–[31].

[65] *Ethiopian Orthodox Tewahedo Church of Canada St Mary Cathedral v Aga*, 2021 SCC 22 [48] (hereinafter '*Aga*').

[66] *cf Shergill v Khaira* [2014] UKSC 33, [2015] AC 359 (SC). The Supreme Court of Canada distinguished *Shergill* in *Wall*, holding that *Shergill* had required procedural fairness as 'a way of enforcing a contract': *Wall* (n 54) [26]. However, the Court did not cite *Shergill* in *Aga*, even though the UK Supreme Court's discussion of the contractual source of the powers of religious associations was directly on point: see *Shergill* at [45]–[48].

[67] *Syndicat Northcrest v Amselem*, 2004 SCC 47, [2004] CarswellQue 1543 [50]; *Demiris v Hellenic Community of Vancouver*, 2000 BCSC 733, [2000] CarswellBC 974 [33].

[68] See, eg, Rick Garnett, 'The Freedom of the Church: (Toward) an Exposition' in M Schwartzman, C Flanders and Z Robinson (eds), *The Rise of Corporate Liberty* (Oxford University Press, 2015) 49 ('Freedom of the church should be seen as requiring not only that secular authorities "abstain" from interfering in religious matters but also they acknowledge the limits on their jurisdiction over such matters'). See also *Hart* (n 52) [11]–[12].

In my view, *Lakeside Colony* illustrates how justiciability and jurisdiction have been elided in judicial considerations of religious membership disputes, and *Wall* represents an attempt to distinguish the two concepts and to identify matters that the courts cannot decide. However, it remains a somewhat open question whether the Canadian judiciary's general avoidance of religious disputes is better understood as a practice of discretion or a principle of law.[69]

The concepts of justiciability and jurisdiction both play a role in delineating the boundaries of judicial intervention in religious disputes. Courts sometimes appear to use the two terms interchangeably in legal judgments, and courts in different jurisdictions define the terms in slightly different ways.[70] However, despite their similarities, the terms 'justiciability' and 'jurisdiction' have somewhat different subtexts. Legal dictionaries generally define 'jurisdiction' as the power or authority to make legal decisions.[71] To say that a court has no jurisdiction over a matter is to imply that *the court cannot adjudicate that matter*. In North America, litigants of religious membership disputes often pair the claim that a civil court lacks jurisdiction to resolve the dispute with a claim that a religious association shares sovereignty with the state. The language of sovereignty and jurisdiction is invoked to support the claim that there is a 'presumptively autonomous sphere within which [religious associations] may act largely unimpeded', free from government interference.[72] In the US, constitutional law goes some way towards setting a jurisdictional boundary between the respective spheres of religious associations and civil courts. For example, the American ministerial exception prohibits the judiciary from intervening where religious institutions hire and fire ministerial employees on discriminatory grounds, 'even when the discrimination is wholly unrelated to the employer's religious beliefs or practice'.[73]

However, at least in Canadian law, justiciability has a different connotation. Lorne Sossin defines justiciability 'as a set of judge-made rules, norms and principles delineating the scope of judicial intervention in social, political and economic life'.[74] In *Canada (Auditor General) v Canada (Minister of Energy, Mines & Resources)*, Dickson CJ described an inquiry into justiciability as 'first and foremost, a *normative* inquiry into the appropriateness as a matter of constitutional judicial policy of the courts deciding a given issue'.[75] The results of this normative inquiry may vary from context to context, Canadian scholars have explained, depending on prevailing views about 'the role of the judiciary in a given place at a given time as well as on its changing character

[69] *Shergill* (n 66) [38].

[70] See the discussion in ibid [41]–[43].

[71] See, eg, *Black's Law Dictionary*, 10th edn (Thomson Reuters, 2014) 980 ('jurisdiction').

[72] SD Smith, 'The Jurisdictional Conception of Church Autonomy' in *The Rise of Corporate Religious Liberty* (Oxford University Press, 2016) 22. For a discussion of religious jurisdictional claims in a Canadian context, see K Chan, 'Religious Institutionalism: A Feminist Response' (2021) 71 *University of Toronto Law Journal* 443.

[73] *Our Lady of Guadalupe School v Morrisey-Berru*, 140 S Ct 2049 (2020), 2072, Sotomayor J and Ginsburg J dissenting.

[74] L Sossin, *Boundaries of Judicial Review*, 2nd edn (Thomson Reuters Canada, 2012) 7. Elliott and Thomas consider justiciability and deference to be different points on the same continuum: see M Elliott and R Thomas, *Public Law*, 3rd edn (Oxford University Press, 2017) 563.

[75] *Canada (Auditor General) v Canada (Minister of Energy, Mines & Resources)* [1989] 2 SCR 49 (SCC), 90–91.

and evolving capability'.[76] The determination of whether a matter is justiciable or non-justiciable is within the discretion of the Court.[77] To say that a matter is non-justiciable, therefore, is not to imply that *a court cannot adjudicate that matter*, but rather to imply that *a court has decided to abstain from adjudicating the matter* based on its unsuitability for judicial determination.

The Supreme Court of Canada described its decision to intervene in *Lakeside Colony* as a decision about jurisdiction. However, a close reading of the judgment suggests that the majority understood itself to be delineating a boundary not between what courts can and cannot decide, but between 'what courts should and should not decide'.[78] The majority framed the jurisdictional question in *Lakeside Colony* as a question about when the courts had historically 'exercised' jurisdiction over religious membership disputes,[79] a framing that suggested the jurisdiction was the Court's to decline.[80] It also depicted the question about whether to intervene in the Colony's dispute as a normative question, stating that the decision turned not so much on the legal characterisation of the expelled members' asserted right as on whether the right was 'of sufficient importance to deserve the intervention of the court'.[81] In considering whether it should intervene in the Colony's dispute, the majority appeared less concerned with whether the Court was barred from deciding the matter than whether it should abstain.

Set against the background of *Lakeside Colony*, the Court's decision in *Wall v Highwood Congregation* reads as an attempt to clarify the distinction between jurisdiction and justiciability, and to more clearly associate 'jurisdiction' with mandatory limits on what civil courts can decide. *Wall* outlined three limits on review for procedural fairness: the restriction of (public law) judicial review to state action; the restriction of (private law) review to cases involving the vindication of a legal right; and the refusal of courts to consider issues of theology.[82] The Court identified the first two of these as jurisdictional limits and the third as a 'supplementary' justiciability issue. Unlike in *Lakeside Colony*, the Court depicted the jurisdictional limits as establishing a hard boundary between what the Court could and could not do. For instance, the Court in *Wall* did not frame the jurisdictional question before it as a question about when the practice of the courts was to 'exercise' jurisdiction over religious membership disputes. Rather, the Court identified the central question as being when 'courts *have* jurisdiction to review the decisions of religious organizations' in cases where procedural fairness concerns are raised.[83]

[76] P Macklem and C Scott, 'Constitutional Ropes of Sand or Justiciable Guarantees? Social Rights in a New South African Constitution' (1992) 141 *University of Pennsylvania Law Review* 1, 27, cited in Sossin (n 74) 7.

[77] *Reference re Canada Assistance Plan (BC)* [1991] 2 SCR 525, 545: 'In exercising its discretion whether to determine a matter that is alleged to be non-justiciable, the Court's primary concern is to retain its proper role within the constitutional framework of our democratic form of government.'

[78] Sossin (n 74) 9. See also *Hart* (n 52) [11]: 'The question of jurisdiction in cases such as *Lakeside* and *Wall* is more precisely understood as a question of *justiciability*.' As will be seen, my view of *Wall* is somewhat different.

[79] *Lakeside* (n 5) [6].

[80] Although it should be noted that the Court devoted little attention to this issue, perhaps because both parties were seeking judicial intervention: *Hart* (n 52) [11].

[81] *Lakeside* (n 5) [9].

[82] *Wall* (n 54) [2].

[83] ibid [1].

The comments addressed to the third limit – ie, the Court's supplementary comments on justiciability – are the only ones directly addressed to the religious nature of the dispute between Mr Wall and the Highwood Congregation, and are somewhat more ambiguous. At one point, the Court seems to identify justiciability as a limit on its own authority, stating that 'justiciability limits the extent to which courts may engage with decisions by voluntary associations'.[84] It also suggests that a religious group's procedural as well as substantive rules may be non-justiciable.[85] Ultimately, however, *Wall* describes justiciability as a flexible and contextual judicial decision 'whether to decide a matter in the courts'.[86] If the court's reluctance to adjudicate religious matters is to be understood as a legal principle rather than a practice of discretion, it may need to be linked more explicitly with the constitutional protection of religious freedom, a matter to which I will return in the concluding section.

B. Religious Law as Law

A second important theme that emerges from *Lakeside Colony* concerns the juridical status of religious customs and laws. *Lakeside* provides an early example of the Supreme Court of Canada considering, in some detail, the customs and traditions of a non-state legal order.[87] At a time when courts and scholars are increasingly grappling with the challenges of legal pluralism and interlegality,[88] the decision offers insights on both the perils and the importance of seeking to understand non-state laws.

We have seen that the *Lakeside* court identified four sources of authority governing Colony disputes: the tradition and custom of Hutterites; the Articles of Association of the Lakeside Colony; the Constitution of the Hutterian Brethren Church and Rules as to Community of Property; and a federal act incorporating the Hutterian Brethren Church. The Court devoted considerable attention to the legal status of each of these sources and the relationships between them before determining whether the expulsion of Hofer Sr and his followers was carried out fairly and in accordance with the applicable rules.[89]

Along the way, the Court had to confront some of the complexities of the Lakeside Colony's institutional framework. For example, the Colony Articles of Association and the Church Constitution appeared to have inconsistent positions on whether a

[84] ibid [32].

[85] ibid [38]. Chowdury ((n 60) 5) refers to this as an 'additional gloss' to the case law on justiciability.

[86] *Wall* (n 54) [32]–[34].

[87] Ogilvie (n 50) 250 (describing *Lakeside* as the first case in which the Supreme Court of Canada considered the legal status of and interrelationship among the governing documents of a religious organisation in this way).

[88] Sousa Santos refers to interlegality as 'legal porosity' and 'the intersection of multiple legal orders': Bonaventura de Sousa Santos, 'Law: A Map of Misreading. Toward a Postmodern Conception of Law' (1987) 14 *Journal of Law & Society* 279, 298. See also J Webber et al, 'Sally Engle Merry, Legal Pluralism, and the Radicalization of Comparative Law' (2020) 54:4 *Law Society Review* 846; A Hanna, 'Spaces for Sharing: Searching for Indigenous Law on the Canadian Legal Landscape' (2018) 51 *University of British Columbia Law Review* 105; H Kislowicz, 'Sacred Laws in Earthly Courts: Legal Pluralism in Canadian Religious Freedom Litigation (2013) 39 *Queen's Law Journal* 175.

[89] Ogilvie (n 50) 250.

vote was always required for a colony to expel a member. The Court reconciled the conflicting provisions by reference to the Hutterian custom of operating by consensus, finding that a vote was always required for expulsion, but that the vote need not be formal.[90] The Court also addressed the complex relationship between the Constitution and the Church's private Act of Incorporation. The Act suggested that only the Church's Board of Managers had authority to expel a Hutterite, an interpretation that would have rendered the Colony's expulsion of Hofer Sr invalid.[91] The Court avoided this result by holding that the 'Church' incorporated by the statute and the 'Church' created by the Constitution were 'neither wholly identical nor wholly distinct'.[92] The technical distinction between the 'Church corporation' and the 'Church' meant that the authority to expel was not limited to the Board of Managers in the way the Act described.

The Court's discussion of the sources of authority in Lakeside Colony has two noteworthy features. First, the majority opinion recognises the responsibility that attends a judicial decision to intervene in a religious dispute. Justice Gonthier acknowledges that interpreting the tradition and custom of a religious community is difficult. In many instances, courts that interfere in internal disputes end up 'writing very long opinions on questions which they could not well understand'.[93] This difficulty provides a reason for a court to avoid assuming jurisdiction over an internal dispute in the first place. However, once the court assumes jurisdiction, 'there is no alternative but to come to the best understanding possible of the applicable tradition and custom'.[94] In many cases, expert evidence will assist the court in this task.[95]

Second, *Lakeside Colony* is noteworthy for the emphasis that the decision places on unwritten sources of law. The status of unwritten Hutterian traditions was at issue in *Lakeside* because the expelled members argued that the custom by which the Senior Elder referred questions to a small group of ministers for binding determination was an impermissible subdelegation of a power that the Constitution accorded to the Conference Board. While this argument was based on plausible textuality and was thus familiar to the Supreme Court of Canada's judges, the majority wrote that:

> [T]o rely exclusively on the written documents without reference to the tradition and custom of Hutterites would seem unwise. From a point of view inside the Hutterite society, it seems probable that tradition and custom are in fact the highest source of authority, and the written documents are merely imperfect attempts to capture these sources. Indeed, the Senior Elder of the Hutterite Church testified to this effect …
>
> It is only from an external viewpoint that the written documents and the authority which they outline seem primary. Indeed, it is difficult for a court to come to a firm conclusion as to what the tradition and custom are, and correspondingly easier to analyze the formal legal documents.[96]

[90] *Lakeside* (n 5) [74].
[91] ibid [47].
[92] ibid [58].
[93] ibid [63], citing Z Chafee Jr, 'The Internal Affairs of Associations Not for Profit' (1930) 43 *Harvard Law Review* 993, 1024.
[94] *Lakeside* (n 5) [64], cited in *Bruker v Marcovitz*, 2007 SCC 54 [45].
[95] ibid [65].
[96] ibid [62]–[63].

The majority held that a sufficiently well-established tradition or custom may be considered an implied contractual term of the articles of a voluntary association.[97] It may also provide 'a kind of notice' to members of the rules the association will follow. The majority concluded that the unwritten tradition that a group of ministers appointed by the Senior Elder could finally decide issues referred to them was a valid rule. In the absence of any written provision forbidding the delegation, the undisputed tradition was 'sufficient to authorize the further delegation of the power'.[98]

V. Conclusion

Lakeside Colony v Hofer is an important adjunct to the section 2(a) case law that is the centrepiece of the Canadian law and religion jurisprudence. The decision neither applies nor interprets the Charter's constitutional guarantee of religious freedom. However, it does engage with two enduring questions of religion–state relations in Canada. The first concerns the relationship between justiciability and jurisdiction: is the Canadian judiciary's customary avoidance of religious disputes better understood as a practice of discretion or a principle of law? The second concerns the juridical status of non-state legal norms: what weight ought a secular state institution give to such written and unwritten norms?

Lakeside Colony's contributions to debates over justiciability, jurisdiction and the juridical status of non-state legal norms are likely sufficient to merit its place in the Canadian law and religion canon. However, the decision's connection to Canada's core religious freedom cases is also closer than it might appear at first sight. While *Lakeside Colony* does not directly address religious freedom, the fundamental freedom arguably lurks just below the surface of the case. Indeed, it is plausible to suggest that questions of religious freedom underlie all cases that ask whether the court should intervene in an internal religious matter.

We have seen that, at least until *Wall*, the case law suggested that Canadian courts had the authority to review the decisions of religious associations, even though their consistent practice was to consider the appropriateness of doing so. Despite this position, litigants have persisted in arguing that 'civil courts have no jurisdiction to determine disputes from religious institutions'.[99] In recent years, despite the principle that the Charter does not apply to disputes between private parties, litigants have increasingly identified section 2(a) as the source of this jurisdictional limit. This argument was made in *Wall*, where the Highwood Congregation and its Judicial Committee of Elders cast the potential review of Mr Wall's expulsion as a violation of their community's religious freedom.[100] Interveners offered variations on the Congregation's arguments, submitting that the common law and section 2(a) provided independent bases for a court to

[97] ibid [64].

[98] ibid [66].

[99] MH Ogilvie, 'Three Recent Cases Confirm Canadian Approach to Church Property Disputes' (2015) 93 *Canadian Bar Review* 537, 547.

[100] *Wall* (n 54). (Factum of the Appellant), identifying four 'fundamental constitutional principles' that militated against review.

refrain from adjudicating church membership,[101] and that religious freedom permits religious communities to self-define.[102] The dissenting member of the Alberta Court of Appeal accepted the Congregation's argument about the constitutional source of the jurisdictional limit, holding that a court's common law jurisdiction to interfere with the decision of a religious tribunal 'may be abridged by the values on which s 2(a) … is based'.[103]

These arguments appear to have gained a certain amount of traction before the Supreme Court of Canada in *Wall* and in *Aga*. In both cases, the Court associated 'jurisdiction' with mandatory limits on what civil courts can decide. In both cases, the Court emphasised the difficulty of establishing legal relations 'in a religious context', in this way suggesting that the availability of review is even more limited for religious groups than for other voluntary associations.[104] However, in neither case did the Court accept a party's invitation to explicitly base its decision on religious freedom principles. Religious freedom arguments appear only at the end of the Court's judgment in *Wall*, functioning as a sort of a postscript to its comments on the justiciability of religious procedures and disputes.[105] Nevertheless, it seems likely that parties will continue to appear in the courts, arguing that religious freedom precludes civil courts from determining internal disputes involving religious associations. The relationship between religious membership disputes and religious freedom, a submerged theme in *Lakeside Colony*, is likely to crest the surface before long.

[101] ibid (Factum of the Intervener, Seventh-Day Adventist Church in Canada at [2]–[7]).
[102] ibid (Factum of the Intervener, EFC/CCRL at [24]).
[103] *Wall v Judicial Committee of the Highwood Congregation of Jehovah's Witnesses*, 2016 ABCA 255 [114], cited in *Hart* (n 52) [24].
[104] *Wall* (n 54) [29]; *Aga* (n 65) [41]. Ironically, in expanding the autonomy of religious communities in this way, the Court also undermined the juridical status of religious legal norms: see *Aga* (n 65) [41].
[105] See *Wall* (n 54) [39], where the Court acknowledged the particular justiciability concerns raised by theological disputes and briefly mentioned section 2(a).

15

Minister of Home Affairs and Another v Fourie and Another

A Jurisprudence of Engagement

IAIN T BENSON*

I. Introduction

South Africa is a country that has embraced the importance of religion to culture, in its legal decisions and its constitutional framework more openly than many others. The landmark case of *Minister of Home Affairs and Another v Fourie and Another; Lesbian and Gay Equality Project and Others v Minister of Home Affairs and Others*,[1] the subject of this chapter, took a bold approach stating that religion matters to its society more than, say, Canada or Australia – two other former colonies of the UK. In its 1996 *Constitution*, South Africa created a means for a civil society charter whose first use was long recognised to be the creation of the *Charter of Religious Rights and Freedoms*. The *Charter* was signed by all the religions and many interested organisations in 2010. The combination of South Africa's *Charter* and case law models robust expressions of the significance of religions to the society. Nowhere is this more clear than in *Fourie*, which provides us with an exemplar for a rich jurisprudence of engagement.

In the decision of *Fourie*, the Constitutional Court of South Africa (CCA) examined the significant issue of whether the common law and the *Marriage Act 1961*[2] were inconsistent with the *Constitution* by not providing a means for same-sex couples to access the institution of marriage. On one level, *Fourie* is a case that examines the claims of unconstitutionality and the rights of same-sex couples; on a deeper level, it is a case that provides us with a jurisprudence that attempts to address the difficult philosophical and practical questions of pluralism, accommodation and the nature of an open society. Although the legal issue of marriage between gay and lesbian couples

* The author would like to acknowledge the assistance of Tara Veness BA (Hons) in the preparation of this chapter.

[1] *Minister of Home Affairs and Another v Fourie and Another; Lesbian and Gay Equality Project and Others v Minister of Home Affairs and Others* [2005] ZACC 19 (hereinafter '*Fourie*').

[2] No 25 1961.

was addressed in other countries, nowhere was it done with such attention to the surrounding associational aspects and, in particular, how a post-same-sex marriage inclusion would function alongside religious associations (and others) that would not and could not accept the new inclusions. In Canada, this issue has been handled in ways that have left some commentators alleging there was, in fact, no functional modus vivendi created of the 'live and let live' sort anticipated in *Fourie*.[3] In other words, Sachs J's attempt to navigate a way for law to accommodate differing beliefs and practices without falling into the trap in which many liberal democracies find themselves, namely, a jurisprudence of avoidance, exclusion or subordination of differing views. For the present purposes, we must examine Sachs J's obiter comments on engaging with religious objections to same-sex marriage, where he illustrates a way in which we can manoeuvre within a liberal society to co-exist in a manner that is not mutually destructive, but rather accommodate different worldviews in a reasonable manner. The importance of Sachs J's obiter comments in *Fourie* should not be overlooked – a juxtaposition of his sensitive and more nuanced approach compared with the less nuanced approach of the Supreme Court of Canada (for example) demonstrates a significant tension within certain approaches to liberalism in contemporary jurisprudence. For liberalism to survive, even on its own terms, it is necessary to examine how we retain the lofty goals of achieving dignity for all people and not the 'elimination or suppression of difference'.[4] The analysis of *Fourie* helps guide us to address key questions within the complex framework of a 'liberal democracy'. First, it is useful to address how Sachs J attempts to curb liberalism's tendency for convergence and why such a restriction is essential for the continuation of civil society. Second, it is useful to suggest that: (a) commentators and courts alike reflexively invoke a rather reductive conception of 'the secular'; and concomitantly (b) this reductive conception is generally 'anti-religious'; and (c) the *South African Constitution* ought to be read so as to

[3] The Canadian approach to co-existence between associations with differing beliefs has been heavily criticised as offering no co-existent difference whatsoever. An obvious example of the subordination of a religious association's own beliefs in relation to marriage to that of a 'one-size-fits-all model' is viewed in the majority judgment of the Supreme Court of Canada in *Trinity Western University v Law Society of British Columbia* and *Law Society of British Columbia v Trinity Western University and Brayden Volkenant* [2018] 2 SCR 293 and *Trinity Western University and Brayden Volkenant v Law Society of Upper Canada* [2018] 2 SCR 453. The superior analysis of the British Columbia Court of Appeal is in that court's unanimous judgment: *Trinity Western Law School and the Law Society of British Columbia* (BCCA, 2016). I have written about the risk of a homogenising tendency elsewhere in IT Benson, 'Subsidiarity: Origins and Contemporary Aspects' in N Aroney and I Leigh (eds), *Christianity and Constitutionalism* (Oxford University Press, 2021). In essence, while the British Columbia Court of Appeal urged the necessity of an approach to diversity that allowed for religious associations to have their own ethos and access to public accreditation, the majority judges of the Supreme Court of Canada ignored this without serious analysis and forced the views of same-sex advocates onto the religious association, denying it any public recognition space. The result was that the Evangelical University was not allowed to have its law school accredited owing to a religious ethos on its own campus that denied validity to same-sex marriages. This subordination approach, rather than sphere sharing, was rejected by Sachs J in *Fourie* for reasons that are discussed in this chapter. On the majority of the Supreme Court of Canada's judgment in *Trinity Western University*, see C Dielemann, 'Accommodating Rights in Administrative Law: A Critique of the Doré /Loyola Framework' (2021) 34 *Canadian Journal of Administrative Law & Practice* 197. Had the approach of Sachs J been used by the Supreme Court of Canada – for it was the approach of the five-justice division of the unanimous British Columbia Court of Appeal – there is little doubt that the law school would have received its accreditation.

[4] *Fourie* (n 1) 38–39 [60] (Sachs J).

recognise that religions and religious practice occupy an important role in the formation of public discourse and the support of public institutions. Religions are not merely to be tolerated, but should be recognised as important and even embraced once their nature and benefits are properly understood – sometimes an achievement in secularised societies. Finally, it will be useful to demonstrate that the failure to take religions and cultural communities with comprehensive understandings of the good seriously results in a body of jurisprudence of avoidance or exclusion. However, we should aim for a rich jurisprudence of engagement and genuine inclusion without homogenisation – as we find in *Fourie*.

II. The Facts and Judgment in *Fourie*

To best frame Sachs J's obiter comments on the interplay between religion and competing beliefs, we must first understand the facts and the judgment in *Fourie*. Ms Fourie and Ms Bonthuys were a same-sex couple that were the applicants in this case. After many years of considering themselves to be a couple, they wished to publicly recognise their relationship through marriage and thus embrace the rights and responsibilities that flow from that status.[5] However, they were unable to legally do so because the common law and the *Marriage Act* excluded them as a same-sex couple from getting married. Furthermore, they argued, the law not only excluded them from marriage, but also did so unfairly and unconstitutionally.[6]

The common law definition of marriage in South Africa was 'a union of one man with one woman, to the exclusion, while it lasts, of all others'.[7] This formulation of marriage was then enforced through the *Marriage Act*. Section 30(1) of the *Marriage Act* excluded same-sex couples because of the reference to 'wife (or husband)'. This section requires a marriage officer to ask each party the following question:

> Do you, AB, declare that as far as you know there is no lawful impediment to your proposed marriage with CD here present, and that you call all here present to witness that you take CD as your lawful *wife (or husband)?*', and thereupon the parties shall give each other the right hand and the marriage officer concerned shall declare the marriage solemnized in the following words: 'I declare that AB and CD here present have been lawfully married.' (Emphasis added)

There was no dispute between the parties as to whether section 30(1) excluded same-sex couples. The dispute arose as to whether this exclusion was unconstitutional – particularly because the *Constitution* expressly prohibits sexual orientation discrimination:

> Section 9 (1) Everyone is equal before the law and has the right to equal protection and benefit of the law …
>
> Section 9 (3) The state may not unfairly discriminate directly or indirectly against anyone on one or more grounds, including race, gender, sex, pregnancy, marital status, ethnic or social origin, colour, sexual orientation, age, disability, religion, conscience, belief, culture, language and birth.

[5] ibid 2 [2].
[6] ibid.
[7] *Mashia Ebrahim v Mahomed Essop*, 1905 TS 59 [61] (Innes CJ).

The court had to consider whether the common law and *Marriage Act* amounted to a denial of equal protection of the law and unfair discrimination by the state due to the applicants' sexual orientation.

A. The History of Litigation

The applicants first appeared at the Pretoria High Court and the Supreme Court of Appeal (SCA). Initially, they litigated on the basis that the common law needed to be developed, but did not link this with a challenge to the *Marriage Act*.[8] In the SCA, all five judges held that the common law definition of marriage, by excluding same-sex couples, constituted unfair discrimination. Two separate judgments were written, and Cameron JA, writing for the majority, highlighted some significant points which are relevant to the subsequent decision made by Sachs J.

Cameron JA wove together three fundamental points: first, the *Constitution* grants powers to the Constitutional Court, the SCA and the High Courts to develop the common law, taking into account the interests of justice;[9] second, to apply the Bill of Rights, it 'must apply or, if necessary, develop the common law to the extent that legislation does not give effect to that right';[10] and, third, the *Constitution* also provides that when developing the common law, the Court must promote the spirit, purport and objects of the Bill of Rights.[11] Subsequently, Sachs J took these comments to their ultimate conclusion in *Fourie* – together, 'these provisions create an imperative normative setting that obliges courts to develop the common law in accordance with the spirit, purport and objects of the Bill of Rights. Doing so is not a choice. Where the common law is deficient, the courts are under a general obligation to develop it appropriately'.[12]

Ultimately, in the SCA, it was held that the common law definition of marriage should be developed to include same-sex couples; however, the *Marriage Act* could not be read in such a way as to embrace this change in the common law. The right of same-sex couples to celebrate their marriage fully – that is, in a non-religious and publicly recognised sense – needed to await a challenge to the *Marriage Act*.

Subsequently, the Lesbian and Gay Equality Project (hereinafter 'the Equality Project') and 18 others launched an application to the Johannesburg High Court to challenge the constitutional validity of the *Marriage Act*. They sought to have the words 'or spouse' added to the prescribed marriage formula in section 30(1) of the *Marriage Act* immediately after the words 'or husband'. The Equality Project then applied for direct access to the Constitutional Court to enable its challenge to the statute as well as to the common law definition of marriage to be heard together with the appeal in the *Fourie* case. The Constitutional Court, as a general rule, does not act as a court of first and final instance in relation to constitutional matters that may be heard in

[8] *Fourie and Another v Minister of Home Affairs and Another*, 2003 (5) SA 301 (CC), 2003 (10) BCLR 1092.
[9] *Fourie* (n 1) 8 [13].
[10] Section 39(2) of the *Constitution*.
[11] *Fourie and Another* (n 8).
[12] *Fourie* (n 1) 8 [13].

other courts.[13] However, Sachs J stated that to deal with each case separately would be 'highly artificial and abstract' as the 'essence the enquiry into the common law definition of marriage and the constitutional validity of section 30(1) of the *Marriage Act* is the same'.[14] Thus, Sachs J stated: 'There would be grave disadvantages to all concerned if the issues raised were to be decided in a piecemeal way.'[15] Therefore, in the circumstances of this case, it was in the interests of justice that *Fourie* and the Equality Project matters be heard together.

B. Arguments by the State and Sachs J's Reasoning

The state argued that the *Constitution* did not expressly protect the right to marry; rather, it simply granted same-sex couples the right to establish their own forms of family without interference from the state.[16] Further, through historical development, marriage was heterosexual by nature, so same-sex couples had no constitutional right to change the institution of marriage.[17]

Sachs J found that although the Bill of Rights does not expressly include a right to marry, it does not follow that the *Constitution* does nothing to protect the right, while at the same time protecting the enshrined 'values of human dignity, equality and freedom'.[18] The forms of 'family' in South Africa are diverse and complex, and are evolving as society develops. Therefore, it would be inappropriate to entrench any one particular form as the only legally acceptable one.[19] Further, given South Africa's unique *Constitution*, insofar as it represents 'a radical rupture with the past based on intolerance and exclusion', there is an imperative need for the *Constitution* to uphold the goals of the liberal society – 'democratic, universalistic, caring ... and accepts people for who they are'.[20] Fundamental to the reasoning of *Fourie* and also for our analysis of the relationship between law and religion, Sachs J stated:

> To penalise people for being who and what they are is profoundly disrespectful of the human personality and violatory of equality. Equality means equal concern and respect across difference. It does not presuppose the elimination or suppression of difference. Respect for human rights requires the affirmation of self, not the denial of self. Equality therefore does not imply a levelling or homogenisation of behaviour or extolling one form as supreme, and another as inferior, but an acknowledgement and acceptance of difference. At the very least, it affirms that difference should not be the basis for exclusion, marginalisation and stigma. At best, it celebrates the vitality that difference brings to any society ... Accordingly, what is at stake is not simply a question of removing an injustice experienced by a particular section of the

[13] *Mkontwana v Nelson Mandela Metropolitan Municipality and Another; Bissett and Others v Buffalo City Municipality and Others; Transfer Rights Action Campaign and Others v MEC, Local Government and Housing, Gauteng and Others*, 2005 (1) SA 530 (CC), 2005 (2) BCLR 150 (CC).

[14] *Fourie* (n 1) 26 [42], [44].

[15] ibid 26 [42].

[16] ibid 27 [46].

[17] ibid.

[18] ibid 28 [47].

[19] ibid 37 [59].

[20] ibid 38 [59]–[60].

> community. At issue is a need to affirm the very character of our society as one based on tolerance and mutual respect. The test of tolerance is not how one finds space for people with whom, and practices with which, one feels comfortable, but how one accommodates the expression of what is discomfiting.[21]

Sachs J illustrated his reasoning through the metaphor of a national tapestry, stating that diversity is now understood as weaving together beliefs of traditional religions and other belief frameworks that encompass different views about human sexual behaviour that, in his view, would lead to a richer framework for a flourishing society.[22] To deny same-sex couples access to marriage is to reinforce the notion that they do not qualify for the 'full moral concern that our Constitution seeks to secure for everyone' and their capacity for love and commitment is 'by definition less worthy of regard than that of heterosexual couples'.[23] Therefore, the exclusion of same-sex couples from the definition of common law marriage and the *Marriage Act* is, he reasoned, in direct conflict with section 9(1) and (3) of the *Constitution*:

> It is equally evident that same-sex couples are not afforded equal protection not because of oversight, but because of the legacy of severe historic prejudice against them. Their omission from the benefits of marriage law is a direct consequence of prolonged discrimination based on the fact that their sexual orientation is different from the norm.[24]

The *Constitution*, on this reading, does not merely protect same-sex couples from stigmatisation; rather, it protects their right to be 'acknowledged as equals and to be embraced with dignity by the law'.[25] On this reasoning, to deny same-sex couples access to marriage is to deny them equal protection under the law (section 9(1)) and subject them to unfair discrimination (section 9(3)), as the law makes no provision for them to 'achieve the dignity, status, benefits, and responsibilities available to heterosexual couples through marriage'.[26] What does this approach do to the public place of religious and other believers (and their communities) who do not accept this approach to human sexuality as valid? This important question is addressed more by implication by Sachs J in his comments rather than head-on or in sufficient detail to delineate just how the shared public sphere is to function.

III. Obiter Comments: Framework for Jurisprudence of Engagement

Sachs J considered the following issues surrounding the question of same-sex marriage which were raised by the state as objections, namely, the procreation argument,[27]

[21] ibid 38–39 [60]. It should be noted that this approach runs counter to the idea, current in some quarters, that public pronouncements must not make others feel 'judged', 'insecure' or 'unsafe'; disagreement, with its consequent 'hurt feelings', is part and parcel of life in an open (and mature) society.
[22] ibid 40 [61].
[23] ibid 45 [71].
[24] ibid 48 [76].
[25] ibid 49 [78].
[26] ibid 51 [79].
[27] ibid 54 [85].

the respect for religion argument,[28] the international law argument[29] and the family law pluralism argument.[30] It is the respect for religion argument to which I wish to draw special attention. He articulated a succinct yet strong framework that could provide some guidance on how the accommodation of irreconcilable positions is to occur in the public sphere. Although he rejected the arguments put forward as to why same-sex marriage should not be recognised, he did so in a way that suggests the need to accommodate religious associations without shuffling them out of sight or tearing them down – allowing apparent irreconcilable positions to function alongside each other in the public sphere:

> In the open and democratic society contemplated by the Constitution there must be mutually respectful co-existence between the secular and the sacred. The function of the Court is to recognise the sphere which each inhabits, not to force the one into the sphere of the other. Provided there is no prejudice to the fundamental rights of any person or group, the law will legitimately acknowledge a diversity of strongly held opinions on matters of great public controversy …[31]
>
> The hallmark of an open and democratic society is its capacity to accommodate and manage difference of intensely-held world views and lifestyles in a reasonable and fair manner. The objective of the Constitution is to allow different concepts about the nature of human existence to inhabit the same public realm, and to do so in a manner that is not mutually destructive and that at the same time enables government to function in a way that shows equal concern and respect for all.[32]

Sachs J's approach is consistent with that set out in Article 18 of the *International Covenant on Civil and Political Rights* (*ICCPR*), which reads:

> 1. Everyone shall have the right to freedom of thought, conscience and religion. This right shall include freedom to have or to adopt a religion or belief of his choice, and freedom, either individually or in community with others and in public or private, to manifest his religion or belief in worship, observance, practice and teaching.
> 2. No one shall be subject to coercion which would impair his freedom to have or to adopt a religion or belief of his choice.
> 3. Freedom to manifest one's religion or beliefs may be subject only to such limitations as are prescribed by law and are necessary to protect public safety, order, health, or morals or the fundamental rights and freedoms of others.
> 4. The States Parties to the present Covenant undertake to have respect for the liberty of parents and, when applicable, legal guardians to ensure the religious and moral education of their children in conformity with their own convictions.

Note how, in the following additional key passage from the *Fourie* decision, Sachs J brings together the personal and communitarian dimensions of the *ICCPR* in relation to how a society of irreconcilable belief positions (such as the legitimacy of same-sex marriage) might square the circle and allow both to flourish. He does this by pointing out how important religion is to society itself. The following passage is the most robust

[28] ibid 55 [88].
[29] ibid 62 [99].
[30] ibid 66 [106].
[31] ibid 59 [94].
[32] ibid 60 [95].

description of the importance of the freedom of religion for persons and their communities and the surrounding society that I have seen in any reasons for judgment:

> [I]n the open and democratic society contemplated by the Constitution, although the rights of non-believers and minority faiths must be fully respected, the religious beliefs held by the great majority of South Africans must be taken seriously. As this Court pointed out in *Christian Education*, freedom of religion goes beyond protecting the inviolability of the individual conscience. For many believers, their relationship with God or creation is central to all their activities. It concerns their capacity to relate in an intensely meaningful fashion to their sense of themselves, their community and their universe. For millions in all walks of life, religion provides support and nurture and a framework for individual and social stability and growth. Religious belief has the capacity to awaken concepts of self-worth and human dignity which form the cornerstone of human rights. Such belief affects the believer's view of society and founds a distinction between right and wrong. It expresses itself in the affirmation and continuity of powerful traditions that frequently have an ancient character transcending historical epochs and national boundaries. For believers, then, what is at stake is not merely a question of convenience or comfort, but an intensely held sense about what constitutes the good and proper life and their place in creation. Religious bodies play a large and important part in public life, through schools, hospitals and poverty relief programmes. They command ethical behaviour from their members and bear witness to the exercise of power by state and private agencies; they promote music, art and theatre; they provide halls for community activities, and conduct a great variety of social activities for their members and the general public. They are part of the fabric of public life, and constitute active elements of the diverse and pluralistic nation contemplated by the Constitution. Religion is not just a question of belief or doctrine. It is part of a people's temper and culture, and for many believers a significant part of their way of life. Religious organisations constitute important sectors of national life and accordingly have a right to express themselves to government and the courts on the great issues of the day. They are active participants in public affairs fully entitled to have their say with regard to the way law is made and applied.[33]

For Sachs J, religion is cultural and its importance is, in key ways, greater than politics and therefore the state, both of which are framed by the essential background that religion (and other culture forming dimensions such as race) provides. Few legal judgments anywhere set out this sort of understanding of religion. Sachs J incorporates the key aspects of Article 18 *ICCPR* and in so doing overcomes, or at least gestures towards overcoming, identified key weaknesses in liberal theory – individualism and the privatisation of religion.

It is important to recognise that the associational diversity (and public diversity as well) which religion both instantiates and, at its best, perpetuates requires various viewpoints to co-exist. Consider the following passage on the term 'equality' from Sachs J:

> [E]quality should not be confused with uniformity; in fact, uniformity can be the enemy of equality. Equality means equal concern and respect across difference. *It does not presuppose the elimination or suppression of difference.* Respect for human rights requires the affirmation of self, not the denial of self. *Equality therefore does not imply a levelling or homogenisation of behaviour but an acknowledgment and acceptance of difference.*[34] (Emphasis added)

[33] *Minister of Home Affairs and Another v Fourie and (Doctors for Life International and Others, Amici Curiae); Lesbian and Gay Equality Project and Others v Minister of Home Affairs*, 2006 1 SA 524 (CC) [89]–[90].
[34] *National Coalition for Gay and Lesbian Equality v Minister of Justice* (1998) 1517, 1574–75 (Sachs J).

Canadian and South African jurisprudence tends *in theory* to favour both a religiously inclusivist and plural conception of the public sphere. The practical dimension is sometimes another matter. In terms of theory, the Constitutional Court in *Fourie* held that:

> [T]here are a number of constitutional provisions that underline the constitutional value of acknowledging diversity and pluralism in our society, and give a particular texture to the broadly phrased right to freedom of association contained in section 18. Taken together, they affirm the right of people to self-expression without being forced to subordinate themselves to the cultural and religious norms of others, and highlight the importance of individuals and communities being able to enjoy what has been called the 'right to be different'. In each case, space has been found for members of communities to depart from a majoritarian norm.[35]

Therefore, unlike the Canadian Supreme Court, Sachs' J judgment in *Fourie* allows for religious beliefs to have a public place and differences compared to other prevailing norms, which are themselves now also part of the public sphere. Several central tensions will need to be managed as a result of the following incorporations of the Article 18 *ICCPR* dimensions into the *Fourie* judgment.

IV. Religion is Both Public as Well as Private: A Group as Well as a Personal Right

It should be noted that the rights are not limited to the private sphere, nor are they limited to individuals; they are private and public, personal and communal. This is important when we come to consider the implications of moves to limit both the public dimension (restriction of public charitable work, for example) or group involvement (threatening the associational dimension of religious liberty). Secularism, as originally and most richly understood, was expressly an attempt to limit the role of religion in the public sphere – a point in direct opposition to the language of the *ICCPR* and rejected by Sachs J and the court in *Fourie*.[36]

The reference both to 'community' and 'social stability' in this passage points towards a better framework for locating the right to religion (and also to culture). For it is precisely in the relationship between the person and the community that the importance of the freedom of religion is best viewed. Social stability, after all, is not something achieved by the individual. Its achievement is a function of the coordination of action between and among individuals within a community.

[35] *Fourie* (n 1) 60–61 (Sachs J).

[36] For more on the history of the terms 'secularism' and 'secular' and their relationship to the understanding of the public sphere, see IT Benson, 'Considering Secularism' in D Farrow (ed), *Recognising Religion in a Secular Society* (2004) 83–93; and O Chadwick, *The Secularization of the European Mind in the 19th Century* (Cambridge University Press, 1975) 89–109.

V. How Will the Public Sphere Accommodate Different Belief Systems? The Constitutional Court Judgment in *Pillay v Durban Girls High School*

In the later decision of *Pillay*, questions were raised as to 'the extent of protection afforded to cultural and religious rights in the public school setting and possibly beyond'.[37] The case concerned a uniform dispute between the school and a student (Pillay) as to whether the choice to wear a nose stud, as a voluntary expression of South Indian Tamil Hindu culture, could be forcibly removed through disciplinary action by the school. The CCA held the choice to wear the nose stud was intertwined with the Hindu religion and so recognised and affirmed the right of the student to wear her nose stud as a cultural religious identifier important to her rather than affirm the school's non-accommodating uniform rules. Importantly, religious and cultural practices, even in the public sphere such as at school, ought to be protected because they are core to human identity and thus to human dignity.[38]

Unfortunately, *Pillay* did not draw on Sachs J's obiter comments in *Fourie*. However, if Sachs J's comments were used, it would have provided a richer framework for discerning how to move towards a respectful co-existence between the 'secular and the sacred' in the public sphere. A fundamental issue of living within an open society of the sort described by Sachs J is the continual inability of the state to live up to its professed claim to neutrality or impartiality. Rather than engage deeply with the differing belief systems, it all too often avoids a deeper analysis or, worse, excludes them in the direction of the pseudo-liberalism of convergence critiqued by John Gray. Rather than adhering to Sachs J's principles – 'difference should not be the basis for exclusion, marginalisation and stigma. At best, it celebrates the vitality that difference brings to any society'[39] – liberal states tend towards an evisceration of customs, practices and rituals.[40] This is in part because of liberalism's damaging anthropology of the essentially 'autonomous individual', a conception that is inconsistent with the community and personalist aspects of religious traditions. Too great a focus on the individual's belief runs the risk of trivialising the communal foundation to which any individual belief is invariably related. It is not too strong a statement to say that *Pillay* gets things back to front: the meaning that an individual draws from a religious belief or a religious practice is contingent upon the existence of a pre-existing religious community with well-developed tenets of belief and practice. In other words, in a very important sense, the religious community creates and nurtures the religious believer. Unfortunately, *Pillay* fails to recognise this relationship. Sachs J's comments from *Fourie* evince a conception of society in which there is room for the communal foundation of individual belief in relations with others. In fact, Sachs J greatly

[37] *MEC for Education: KwaZulu-Natal and Others v Navaneethum Pillay* [2007] ZACC 21 [1] (Langa CJ).

[38] For a discussion of the *Pillay* case, see IT Benson, 'Can Law Avoid Creating Culture and Religion in its Own Image? The Context for Diversity, Religion and Culture in *MEC for Education: KwaZulu-Natal and Others v Navaneethum Pillay*: Reflections a Decade Later' (2017) 42 *Journal for Juridical Science* 2.

[39] *Fourie* (n 1) 38–39 [60].

[40] PJ Deneen, *Why Liberalism Failed* (Yale University Press, 2018) 64.

contributes a richer conception of a liberal society to jurisprudence than autonomous individualism can provide. Though beyond the scope of the analysis here, it is useful to point out that in 2010, South Africa became the first nation to develop a civil society charter – the *South African Charter of Religious Rights and Freedoms* – that in its Preamble and in its substantive sections recognises genuine pluralism alongside a personalist and communitarian social anthropology.[41] *Pillay* could have provided us with a more nuanced and insightful jurisprudence if the court had engaged with the pervasive issues of liberalism's tendency for homogenisation of behaviour rather than simply viewing the case through the somewhat narrower lens of the accommodation of a nose stud in a school whose uniform rules precluded it.

VI. The Crisis of Liberalism

Indeed, the inclination of courts to dance around, or omit, liberalism's tendency for homogeneity results in a jurisprudence which subtly reinforces aspirations for uniformity. This silences places greater tension on the interplay between law and religion in most liberal democracies. Liberalism's central aim is to pursue the goal of a just society, not through the state promoting any particular ends, but, so the theory goes, by enabling its citizens the liberty to pursue their own ends.[42] Therefore, the liberal state 'must govern by principles that do not presuppose any particular conception of the good'.[43] In other words, the rights of citizens to pursue their own ends are held prior to any normative moral claims as to what is good. The state must create laws that aim to accommodate individual rights to choose their own individual goods rather than creating laws that choose between competing purposes/goods. One consequence of this is the all too familiar claim that what constitutes 'morally good' is merely an opinion, to which we must 'agree to disagree' or not engage with at all. The state must remain agnostic to competing claims of 'the good life'. In restraining our individual rights, the artificial state is required to step in and thus the only constraints acceptable are those that the state provides – 'the assumption is that legitimate limits upon liberty can arise only from the authority of the consent-based liberal state'.[44]

[41] The *South African Charter of Religious Rights and Freedoms* is available at: https://www.strasbourgconsortium.org/content/blurb/files/South%20African%20Charter.pdf. For the process and background to the *Charter*, see IT Benson, 'The South African Charter of Religious Rights and Freedoms' (2011) 4(1) *International Journal of Religious Freedom* 125. See also P Coertzen, 'Constitution, Charter and Religions in South Africa' (2014) 7(1) *African Human Rights Law Journal* 8; and R Malherbe, 'The Background and Context of the Proposed South African Charter of Religious Rights and Freedoms' [2011] *Brigham Young University Law Review* 612. All three of these authors were involved in the drafting of the *Charter*. The original intention of the framers was to take the *Charter* to the government for passage, but on later consideration, it was decided that to do so would endanger its status and integrity as a 'civil society' document, so that course was abandoned as ill advised. Section 234 of the *Constitution of the Republic of South Africa* speaks, after all, of the 'adoption' of charters created pursuant to the section, not passage by law in the usual sense.

[42] M Sandel, 'The Procedural Republic and the Unencumbered Self' in SM Cahn (ed), *Political Philosophy* (Oxford University Press, 2015) 944.

[43] ibid.

[44] Deneen (n 40) 69.

Many scholars have written extensively on the theories underlying liberalism and what has increasingly been identified at a 'crisis' at the core of liberal theories, but a detailed discussion of this is beyond the scope of this chapter.[45] For our purposes – that is, to examine the case of *Fourie* as an example of how to manoeuvre within a liberal state between competing and seemingly incompatible belief systems in the area of law and religion – we must understand the background of the case and what Sachs J was aspiring towards. The question is as follows: regardless of liberalism's failures, we are situated within a state that is aiming towards liberalism's goal – to establish rights prior to any conception of the good. And yet, what does this look like on a practical level in the court? If liberalism has any hope of lasting as the prevailing political philosophy, we must learn how to accommodate: 'The test of tolerance is not how one finds space for people with whom, and practices with which, one feels comfortable, but how one accommodates the expression of what is discomfiting.'[46] As Paul Horwitz notes in *The Agnostic Age:*

> [W]e are now in the twilight of the liberal consensus as we have known it. It may survive, with important revisions. Or it may collapse all together, and new prophets will arise to predict what will come after it. One thing, however, seems certain: the liberal consensus that emerged after the enlightenment, gelled in the nineteenth century, and reached a more or less stable form in the twentieth century, cannot last much longer as a basic, unquestioned assumption about the way we live.[47]

If liberalism is to hold true to its own theory, it should not be hostile, suspicious or even find religious groups peculiar. As a theory, it is called to remain agnostic towards difference. Although the reality of the state's ability to be neutral has been penned the 'Noble Lie',[48] we nevertheless find ourselves operating within constitutions that are set up under liberalism's watchful eye. As Patrick Deneen argues: 'There can be no going back, only forward.'[49] In other words, we cannot simply reject liberalism's achievements outright as it has provided a theoretical movement towards greater dignity recognition for all, even if, in practice, it increasingly falls short of delivering it.[50] Moving forward, with the development of a tradition, from our inheritance of Western antiquity, rather than demolishing it for ideologies such as post-Marxism, we must look at how best to accommodate the reality in which we find ourselves – that is, a multifaceted world with various human practices. We must develop a jurisprudence of engagement as opposed to a jurisprudence of avoidance or, worse, of exclusion.

The implementation of liberalism often hides a dark and sinister motive, that is, a 'one-size-fits-all' or 'single culture' conception of the public sphere. The implicit result of the state's attempt to remain agnostic towards a particular conception of the good is

[45] See Sandel (n 42); Deneen (n 40). For a review of recent scholarship on 'the crisis of liberalism', see IT Benson, 'Civic Virtues and the Politics of "Full-Drift Ahead"', 2017 Acton Lecture, Centre for Independent Studies, Sydney, Australia, https://www.cis.org.au/publications/occasional-papers/acton-lecture-2017-civic-virtues-and-the-politics-of-full-drift-ahead.

[46] *Fourie* (n 1) 38–39 [60].

[47] P Horwitz, *The Agnostic Age: Law Religion and the Constitution* (Oxford University Press, 2011) 22.

[48] Deneen (n 40) 180.

[49] ibid 182.

[50] ibid 183.

'the evisceration of culture as a set of generational customs, practices, and rituals that are grounded in local and particular settings'.[51] Or, as John Gray has argued, a 'convergence' approach:

> Liberalism contains two philosophies. In one, toleration is justified as a means to truth. In this view, toleration is an instrument of rational consensus, and a diversity of ways of life is endured in the faith that it is destined to disappear. In the other, toleration is valued as a condition of peace, and divergent ways of living are welcomed as marks of diversity in the good life. The first conception supports an ideal of ultimate convergence on values, the latter an ideal of modus vivendi. Liberalism's future lies in turning its face away from the ideal of rational consensus and looking instead to modus vivendi. The predominant liberal view of toleration sees it as a means to a universal civilisation. If we give up this view, and welcome a world that contains many ways of life and regimes, we will have to think afresh about human rights and democratic government. We will refashion these inheritances to serve a different liberal philosophy. We will come to think of human rights as convenient articles of peace, whereby individuals and communities with conflicting values and interest may consent to coexist.[52]

From Sachs J's comments in *Fourie*, we can see that he does not want to allow convergent liberalism to prevail and is looking for a way to enable genuine difference between practices to co-exist in a diverse public sphere. There is a recognition, within the rich national tapestry of South Africa, that small community and religious practices are more than a collection of self-interested individuals brought together for their own personal gains; rather, it is a network composed of complex practices and traditions 'drawn from a store of common memory and tradition'.[53] However, in an attempt to avoid convergent liberalism, an issue arises regarding the dichotomy of looking for a 'co-existence between the secular and the sacred' – it is the use of the word 'secular' which requires examination.

VII. Secularism

In religiously exclusive liberal discourse, 'secular' often serves as a synonym for 'non-religious'.[54] The nineteenth-century definition of 'secularism' was to exclude religion from public society.[55] It was claimed that secularism was a superior ethical system as it had a much broader appeal to society and thus 'accept[ed] the purely moral teaching of the Bible, and to controvert its theology, in such respects as it contradicts and discourages ethical effort'.[56] Secularism was an alternative to religion[57] and, by

[51] ibid 64.
[52] J Gray, *Two Faces of Liberalism* (New Press, 2000) 105.
[53] Deneen (n 40) 78.
[54] For more on the history of the terms 'secularism' and 'secular', see Benson (n 36). For a useful discussion of models of religion–state relations covering secularism, public/private, the separation of Church and State and versions of 'pluralism' and 'neutrality', see R Ahdar and I Leigh, *Religious Freedom in the Liberal State*, 2nd edn (Oxford University Press, 2013) 88–124.
[55] ibid.
[56] ibid quoting G Holyoake, *English Secularism* (Library of Alexandria, 1896) 91.
[57] ibid 89.

exempting religion from the public, claimed to reach a state of neutrality which was equally accessible to all citizens.[58]

The implications of defining the public sphere and the state as secular, in which the religious is excluded from the public, show that it is not a system of neutrality towards all belief systems, but is 'the process in which religious consciousness, activities and institutions lose social significance. It indicates that religion becomes marginal to the operation of social systems'.[59] The issue of excluding religion from a place in the public is that many religious people in society believe that 'they *ought* to base their decisions concerning fundamental issues of justice on their religious convictions' (emphasis in original).[60] To claim that the person of religious faith cannot do so 'places an undue mental and psychological burden … [which asks them] to split their identity into public and private components as soon as they participate in public debates'.[61] The issue of systems such as the law and politics developing under a 'secularist' view is that the systems become parasitic upon the different moral traditions within society, while denying the basis of such traditions. This happens as lifeworld views like religion rely upon community, and when a secular system restricts the participation in public life, it has ramifications for both the lifeworld and the system.[62] It is important to stop and to examine what we mean when we use terms such as 'secular' or 'secularism'. A failure to do so can clearly lead to fundamentally anti-religious outcomes.

A decision from the Canadian courts provides an illuminating and instructive account of why getting this term right is of such great import. McKenzie J, in the unanimous decision of the British Columbia Court of Appeal in *Chamberlain*, stated that:

> In my opinion, 'strictly secular' in the School Act can only mean pluralist in the sense that moral positions are to be accorded standing in the public square irrespective of whether the position flows out of a conscience that is religiously informed or not. That meaning of strictly secular is thus pluralist or inclusive in the widest sense … No society can be said to be truly free where only those whose morals are uninfluenced by religion are entitled to participate in deliberations related to moral issues of education in public schools. In my respectful view 'strictly secular' so interpreted could not survive scrutiny in light of the freedom of conscience and religion guaranteed by section 2 of the Charter [conscience and religion] and equality rights guaranteed by section 15.[63]

What is said here about moral positions applies equally to religious and cultural beliefs in a public school setting such as *Pillay* or in the attempt to achieve peaceful co-existence in society such as *Fourie*. Simply put, convictions emanating from religious beliefs ought to be at no disadvantage in terms of public respect in comparison to belief sets that emanate from non-religious convictions. When the case reached the Supreme

[58] J Habermas, 'Religion in the Public Sphere' (2006) 14 *European Journal of Philosophy* 1, 7.

[59] BR Wilson, 'Secularisation' in Eliade, *The Encyclopaedia of Religion*, 15, 160.

[60] Habermas (n 58) 9.

[61] ibid 10.

[62] I have written about Habermas' approach and his most helpful distinctions between 'lifeworlds' and 'systems' elsewhere: see IT Benson, 'Pluralism, Lifeworlds, Civic Virtues and Civil Charters' in P Coertzen, MC Green and L Hansen (eds), *Religious Freedom and Religious Pluralism in Africa* (Sun Media, 2016) 287–306.

[63] *Chamberlain v Surrey School Board* (2000) 80 BCLR (3d) 181 (CA) (hereinafter '*Chamberlain*') [33]–[34].

Court of Canada, all nine judges agreed with the reasoning of McKenzie J. 'Secular' in Canadian constitutional jurisprudence embraces a religiously inclusive understanding of the term.

The South African approach might well be said to accept a 'co-operation' of Church and State.[64] In *Pillay*, the Constitutional Court arrived at a similar conclusion about the place of religion in the public sphere to that of the Canadian Supreme Court in *Chamberlain*. This is in line with Sachs J's comments in *Fourie* – there must be a 'mutually respectful co-existence between the secular and the sacred'.[65] Although Sachs J provides us with an excellent framework of how to achieve a modus vivendi liberalism as opposed to a convergent liberalism, utilising the secular/sacred dichotomy confuses the principles at issue. What should be emphasised is the co-operative relationship – between politics and religion – in the same manner as the passage correctly notes the co-operation of the religious and the non-religious within 'the same public realm'. Unfortunately, the distinction between the 'secular' and the 'sacred' at the outset does little to assist South Africa's religiously inclusive position. For a religious citizen, the public order of the state, too, has its own sacred dimension. Why? Because everything within creation flows, in some sense, from 'grace' or 'the holy' or 'the divine'. *Fourie* would have done better to describe the public realm as encompassing believers of all sorts – whether atheist, agnostic or religious – and identifying the role of the law, when certain types of conflicts emerge, as ordering all relationships according to the principles of justice. When most people use the term 'secular', they mean 'public' and non-theocratic, and it would clarify matters greatly if the Constitutional Court (and courts elsewhere) said so in the future.

VIII. The Nature of Belief as Communal Rather than Individual

The reference both to 'community' and 'social stability' points towards a better framework for locating the right to religion (and to culture). For it is precisely in the relationship between the person and the community that the importance of the freedom of religion is best viewed. Social stability, after all, is not something achieved by the individual. Its achievement is a function of the co-ordination of action between and among individuals within a community.

The standard liberal individualistic approach to communities is both epistemologically incorrect and politically unsound: it gets the ontological priority of meaning back to front. Individuals only come to participate in these institutions because a community has – in most instances – already produced them and the meaning that flows from their ongoing reproduction. It is because communities exist that individuals have anything to choose at all.

[64] The principles of such co-operation and useful distinctions about the avoidance of both atheistic and religious theocracy are neatly set out in A Sachs, *Protecting Human Rights in a New South Africa* (Oxford University Press, 1990) 43–49.

[65] *Fourie* (n 1) 59 [94].

To think of a person as first and foremost part of a whole is to flip the liberal conception of the individual on its head. Liberalism's anthropology, particularly in the Hobbesian tradition, holds us to be autonomous and radically free individuals who then come together to form artificial institutions such as government for our own protection. The fundamental nature of humans is defined 'above all by the absence of culture, and that, by contrast, the presence of culture marks existence of artifice and convention'.[66] However, the word 'culture' shows us a deeper meaning – it is a word connected with natural forms and processes, such as 'agriculture' or 'cultivation'. As Patrick Deneen insightfully highlights: 'Just as the potential of a plant or animal isn't possible without cultivation, so it was readily understood that the human creature's best potential simply could not be realized without good culture.'[67] These cultures, such as in *Pillay*, are in danger of being destroyed if liberalism is allowed to move in a convergent manner. In other words, to have a standardising legal regime that replaces widely observed and informal norms denudes society and culture of important traditional resources so well recognised by Sachs J in *Fourie* and to a lesser extent by the Constitutional Court in *Pillay*. To not allow the nose ring to be worn inevitably pushes towards a monoculture that has colonised and is parasitic upon living and breathing lifeworlds – in other words, one that is parasitic on actual cultures rooted in experience and history that, in turn, form the individual.

IX. Conclusion

For many reasons, South Africa has a more respectful legal approach to religious beliefs than many other Western cultures. Frankly, embracing a *co-operation* of Church and State rather than a separation of Church and State (see how the *Constitution* allows expressly for the funding of religious schools, for example), the overall framework for law is, as we might expect, favourable to a more expansive role for religion.

The extensive role of religions in 'social upliftment' projects of all sorts in the face of widely identified governmental failures in South Africa makes religious projects important and widely recognised *to be* important. This social recognition is represented both in the very existence of the *South African Charter of Religious Rights and Freedoms* and the approach to religion set out by Sachs J in both *Fourie* and the earlier decision of *Christian Education*.[68] While in both cases, the rights of religion could be said to be

[66] Deneen (n 40) 67.

[67] ibid.

[68] See *Christian Education South Africa v Minister of Education*, 2000 (4) SA 757 (CC) [36] for Sachs J's earlier judgment, where he states: '[F]reedom of religion goes beyond protecting the inviolability of the individual conscience. For many believers, their relationship with God or creation is central to all their activities. It concerns their capacity to relate in an intensely meaningful fashion to their sense of themselves, their community and their universe. For millions in all walks of life, religion provides support and nurture and a framework for individual and social stability and growth. *Religious belief has the capacity to awake concepts of self-worth and human dignity which form the cornerstone of human rights. It affects the believer's view of society*

somewhat truncated (one in relation to the corporal punishment of children and the other in relation to same-sex marriage), these were not cases in which the religious viewpoints could be said to be severely truncated, as has been seen in other jurisdictions such as Canada.

and founds the distinction between right and wrong. It expresses itself in the affirmation and continuity of powerful traditions that frequently have an ancient character transcending historical epochs and national boundaries' (emphasis added). This passage is the foundation upon which Sachs J builds the central passage in his later reasons in *Fourie*. Clearly, in both cases, Sachs J rightly identified the nature of religious belief – the gravitas of religious belief – to the religious believer. The richer development we find in *Fourie*, building on *Christian Education*, is that Sachs J extended further into the nature of religious belief as a metaphysical reality for a pluralistic society. Indeed, many of the places and activities where 'life' or 'living' happens – schools, hospitals, charity programmes, music, art etc – are so tightly interwoven with religious belief that to exclude arbitrarily religious belief from the public sphere is to cut off one's society from a crucial part of its very being. Sachs J recognised that religion is part of the fabric of public life and to tear it out so as to be 'homogenous' inevitably produces a reduction to the vibrancy of culture. This expansion from the religious believer to the society, from *Christian Education* to *Fourie*, gives us a jurisprudence which recognises the depth of contribution religion gives to its society and, in so doing, shows us that open religious participation in the public sphere is part of the necessary elements for a successful pluralistic culture and nation.

PART IV

Rights, Relationships, Responsibilities and Religion Around the Commonwealth

16

Her Majesty's Attorney-General v Akhter and Others

The Need for Legislative Reform of the Marriage Act 1949

MICHELLE FLYNN

I. Introduction

The judgment of the Court of Appeal in the case of *Her Majesty's Attorney-General v Akhter and Others* (2020)[1] overturned the controversial judgment of the High Court which held that an Islamic marriage ceremony, a *nikah*, could have legal effect notwithstanding that it was an unregistered religious marriage.[2] As the Law Commission has succinctly noted: 'A lack of registration does not invalidate a marriage, but it is a prerequisite for registration that the wedding be conducted according to the requirements of the Marriage Act 1949. The term "unregistered marriages" is sometimes used as a shorthand to refer to ceremonies that would not be capable of registration, ie those that fall outside the statutory scheme.'[3] This chapter will examine the approaches adopted by both the High Court and the Court of Appeal to the issue of unregistered religious marriages in England and Wales. The chapter is divided into three subsequent sections. Section II sets out the factual matrix of this case and places it in its legal context. Section III proceeds to address two novel aspects of the judgments. The first is the extent to which the provisions of the *European Convention on Human Rights* (hereinafter *ECHR* or 'the *Convention*') and other international human rights instruments were considered by both the High Court and the Court of Appeal. The second aspect which marked a departure from previous case law was the strong expression of dissatisfaction by both courts towards the term 'non-marriage'. Section IV will chart the far-reaching implications of this judgment.

[1] *Her Majesty's Attorney-General v Akhter and Others* [2020] EWCA Civ 122.
[2] *Akhter v Khan* [2018] EWFC 54.
[3] *Getting Married: A Consultation Paper on Weddings Law* (Law Com No 247, 2020) [5.5].

II. The Factual and Legal Context

A. The Factual Context

In 1998, the petitioner wife and the respondent husband took part in an Islamic marriage ceremony, a *nikah*, conducted by an Iman in a restaurant in London.[4] A certificate recorded the name of the wife's father as the *wali* and was signed by him, in addition to the names of two witnesses.[5] The family lived in England, apart from a period between 2005 and 2011 when they lived in Dubai and the couple were considered by the authorities there to be validly married. The couple had four children and remained together for 18 years until 2016, when the wife filed for divorce. The husband resisted that petition on the basis that the parties did not have a valid marriage according to English law. Furthermore, the husband denied the wife's assertion that both parties intended to undertake a civil marriage ceremony following the religious wedding. From the outset, it is crucial to note that it was not argued that the *nikah* had created a valid marriage; rather, the wife argued that a presumption of marriage arising out of cohabitation and reputation should be extended to validate the marriage. In the alternative, the wife argued that due to the failure to comply with the requirements in the *Marriage Act 1949*, the marriage was void pursuant to section 11(a)(iii) of the *Matrimonial Causes Act 1973* (*MCA 1973*).

B. The Legal Context

The *Marriage Act 1949* provides the statutory framework for marriages in England and Wales.[6] The *Act* sets out three categories of formalities required for the solemnisation of a marriage: (i) preliminaries; (ii) ceremony; and (iii) registration. Complications arise as different rules apply depending on whether the marriage is a civil marriage or in accordance with a religious denomination. Therefore, in addition to setting out the statutory framework for marriage in England and Wales, the *Marriage Act 1949* also indicates the nature of the relationship between the state and various religions, with certain religions being afforded privileges or recognition in respect of the required formalities.[7]

Within the preliminaries category, there are two principal formalities: the giving of notice of intention to marry and the publication of intent to marry. The requirements

[4] The petitioner and respondent will be referred to as 'wife' and 'husband' respectively.

[5] A *wali* is an Arabic word with a number of meanings, but is generally understood as 'guardian'. In the context of marriage, a *wali* is an authorised agent of the bride who concludes the marriage contract. See generally M Rohe, *Islamic Law in Past and Present* (Brill, 2015) 107.

[6] It should be noted that since the judgment of the Court of Appeal in *Her Majesty's Attorney-General v Akhter and Others* (n 1), the *Registration of Marriages Regulations 2021* have implemented a number of changes to the *Marriage Act 1949* as provided for by the *Civil Partnerships, Marriages and Deaths (Registration etc) Act 2019*. The legislative framework outlined in this section takes these changes into account, thereby providing an overview of the current legal context.

[7] See generally R Probert, 'Getting Married: The Origins of the Current Law and its Problems' (2021) 23(3) *Ecclesiastical Law Journal* 255, which provides an insightful overview of the history of marriage law reform and the background to the *Marriage Act 1949*.

differ in relation to marriages within the Church of England and all other marriages, whether civil or religious. Publication of intent to marry within the Church of England must be carried out in accordance with the religious rites. This entails 'banns of marriage', whereby intent to marry is published during church service on three successive Sundays preceding the solemnisation of the marriage.[8] A clergyman must, after the publication of banns, on the authority of a special licence or on the authority of a common licence issue a 'marriage document' before solemnising the marriage.[9] In respect of all other marriages, parties intending to marry must follow detailed procedural rules in order to obtain a 'marriage schedule' from the superintendent registrar for the registration district in which the marriage is to be solemnised.[10]

Within the ceremony category, the rules vary depending on the type of marriage ceremony. Under the provisions of the *Places of Worship Registration Act 1855*, the owners or trustees of places of worship can certify to the Registrar General for England and Wales that a premises is used as a place of worship. There is no obligation for places of worship to be recorded under this *Act*; however a premises must be recorded as a place of worship before it can be registered for the solemnisation of marriages under the *Marriage Act 1949*. Interestingly, exemptions from the statutory formalities in respect of places of worship as an 'approved premises' arise due to the historical position of certain religious groups in England.[11] For example, Jews and Quakers are not subject to legal regulation as to the venue or content regarding the marriage ceremony once the civil marriage preliminaries are satisfied and the marriage is subsequently registered.[12] Therefore, apart from marriages within the Church of England, Jewish or Quaker traditions, in order for a religious marriage to be legally valid, it must take place in a venue certified as a place of 'religious worship' and be a registered building.[13] The presence of a registrar of marriages or an 'authorised person' is required in order for a valid marriage to take place in a registered building.[14] Couples who wish to celebrate their marriage in a place of worship or elsewhere that has not been registered must undertake an additional civil ceremony in order to be legally married. With regard to Islam, a significant issue arises as few Muslim places of religious worship have been registered.[15] In such circumstances, Muslim couples must undertake a separate civil ceremony if they wish to have a legally recognised marriage.

Civil marriages can take place in a register office or an approved premises.[16] Whilst civil ceremonies must contain no religious elements, couples may have a religious ceremony or blessing after the civil ceremony in the register office; however, this has no further legal effect. There must be a superintendent registrar and a registrar of the

[8] *Marriage Act 1949*, s 7.
[9] ibid s 21A.
[10] ibid s 27.
[11] See Probert (n 7).
[12] *Marriage Act 1949*, s 43.
[13] ibid ss 41 and 43A.
[14] ibid s 44.
[15] See R Probert and S Saleem, 'The Legal Treatment of Islamic Marriage Ceremonies' (2018) 7(3) *Oxford Journal of Law and Religion* 376, 382.
[16] *Marriage Act 1949*, ss 45 and 46B.

district present to ensure compliance with the *Marriage Act 1949* and it is an essential requirement that both parties proclaim the prescribed declaratory words stating that they can freely enter the marriage and the legal words expressing an intention to be bound to the marriage contract.[17] There is also a requirement that the marriage takes place in the presence of two witnesses. Regarding the formal requirements concerning registration, the Registrar General maintains an index of marriages which can be viewed by all members of the public.[18] The 'marriage document' or 'marriage schedule' must be signed and returned to the registrar for the registration district in which the marriage took place. The registrar must then register the marriage by entering the relevant details into the register which must be accessible in electronic form. The clergyman who solemnised the marriage is responsible for returning the marriage document to the registrar,[19] whereas the 'specified person' will be responsible for returning the marriage schedule to the registrar, except where the marriage was solemnised by a registrar.[20]

More generally, a marriage can be categorised as 'valid', 'void' or 'voidable'. Upon the breakdown of a valid marriage, an order for judicial separation or divorce can be made, in addition to financial orders in respect of the division of assets and maintenance. A decree of nullity[21] can be sought in respect of a void or voidable marriage, thereby entitling a party to apply for financial orders under the *MCA 1973*.[22] A void marriage is one deemed to have never existed due to a fundamental defect that renders the marriage *void ab initio*. Section 11 of the *MCA 1973* provides the circumstances in which a marriage will be declared void and includes where parties have married in disregard of certain requirements as to the formation of marriage. It is important to note that the marriage will be deemed to be void only if both parties 'knowingly and willfully' failed to comply with these requirements.[23] In contrast, a voidable marriage is a legally valid marriage which can be annulled by the courts for a specified reason as set out in section 12 of the *MCA 1973*, such as a lack of valid consent due to duress, mistake, unsoundness of mind or otherwise at the time of the marriage.

It is also worth noting that depending on the level of non-compliance with required formalities pursuant to the *Marriage Act 1949*, a presumption of marriage may be extended to the relationship or it may be deemed to be a 'non-marriage'. Two circumstances have been identified as having the potential to give rise to a presumption

[17] ibid s 45(1).
[18] ibid s 65.
[19] ibid s 53D.
[20] A definition of 'specified person' is provided in ibid s 53C(8).
[21] Upon the commencement of the *Divorce, Dissolution and Separation Act 2020*, the term 'decree of nullity' will be replaced by the term 'nullity of marriage order'.
[22] It is essential to note that a decree of nullity in this context is one which is legally recognised and obtained from the civil courts. This differs from a decree of nullity obtained from a Marriage Tribunal within the Catholic tradition, which enables a person to marry within the faith.
[23] See generally Probert and Saleem (n 15) 387, who state that: 'This qualification dates back to the Marriage Act 1823 and was intended to ensure that marriages could not be challenged on the basis of a defect known to one spouse alone, while still potentially invalidating marriages where the parties were deliberately colluding to evade the legal requirements.'

of marriage.[24] The first is a presumption arising from cohabitation and reputation, and is succinctly described as:

> Where there is no positive evidence of any marriage having taken place, where parties have cohabited for such a length of time and in such circumstances so as to have acquired the reputation of being spouses, a lawful marriage may be presumed to exist. This is particularly so when the relevant facts have taken place outside the jurisdiction. Where the presumption of a lawful marriage is fully engaged, it may be rebutted only by strong and weighty evidence to the contrary.[25]

The second presumption arises where a ceremony was followed by cohabitation and is described as:

> Where the court has evidence that the parties have undertaken a ceremony of marriage and have subsequently cohabited then, unless there is cogent evidence to the contrary, the existence or happening of all other things necessary for the validity of the marriage will be presumed.[26]

Contrarily, the term 'non-marriage' refers to a ceremony that falls outside the scope of the *Marriage Act 1949*. As a non-marriage is not recognised, no claim for financial relief can be made by a party upon the breakdown of such a relationship. The parties are treated as if they were cohabitants and upon the breakdown of the relationship, the only financial protection arises under the *Trust of Land and Appointment of Trustees Act 1996*, which enables declarations and orders to be made relating to land or property held in the parties' names. Furthermore, if there are children, it is also possible to make an application for financial relief pursuant to the *Children Act 1989*.[27] The crux of this case was to determine whether a presumption of marriage should be extended or whether the ceremony that took place in 1998 fell within the scope of section 11 of the *MCA 1973*, thereby rendering the marriage void and hence susceptible to the granting of a decree of nullity.

C. The Judgment of the High Court

This case was heard in the High Court Family Division before Williams J on dates in February and July 2018. Initially the case was listed for three days; however, upon its commencement, it became clear that significant human rights issues and matters of wider public policy arose, and so the Attorney-General was invited to intervene in the proceedings. The Attorney-General argued that as the ceremony was of no legal effect, the wife was not entitled to a decree of nullity. Williams J noted that the case was not about whether a *nikah* created a valid marriage in English law, but rather whether a *nikah* created 'an invalid or void marriage in English law'.[28] He posed two central

[24] D Williams, S Trowell, M Thorpe and P Waller (eds), *Rayden and Jackson, Relationship Breakdown, Finances and Children*, 19th edn (LexisNexis Butterworths, 2020). In *Akhter v Khan* (n 2), Williams J referred to this categorisation (at [32]), noted the long history of the presumption of marriage and referred to cases ranging from *Piers v Piers* [1849] 2 HL Cas 331 to *Hyatleh v Mofdy* [2017] EWCA Civ 70.

[25] Williams et al (n 24) [3.154] and [3.155].

[26] ibid [3.156].

[27] Such applications are made pursuant to sch 1 to the Children Act 1989.

[28] *Akhter v Khan* (n 2) [5].

questions: (1) whether the parties were to be treated as validly married under English law by the operation of a presumption of marriage; and (2) if this was answered in the negative, whether the marriage was a void marriage and susceptible to a decree of nullity. On 31 July 2018, he issued a lengthy judgment which set out an account of the relationship between the petitioner and the respondent. In an introductory paragraph, he explained that he would refer to the petitioner as the 'wife' and to the respondent as the 'husband' on the basis that they 'held themselves out to the world at large as husband and wife'.[29] The complexity of the issues and the arduous process of determining disputed facts were explicitly noted.[30]

In respect of the first question as to whether the parties should be treated as validly married under English law by operation of a presumption of marriage, Williams J held that the presumption of marriage was deemed not to operate on the facts of the case. Furthermore, based on the direct evidence of the parties, it could not be presumed that a second ceremony had taken place during the couple's time in Dubai.[31] In respect of the second question as to whether the marriage was void and therefore susceptible to a decree of nullity, Williams J relied upon the *ECHR* and other human rights instruments to conclude that the ceremony that took place in December 1998 was 'a marriage entered into in disregard of certain requirements as to the formation of marriage' and therefore void under section 11(a)(iii) of the *MCA 1973*, thereby entitling the wife to a decree of nullity.[32] More specifically, he held that Articles 8 and 12 *ECHR* in addition to Article 3 of the *United Nations Convention on the Rights of the Child* (*UNCRC*) were engaged and supported an interpretation of section 11(a)(iii) of the *MCA 1973*, which would result in a finding of a void marriage rather than a non-marriage.[33] Given the public interest in this issue and its ramifications for the institution of marriage, the Attorney-General appealed the decision.

D. The Judgment of the Court of Appeal

From the outset, it is essential to note that whilst the wife and husband were the respondents in the appeal, neither took an active part at this stage as they had already agreed a settlement. However, the Court of Appeal gave permission to a first and second intervener, both of whom were represented pro bono. The first intervener was a petitioner in separate nullity proceedings and was allowed to intervene in relation to matters of law. The second intervener was Southall Black Sisters.[34] The Attorney-General also agreed

[29] ibid [3].

[30] Oral evidence was heard from the wife, her sister and the husband, with disputes of fact being resolved on the balance of probabilities. Williams J issued a Lucas direction in respect of his own assessment of the evidence, given his observations in respect of the husband's demeanour and the evidence-based contradictory accounts provided by the wife to challenge the husband's evidence. ibid [20] and [25].

[31] ibid [40].

[32] ibid [96].

[33] ibid [93].

[34] www.southallblacksisters.org.uk/about. The website states that the Southall Black Sisters, 'a not-for-profit, secular and inclusive organisation, was established in 1979 to meet the needs of Black (Asian and African-Caribbean) women. Our aims are to highlight and challenge all forms gender-related violence against women, empower them to gain more control over their lives; live without fear of violence and assert their human rights to justice, equality and freedom'.

to instruct an Advocate to the Court to ensure that any contrary arguments were put before the Court.

The two major issues to be determined by the Court of Appeal were as follows:

(i) Whether there are ceremonies or other acts which do not create a marriage, even a void marriage, within the scope of s 11 of the 1973 Act; and
(ii) If there are, whether the December 1998 ceremony was such a ceremony, currently described as a non-marriage, or whether, as Williams J decided, it created a void marriage.[35]

With regard to the first matter, the Court of Appeal held that there can be ceremonies which do not create a marriage within the scope of the *Marriage Act 1949* and the *MCA 1973*, and therefore do not entitle the parties to a decree of nullity.[36] The classification of a marriage as void is determined at the date of its alleged solemnisation and is thus not dependent on subsequent events such as the intention to undertake a further ceremony, or indeed whether there are children within the relationship.[37]

In relation to the second issue, the Court of Appeal held that the *nikah* ceremony was not a marriage within the scope of the *Marriage Act 1949*. The ceremony would have been permitted under section 44 of the *Marriage Act 1949* had it been performed in a registered building. However, no notice had been given to the superintendent registrar, no certificates had been issued and no registrar or authorised person was present at the ceremony. Both parties understood that the ceremony created no legal consequences and, in order for the couple to be validly married, a further ceremony was required which complied with the requirements of the *Marriage Act 1949*.[38] Whilst the Court of Appeal recognised that Williams J's decision was an attempt to enable the wife to make an application for financial orders,[39] it nonetheless set aside the decree of nullity issued by the High Court and held that no ceremony had taken place in respect of which a decree of nullity could be granted pursuant to the provisions of section 11 of the *MCA 1973*.[40]

III. Novel Aspects of the Judgments

The comprehensive judgments handed down by the High Court and the Court of Appeal point to the complexity of this case. Upon analysing both judgments, two particularly novel aspects become apparent. The first is the extent to which the provisions of the *ECHR* and other international human rights instruments were considered by both courts. The second aspect which marked a departure from previous case law was the

[35] *Her Majesty's Attorney-General v Akhter and Others* (n 1) [5].
[36] *R v Bham* [1965] 3 All ER 124 relied upon.
[37] The Court of Appeal nonetheless acknowledged that such a situation was provided for by s 12 of the *MCA 1973* in respect of a voidable marriage, wherein the nature and effect of a ceremony can change over time: *Her Majesty's Attorney-General v Akhter and Others* (n 1) [124].
[38] *Her Majesty's Attorney-General v Akhter and Others* (n 1) [123].
[39] ibid [102].
[40] ibid [128].

strong expression of dissatisfaction by both courts towards the term 'non-marriage'. Each of these aspects will be considered in turn.

A. The Impact of the *ECHR* and International Human Rights Instruments

During the hearing before the High Court, counsel on behalf of the wife submitted that arguments under the *Human Rights Act 1998* (*HRA 1998*) were absent from relevant precedent case law.[41] Williams J noted that in undertaking an evaluation of whether there had been an attempt to comply with the required formalities to create a valid marriage, and in interpreting section 11 of the *MCA 1973*, the court should take into account fundamental rights under the *ECHR* as brought into effect by the *HRA 1998*. This brought the issue of human rights front and centre in this case. Williams J embarked upon a lengthy consideration of a number of articles of the ECHR and other human rights instruments, in addition to relevant case law from both the European Court of Human Rights (ECtHR) and the national courts.[42] The obligation on states to provide both the substantive and procedural means to ensure effective rights was acknowledged, and the recent Court of Appeal judgment in *Re A (Children) (Contact: Ultra-Orthodox Judaism: Transgender Parent) (Stonewall Equality Limited and Another Intervening)*[43] was noted insofar as it reasserted that a court must act compatibly with *Convention* rights.[44]

With regard to international human rights instruments, Williams J noted the relevance of Article 3 *UNCRC*, which provides that: 'In all actions concerning children, whether undertaken by public or private social welfare institutions, courts of law, administrative authorities or legislative bodies, the best interests of the child shall be a primary consideration.' Authorities were also set out which confirmed that the *UNCRC* was binding and must be complied with in domestic decision making.[45] Upon considering

[41] *Akhter v Khan* (n 2) [57]. It was noted that there was limited reference made to human rights in *AB v HT and Others* [2018] EWCOP 2, which concerned the capacity of a woman and the nature of a religious marriage ceremony that had occurred.

[42] The relevant provisions of the *HRA 1998* were also set out, namely the positive obligation contained in s 3 requiring that in 'so far as it is possible to do so, primary legislation and subordinate legislation must be read and given effect in a way which is compatible with the Convention rights'. Section 6, concerning the acts of public authorities, was noted insofar as it applied to the obligation placed upon courts to interpret legislation in a manner that is consistent with the rights protected under the *Convention*.

[43] *Re A (Children) (Contact: Ultra-Orthodox Judaism: Transgender Parent) (Stonewall Equality Limited and Another Intervening)* [2017] EWCA Civ 2164.

[44] *Akhter v Khan* (n 2) [65].

[45] The *UNCRC* was ratified by the UK on 16 December 1991 and came into effect on 15 January 1992. In *Akhter v Khan* (n 2) [68], Williams J noted that: 'It has not been incorporated by statute into domestic law and does not, as such, form part of the law of England and Wales, but decisions of the Supreme Court of the UK make clear that the rights set out in the UNCRC are binding and must be complied with in domestic decision making.' Reliance was placed upon the decisions of *ZH (Tanzania) v Secretary of State for the Home Department* [2011] UKSC 4 and *HH v Deputy Prosecutor of the Italian Republic, Genoa (Official Solicitor Intervening)* [2012] UKSC 25 [33] and [155], where the Supreme Court stated that *ECHR* rights had to be considered through the prism of art 3.1 *UNCRC*. In *Her Majesty's Attorney-General v Akhter and Others* (n 1) [109] and [110], the Court of Appeal also referred to these authorities in its judgment.

precedent case law, Williams J deemed the action to be 'properly described as an action concerning children both because a direct consequence will be the availability or non-availability of a financial remedy of quite a different character to that which is available under the Children Act 1989'.[46] It was concluded that the courts should, where appropriate, take into account the best interests of children as a primary consideration and weigh it against other Article 8 rights of the parties.[47] The Court of Appeal, in rejecting this conclusion, noted that 'whilst there is inevitably a tangential impact upon a child dependent upon the status of his or her parents' relationship, an application brought before the court made in order to establish the status of that relationship cannot properly be regarded as an "action concerning children"'.[48] The *Family Law Reform Act 1987* was noted as providing equality for all children irrespective of parental marital status. Whilst the Court of Appeal accepted that a claim for provision under the *MCA 1973* differed in nature to a claim under the *Children Act 1989*, the former amounting to a 'freestanding claim made in the capacity of wife as well as in the capacity of mother' and the latter being a claim on behalf of only the child, it took the view that 'each route however provides for all the same essential elements necessary in order properly to provide for that child'.[49]

Interestingly, counsel on behalf of the wife had placed reliance upon the *United Nations Convention on the Elimination of all Forms of Discrimination Against Women* (*CEDAW*), in particular Article 16, which provides that:

> States Parties shall take all appropriate measures to eliminate discrimination against women in all matters relating to marriage and family relations and in particular shall ensure, on a basis of equality of men and women … (c) The same rights and responsibilities during marriage and at its dissolution … (h) The same rights for both spouses in respect of the ownership, acquisition, management, administration, enjoyment and disposition of property, whether free of charge or for a valuable consideration.

However, Williams J ultimately declined to be persuaded by this argument on the basis that 'at its simplest level the law in relation to invalid marriages applies equally to men and women', and thus he held that Article 16 did not provide additional assistance in interpreting section 11 of the *MCA 1973*.[50]

The main human rights arguments arose in respect of the *ECHR*. Counsel on behalf of the wife submitted that a number of *Convention* rights were engaged in this case, namely, Article 6 (the right to a fair trial), Article 8 (the right to respect for private and family life), Article 12 (the right to marry), Article 1 of Protocol 1 (the right to peaceful enjoyment of one's possessions) and Article 14 (prohibition of discrimination). Regarding Article 6, counsel on behalf of the wife argued that:

> [T]he existence of a law of non-marriage and the resulting inability to make a financial claim is indirectly discriminatory in respect both of women and in particular Muslim women; both being disproportionately affected given the likelihood that men will usually hold the majority

[46] *Akhter v Khan* (n 2) [72].
[47] ibid [93].
[48] *Her Majesty's Attorney-General v Akhter and Others* (n 1) [118].
[49] ibid [117].
[50] *Akhter v Khan* (n 2) [89].

> of financial assets and Muslim women are more likely to be held to be in a non-marriage given the current state of the law.[51]

Counsel on behalf of the Attorney-General had argued that Article 6 guarantees procedural rights and does not create a substantive right where none exists in domestic law. Williams J held that no violation of Article 6 or Article 14 arose as there was no direct or indirect discrimination against a Muslim woman in bringing a financial remedy claim upon obtaining a decree of nullity.

With regard to Article 8 of the *Convention*, counsel on behalf of the wife had argued that the right to respect for private and family life incorporated a right to respect for the status of the parties as a married couple.[52] It was counsel's submission that 'categorising their relationship as a non-marriage and thus excluding them from the ambit of nullity' amounted to a breach of Article 8.[53] The Attorney-General argued that it had not been demonstrated that the state had failed to comply with its positive obligation to ensure respect for family life, or that there had been interference with the right to respect for family life and placed reliance upon the decision of the ECtHR in *Şerife Yiğit v Turkey*.[54] Williams J accepted the submissions of the Attorney-General that Article 8 did not distinguish between those who cohabit and choose not to marry, and those who knowingly undertake a religious-only ceremony without undertaking the additional formalities required to create a legally valid marriage.[55] However, Williams J opined that 'in respect of those who sought to effect or intended to effect a legal marriage', Article 8 supported an approach to interpretation and application which would result in the finding of a void marriage rather than a wholly invalid marriage.[56] The Court of Appeal disagreed with this view and concluded that whilst Article 8 was engaged, the failure of the state to recognise the *nikah* as a legal marriage did not breach those rights.[57] The Court of Appeal considered at length the approach adopted by the High Court in respect of the role of Article 8 in the interpretation of section 11 of the *MCA 1973* and concluded that neither Article 8 *ECHR* nor Article 3 *UNCRC* provided a basis to change the legal effect of a ceremony and alter the status of a 'non-marriage' to a 'void marriage'.[58]

Regarding the role of Article 12 *ECHR*, both counsel on behalf of the wife and the Attorney-General accepted that national law may properly regulate marriages and Article 12 did not oblige a state to recognise a religious marriage.[59] Nevertheless, Williams J concluded that:

> [T]here may be circumstances where Article 12 also has relevance in terms of its horizontal effect. In this case where the husband led the wife to believe that they would undertake a

[51] ibid [75].

[52] Article 8 *ECHR* provides: '1. Everyone has the right to respect for his private and family life, his home and his correspondence. 2. There shall be no interference by a public authority with the exercise of this right except such as is in accordance with the law and is necessary in a democratic society in the interests of national security, public safety or the economic well-being of the country, for the prevention of disorder or crime, for the protection of health or morals, or for the protection of the rights and freedoms of others.'

[53] *Akhter v Khan* (n 2) [78].

[54] *Şerife Yiğit v Turkey* (2011) 53 EHRR 25.

[55] *Akhter v Khan* (n 2) [80].

[56] ibid.

[57] *Her Majesty's Attorney-General v Akhter and Others* (n 1) [106].

[58] ibid [103].

[59] Article 12 *ECHR* provides that men and women of marriageable age have the right to marry and to found a family, according to the national laws governing the exercise of this right.

> civil ceremony as part of the process of marrying and has thus left her in the situation where she does not have a marriage which is valid under English law the husband himself has infringed her right to marry. Once she had embarked on the process going through the Nikah ceremony and consummating the marriage, notwithstanding Ms Rhone-Adrien's [counsel on behalf of the husband] assertion that she could have left the marriage at any stage, the reality for this wife and I suppose many others in her situation is that this was not a realistic option for her. Thus if this marriage is not a valid marriage according to English law nor a void marriage she is left without the remedies which arise from divorce or nullity. It seems to me this must be a relevant consideration in the evaluation of whether on these facts this should be treated as a void marriage.[60]

Notwithstanding his acknowledgement that the equitable maxims that equity treats as done that which ought to be done and that equity focuses on intent not form usually apply in the context of property rights, Williams J noted that it might be capable of informing the court's approach to the interpretation of section 11 and concluded that whilst it could not create a valid marriage, it supported:

> [T]he conclusion that in determining whether on the facts of this case whether what happened created a void marriage I can treat the joint intention of the parties to undertake a civil ceremony which was not then seen through by the husband's as supporting the conclusion that this was a void marriage.[61]

The conclusion drawn by Williams J that the ceremony that took place in 1998 fell within the parameters of section 11 on the basis of a 'horizontal effect' of Article 12 and, in light of general principles of fairness or equity, was described as 'unconventional' by the Court of Appeal.[62] The Court of Appeal held that Article 12 was not engaged and even if it were, there would be no breach on the facts of this case. Agreement was expressed with the submissions made by counsel for the Attorney-General that sections 3 and 6 of the *HRA 1998* imposed obligations on public authorities, including courts, but not on individuals. Whilst those obligations can require the state through the courts to regulate relations between private individuals, in the present case the wife did not have any type of private law right against the husband requiring him to marry her lawfully or have any claim against him for refusing to do so.[63] The Court of Appeal unequivocally stated that:

> No one can be forced to marry; indeed to force someone to marry is a criminal offence. Further, a person can change their mind and break their promise to do so right up to the last minute before the proposed marriage ceremony (or, even, during the ceremony). From a legal perspective, it does not matter how badly that refusal may reflect on the person who changes their mind, or indeed how deeply hurtful it is to their intended spouse. That this is the case is reflected in the fact that agreements to marry do not give rise to legal rights, and that no action lies for their breach: see s 1 of the Law Reform (Miscellaneous Provisions) Act 1970 ('the 1970 Act') which abolished 'breach of promise' actions.[64]

The Court of Appeal also expressed agreement that a finding of a void marriage would not logically remedy a determination that the right to marry was infringed.

[60] *Akhter v Khan* (n 2) [83].

[61] ibid [83].

[62] *Her Majesty's Attorney-General v Akhter and Others* (n 1) [77].

[63] ibid [84] and [85]. The Court of Appeal also analysed *Johnston and Others v Ireland* (1986) 9 EHRR 203, *Babiarz v Poland* (2017) ECHR 13 and *Owens v Owens* [2018] UKSC 41.

[64] *Her Majesty's Attorney-General v Akhter and Others* (n 1) [88].

Regarding the submission that the wife's right to peaceful enjoyment of her possessions as provided by Article 1 of Protocol 1 had been infringed, Williams J concluded that it must first be established that there was a valid or void marriage before any potential property right could be deemed to be infringed.[65] The Court of Appeal agreed with this analysis concluding that Article 1 of Protocol 1 'cannot be used as a basis for, or to bolster other, human rights arguments'.[66]

Ultimately, Williams J concluded that Articles 8 and 12 *ECHR* in addition to Article 3 *UNCRC* mandated a 'slightly more flexible interpretation' of section 11 of the *MCA 1973*, which sets out the grounds upon which a marriage may be deemed void.[67] Williams J, in taking 'a holistic view of a process rather than a single ceremony', concluded that the ceremony that took place in December 1998 fell within the scope of section 11 of the *MCA 1973*, thereby entitling the wife to a decree of nullity.[68] The Court of Appeal rejected this approach and held that the failure of the state to recognise the *nikah* as a legal marriage was not in breach of the *ECHR*. The Court noted that at no time did the parties seek to effect a legal marriage, but rather that the 'judge has, instead, relied upon the continuum argument, namely the parties' agreement at the date of the Nikah that they would have a civil ceremony at some future date with the intention to effect a legal marriage'.[69] The Court concluded that this approach failed to uphold section 1(1) of the *Law Reform (Miscellaneous Provisions) Act 1970*, which provides that agreements to marry are not enforceable in law.[70] The determination of whether a marriage is void depends on the facts at the date of the alleged marriage and not on future events, such as the intention to undertake another ceremony or whether there are children within the relationship.

Both judgments gave significant consideration to the effects of the *ECHR* and other human rights instruments upon the interpretation of section 11 of the *MCA 1973*. Williams J in the High Court engaged rigorously with the human rights legal framework and left the Court of Appeal with no option but to step into the discussion.[71]

B. Dissatisfaction with the Term 'Non-Marriage'

The expression of dissatisfaction by both the High Court and the Court of Appeal towards the term 'non-marriage' emerges as the second novel aspect of both judgments.[72]

[65] *Akhter v Khan* (n 2) [88].

[66] *Her Majesty's Attorney-General v Akhter and Others* (n 1) [73].

[67] *Akhter v Khan* (n 2) [96].

[68] ibid [94].

[69] *Her Majesty's Attorney-General v Akhter and Others* (n 1) [102].

[70] Section 1(1) of the *Law Reform (Miscellaneous Provisions) Act 1970* provides that: 'An agreement between two persons to marry one another shall not under the law of England and Wales have effect as a contract giving rise to legal rights and no action shall lie in England and Wales for breach of such an agreement, whatever the law applicable to the agreement.'

[71] In *Her Majesty's Attorney-General v Akhter and Others* (n 1), the Court of Appeal noted at [120] that: 'Whilst the judge set out the terms of Article 14, at [66], the focus of his judgment was upon the matters set out above and there is little consideration or analysis of Article 14 nor is it a ground of appeal. It is not therefore necessary or appropriate for the disposal of this particular appeal to consider the issue of Article 14 discrimination.'

[72] See generally R Probert, 'The Evolving Concept of "Non-Marriage"' (2013) 25(3) *Child and Family Law Quarterly* 314. See also C Barton and R Probert, 'The Status of a Religious-Only Marriage: Valid, Void, or "Non"? *Akhter v Khan*' (2018) 48 *Family Law* 1540.

Williams J noted that the application of the term 'non-marriage' to cases such as this one felt 'instinctively inappropriate'.[73] He also observed that as the term originated from the courts, it is an act of a public authority and 'either does, or risks, infringing the Article 8 rights of couples to respect for their private and family life'.[74] Setting out the potential impact of the use of such a term, he expressed the view that:

> Those who have religiously married and have lived for many years, raised families and been treated by the family community and state authorities as married should not have the term non-marriage applied to them … In my view the expression non-marriage should be reserved only to those situations such as acting or children playing where there has never been any intention to genuinely create a marriage.[75]

Williams J proposed that a more appropriate term may be 'invalid marriage'.[76] The Court of Appeal concurred with the High Court with regard to the use of the term 'non-marriage'.[77] Whilst continuing to use the term throughout its judgment for consistency, the Court of Appeal proposed that such a ceremony should be referred to as a 'non-qualifying ceremony' to signify that it fell outside the scope of both the *Marriage Act 1949* and the *MCA 1973*.[78]

IV. Implications of the Judgment

Permission to appeal to the Supreme Court was refused, so the judgment of the Court of Appeal in *Her Majesty's Attorney-General v Akhter and Others* remains the leading case in this area.[79] The judgment has already been cited in a number of cases and has been frequently referred to in the Law Commission Consultation Paper on Weddings Law issued in September 2020.[80] Given its importance, it is worth considering some of the far-reaching implications of this judgment.

The first consequence is that whilst both courts conveyed their dissatisfaction in respect of the term 'non-marriage', the Court of Appeal re-affirmed that it should nonetheless remain as a category within the law, albeit with a more palatable term as a 'non-qualifying ceremony'. Despite Williams J's attempts to adopt a 'flexible approach' through the engagement of international human rights instruments, namely Article 8

[73] *Akhter v Khan* (n 2) [9].

[74] ibid [81].

[75] ibid.

[76] ibid.

[77] *Her Majesty's Attorney-General v Akhter and Others* (n 1) [7].

[78] ibid [64]. Nevertheless, when referring to this specific ceremony (at [122] and [123]), the Court of Appeal referred to the ceremony as a 'non-qualifying ceremony'.

[79] The application to the Supreme Court by the second intervener for permission to appeal from the decision of the Court of Appeal was refused by a decision dated 6 August 2020.

[80] See, eg, *R (on the Application of Harrison and Others) v Secretary of State for Justice* [2020] EWHC 2096 (Admin); *Padero-Mernagh v Mernagh* [2020] EWFC 27; *AR v Secretary of State for Work and Pensions* [2020] PTSR 2162; *Shahzad v Mazher (Queen's Proctor Intervening)* [2020] EWCA Civ 1740. See also *Getting Married* (n 3).

ECHR and Article 3 *UNCRC*, the Court of Appeal reasserted the need for clarity in the regulation of marriages. The continuum approach adopted by Williams J was indeed flawed and apart from any considerations concerning international human rights instruments, it is clear that no person can be forced to legally marry irrespective of any promises previously made to do so. In this case, it was clear that both parties knew that there was no legal effect arising from their *nikah* ceremony and that a civil ceremony was required to effectuate a legal marriage. The husband's unilateral refusal to undertake a civil ceremony must be respected in accordance with section 1(1) of the *Law Reform (Miscellaneous Provisions) Act 1970*, which provides that agreements to marry are not enforceable in law. Whatever the merits of the decision of the Court of Appeal, the harsh result remains that non-recognition in respect of unregistered religious marriages that are conducted outside the legal framework effectively excludes individuals, predominantly women, from having such disputes adjudicated by the civil courts. Undoubtedly, this has significant societal impacts, such as increasing the demand for religious tribunals to adjudicate on such issues.

The second observation relates to the application of international human rights instruments in relation to marriage law in England and Wales. The conclusions drawn by the Court of Appeal – that Article 12 was simply not engaged, that no breach of Article 8 arose, and that an action concerning marital status was not a matter concerning children and therefore did not engage Article 3 *UNCRC* – shine a light upon the utility of such arguments in cases of this nature. More recently, the case of *R (on the Application of Harrison and Others) v Secretary of State for Justice*[81] focused on an alleged breach of Article 9 (freedom of thought, conscience and religion) in conjunction with Article 14 (prohibition of discrimination) *ECHR*. Eady J in the High Court dismissed the claim brought by six couples who claimed that the legal regime in England and Wales was discriminatory as it failed to give legal recognition to marriage conducted by way of humanist ceremony. *Her Majesty's Attorney-General v Akhter and Others* was considered by Eady J in addition to other case law. Eady J concluded that the case fell within the scope of Article 9 and Article 14 as it had been shown that there was a difference in treatment on the ground of belief.[82] Nevertheless, the defendant's arguments that there was a legitimate aim in awaiting the publication of the Law Commission review of the law governing weddings was accepted as a reason to dismiss the claim.[83]

The third observation relates to the anticipated recommendations of the Law Commission. In *Her Majesty's Attorney-General v Akhter and Others* (2020), the Court

[81] *R (on the Application of Harrison and Others) v Secretary of State for Justice* (n 80).

[82] Article 14 provides that: 'The enjoyment of the rights and freedoms set forth in this Convention shall be secured without discrimination on any ground such as sex, race, colour, language, religion, political or other opinion, national or social origin, association with a national minority, property, birth or other status.' As 'belief' is not a prescribed ground within art 14, Eady J noted that it falls under the category of 'other status'; *R (on the Application of Harrison and Others) v Secretary of State for Justice* (n 80) [95].

[83] See generally M Welstead, 'No Right (as Yet) to Be Married Legally in a Humanist Ceremony: *R (on the Application of Harrison and Others) v Secretary of State for Justice* [2020] EWHC 2096 (Admin)' [2020] *Family Law* 1694.

of Appeal referred to the Law Commission review of the law governing weddings and since its judgment, the Law Commission launched its Consultation Paper on Weddings Law in September 2020.[84] Offering crucial insight, the Consultation Paper notes that: 'Religious-only weddings are a specific instance of a wider difficulty that arises at the end of a relationship between a couple who were never married in the eyes of the law … We consider that the correct approach in such cases is to focus on the consequences of the relationship coming to an end, rather than on the ceremony.'[85] The Consultation Paper argues that reform of the law relating to cohabitation would ensure protection of those whose religious ceremonies have no legal consequences, as well as those who have had a non-religious ceremony or no ceremony at all.[86] Indeed, this approach has been advanced by various academics.[87] It has also been noted that 'it cannot simply be assumed that religious-only marriages are a problem that needs to be eliminated either by universal recognition or a blanket ban.'[88] Religious-only marriages have different meanings and functions for faith adherents. For instance, within the Muslim context, religious-only marriages allow for 'halal' cohabitation, which enables a couple to live together without social stigma within their faith communities prior to any legally binding marriage.[89] The Law Commission has put forward various provisional proposals, including a move from a registered buildings-based system towards an officiant-based system and a removal of the prescribed words so as to ensure that different religious practices are accommodated.[90] The Law Commission has also made proposals about the consequences of a ceremony that fails to comply with the revised requirements, with the aim of making it 'more likely that a marriage will be void, rather than non-qualifying'.[91] Overall, it is thus clear that a significant consequence of the Court of Appeal judgment in *Her Majesty's Attorney-General v Akhter and Others* is the confirmation that legislative reform concerning marriage law in England and Wales is urgently needed.

[84] *Getting Married* (n 3). It is worth noting that this process commenced in December 2014. The Scoping Paper was published in December 2015 and, after agreeing Terms of Reference, the review began in July 2019.

[85] ibid [10.204].

[86] ibid [10.205]; reference made to *Cohabitation: The Financial Consequences of Relationship Breakdown* (Law Com No 30, 2007).

[87] See especially R Sandberg, 'Unregistered Religious Marriages are Neither Valid nor Void' (2020) 79(2) *Cambridge Law Journal* 237; R Sandberg and S Thompson, 'The Sharia Law Debate: The Missing Family Law Context' (2016) 177 *Law & Justice* 181.

[88] Probert and Saleem (n 15) 377.

[89] ibid.

[90] *Getting Married* (n 3) [10.181] and [10.182]. N Hopkins, E Welch and S Hussaini, 'The Law Commission's Project on Weddings Law Reform' (2021) 23(3) *Ecclesiastical Law Journal* 267 describes at 273: 'Under the scheme, there would be a new role of "officiant": all officiants would have the same legal duties and responsibilities, and all weddings would have to be attended by one officiant. The focus of the regulation would be on this person and their responsibilities. All officiants would have the duty to ensure that the parties freely expressed consent to marry each other, that the other requirements of the ceremony (discussed below) were met and that the schedule was signed. Officiants would also be responsible for upholding the dignity and solemnity of marriage.'

[91] *Getting Married* (n 3) [10.185]. See also R Sandberg, 'Marital Problems: The Law Commission's "Getting Married" Consultation Paper and Non-Qualifying Wedding Ceremonies' (2021) 23(2) *Ecclesiastical Law Journal* 140, which critiques some of the proposals put forward by the Law Commission.

V. Conclusion

Legally recognised marriages create a variety of rights and obligations, and the state undoubtedly has an interest in its regulation. The *Marriage Act 1949* establishes various thresholds that must be reached in order for marriage ceremonies to come within the scope of the legislative framework. The judgment by Williams J confirms the benefit of the position of a judge, having heard evidence from the parties, to appreciate the complexity of familial structures within a religious community and, more broadly, within a multicultural society. Whilst the decision was to be anticipated, the conclusion of the Court of Appeal that 'Although the overall system might be described as complex, we would suggest that it is not difficult for parties who want to be legally married to achieve that status'[92] points to a lack of understanding of the lived experience of individuals, especially women, within certain cultural or religious groups.

Some academics have argued that only civil marriage should be recognised on the basis that this would provide the same framework for everyone and preserve the institution of religious marriage. Other academics have gone so far as to argue for the abolition of the institution of marriage and the introduction of a regime of civil partnerships for all couples,[93] while others have called for legal pluralism to be explored and even going so far as to advocate for minority legal orders.[94] There has also been criticism that the focus of the debate needs to shift from whether religious legal pluralism exists to the conditions under which it should exist.[95] Irrespective of one's view, it is clear that the regulation of marriage and divorce by the state is a matter of huge practical significance, especially for individuals whose religious prescripts concerning marriage and divorce fall outside the ambit of state law. Given the profound consequences of a determination of 'non-marriage' both in a social and a legal context, the current legislative framework concerning marriage is clearly questionable. Occurring with considerable frequency in respect of Islamic marriages is a finding of non-compliance with the statutory formalities.[96] Therefore, in tandem with calls for legislative reform, it is crucial that there are initiatives within these religious communities identifying ways for faith adherents to remain faithful to their religious prescripts and cultural traditions, whilst simultaneously encouraging compliance with the state law.[97] Whilst the Law Commission review

[92] *Her Majesty's Attorney-General v Akhter and Others* (n 1) [12]. This runs counter to the views expressed by the Law Commission that 'there are clear problems with the law: it is unduly complex, uncertain, and inefficient; and it is also perceived to be unfair and overly restrictive': *Getting Married* (n 3) [1.32].

[93] See, eg, PW Edge, 'Let's Talk about a Divorce: Religious and Legal Weddings' in J Miles, P Mody and R Probert (eds), *Marriage Rites and Rights* (Hart Publishing, 2015) 255; C Chambers, *Against Marriage: An Egalitarian Defence of the Marriage-Free State* (Oxford University Press, 2017).

[94] See, eg, A Shachar, *Multicultural Jurisdictions: Cultural Differences and Women's Rights* (Cambridge University Press, 2001).

[95] R Sandberg (ed), *Religion and Legal Pluralism* (Routledge, 2017) 9.

[96] See, eg, *Al-Saedy v Musawi* [2010] EWHC 3293 (Fam); *Dukali v Lamrani* [2012] EWHC 1748; *Sharbatly v Shagroon* [2012] EWCA Civ 1507; and *Her Majesty's Attorney-General v Akhter and Others* [2020] EWCA Civ 122.

[97] The 'Register Our Marriage' campaign was started in 2014 to raise awareness of the lack of legal protection for unregistered religious marriages and focuses particularly on religious marriages within the Muslim community. In February 2019, the UK government funded the Register Our Marriage campaign to run awareness-building programmes nationwide. The campaign also advocates for amendments to the *Marriage Act 1949*. See www.registerourmarriage.org.

is to be welcomed, its scope is confined to the law governing weddings.[98] Thus, questions concerning the substance of the law of marriage remain and it is essential that the complexities of these issues are treated in a nuanced and practical fashion by the legislature, upon whom this issue firmly rests.[99]

[98] The law governing weddings includes preliminaries, location, content of the ceremony, officiants, registration and criteria for a valid marriage ceremony. *Getting Married* (n 3) [1.12] and Appendix 1.

[99] For a broad overview of recent government responses and strategies regarding Islamic marital matters, see C Fairbairn, *Islamic Marriage and Divorce in England and Wales*, House of Commons Library, Briefing Paper 08747 (2020), www.researchbriefings.files.parliament.uk/documents/CBP-8747/CBP-8747.pdf. See also N Hopkins, E Welch and S Hussaini, 'The Law Commission's Project on Weddings Law Reform' (2021) 23(3) *Ecclesiastical Law Journal* 267, which notes that the Law Commission had been due to publish the final report at the end of 2021 and at 279 highlights that 'It will then be for Government to consider whether to pass legislation to implement the recommendations. Under the Protocol between the Lord Chancellor and the Law Commission, there is an expectation that Government will provide an interim response within six months and a final response within a year. But, ultimately, timing is in Government's hands.'

17

Christian Youth Camps Ltd v Cobaw Community Health Services Ltd

Balancing Discrimination Rights with the Religious Freedom of Organisations

NEIL FOSTER

I. Introduction

One of the important ways in which religious freedom is protected by the law around the Commonwealth, especially in countries (such as Australia) where there is no overarching human rights statute, is through the inclusion of 'balancing clauses' or 'exemptions' into laws forbidding unjust discrimination on various grounds.[1] Questions involving sexual orientation discrimination present these issues very sharply. In Australia, the decision of the Victorian Court of Appeal in *Christian Youth Camps Ltd v Cobaw Community Health Service Ltd*[2] is a landmark decision of an appellate court delineating the extent of the protection provided under state discrimination law to groups claiming that their religious beliefs should be protected by such clauses.[3] This chapter will describe the background to the litigation, its progress through the courts and its implications for future Australian consideration of these issues. It concludes that a number of features of the decision do not adequately balance the various rights involved and suggests that clarification on these matters will need to be provided by Parliaments and the High Court of Australia in the future.

The decision was handed down on appeal from a Tribunal decision fining Christian Youth Camps Ltd (CYC), and one of its officers, for declining an

[1] See N Foster 'Freedom of Religion and Balancing Clauses in Discrimination Legislation' (2016) 5 *Oxford Journal of Law and Religion* 385.

[2] *Christian Youth Camps Ltd v Cobaw Community Health Service Ltd* (2014) 50 VR 256, [2014] VSCA 75 (hereinafter '*CYC v Cobaw*').

[3] See B Murphy, 'Balancing Religious Freedom and Anti-discrimination: *Christian Youth Camps Ltd v Cobaw Community Health Services Ltd*' (2016) 40 *Melbourne University Law Review* 594, 596: '*Cobaw* was a landmark case'.

accommodation booking from a support group for same-sex-attracted young people.[4] The Court of Appeal, by a 2:1 majority, said that the organisation (CYC) was liable, but by a different 2:1 majority ruled that Mr Rowe, the individual who had declined the booking, was *not* liable.

After setting out the factual background for the decision, this chapter will review the issues on appeal that related to 'law and religion' interests and how the Victorian Court of Appeal dealt with those issues, the attempt to appeal the decision to the High Court, the subsequent impact of the decision, and the possible ramifications for the future consideration of the interaction of religious freedom and discrimination issues in Australia.

II. Background Facts

The complainant organisation, Cobaw, ran a project called 'WayOut', designed to provide support and suicide prevention services to 'same-sex-attracted young people'. The co-ordinator of the project approached CYC (a camping organisation connected with the Christian Brethren denomination) to inquire about making a booking at a Phillip Island campsite that was generally made available to community groups. Mr Rowe, to whom she spoke, informed her that the organisation would not be happy about making a booking for a group that encouraged a homosexual 'lifestyle', as he later put it.

There was some factual dispute about what was said in the telephone conversation. However, in the end, the issues were fairly clear: there had been a refusal to proceed with a booking; the reason for the refusal was connected with CYC's view of the philosophy of support for homosexuality as a valid expression of human sexuality; its opposition to this view was a result of what was seen by CYC to be required by the Scriptures. The Tribunal (constituted by Judge Hampel of the Victorian County Court) ruled against CYC and Mr Rowe, finding that they had unlawfully discriminated and should be jointly liable to pay a fine of $5,000.

The primary liability imposed was under sections 42(1)(a) and (c), and 49 of the *Equal Opportunity Act 1995* (Vic) (hereinafter '*EO Act 1995*'). These provisions prohibited discrimination on certain grounds (among which were same-sex sexual orientation, and personal association with persons of same-sex sexual orientation) in the areas of 'services', 'other detriments' and accommodation.[5] But the Tribunal said that it also had to take into account the *Charter of Human Rights and Responsibilities Act 2006* (Vic) (hereinafter 'the *Charter*'), which in effect is a general 'Bill of Rights' for Victoria. The *Charter* contains a general prohibition on discrimination in section 8; importantly, it also contains a right to freedom of religion and religious practice in section 14, and a right to freedom of expression in section 15.

[4] The Tribunal decision appealed from was *Cobaw Community Health Services Ltd v Christian Youth Camps Ltd and Rowe* [2010] VCAT 1613 (hereinafter '*Cobaw v CYC VCAT*').

[5] The previous legislation has now been replaced by the *Equal Opportunity Act 2010* (Vic), which contains provisions to similar effect, most of which came into operation on 1 August 2011.

The *EO Act 1995* contained two exemptions based on religion. Section 75(2) provided:

(2) Nothing in Part 3 applies to anything done by a body established for religious purposes that –

(a) conforms with the doctrines of the religion; or
(b) is necessary to avoid injury to the religious sensitivities of people of the religion.

And section 77 provided:

> Nothing in Part 3 applies to discrimination by a person against another person if the discrimination is necessary for the first person to comply with the person's genuine religious beliefs or principles.

However, the Tribunal held that neither of these provisions assisted either CYC or Mr Rowe.[6]

III. The Victorian Court of Appeal

The main issues[7] that the Court of Appeal dealt with can be summarised as follows:

1. Was the Victorian *Charter* relevant to the case?
2. Was the relevant refusal discriminatory on the basis of the sexual *orientation* of the participants or could it be seen as based on the support that the weekend was to offer for homosexual *activity*?
3. Was CYC alone liable under the *Act* or were both CYC and Mr Rowe potentially liable?
4. Could CYC rely on the section 75 defence applying to a 'body established for religious purposes'?
5. Could Mr Rowe rely on the section 77 defence on the basis of the necessity to comply with his 'genuine religious beliefs or principles'?
6. Could CYC as an incorporated body rely on the section 77 defence?

A. Application of the *Charter*

The Tribunal member, Judge Hampel, had ruled that the *Charter* was relevant, even though it had commenced on 1 January 2008 and the events at issue here occurred before then. In the Court of Appeal, Maxwell P ruled that this was a mistake; while the *Charter* required courts dealing with issues that arose after 1 January 2008 to interpret

[6] For earlier comments on the Tribunal decision, see N Foster, 'Freedom of Religion in Practice: Exemptions under Anti-discrimination Laws on the Basis of Religion' (paper presented at Law and Religion: Legal Regulation of Religious Groups, Organisations and Communities – Melbourne Law School, University of Melbourne, 15–16 July 2011), http://works.bepress.com/neil_foster/46.

[7] In this note I have omitted some other minor preliminary issues, most of which were resolved by Maxwell P, with whom on these points the other Judges agreed.

legislation passed before that date in accordance with its principles, it was not fully retrospective. Matters that had taken place before its commencement should be dealt with under pre-*Charter* law.[8]

B. Discrimination Based on Orientation or Behaviour?

The CYC argued that the decision not to accept the booking from Cobaw was not based on the 'sexual orientation' of the participants, but upon the advocacy of homosexual activity which the event would involve.[9]

This argument was rejected by Maxwell P, who supported comments that had been made by the Tribunal which were to the effect that sexual orientation is 'part of a person's being or identity' and that:

> To distinguish between an aspect of a person's identity, and conduct which accepts that aspect of identity, or encourages people to see that part of identity as normal, or part of the natural and healthy range of human identities, is to deny the right to enjoyment and acceptance of identity.[10]

In essence, his Honour said that to criticise homosexual sexual *activity* is to attack those *people* who identify as homosexual. In particular, he supported the UK Supreme Court decision in *Bull and Bull v Hall and Preddy*,[11] in which Lady Hale said: 'Sexual orientation is a core component of a person's identity which requires fulfilment through relationships with others of the same orientation.'[12]

The view that decisions made on the basis of same sex sexual activity, or support for such, are in effect decisions that discriminate against *persons* who identify as homosexual seems to be impliedly supported by Neave JA[13] and Redlich JA. Redlich JA gave more detailed consideration to the issues, but essentially took the same position put forward by Maxwell P that 'sexual orientation [is] inextricably interwoven with a person's identity'.[14] His Honour then went on to consider a Canadian decision[15] holding that a printing company was guilty of sexual orientation discrimination when it refused to print leaflets which were 'promoting the causes of' homosexual persons and said:

> Efforts to promote an understanding and respect for those possessing such a characteristic should not be regarded as separate from the characteristic itself. To draw such a distinction was inconsistent with the prohibition against discrimination under the Code.[16]

[8] *CYC v Cobaw* (n 2) [176]–[179]. Redlich JA at [510] agreed on this point; Neave JA should probably be seen as impliedly agreeing, as she made no specific comment on the issue.

[9] ibid [52].

[10] ibid, per Maxwell P at [57], quoting Judge Hampel in *Cobaw v CYC VCAT* (n 4) [193]. See also *CYC v Cobaw* (n 2) [59]: 'her Honour was right to reject the distinction between 'syllabus' [the teaching to be conveyed on the weekend] and 'attribute', for the reasons which her Honour gave'.

[11] *Bull and Bull v Hall and Preddy* [2014] 1 WLR 3741 (hereinafter '*Bull v Hall*').

[12] ibid 3755 [52].

[13] Her Honour simply said at one point that, apart from the question of personal liability, she dismissed the appeal for 'substantially the same reasons' as the President': *CYC v Cobaw* (n 2) [360].

[14] ibid [443]–[448]; the quote is from [443].

[15] *Ontario (Human Rights Commission) v Brockie* (2003) 222 DLR (4th) 174 (Ontario Superior Court of Justice (Divisional Court)) (hereinafter '*Brockie*').

[16] *CYC v Cobaw* (n 2) [447].

As will be noted later, Redlich JA also relied heavily on other aspects of that same Canadian decision in finding that in fact CYC and Mr Rowe could rely on the section 77 defence. But on this issue of whether there had been discrimination or not, his Honour agreed with the other members of the Court.

In the end, then, all members of the Court of Appeal in *CYC v Cobaw* took the view that a refusal to support an activity providing support for homosexual sexual *activity* was the same as discrimination against homosexual *persons*. The view that sexual 'orientation' is a fundamental part of human 'identity', and the view that this must then be allowed expression in sexual activity, seems to be accepted.

C. Institutional or Individual Liability?

The third major issue in the decision was whether CYC alone, or both Mr Rowe and CYC, should be held liable for whatever discrimination had occurred. This is an issue that took up a large part of the judgments in the Court, and it is a fascinating legal question about how legislation applying to corporate bodies should be viewed.[17] However, given that the focus of our immediate interest in this chapter is the law and religion question, it will only be briefly summarised here.

In short, Maxwell P took the view that the liability of a corporation under the Victorian legislation was 'direct', based on the actions of officers and employees of the corporation whose actions are deemed, under a relevant 'attribution rule', to be those of the company.[18] His Honour said that the provision of the legislation headed 'vicarious liability', section 102 of the *EO Act 1995* did not deal with these standard cases of employees discriminating in the course of carrying out their normal duties.[19] He then also came to the view that since corporations are 'directly' liable for the actions of officers or employees, this means that the legislation did *not* intend to also make those individuals personally liable.[20] On this basis, he overturned the Tribunal's finding against Mr Rowe, while upholding the liability of CYC.

By contrast, both the other members of the Court found that *both* CYC and Mr Rowe could be held jointly and severally liable for discrimination. Neave JA noted that the term 'vicarious liability', used in the heading to section 102, did not necessarily have to have all the implications of the common law doctrine of vicarious liability.[21] Even if, as seems plausible, a corporation could be 'directly' liable for breach of the

[17] See N Foster, 'Personal Civil Liability of Company Officers for Company Workplace Torts' (2008) 16(1) *Torts Law Journal* 20; N Foster, 'Manslaughter by Managers: The Personal Liability of Company Officers for Death Flowing from Company Workplace Safety Breach' (2006) 9 *Flinders Journal of Law Reform* 79; N Foster, 'Personal Liability of Company Officers for Corporate Occupational Health and Safety Breaches: Section 26 of the *Occupational Health and Safety Act 2000* (NSW)' (2005) 18 *Australian Journal of Labour Law* 107.

[18] *CYC v Cobaw* (n 2) [97]–[122].

[19] ibid [124]–[138].

[20] ibid [123].

[21] ibid [371] – this is 'not a true example of vicarious liability'. Maxwell P at [126] had supported his view that section 102 did not deal with the 'ordinary' case of an employee acting on behalf of an employer partly by noting that at common law, vicarious liability only applied where the employer was not personally liable. But Neave JA, with respect, seems to be correct to have noted that the phrase is not necessarily intended here to have all the implications of the common law doctrine.

EO Act 1995,[22] this did not automatically mean that the employee whose actions are deemed to create direct liability for the company would then be excused.[23] With respect, it is submitted that Neave JA is correct at this point. Maxwell P moved too quickly from the imputation of direct liability to the company, to the view that the employee should therefore be immune.

Neave JA then also supported this view from her consideration of section 102, the 'vicarious liability' provision. As her Honour noted, by reference to academic commentary, the term 'vicarious liability' is often used loosely in anti-discrimination legislation to refer to different forms of 'attributed liability'.[24] As such, there was no need to assume that the Act used the term only in situations where the corporate employer would be otherwise innocent of wrongdoing, as the common law usage would imply.[25]

Redlich JA agreed with Neave JA generally on this issue, holding that both CYC and Mr Rowe could be held liable for any discrimination that had occurred. Redlich JA said that there was, in effect, no need to search for an 'attribution rule' for direct liability for CYC when section 102 provided the relevant rules.[26]

The result is that there was a 2:1 majority in the Court of Appeal judgment in favour of the proposition that both the company and the employee who commits the relevant direct act can be held liable for discrimination. However, as we will see below, since one of those in favour of this view (Redlich JA) was not in favour of the final order that was made, it could be argued that the precedential status of this proposition is unclear. Nevertheless, it is submitted that as a matter of law, the view of Neave JA and Redlich JA is to be preferred.

D. Could CYC Rely on the Section 75 Defence?

While both parties could be potentially held liable for discrimination, only CYC could rely on the section 75 defence, which applied to 'a body established for religious purposes' (the word 'body' clearly implied a corporate entity of some sort, not an individual).[27]

The Tribunal had ruled that CYC could not rely on the section 75 defence for a number of reasons: that it was not a body 'established for religious purposes', and in any event that the refusal of accommodation did not 'conform with the doctrines' of any relevant religion, nor was it necessary to 'avoid injury to the religious sensitivities' of believers. In effect, for similar reasons, the Court of Appeal agreed. This is arguably one of the most problematic aspects of the decision. It is also the feature of the decision that is likely to have the most impact in other jurisdictions around Australia, most of which have a provision similar to section 75 as a defence.[28]

[22] ibid [378].

[23] ibid [371].

[24] See ibid [385], citing N Rees, K Lindsay and S Rice, *Australian Anti-discrimination Law* (Federation Press, 2008).

[25] See the comment of Maxwell P at *CYC v Cobaw* (n 2) [126] on this issue.

[26] ibid [456]–[458].

[27] In this area Maxwell P (ibid [158]) correctly noted that Mr Rowe himself could not have directly relied on section 75 and would need (if he otherwise discriminated) to rely on section 77.

[28] For an overview of 'balancing clauses' in Australian discrimination laws recognising the religious freedom rights of religious bodies, see N Foster, 'Protecting Religious Freedom in Australia through Legislative Balancing Clauses' (2017), http://works.bepress.com/neil_foster/111.

i. *Was CYC a 'Body Established for Religious Purposes'?*

Maxwell P agreed with the decision of Judge Hampel that CYC was not a body 'established for religious purposes'.[29]

Features which, on the one hand, pointed to the 'religious purposes' of CYC were its establishment by the Brethren denomination, the fact that it was required to operate 'in accordance with the fundamental beliefs and doctrines of the Christian Brethren', that it had to aim to create an 'obviously Christian' atmosphere, that its provision of camping facilities was to provide 'an opportunity to communicate the Christian faith', that those who visited the campsites should 'experience Christian life and values' and that it had the power to advance to the Trustees of the Brethren church money for 'charitable' purposes.[30] Members of the Board of CYC were to subscribe to the Brethren declaration of faith.[31]

On the other hand, Maxwell P regarded a number of other features of the way in which CYC operated as counting against the body being one that was operated 'for religious purposes': advertising on the website and brochures did not contain any explicit reference to Christianity; the site was regularly booked by secular groups; there was no prohibition of any particular type of activity offered in its advertising, and camps were not required to have any Christian content (even though Christian groups did also occasionally use the site).

Maxwell P quoted at length from a judgment of Dixon J in an old case dealing with a testamentary bequest, *Roman Catholic Archbishop of Melbourne v Lawlor*,[32] where he said that to establish the charitable category of a trust for religious purposes, the actual activities themselves must be 'religious'. From the examples given by Dixon J, this meant 'directly' religious-spiritual teaching, support of clergy or church buildings, or gifts to religious societies. Undertaking a 'secular' activity could not be a 'religious' purpose, even if motivated by religious reasons.[33]

However, it is worth noting that the *Lawlor* decision was in fact an evenly divided 3:3 split on this very issue of religious purpose, and hence cannot amount to a binding precedent.[34] In any case, the very specific issue was whether a bequest was for 'the advancement of religion' in the context of the law of charities, and it was not intended to be a 'one-size-fits-all' definition of 'religious purposes' for all contexts.

In the *CYC v Cobaw* decision, Maxwell P distinguished[35] the decision of the High Court in *Federal Commissioner of Taxation v Word Investments*,[36] which had held that a body which was itself clearly set up for religious purposes (Bible translation in

[29] There is a long discussion and review of the evidence in *CYC v Cobaw* (n 2) [199]–[254].

[30] ibid [204]–[205].

[31] ibid [206].

[32] *Roman Catholic Archbishop of Melbourne v Lawlor* (1934) 51 CLR 1.

[33] Maxwell P in *CYC v Cobaw* (n 2) [231]–[232].

[34] See the comments on this aspect of *Lawlor* (n 32) in *Federal Commissioner of Taxation v Word Investments* (2008) 236 CLR 204, per Kirby J at [171], noting that as a result of the even split, the decision of the court being appealed from, *In re Lawlor; National Trustees Executors & Agency Co of Australasia Ltd v Lawlor* [1934] VLR 22, was affirmed.

[35] *CYC v Cobaw* (n 2) [234]–[236].

[36] *Federal Commissioner of Taxation v Word Investments* (2008) 236 CLR 204 (hereinafter '*Word Investments*').

that case) could still be regarded as 'charitable' even though it engaged in secular commercial enterprises to provide funding for those religious purposes. The implication seems to be that if the Christian Brethren Church had *directly* run the camping activities rather than setting up CYC as a separate organisation, it would have been able to rely on section 75(2).

Yet, with respect, it seems as though Maxwell P was very much relying on a narrow view of what 'religion' requires in saying that CYC was not established for 'religious purposes'. For example, he characterised the 'very purpose for which CYC exists' as 'the commercial activity of making campsite accommodation available to the public for hire'.[37] However, that is not what CYC's founding documents said. Of the 10 substantive objects, four contain an explicit reference to CYC's religious goals.[38] Maxwell P acknowledged that these existed, but still concluded that the 'main' activity was a secular one and suggested that only if CYC were offering 'avowedly religious' camps could it have been described as having religious purposes.[39]

In so reasoning, it seems arguable that his Honour was making the same mistake identified by the majority of the High Court in *Word Investments* as having been made by the Commissioner of Taxation in that case. There the majority said that the Commissioner had made the mistake of reading the different possible activities carried out by Word on its own rather than reading the list as a whole.[40] The Commissioner had also been mistaken in assuming a sharp dichotomy between 'commercial' activities and 'charitable' activities, when the commercial activities were being carried out solely in aid of the charitable purposes:

> Word endeavoured to make a profit, but only in aid of its charitable purposes. To point to the goal of profit and isolate it as the relevant purpose is to create a false dichotomy between characterisation of an institution as commercial and characterisation of it as charitable.[41]

On the question as to whether freedom of religion should receive a 'broad' or 'narrow' interpretation, Maxwell P said at one point that the exemptions in sections 75–77 should not be 'read down' and that neither one of the 'co-existing rights' (that is, freedom from discrimination or freedom of religion) should be 'privileged over the other'.[42] On the other hand, he seemed critical of the approach of French J (as he then was) in the earlier decision of *Bropho v Human Rights and Equal Opportunity Commission*[43] in giving a broad reading to a 'freedom of speech' defence in the *Racial Discrimination Act 1975* (Cth).[44] French J had taken into account the strength of free speech as a value in human rights instruments and the common law to conclude that a free speech 'defence' in section 18D of that *Act* was 'not in substance an exemption, but rather defines areas of freedom of speech and expression not subject to the proscription imposed by section 18C'.[45]

[37] *CYC v Cobaw* (n 2) [246].
[38] Set out in ibid [205].
[39] ibid [249].
[40] *Word Investments* (n 36) [23].
[41] ibid [24].
[42] *CYC v Cobaw* (n 2) [188].
[43] *Bropho v Human Rights and Equal Opportunity Commission* (2004) 135 FCR 105.
[44] See *CYC v Cobaw* (n 2) [183]: 'the views expressed by French J were not adopted by the other member of the majority in that case'.
[45] *Bropho* (n 43) [76].

While there is lip service paid in the judgment of Maxwell P to the equal status of the rights concerned, it is hard to avoid the conclusion that indeed the 'anti-discrimination' right in *CYC v Cobaw* was given a much broader reading than that of freedom of religion.

Neave JA seemed to support Maxwell P's comments on the question of whether CYC was a body established for religious purposes.[46] Redlich JA also indicated his agreement that CYC was not a 'religious body established for religious purposes' (although it should be noted that the first occurrence of the word 'religious' in that phrase is not to be found in section 75(2)).[47] With respect, his Honour later made a number of important points about section 77 (noted below) which seem to imply that he ought perhaps to have been more willing to revisit the question of whether CYC was a body 'established for religious purposes'.[48]

The result of the unanimity on this point in the decision seems to be that even a body with explicitly faith-driven objects may be found not to be a body 'established for religious purposes' if it engages in a wide range of community services which do not explicitly require a faith commitment from the recipients. It may be queried whether this is indeed consistent with the comments of the High Court in *Word Investments* noted previously, or a good policy outcome. Well-known service bodies such as the Salvation Army or St Vincent de Paul regularly offer services to members of the public without inquiring as to their faith stances. Is it really the case that these bodies cannot be said to be established for 'religious purposes'? They would presumably argue that Jesus' teaching in the parable of the Good Samaritan[49] and a range of other teachings in the Bible make 'care for widows and orphans'[50] and other community activities a 'religious purpose' for those who are committed to Christ, especially when done by an organisation which formally acknowledges its Christian purposes in its governance documents.

If a distinction between these bodies and groups like CYC is sought in the fact that CYC charged commercial rates for its services, this seems to be committing the error that the High Court noted in *Word Investments*, and which Redlich JA pointed out in his Honour's discussion of section 77, of assuming that commercial involvement and religious commitment are incompatible. Does the fact that a Salvation Army fundraiser may charge a small amount for sandwiches really preclude them from being a body

[46] See *CYC v Cobaw* (n 2) [360], where her Honour stated in effect that where she made no other comment on issues, she agreed with the President.

[47] ibid [440] point (4). In this respect, if his Honour was applying that incorrect phrase to his analysis (ie, the legislation does not require the body to be characterised as a 'religious' body), it might be said that his decision on this point proceeded on the basis of a misunderstanding.

[48] For example, in ibid [550], his Honour correctly pointed out that, unlike some decisions of the European Court of Human Rights (as to which see the discussion below when s 77 is considered), the defence in s 77 'operate[s] in the commercial sphere' and 'permits a person's faith to influence them in their conduct in both private and secular and public life'. While these comments relate to s 77, the logic of his Honour's remarks apply to s 75 as well. The emphasis on the commercial aspects of CYC's activities was allowed to undercut the fact that all these activities were explicitly grounded in Christian faith and aimed at supporting the religious activities of the Christian Brethren denomination.

[49] Luke 10:25–37.

[50] James 1:27 – 'Religion that God our Father accepts as pure and faultless is this: to look after orphans and widows in their distress and to keep oneself from being polluted by the world' (New International Version).

'established for religious purposes'? Nevertheless, this outcome seems arguable when this aspect of the *CYC v Cobaw* decision is taken into account.

ii. Was the Refusal of Accommodation Justified?

Despite finding that CYC was not entitled to rely on section 75 defences, Maxwell P went on to consider whether, if it were, it could have justified the refusal of the booking on doctrinal or other grounds under section 75(2).

Yet again, Maxwell P operated on a narrow view of 'religious activity' which virtually excluded anything except church services and Bible studies. Even if CYC had been a religious body, his Honour held that the doctrinal defences could not apply to 'secular' activities. CYC's decision to 'voluntarily enter the market for accommodation services' meant that it had to behave in a way that did not allow any consideration of 'doctrinal' issues.[51]

However, in case this was in error, Maxwell P considered whether there would have been any clash with doctrine. He accepted the reasoning of Judge Hampel in the Tribunal, who had adopted the submission of a theological expert that 'doctrines' of the Christian faith were to be confined to matters dealt with in the historic Creeds, none of which mentioned sexual relationships.[52]

Maxwell P then went on to consider what result would have followed were he to accept the idea that views about the exclusivity of sexual relationships to marriage, and the nature of marriage as between a man and a woman, were in fact 'doctrines'. He noted that these views functioned as moral guidelines for those within the Church and that no doctrine of Scripture required interference with those outside the Church who chose to behave otherwise.[53] Hence, in his Honour's view, a refusal of accommodation cannot have been 'required' by Christian doctrine. On this point, he held that 'conforms to' doctrine must mean that there is 'no alternative' but to act in this way.[54] Indeed, he went on to helpfully explain to CYC what measures it should have taken if it was serious about this doctrine, such as warning guests that sexual activity outside marriage should not take place on the campsite.[55]

There are a number of serious problems with this whole passage of the judgment. One is that the passage suggests that the question of what is a 'doctrine' should be resolved by a comparison of expert evidence by a judge who has no real familiarity with the faith concerned. It surely was not Parliament's intention that judges of secular courts should make a decision as to what is a 'core' doctrine or not of a particular faith.[56]

[51] *CYC v Cobaw* (n 2) [269].
[52] ibid [276]–[277].
[53] ibid [284].
[54] ibid [287].
[55] ibid [290].
[56] On this point, see the comment of Redlich JA when discussing the s 77 defence (ibid [526]): 'Neither human rights law nor the terms of the exemption required a secular tribunal to attempt to assess theological propriety (citing *Catch the Fire Ministries Inc and Others v Islamic Council of Victoria Inc* (2006) 15 VR 207, 220 [36] (Nettle JA)). The Tribunal was neither equipped nor required to evaluate the applicants' moral calculus.' For a general discussion of this issue, see N Foster, 'Respecting the Dignity of Religious Organisations: Courts Deciding Theology?' (2020) 47 *University of Western Australia Law Review* 175.

In addition, the view that action in 'conformity' with doctrine must be 'required' or 'compulsory' seems far too narrow.[57] This very view was decisively rejected by the European Court of Human Rights (ECtHR) in the case of *Eweida v UK*.[58] There the action of British Airways in ordering its staff member not to display a cross was at one stage defended on the basis that wearing a cross was not 'required' by Christian doctrine. The ECtHR, in considering a claim under the freedom of religion provision in Article 9 of the *European Convention on Human Rights* (*ECHR*), ruled that it was not necessary to establish a breach of religious freedom to show that the action in question was religiously 'compulsory':

> In order to count as a 'manifestation' within the meaning of Article 9, the act in question must be intimately linked to the religion or belief. An example would be an act of worship or devotion which forms part of the practice of a religion or belief in a generally recognised form. However, the manifestation of religion or belief is not limited to such acts; the existence of a *sufficiently close and direct nexus* between the act and the underlying belief must be determined on the facts of each case. In particular, there is *no requirement on the applicant to establish that he or she acted in fulfilment of a duty* mandated by the religion in question. (Emphasis added).[59]

In that case, the wearing of a cross, while not a 'duty', was clearly a 'manifestation' of religious commitment. While the language of section 75(2) is not the same as that of Article 9, a similar approach would seem to be desirable (and it should be noted that Maxwell P accepted that international human rights jurisprudence on freedom of religion was, while not binding, certainly a relevant source to which Australian courts should look).[60]

Another point that should be noted is that Maxwell P's discussion of Christian moral doctrine not requiring the 'shunning' of non-Christian persons who do not conform to it (which is clearly correct) fails to deal with the completely different question of whether an organisation should be required to provide support for a particular *viewpoint* which has been announced when a booking is made. This point was picked up by Redlich JA in his discussion of section 77 (see below) and is also applicable to the question of whether providing a booking here would have involved CYC providing encouragement and a platform for teaching which they perceived to be contrary to an important part of Christian belief.

Maxwell P took a similar approach to the section 75(2)(b) question of an injury to 'religious sensibilities'. The fact that previously no inquiry had been made of the sexual practices of those attending the camps was taken to mean that simply allowing homosexual persons to attend was not of itself an interference with religious sensibilities. His Honour failed to consider the issues raised by a clear declaration on the part of the person booking that the very aim of the camp included an aim of 'normalising' homosexual activity, which CYC considered sinful.

[57] This view is shared by a commentator who was otherwise supportive of the majority decision: see A Gray, 'The Reconciliation of Freedom of Religion with Anti-discrimination Rights' (2016) 42 *Monash University Law Review* 72, 93: 'The natural meaning of the word "conformity" in this context does not, in my view, contemplate compulsion.'

[58] *Eweida v UK* [2013] ECHR 37.

[59] ibid [82].

[60] *CYC v Cobaw* (n 2) [192]–[198]. See also Neave JA at [411], who noted that the Court 'can also take account of international jurisprudence on the right to freedom of religion'.

Since Neave JA agreed with Maxwell P that CYC were not a 'religious' body, her Honour did not discuss the possible application of section 75 to the corporation. Redlich JA very briefly expressed his agreement with Maxwell P that, for the purposes of section 75, 'the beliefs or principles upon which CYC relied were not "doctrines" of the religion'.[61] It seems that his Honour was adopting the very narrow view of 'doctrines' as purely stemming from the historic Creeds, although his remark is so brief that one cannot be sure. As will be seen, his Honour later took a broader view of 'beliefs' under section 77.

The view that 'doctrine' can be confined to the 'bare minimum' of the historic Creeds is unlikely for many reasons, not least of which is that there have been many significant splits and divergences between branches of the Christian Church since the Creeds were established.

E. Could the Section 77 Defence Apply?

For those judges who considered that Mr Rowe was potentially personally liable, the defence in section 77 also required consideration. Maxwell P, while holding that in fact Mr Rowe was not personally liable, also offered his views on the interpretation of section 77.

For Maxwell P, any possible section 77 defence (which authorises actions by a person where 'necessary … to comply with the person's genuine religious beliefs or principles') was ruled out for reasons similar to those which his Honour thought would have ruled out the section 75(2) defence applicable to CYC: because it was not 'necessary' to refuse a booking for Mr Rowe to comply with his religious beliefs. The rule that sex should only be between a heterosexual married couple was a rule of 'private morality' and even on its own terms did not have to be applied to others.[62] As noted above, this of course ignored the fact that Mr Rowe was being asked to support a *message* of the 'normality' of homosexual activity, with which he fundamentally disagreed.

Neave JA's discussion of the section 77 point is important because for her Honour, section 77 was a live issue, given that Mr Rowe could be personally liable. Her Honour's judgment warrants careful attention, especially since it has to be said that, with respect, she has misunderstood some of the UK and European jurisprudence to which she referred in reading the Victorian legislation.

Yet, one point which seems correct is that the standard of 'necessity' must be objectively rather than entirely subjectively determined. Her Honour's view that the phrase 'necessary to comply' means 'what a reasonable person would consider necessary for Mr Rowe to comply with his genuine religious belief" sums this up well.[63]

However, there was never any dispute about the *content* of the relevant Christian teaching, or that Mr Rowe was *genuinely* motivated by that content. What is unfortunate is that her Honour moves from this issue of the 'objectivity' of the relevant necessity into other more debatable propositions.[64] While it is true that 'subjectively

[61] ibid [440] point (4).
[62] ibid [330].
[63] ibid [425].
[64] This can be seen in ibid [426].

held religious beliefs of one individual do not always override the human rights of others',[65] this is not what Lord Walker was referring to in the quote then given from *R v Secretary of State for Education and Employment ex parte Williamson*.[66] Lord Walker's comment that 'not every act which is in some way motivated or inspired by religious belief is to be regarded as the manifestation of religious belief'[67] is not concerned with the question of subjectivity or objectivity. His Lordship was discussing the meaning of 'manifestation' and considering whether the fact that some behaviour was 'motivated' or 'inspired' by belief (rather than 'required' or 'compelled') could always be regarded as a 'manifestation' of that belief.

In fact, it has to be said that Neave JA's reliance on *Williamson* and some older UK and ECtHR decisions shows a lack of familiarity with more recent European law and religion jurisprudence. For example, her Honour suggested that Lord Walker's remark noted above related to the 'distinction between the freedom to hold a belief and the freedom to manifest that belief' playing an 'important part' in European and UK cases.[68] That may well have been true at one time. In particular, there were European and UK decisions which came very close to holding the very harsh view that the right to freedom of religion in the employment context, for example, could be perfectly well protected by the fact that an employee whose religious freedom was impaired could leave and find another job.

But since the important decision of the ECtHR in *Eweida*,[69] it has been clear that this is no longer the approach to be followed in Europe in dealing with Article 9 *ECHR*. The Court commented:

> [I]n cases involving restrictions placed by employers on an employee's ability to observe religious practice, the Commission held in several decisions that the possibility of resigning from the job and changing employment meant that there was no interference with the employee's religious freedom ... However, the Court has not applied a similar approach in respect of employment sanctions imposed on individuals as a result of the exercise by them of other rights protected by the Convention, for example the right to respect for private life under Article 8; the right to freedom of expression under Article 10; or the negative right, not to join a trade union, under Article 11 ... Given the importance in a democratic society of freedom of religion, the Court considers that, where an individual complains of a restriction on freedom of religion in the workplace, *rather than holding that the possibility of changing job would negate any interference with the right, the better approach would be to weigh that possibility in the overall balance* when considering whether or not the restriction was proportionate. (Emphasis added, references omitted)[70]

As a commentator on this decision has noted:

> *Eweida* was an important turning point in Article 9 jurisprudence, with the Strasbourg Court recognising that an individual's desire to express their religious belief *publicly*, beyond the context of church and home, could outweigh the secular interests of an employer. The case

[65] ibid.
[66] *R v Secretary of State for Education and Employment ex parte Williamson* [2005] 2 AC 246 (hereinafter '*Williamson*').
[67] ibid [63].
[68] *CYC v Cobaw* (n 2) [428].
[69] *Eweida* (n 58).
[70] ibid [83].

> stands as an important recognition of the need to attribute a basic weight to individuals' desires to manifest their religion.[71]

I have taken the time to comment on these developments because Neave JA justifiably notes that courts in Australia should be aware of international developments. However, in doing so, they need to be aware of the current state of the law in these areas.

While Neave JA does refer to the *Eweida* decision, her Honour has not captured the complexity of the issues and the important changes in EU jurisprudence signalled by the decision.[72] In particular, her comment that it was important to consider whether the discriminatory act arose from a 'core feature' of the discriminator's religious beliefs[73] is contradicted by the finding of the *Eweida* court noted previously that the particular behaviour need not be 'mandated' by religious belief.[74]

Neave JA, taking the 'narrow' view of religious belief that mainly sees it as applicable to 'church services' or 'religious rules', nevertheless accepted that there could be serious issues where a secular law on discrimination:

> [C]ompels the alleged discriminator to refrain from conduct which is required by their religion (for example participation in religious ceremonies or observance of dietary laws) or to actively participate in an act prohibited by their religion, for example celebrating a marriage between a same sex couple. However, the appropriate balance between religious freedom and freedom from discrimination would be struck by holding that the exemption does not apply in situations where it is not necessary for a person to impose their own religious beliefs upon others, in order to maintain their own religious freedom.[75]

There are a number of comments to be made about this somewhat disturbing paragraph. For example, it seems hard to imagine a circumstance where anti-discrimination laws would otherwise require someone to not participate in a religious ceremony or observance of a dietary rule. But the rule that Neave JA saw as 'striking the right balance' had to do with it not being necessary for 'a person to impose their own religious beliefs upon others, in order to maintain their own religious freedom'. Presumably her Honour saw the refusal of Mr Rowe here as amounting to such an 'imposition'.

Yet to reframe the question in this way seems wrong for two reasons. The first and most obvious is that Mr Rowe was not seeking to 'impose' anything on Cobaw; it was Cobaw that was seeking to enter into a contract with CYC through Mr Rowe. Indeed,

[71] J Maher, 'Proportionality Analysis after *Eweida and Others v UK*: Examining the Connections between Articles 9 and 10 of the ECHR' *Oxford Human Rights Hub* (21 June 2013), http://ohrh.law.ox.ac.uk/?p=2019.

[72] In particular, it must be said that her Honour's summary of the *Ladele* proceedings in *CYC v Cobaw* (n 2, fn 285 to [431]) is somewhat misleading. To say that the registration of civil partnerships was a 'secular task which was not protected by the right to religious freedom' may capture the flavor of some comments by Lord Neuberger in the Court of Appeal decision in *Islington London Borough Council v Ladele* [2010] WLR 955 [52] (see the critique in Foster (n 6)), but it does not represent the views on appeal in the ECtHR *Eweida* decision (where the *Ladele* case was joined in the appeal). In *Eweida* (n 58), it was clearly acknowledged, for reasons noted above, that the directive that Ms Ladele register civil partnerships *did* have a serious impact on her religious freedom and required justification under the principles set out in arts 9 and 14 of the Convention – see [104]. That in the end the Court ruled that the directive was justified and proportionate in achieving other aims, did not detract from the fact that it was actually found have an impact on Ms Ladele's religious freedom. This was not a simple case where a 'secular task' was 'not protected' as Neave JA suggests.

[73] *CYC v Cobaw* (n 2) at [433].

[74] See above, text near n 67.

[75] *CYC v Cobaw* (n 2) [434].

if either side of the relationship were 'imposing' on the other, it was Cobaw that was demanding that CYC make its facilities available to facilitate a camp whose avowed message of support for the normality of homosexual relationships flew in the face of CYC's stated commitment to orthodox Christianity.

However, second, and more importantly, this statement of how the relevant balance should be struck assumes that it is up to the Court of Appeal to do the 'striking'. But, as Redlich JA powerfully argued, that is to misunderstand how the legal norms here are spelled out. Yes, there is a need to strike a balance between competing human rights. But it is *Parliament* which has struck that balance by spelling out the situations in which a person's religious commitment may override the law of discrimination. However, here Neave JA seemed to be endeavouring to formulate the appropriate balance herself.[76]

Again, as with the comments of Maxwell P noted previously, there is no attention paid to the imposition upon Mr Rowe of a course of behaviour that supported a view he opposed on religious grounds. That this seems to have been forgotten emerged when Neave JA regarded it as inconsistent of Mr Rowe to have conceded that he would not have refused accommodation to lesbian parents who were attending a school camp of some sort.[77] To say that this 'contradicted' his assertion that he regarded the denial of a booking as necessary to comply with his beliefs was odd. It almost seemed that her Honour had decided that, whatever Mr Rowe and CYC said, their 'real' reason for refusing the booking was a dislike of homosexual persons. In reality, there was nothing inconsistent in Mr Rowe's assertion that he would have been happy to accept a booking for an ordinary school camp even if he knew there were same-sex parents who were part of the group, while being unwilling to accept a booking from a group whose very raison d'etre was the 'normalisation' of behaviour seen by him as contrary to God's word.

Finally, the comparison that Neave JA found apt is telling.[78] Her Honour conceded that the case of *Bull v Hall* was 'not on all fours' with the *Cobaw* case.[79] This is an understatement. In *Bull v Hall*, Christian proprietors of a boarding house had declined double bed accommodation to a same-sex couple. A fundamental difference between the UK and the Victorian legislation was that the UK law concerned had *no* general defence provision applying to individuals, unlike section 77 of the Victorian *EO Act 1995*.[80] Thus, it was not very surprising that the boarding house proprietors were found to have unlawfully discriminated.[81] When Neave JA said that this case reassured her that section 77 'achieves an appropriate balance', she must, with respect, have been wrong; there was no equivalent provision at all at issue in the *Bull* case. Her Honour's comment would only be true if section 77 provided no effective protection whatsoever.

[76] See also Gray (n 57) 76: 'Parliament, rather than courts, reconciles these competing fundamental human rights in legislation.'

[77] *CYC v Cobaw* (n 2) [436].

[78] *CYC v Cobaw* (n 2) [437].

[79] *Bull v Hall* (n 11).

[80] A fact noted by Maxwell P in *CYC v Cobaw* (n 2) [311] fn 177.

[81] Arguably the majority decision in *Bull* can still be criticised for giving little weight to the fact that the criterion used by the Halls was not explicitly whether the couple concerned were of the same sex, but whether they were married. However, it seems that even on this view, the minority in *Bull* were correct to find that there would have been 'indirect discrimination'.

In contrast to the decisions of the other members of the Court, Redlich JA considered that not only was section 77 theoretically applicable to Mr Rowe, but that it also actually applied to give him a defence against the claim for discrimination. His Honour's comments are, in my view, very important for a proper application of a religious freedom defence in Australia.

Redlich JA commented that the Tribunal had been wrong to conclude that the section 77 defence did not apply for four reasons:

- a too-narrow construction of the defences;
- an insistence on an 'objective' test as to whether the religious beliefs 'compelled' action;
- holding that commercial activity was an area with limited scope for religious freedom; and
- inferences that were drawn about CYC's commercial activity.[82]

On the issue of the *construction* of the defences, Redlich JA noted that the Tribunal had explicitly taken guidance from the Victorian Charter in ruling that it (the Tribunal) needed to strike the appropriate balance between freedom from discrimination and freedom of religion.[83] In particular, the Tribunal held that since the defences in sections 75–77 'impaired the full enjoyment' of a Charter right to non-discrimination, they should be read very 'narrowly'.[84] This, his Honour held, was an error.

It was an error because the *EO Act 1995* cannot be said to have only one purpose, as if freedom from discrimination was its sole object. It is Parliament that has set up a system to balance these rights with other important rights, such as religious freedom. It is not up to the Tribunal (or, one may add, a Justice of Appeal) to undertake the balancing process as they see fit. Redlich JA commented:

> When, as is so obviously the case with section 77, Parliament adopts a compromise in which it balances the principal objectives of the Act with competing objectives, a court will be left with the text as the only safe guide to the more specific purpose.[85] Ultimately, it is the text, construed according to such principles of interpretation as provide rational assistance in the circumstances of the particular case, that is controlling.[86]

As his Honour said, the Tribunal had adopted an 'unworkably narrow interpretation of the exemption in section 77, calculated to frustrate the very purpose of the exemption'.[87]

On the question of the 'objective' test as to whether behaviour was 'compelled' by religion, Redlich JA noted the inappropriateness of a secular tribunal or court weighing up moral obligations under a religious set of doctrines or beliefs.[88] Instead, while not arguing for a completely 'subjective' test, his Honour said that the subjective beliefs held

[82] *CYC v Cobaw* (n 2) [503].
[83] ibid [511].
[84] ibid [513].
[85] *Kelly v The Queen* (2004) 218 CLR 216, 235 [48] (Gleeson CJ, Hayne and Heydon JJ).
[86] *CYC v Cobaw* (n 2) [516], citing *Nicholls v The Queen* (2005) 219 CLR 196, 207 [8] (Gleeson CJ).
[87] *CYC v Cobaw* (n 2) [518].
[88] ibid [523], citing a passage from R Adhar and I Leigh, *Religious Freedom in the Liberal State* (Oxford University Press, 2005) 164, referring ironically to the 'amateur theologian-cum-Tribunal'.

by the alleged discriminator required at least some consideration.[89] In part, he relied on the fact that the provisions of section 77 had actually previously been criticised by a parliamentary scrutiny body as too easy to satisfy and that in later legislation – the *Equal Opportunity Act 2010* (Vic) – the equivalent provision required discrimination to be 'reasonably necessary'. However, he went on to note that even a requirement that discrimination be 'reasonably necessary' would not be so narrow as the approach to section 77 adopted by the Tribunal in this case.[90]

In particular, Redlich JA rejected the view that activity in the *commercial* sphere was somehow not covered by the section 77 defence. Again, his Honour criticised the tendency of the Tribunal (and, it may be implied, his Honour's colleagues on the Court of Appeal) to give too much attention to international jurisprudence that required the balancing process to be undertaken by judicial or tribunal officers. In particular, he noted that the ECtHR in Europe had interpreted the Article 9 right there in a narrow way where a person chose to engage in the commercial marketplace such as by employment.[91]

Redlich JA's point about the need for courts to observe the balance struck by Parliament, and not to strike out on a balancing process themselves unless invited to do so by Parliament, seems clearly correct.

Redlich JA then undertook a careful analysis of the Canadian *Brockie* case,[92] in which he stressed that the outcome of the case was that the court held that there could be the refusal of a service in the commercial sphere 'where its use would reasonably be seen to be in conflict with core elements of the belief'.[93]

It is worth noting the facts of *Brockie* in more detail. The Board of Inquiry there had found Mr Brockie guilty of discrimination because he declined to print leaflets for an organisation whose literature indicated that it 'represented [the] interests of gays and lesbians'.[94] The Board ordered that Mr Brockie was to provide printing services to 'lesbians and gays and to organizations in existence for their benefit'.[95] In the course of their decision on appeal, as noted above, the Judges of the Divisional Court ruled that 'efforts to promote an understanding and respect for those possessing any specified characteristic should not be regarded as separate from the characteristic itself'.[96]

But Mr Brockie argued that to require him to go further and to *support and promote* the cause of homosexuality would require him to behave in a way which conflicted with his Christian beliefs and would be a breach of his right to freedom of religion under the Canadian *Charter*.[97] The Divisional Court agreed that in some circumstances the very broad order of the Board – that Mr Brock publish whatever the organisation requested – would indeed amount to a disproportionate burden on his freedom of religion. In doing

[89] *CYC v Cobaw* (n 2) [527].

[90] ibid [533].

[91] ibid [539]. As noted above, while his Honour's views about the narrow approach of the European and UK courts to these questions were correct at one stage, the courts since *Eweida* have adopted a much broader approach.

[92] *Brockie* (n 15).

[93] *CYC v Cobaw* (n 2) [543] ff.

[94] *Brockie* (n 15) [6].

[95] See ibid [17].

[96] See ibid [31].

[97] See ibid [37].

so, they impliedly rejected the narrow view that rights to freedom of religion could not operate in the 'commercial' sphere:

> However, the order [of the Board] would also extend to other materials such as brochures or posters with editorial content espousing causes or activities clearly repugnant to the fundamental religious tenets of the printer. The Code prohibits discrimination arising from denial of services because of certain characteristics of the person requesting the services, thereby encouraging equality of treatment in the marketplace. It encourages nothing more. If the order goes beyond this, the order may cease to be rationally connected to the objective of removing discrimination.[98]

The Divisional Court then provided some examples of the distinctions it thought needed to be drawn:

> If any particular printing project ordered by Mr Brockie (or any gay or lesbian person, or organization/entity comprising gay or lesbian persons) contained material that conveyed a message *proselytizing and promoting the gay and lesbian lifestyle* or ridiculed his religious beliefs, such material might reasonably be held to be in direct conflict with the core elements of Mr Brockie's religious beliefs. On the other hand, if the particular printing object contained a directory of goods and services that might be of interest to the gay and lesbian community, that material might reasonably be held not to be in direct conflict with the core elements of Mr Brockie's religious beliefs. (Emphasis added)[99]

The Board's order that the specific printing project go ahead was upheld, but it was to be qualified by the addition of extra words:

> Provided that this order shall not require Mr Brockie or Imaging Excellence to print material of a nature which could reasonably be considered to be in direct conflict with the core elements of his religious beliefs or creed.[100]

When this aspect of the decision is taken into account, it can be seen that the final order of the Court in *Brockie* is more in line with the submissions of CYC than those of Cobaw. Redlich JA noted that Judge Hampel in the Tribunal in *Cobaw* had found that the aims of the proposed camp included 'conduct … which accepted or condoned same sex attraction, or encouraged people to view same sex attraction as normal, or a natural and healthy part of the range of human sexualities'.[101] In this way, requiring CYC to make its camping facilities available to Cobaw was indeed to 'convey a message' that was contrary to CYC's beliefs (and hence to fall within the area that the Divisional Court in *Brockie* said would have been going too far and beyond the power of the Court).

Redlich JA commented that, consistently with the outcome in *Brockie*, section 77 'protects such an obligation when it arises in similar circumstances'.[102] Any judicially created limit which would restrict the operation of section 77 in the commercial sphere would undermine the very balance that Parliament itself has chosen to strike:

> The section does not confine the right to manifest religious beliefs to those areas of activity intimately linked to private religious worship and practice. The legislature intended that it

[98] ibid [49].
[99] ibid [56].
[100] ibid [59].
[101] *CYC v Cobaw* (n 2) [444].
[102] ibid [544].

> operate in the commercial sphere. The approach of the Strasbourg institutions confining freedom of religion to freedom to believe and to worship is not reflected in the legislative policy of the Act, or in the text of the exemption, which permits a person's faith to influence them in their conduct in both private and secular and public life.[103]

Redlich JA's concluding discussion of how section 77 ought to have been applied in the particular circumstances of this case brought together these themes and clearly demonstrated the error of the Tribunal. His Honour noted that it is not necessary for an activity to be a 'religious' one, such as a church service or evangelism, for it to be an activity that is motivated by religious belief. While CYC may not, in his Honour's view, have been a body 'established for religious purposes', it was a body with a religious character, and Mr Rowe of course had his personal religious commitments. He was entitled to the benefit of section 77.

In particular, Redlich JA clearly brought out the point made above that refusing the booking was appropriate once the purpose of the seminar was made known to Mr Rowe. It was reasonable of CYC to offer its services to all without making any particular enquiries about their personal beliefs. However:

> What enlivened the applicants' obligation to refuse Cobaw the use of the facility was the *disclosure of a particular proposed use* of the facility for the purpose of discussing and *encouraging views repugnant to the religious beliefs of the Christian Brethren*. The purpose included raising community awareness as to those views. It was the facilitation of purposes antithetical to their beliefs which compelled them to refuse the facility for that purpose. To the applicants, acceptance of the booking would have made them *morally complicit* in the message that was to be conveyed at the forum and within the community. (Emphasis added)[104]

As Redlich JA noted, it could hardly be doubted that if told that a seminar to be run at the campsite would be aiming to persuade the attendees to deny the Christian faith, CYC would have been entitled to decline the booking.[105] The proposed purpose here was seen as just as antithetical to the beliefs of the members of the organisation.

Hence, Redlich JA held that section 77 excused Mr Rowe from liability. He also went on briefly to note that once section 77 operated in relation to an employee whose actions had made the employer liable, then the employer was also not liable.[106]

F. Could CYC as an Incorporated Body Rely on the Section 77 Defence?

This brings us the final of the major issues in the case: could the corporate body CYC rely on the section 77 defence 'directly'? That is, since section 77 applies to a 'person' and since under established principles of interpretation 'person' usually includes an

[103] *CYC v Cobaw* (n 2) [550]: 'See P Parkinson, "Accommodating Religious Belief in a Secular Age: The Issue of Conscientious Objection in the Workplace" 34(1) *UNSW Law Journal* 281. See his criticisms of *Ladele* and *McFarlane*, and the jurisprudence on religious freedom under the ECHR that has shown little recognition of conscience-based claims in the workplace.'

[104] ibid [567].

[105] ibid [571].

[106] ibid [578].

incorporated body, could CYC argue that it had relevant 'religious beliefs or principles' which were protected?

Maxwell P took the view that the section 77 defence was not applicable at all to a corporate body.[107] His Honour's main reasons for this were by reference to the scheme of sections 75–77, which seemed to distinguish between rights given to 'bodies' and those to 'persons'. In particular, he said that it would be odd if a corporate body could rely on the apparently wider defence in section 77 if it did not satisfy the description of a 'body established for religious purposes' under section 75. He conceded that 'churches' had been said in European jurisprudence to have 'rights of religious freedom', but disputed that those rights were appropriate for other incorporated bodies.[108]

Neave JA agreed with Maxwell P on this issue.[109] Redlich JA did not; he noted that corporations are regularly held liable for various 'states of mind' attributed from their controllers. While there might be problems in other cases, in this situation all the directors of CYC were required to subscribe to a statement of faith.[110] The different provisions in section 75 and section 77 operated in different areas, and to exclude corporations from section 77 would produce anomalous results, particularly for small businesses where the defence would be excluded if they decided to adopt a corporate structure for other reasons.[111]

G. Summary of the Decision

In brief, the result of the *CYC v Cobaw* decision on the six points noted above was:

1. Was the Victorian *Charter* relevant to the case? No, by all members of the Court.
2. Was the relevant refusal discriminatory on the basis of the sexual *orientation* of the participants or could it be seen as based on the support that the weekend was to offer for homosexual *activity*? All members of the Court rejected the distinction. A decision based on activity, or support for the activity, would be seen as a decision based on sexual orientation.
3. Was CYC alone liable under the *Act* or were both CYC and Mr Rowe potentially liable? By a 2:1 majority (Neave JA and Redlich JA), both CYC and Mr Rowe were potentially liable.
4. Could CYC rely on the section 75 defence applying to a 'body established for religious purposes'? No, because (by all members of the Court) it was not established for such purposes. Nor, apparently, was it necessary to decline the booking based on its 'doctrines' (although Redlich JA found that it had a defence based on its 'beliefs' under section 77).
5. Could Mr Rowe rely on the section 77 defence on the basis of the necessity to comply with his 'genuine religious beliefs or principles'? Neave JA said that the

[107] ibid [309] ff.
[108] ibid [322].
[109] ibid [413]–[422].
[110] ibid [480].
[111] ibid [491].

section 77 defence was not made out; Redlich JA that it was. As Maxwell P had ruled that the obligations did not apply to Mr Rowe personally, the decision fining Mr Rowe was overturned, though for two completely different reasons.

6. Could CYC as an incorporated body rely on the section 77 defence? By a 2:1 majority (Maxwell P and Neave JA), no – a body that did not fall within section 75 could not rely on a general section 77 defence.

The fact that the Court was split in different ways on different issues makes the precedential value of some of its comments problematic. For the purposes of a future court wanting to know what principle of law flows from this case, where different reasons are offered by different members of an appellate court for coming to the same outcome, it is not possible to say that there is any specific *ratio* of the decision. Kirby J in *XYZ v Commonwealth* summed up the principle in this way: 'the binding rule is to be derived from the legal principles accepted by those members of the Court who, for common reasons, agreed in the Court's orders'.[112]

There are some propositions in *CYC v Cobaw* for which there is no majority among those Justices who concurred in the final outcome (support for a proposition offered by members of the Court who did not agree in the outcome cannot be aggregated under this principle). So, there is no majority *ratio* here on the question as to whether under the legislation a corporate body has 'direct' liability or whether its liability is 'vicarious' based on the specific statutory version of attributed liability. Of those members of the Court who found CYC liable, Maxwell P favoured direct liability and Neave JA vicarious liability; since Redlich JA found that CYC was not liable, his Honour's support for vicarious liability cannot be counted.

However, there do appear to be relevant majorities for the following views:

- That a corporation cannot rely on the section 77 defence applying to 'persons' – this view was adopted by Maxwell P and Neave JA, who agreed that CYC was liable.
- That a body situated similarly to CYC is not a 'body established for religious purposes' and hence cannot rely on the section 75 defences – a view shared by all members of the Court. Of course, it will be necessary to isolate which characteristics of such a body preclude 'religious purposes', but it seems that operating competitively in a commercial marketplace may do so.
- There may, it seems, be majority support for a related issue, which is that a body established for religious purposes needs to find its 'doctrines' in official doctrinal statements. However, since, as noted below, on this issue the *CYC v Cobaw* court seems to ignore previous comments made in a New South Wales (NSW) Court of Appeal decision, the precedential value of this ruling may be in doubt.[113]
- That the Victorian *Charter* does not apply to events occurring before its commencement.
- That discrimination on the basis of sexual orientation occurs when differentiation on the basis of homosexual activity, or support for homosexual activity, takes place.

[112] *XYZ v Commonwealth* [2006] HCA 25, (2006) 227 ALR 495, (2006) 80 ALJR 1036 [71].
[113] See the discussion below near n 131.

Of these matters, the fourth is likely not to be of much continuing relevance, given that the *Charter* has now been in effect for some time, but the first, second, third and fifth are important propositions that are likely to have a future impact. The practical effect of these views on faith-based organisations in the future may be significant.

It would be unfortunate if *the unavailability of the section 77 defence to an incorporated body* in this case were taken to mean that a general freedom of religion defence applying to 'persons' can never apply to incorporated bodies. Since the decision in *CYC v Cobaw*, the Supreme Court of the United States has ruled in *Burwell v Hobby Lobby Stores Inc* that a 'closely held corporation', even one that is explicitly a commercial entity, has rights of religious freedom that can be protected under the US *Religious Freedom Restoration Act*.[114]

In their comment on the issue, Rajanayagam and Evans argue that the majority in *CYC v Cobaw* were correct to rule that a corporate body could not use the defence in section 77 applying to a 'person', and compare that outcome to decision in *Burwell*.[115] However, their article does recognise that, broadly, a 'religious' incorporated body such as a church (as opposed to a profit-making body) ought to have a right to religious freedom under statute, while acting on behalf of its members.

However, Rajanayagam and Evans' article illustrates the complexity of trying to define a certain type of corporate body that may, and one that may not, exercise such rights. For example, it argues that the decision in *CYC v Cobaw* was correct because CYC (like the two companies in the *Hobby Lobby* case) 'advanced religious ends in a manner that was ancillary to their principal purpose of profit maximisation'.[116] But, with respect, it was clear from the objects clause of the Constitution of CYC that its 'principal purpose' was not to make profits for individuals, but to support the work of the Christian Brethren denomination. The fact that it did this through making a profit in the camping business should not alone have disqualified it from having an essentially religious purpose.[117]

Another area of concern is that the very narrow view adopted in *CYC v Cobaw* as to the characteristics that a body has to have before it will be held to be 'established for religious purposes' will have an impact on the application of defences similar to section 75 of the *EO Act 1995*, which are in place around Australia. While this will clearly be a question of fact to be dealt with on a case-by-case basis, the fact that a body all of whose board were required to subscribe to a statement of faith, and 40 per cent of whose direct objects made a reference to its desire to act in accordance with faith principles, was found not to be established for such purposes will be of great concern to similar bodies which operate in the commercial sphere with an aim of showing Christian love and concern to the community at large.

[114] *Burwell v Hobby Lobby Stores Inc* 134 S Ct 2751 (2014), holding, by a 5:2 majority, that a reference to a 'person' in the *Federal Religious Freedom Restoration Act*, 42 USC § 2000bb (2012), gave a right under that *Act* to a closely held for-profit company.

[115] S Rajanayagam and C Evans, 'Corporations and Freedom of Religion: Australia and the United States Compared' (2015) 37 *Sydney Law Review* 329.

[116] ibid 350.

[117] See the discussion above of the High Court decision in *Word Investments* (n 36); for example, the comment of the majority in that decision at [24] describing the error made by the Commissioner in determining that a business whose profits went entirely to Bible translation was not a 'charitable' organisation.

It will also be of some concern that a policy based on upholding traditional Christian views about human sexuality *based on behaviour* was interpreted as amounting to discrimination against the *persons* involved.

Related to this point, there are some comments of the Maxwell P here that could be so dangerous if misread and taken out of context that it is worth highlighting them and clarifying what they actually mean. They are as follows:

> Both in his statement and in his oral evidence, Mr Rowe expressed the view that it was *not 'homophobic discrimination' for him to hold (on religious grounds) a different view from Ms Hackney regarding homosexuality.* The same point was raised by the grounds of appeal. This *contention must also be rejected.* What occurred on 7 June 2007 was not merely the expression of a difference of opinion. Plainly enough, *that would not have constituted discrimination.* Rather, what occurred was that, because of his strong belief that homosexual sexual activity was morally wrong, Mr Rowe on behalf of CYC refused to allow the Resort to be used by SSAYP for an activity in which their identity as such would be expressed and affirmed. (Emphasis added)[118]

If the highlighted words in the first sentence are simply read on their own, they may be taken to suggest that his Honour is rejecting the proposition that simply holding that a different view on homosexuality does not amount to 'homophobic discrimination'. In other words, his Honour may be read as saying that it *is* homophobic to hold a private opinion on religious grounds that homosexuality is wrong.

But when the extract provided above is read as a whole, this is clearly *not* what his Honour is saying. What is being 'rejected'[119] is the *implication* of the quoted statement in the prior paragraph that the decision of the Tribunal is simply based on a privately held religious opinion alone. Indeed, his Honour explicitly goes on to say that 'expression of a different opinion … would not have constituted discrimination'.[120]

So, despite what seems to be the case on a first reading, it is clear that neither simply holding nor 'expressing' a view about appropriate sexual activity or 'orientation' will of itself amount to 'homophobic discrimination'.

A number of questions still remain after this important decision. The case was an important one dealing with highly contested issues. Maxwell P himself noted at the outset that the litigation raised novel (for Australia) and inherently difficult issues of the conflict of rights.[121] Yet the High Court of Australia declined an application for special leave to appeal.[122] A few comments on the significance of that decision are in order.

IV. The Refusal of Special Leave

Most final appellate courts in the common law world have a 'filtering' process to manage the immense number of possible appeals that might be brought from lower court

[118] *CYC v Cobaw* (n 2) [65]–[66].

[119] ibid [65].

[120] ibid [66].

[121] ibid at [14].

[122] *Christian Youth Camps Ltd v Cobaw Community Health Services Ltd and Others* [2014] HCATrans 289 (12 December 2014) (hereinafter '*CYC v Cobaw Special Leave*').

decisions. In each system, the 'aspirational' goal of perfect justice (even expressed in the fairly modest form that every case receives the best possible consideration from all relevant judicial bodies) has to be balanced with pragmatic considerations of workload and, indeed, the need not to waste valuable judicial time and energy on hopeless cases.[123]

The High Court of Australia is the final appellate tribunal in the country and can hear decisions on both federal and state law. In civil cases, the filtering mechanism used is that of application for special leave to appeal.[124] An attenuated panel of the Court (two or three Justices) will hear arguments from the parties as to whether or not a full appeal will be heard.[125]

The *CYC v Cobaw Special Leave* decision was heard by a three-member bench, made up of Crennan, Kiefel and Bell JJ. After a one-hour hearing, Crennan J announced the decision to refuse special leave, effectively on the basis that the case merely involved an issue of statutory interpretation of the repealed *EOA 1995*, which had later been replaced by the *Equal Opportunity Act 2010* (Vic) (hereinafter '*EOA 2010*'). The implication was that since the statute had now been repealed, it was no longer appropriate to spend court time considering its proper interpretation. This suggests that the relevant grounds for the granting of special leave being considered were that a matter is 'of public importance, whether because of its general application or otherwise'.[126] Her Honour also added that their Honours were not persuaded that 'the interests of the administration of justice, either generally or in the particular case' required a grant of leave.[127]

It is submitted that this decision was, with respect, incorrect. Counsel for CYC, Mr MR Pearce SC, made a number of valuable points that were not accepted by the Court. Importantly, however, it seems that a key point which Mr Pearce did *not* mention ought to have had a great deal of weight with the Court, as required by section 35(a)(ii) of the *Judiciary Act*, and was not considered.

Under section 35(a)(ii), in deciding whether or not to grant special leave, the High Court is to consider whether the proceedings involve a question of law 'in respect of which a decision of the High Court, as the final appellate court, is required to resolve differences of opinion between different courts … as to the state of the law'.[128]

In any federation such as Australia, the potential arises for state appellate courts to differ on legal issues. A key part of the role of the High Court as the final appellate court in the country is in the resolution of those differences. In this area, it seems strongly arguable that there is now a fundamental legal issue in relation to which state appellate courts differ and on which the High Court should have offered a definitive opinion.

[123] See M Kirby, 'Maximising Special Leave Performance in the High Court of Australia' (2007) 30 *UNSW Law Journal* 731, 733, who notes that the system aims to ensure that 'the Court selects its business wisely and deploys the relatively scarce judicial resources appropriately for the performance of the functions of the nation's final appellate and constitutional tribunal'.

[124] See *Judiciary Act 1903* (Cth), ss 35, 35A.

[125] The equivalent system in the US Supreme Court is an application for 'certiorari', an ancient administrative law remedy that is also applied as a filter in that system.

[126] See *Judiciary Act 1903* (Cth), s 35(a)(i).

[127] ibid s 35(b).

[128] ibid s 35(a)(ii).

The difference of opinion arises from the somewhat similar issue raised in NSW litigation in *OV and OW v Members of the Board of the Wesley Mission Council*.[129] The case involved a child welfare agency run by a church, which declined to accept a same-sex couple as potential foster parents. In particular, one of the issues in that case was whether a belief that marriage between a man and a woman was the ideal way for a child to be raised could be justified as being a 'doctrine' of the Wesley Mission. After an initial Tribunal finding to the contrary, the Court of Appeal directed a new hearing, noting that there was a need to consider 'all relevant doctrines' of the body concerned.[130] On referral to the Tribunal, it held that the word 'doctrine' was broad enough to encompass not just formal doctrinal pronouncements such as the Nicene Creed, but also effectively whatever was commonly taught or advocated by a body, and included moral as well as religious principles.[131] It may be that the Victorian Court of Appeal considered that this final decision, being one of an administrative tribunal rather than a superior court, was not binding. But, with respect, it seems to have been a serious error of law for the Victorian Court of Appeal to have ignored the substantive comments on this issue offered by the NSW Court of Appeal.[132] Those comments of the NSW Court of Appeal were relevant to the matters discussed in *CYC v Cobaw* and in accordance with the High Court's directions to intermediate appellate courts in Australia to follow other appellate decisions on nationally similar laws,[133] should have been taken into account unless regarded as 'plainly' wrong.[134]

In brief, then, the NSW Court of Appeal said that it would allow the particular religious group to determine what its own relevant 'doctrines' are, rather than to have that matter determined by a secular tribunal or court. This is contrary to the decision in *CYC v Cobaw*.[135]

While the two decisions relate to different pieces of legislation, the relevant provisions are so close to each other that it is clear that a court that must now apply these provisions will be in some doubt as to which approach should be applied.[136] It is also odd that the High Court's attention was not drawn to this question.

[129] *OV and OW v Members of the Board of the Wesley Mission Council* (2010) 79 NSWLR 606, [2010] NSWCA 155 (hereinafter '*OV & OW CA*'). See also the final stage of that litigation in *OW and OV v Members of the Board of the Wesley Mission Council* [2010] NSWADT 293. The one and only reference to the litigation in the *CYC v Cobaw* appeal is to be found in a very brief footnote – *CYC v Cobaw* (n 2) [223] fn 141 – in the judgment of Maxwell P on the fairly technical issue of what 'established' means.

[130] *OV and OW CA* (n 131), per Allsop P at [9].

[131] *OW and OV v Wesley Mission* (n 129) [32]–[33].

[132] See above at n 131. However, the fact that the reference is there brings out very sharply the oddness of the Victorian court's failure to refer to the major issues dealt with in that litigation, which closely related to those dealt with in *CYC v Cobaw*.

[133] See *Farah Constructions Pty Ltd v Say-Dee Pty Ltd* [2007] HCA 22, [135] – while the comment relates directly to 'uniform national legislation', it would seem to apply here where legislation in most states, while not completely uniform, usually includes some defence relating to 'doctrine'.

[134] Another commentator, who is also generally supportive of the decision, also draws attention to the curious absence of discussion of the *OV and OW* case here: see Murphy (n 3) 612: 'this lack of engagement leaves an unfortunate lack of clarity in what will constitute a religious doctrine for the purposes of the EOA 1995 and its current form in EOA 2010'.

[135] See Maxwell P in *CYC v Cobaw* (n 2) [276]–[277], approving the reasoning of the lower Tribunal in adopting the evidence of a theological expert relied in *Cobaw*, to the effect that the 'doctrines' of the Christian faith were to be confined to matters dealt with in the historic Creeds (and rejecting contrary evidence provided by another theologically qualified expert on behalf of CYC).

[136] See also the comment from L Elphick, 'Sexual Orientation and "Gay Wedding Cake" Cases under Australian Anti-discrimination Legislation: A Fuller Approach to Religious Exemptions' (2017) 38 *Adelaide*

V. Conclusion: Implications for the Future

What are the implications of the rejection of the special leave application in *CYC v Cobaw*? It is clear that a decision of the High Court not to grant special leave to appeal does *not* mean that the decision of the lower court has been approved by the Court. As McHugh J commented in *North Ganalanja Aboriginal Corporation v Queensland*: 'Refusal of special leave creates no precedent and is binding on no one.'[137]

The effect of a refusal to grant special leave, then, neither affirms the validity of the decision of the lower appellate court nor in any way strengthens it. It remains as it was previously, as an authority of full precedential force within the jurisdiction within which it was decided (here, Victoria). It also continues to have whatever persuasive force it held for courts in other jurisdictions before the application for special leave was made.[138] But, as Sir Anthony Mason put it writing extracurially: 'The refusal of special leave is not an affirmation of the decision or of the reasons for decision below.'[139]

As such, it remains open for a future litigant in another state to argue that *CYC v Cobaw* was 'plainly wrong', or of course for a future Victorian litigant to refer to features of the new *EOA 2010*, or relating to the Victorian *Charter* (which, it should be recalled, contains a right to freedom of religion), which would distinguish a possible future case from the earlier one.

Since it was handed down, *CYC v Cobaw* has been briefly cited in subsequent cases, but not in relation to its 'law and religion' issues. Cases have referred, for example, to the decision on the question of how to attribute liability to a corporation based on the state of mind of individuals,[140] but so far there seems to have been no occasion to apply its logic directly to a possible clash between religious freedom and discrimination rights. Such cases may, of course, arise in the future.

In conclusion, the refusal of special leave to appeal the *CYC v Cobaw* decision was unfortunate and arguably wrong. But, while leaving the current law of Australia in some confusion, it still leaves open the possibility for Australian courts to move forward with a clearer set of guidelines in other cases that may arise in the future. And it leaves open the possibility of a future High Court decision which may resolve some of these issues in a way which strikes an appropriate balance between the important rights of non-discrimination and the fundamental rights of religious freedom.

Law Review 149, 166, who notes both decisions: 'the vast judicial disagreement and inconsistency in interpreting then-similar general religious exemption provisions in Victoria and New South Wales is evident'.

[137] *North Ganalanja Aboriginal Corporation v Queensland* (1996) 185 CLR 595, 643.

[138] In other words, as noted above, in accordance with the decision in *Farah v Say-Dee*, other state courts should normally follow it unless persuaded that it is plainly wrong. But the added complication here comes from the fact that NSW courts will be obliged to apply the decision in *OV and OW* where the two decisions clash.

[139] The Hon Sir Anthony Mason, 'The Use and Abuse of Precedent' (1988) 4 *Australian Bar Review* 93, 96. For further comments on the precedential value of special leave refusals, see M Kirby, 'Precedent in Australia' (paper presented at the International Academy of Comparative Law Conference, Utrecht, the Netherlands (10–16 July 2006)) 18–19; D O'Brien, *Special Leave to Appeal*, 2nd edn (Supreme Court of Queensland Library, 2007) 48–50; M Leeming, *Authority to Decide: The Law of Jurisdiction in Australia* (Federation Press, 2012) 300. This follows the practice of the House of Lords in the UK, as spelled out, for example, in *Wilson v Colchester Justices* [1985] 2 All ER 97, 100.

[140] See *Perpetual Ltd v Myer Pty Ltd* [2018] VSC 2 [104].

Whether or not the specific Victorian legislation was correctly interpreted, was the outcome of the decision in *CYC v Cobaw* a good result? Most of the previously published commentators have supported the decision.[141] One's view of the outcome will obviously be coloured by one's view of the proper purpose of discrimination law and the importance of religious freedom. Murphy supports the decision with specific reference to a shift which has been identified in the purpose of discrimination law as now being protection of 'dignity' interests and not just economic harm and denial of services. She suggests that 'the focus of anti-discrimination law shifts from access and distribution to self-identity'.[142] She adds that 'it seems a matter of common sense that the right to have a particular identity is worth very little if it cannot be affirmed and embraced in a public context'.[143]

The critique offered by this chapter suggests that a question that needs to be asked in this context is: what about the right to have a religious identity? Is that an 'identity' which may be affirmed and embraced? Achieving the appropriate balance in this area in Australia is a task which will require much careful thought from Parliaments and goodwill from courts in implementing the provisions which strike that balance. In that debate, the landmark decision in *CYC v Cobaw* will continue to be debated.

[141] See Murphy (n 3); Gray (n 57); D Glasgow, 'Making Room at the Inn: Protecting the Expression of Sexual Identity in Anti-discrimination Law' (2015) 40 *Alternative Law Journal* 9; Elphick (n 136) 162–64 (though this last piece is careful to note that criticisms of the majority decision have been made).

[142] Murphy (n 3) 597, quoting J Harrison and P Parkinson, 'Freedom Beyond the Commons: Managing the Tension between Faith and Equality in a Multicultural Society' (2014) 40 *Monash University Law Review* 413, 414.

[143] Murphy (n 3) 606.

18

Indian Young Lawyers Association v State of Kerala and *Shayara Bano v Union of India*

Understanding Religious Freedom and Women's Rights in the Twenty-First Century Using the Lenses of Sabarimala *and* Shayara Bano

PREETI NALAVADI

I. Introduction

Article 14 of the *Constitution of India*[1] guarantees equality before the law and equal protection of the laws, while Article 15[2] prohibits discrimination on the basis of religion, caste, sex, race or place of birth. Article 25[3] guarantees the right to practise the religion of one's choice and prohibits the state from making any laws infringing such rights. Conflicts inevitably emerge. This chapter will explore these outstanding conflicts and the challenges facing the Indian state with a focus on the rights of women. Two landmark cases stand out as demonstrating the judicial approach in mediating these conflicts. In the first, *Sabarimala*,[4] the Supreme Court of India upheld the rights of women and granted access to women in the shrine of a temple in the State of Kerala. In the second, *Shayara Bano*,[5] the Court struck down the instant triple *talaq* system of divorce found in Sharia law and in doing so upheld the rights of Muslim women.

This chapter examines these two leading cases, arguing that while the Indian judiciary has played an impressive role in protecting the rights of women, there remain

[1] *Constitution of India 1950*.
[2] ibid art 15.
[3] ibid art 25.
[4] *Sabarimala* (2019) 11 SCC 1. See also *Indian Young Lawyers Association and Others v State of Kerala and Others*, Writ Petition (Civil) 373 of 2006.
[5] *Shayara Bano v Union of India*, AIR 2017 SC 4609.

disputes between the equality and anti-discrimination provisions and the free exercise protections of the *Indian Constitution* that remain unresolved.

II. Sabarimala

The Temple of Sabarimala is located in the Pathanamthitta District of the State of Kerala, India, and is the famous abode of *Lord Ayyappa*. It is one the largest pilgrimage places in the world, with approximately 50 million devotees visiting the temple each year.[6] The Deity, as the story goes, was the son of Lord Shiva and Lord Vishnu (while in the form of Mohini); the child was adopted by the local king. This king, upon realising the divine origin, ordered a temple to be built on the Hills of Sabarimala.[7] This temple is the place of Lord Ayyappa and it is believed that he is in the state of 'the teenage god and a yogi with an oath of celibacy'. It is a popular belief that the acts of those men who undertake strict austerities for 41 days in certain months of the year and visit the abode of the Lord are considered to be holy acts that could fulfil all worldly desires. However, both the rituals as well as entry into the temple are prohibited for women of menstruating age. There is a strong belief that the entry of such women could affect the 'celibacy' of the Lord and the devotees who follow the rituals. The faithful believe that the successful completion of all prayers, preserving the celibacy of the Lord and his devotees, is of paramount importance. Hence, the restriction of women aged 10 to 50 was considered essential[8] by the Travancore Devaswom Board.[9] This section examines the controversy which emerged, the constitutional issues raised, and the majority and dissenting judgments delivered in the Supreme Court.

A. Controversy

The Travancore Devaswom Board issued two controversial notifications in 1955 and 1956 that prohibited the entry of women between the ages of 10 and 50 under the guise of ancient practice on certain occasions. Further, section 4 of the *Kerala Hindu Place of Public (Authorisation of Entry) Act 1965*[10] granted power to the authority to frame rules; Rule 3 prohibited women who fell into this group from entry. *Mahendran*[11] challenged the legality of this prohibition.

The High Court of Kerala upheld the rules laid down, observing:

> Our conclusions are as follows: (1) the restriction imposed on women aged above 10 and below 50 from trekking the holy hills of Sabarimala and offering worship at Sabarimala

[6] R Kumari, 'Menstruating Women and Celibate Gods: A Discourse Analysis of Women's Entry into Sabarimala Temple in Kerala, India' (2019) 4 *Third World Thematics* 288.

[7] ibid.

[8] *Sabarimala* (n 4).

[9] The Board was constituted under the *Travancore Cochin Hindu Religious Institutions Act XV of 1950*.

[10] See *Kerala Hindu Place of Public (Authorisation of Entry) Act 1965*, s 4, r 3.

[11] See *S Mahendran v The Secretary, Travancore Devaswom Board, Thiruvananthpuram and Others*, AIR 1993 Kerala 42.

> Shrine is in accordance with the usage prevalent from time immemorial. (2) Such restriction imposed by the Devaswom Board is not violative of Articles 15, 25 and 26 of the *Constitution of India*. (3) Such restriction is also not violative of the provisions of *Hindu Place of Public Worship (Authorisation of Entry) Act, 1965* since there is no restriction between one section and another section or between one class and another class among the Hindus in the matter of entry to a temple whereas the prohibition is only in respect of women of a particular age group and not women as a class.[12]

Appeal to the Supreme Court of India[13] raised five central questions:

1. Was the exclusionary practice which is based upon a biological factor exclusive to the female gender amounts to 'discrimination' and thereby violates the very core of Articles 14, 15 and 17 and was not protected by 'morality' as used in Articles 25 and 26 of the *Constitution*?
2. Did the practice of excluding such women constitute an 'essential religious practice' under Article 25 of the *Constitution* and could a religious institution assert a claim in that regard under the umbrella of the right to manage its own affairs in matters of religion?
3. Did Ayyappa Temple has a denominational character and, if so, was it permissible on the part of a 'religious denomination' managed by a statutory board and financed under Article 290-A of the *Constitution of India* out of the Consolidated Fund of Kerala and Tamil Nadu to indulge in practices that violated constitutional principles/morality embedded in Articles 14, 15(3), 39(a) and 51-A(e)?
4. Did Rule 3 of the *Kerala Hindu Places of Public Worship (Authorisation of Entry) Rules, 1965* permit a 'religious denomination' to ban entry of women between the ages of 10 to 50? If so, would it not run afoul of Articles 14 and 15(3) of the *Constitution* by restricting the entry of women on the ground of sex?
5. Was Rule 3(b) of the *Kerala Hindu Places of Public Worship (Authorization of Entry) Rules, 1965* ultra vires the *Kerala Hindu Places of Public Worship (Authorisation of Entry) Act, 1965* and, if it was intra vires, would it violate the provisions of Chapter III of the *Constitution*?[14]

In response, the Temple authorities contended that:

1. Exclusion of certain group of women is not based on gender and it is a permissible practice considering intelligible differentia[15] and its nexus to the object sought to be achieved.
2. The inapplicability of the law on untouchability in Article 17 of the *Constitution*.[16]
3. The temple was protected under Article 26 of the *Constitution*,[17] making the exclusion permissible.

[12] ibid.
[13] *Sabarimala* (n 4).
[14] ibid.
[15] See *State of West Bengal v Anwar All Sarkar Habib*, 1952 SCR 284; *EP Royappa v State of Tamil Nadu and Another*, 1974 SCR (2) 348.
[16] *Constitution of India 1950*, art 17.
[17] ibid art 26.

4. Custom and usage permitted the exclusion of a category of women from the temple and no fundamental rights were violated by such exclusion.
5. This exclusion was well within the scope of Article 25 of the *Constitution* and the character of the deity *Naishtika Brahmacharya*.[18]
6. The inapplicability of Articles 14[19] and 15 of the *Constitution*.
7. The practice was an *essential religious* one and was in conformity with the character of the Deity in context.

In short, the case turned on whether the fundamental rights of such groups of women as enshrined in Chapter III of the *Constitution*[20] were infringed. This in turn required the Supreme Court to consider: (i) essential religious practices; (ii) the religious denomination of the temple; (iii) the exclusion of women of a certain age;[21] (iv) the doctrine of ultra vires; and (v) custom and personal law. This section considers each of these points in turn, before considering two alternative approaches: those of Chandrachud J and of Malhotra J.

B. Issues

i. Essential Religious Practice

The issue facing the Supreme Court of India thus involved a consideration of whether the ban on the entry of women of menstruating age constituted an infringement of an essential religious practice. The Court considered a range of precedents,[22] from which it derived a principle for determining essential religious practice:

> What constitutes the essential part of a religion is primarily to be ascertained with reference to the doctrines of that religion itself. If the tenets of any religious sect of the Hindus prescribe that offerings of food should be given to the idol at particular hours of the day … all these would be regarded as parts of religion and the mere fact that they involve expenditure of money or employment of priests and servants or the use of marketable commodities would not make them secular activities partaking of a commercial or economic character; all of them are religious practices and should be regarded as matters of religion within the meaning of Article 26(b).[23]

In *Ratilal*,[24] the Court applied the formula laid down in *Shirur Math*,[25] which concluded that complete autonomy is to be given to the religious denominations

[18] As per Hindu mythology, the term *Naisthika Brahmacharya* denotes he who has renounced the worldly pleasures and lives in celibacy. See RK Sharma, *Indian Society, Institutions and Change* (Atlantic Publishers, 2004).

[19] *Constitution of India 1950*, art 14.

[20] ibid. See also ch III.

[21] *Sabarimala* (n 4).

[22] Including *Adelaide Company of Jehovah's Witnesses v Commonwealth* (1943) 67 CLR 116.

[23] ibid; see *Constitution of India 1950*, art 26(b).

[24] See *Ratilal Panachand Gandhi v State of Bombay and Others*, 1954 SCR 1055.

[25] See *The Commissioner, Hindu Religious Endowments, Madras v Sri Lakshmindra Thirtha Swamiar of Sri Shirur Mutt*, 1954 SCR 1005.

in order to determine essential religious practice. Subsequently, the test tightened and narrowed in *Devaru*,[26] leading to *Durgah*,[27] in which the Court applied strict scrutiny,[28] writing that:

> [I]n order that the practices in question should be treated as a part of religion they must be regarded by the said religion as its essential and integral part; otherwise even purely secular practices which are not an essential or an integral part of religion are apt to be clothed with a religious form and may make a claim for being treated as religious practices within the meaning of Article 26. Similarly, even practices though religious may have sprung from merely superstitious beliefs and may in that sense be extraneous and unessential accretions to religion itself. Unless such practices are found to constitute an essential and integral part of a religion their claim for the protection under Article 26 may have to be carefully scrutinised; in other words, the protection must be confined to such religious practices as are an essential and an integral part of it and no other.[29]

Adi Saiva[30] went a step further:

> The requirement of constitutional conformity is inbuilt and if a custom or usage is outside the protective umbrella afforded and envisaged by Articles 25[31] and 26,[32] the law would certainly take its own course. The constitutional legitimacy, naturally, must supersede all religious beliefs or practices.

Sharaya Bano[33] finally adopted a strict standard: mere practice, even if long and continuous, would not be classified as valid if such acts do not withstand scrutiny under the *Constitution*. Thus, the approach taken to freedom of religion under Articles 25 and 26 involved a consideration of whether the freedom claimed constituted an essential religious practice.

The jurisprudence of the Supreme Court of India thus upheld the constitutional values of individual freedom and dignity in the context of essential religious practice. The courts hold the paramount duty to ensure that fundamental constitutional values and guarantees are protected in accordance with constitutional morality. This morality comprises the core components of individual liberty, dignity and equality. Governmental acts or practices that do not meet this strict constitutional morality requirement cannot be considered valid in the eyes of the law. The Supreme Court clearly enunciated this approach in *Government of NCT of Delhi v Union of India and Others*,[34] in which Chandrachud J observed that:

> Constitutional morality in its strictest sense of the term implies strict and complete adherence to the constitutional principles as enshrined in various segments of the document. When a country is endowed with a Constitution, there is an accompanying promise which stipulates

[26] See *Sri Venkataramana Devaru and Others v State of Mysore and Others*, 1958 SCR 895.

[27] See *Durgah Committee, Ajmer and Another v Syed Hussain Ali and Others* (1962) 1 SCR 383.

[28] The doctrine of strict scrutiny is not applied by the Indian courts as it is in the US; rather, it is little more than a passing remark. See *Saurabh Chaudri and Others v Union of India and Others* (2003) 11 SCC 146 (VN Khare CJ).

[29] ibid.

[30] *Adi Saiva Sivachariyargal Nala Sangam v Government of Tamil Nadu* (2016) 2 SCC 725.

[31] *Constitution of India 1950*, art 25.

[32] ibid art 26.

[33] *Shayara Bano* (n 5).

[34] *Government of NCT of Delhi v Union of India and Others* (2018) 8 SCALE 72.

> that every member of the country right from its citizens to the high constitutional functionaries must idolize the constitutional fundamentals. This duty imposed by the Constitution stems from the fact that the Constitution is the indispensable foundational base that functions as the guiding force to protect and ensure that the democratic setup promised to the citizenry remains unperturbed.[35]

This was elaborated further in *Navtej Singh Johar*,[36] in which the Supreme Court held:

> The concept of constitutional morality is not limited to the mere observance of the core principles of constitutionalism as the magnitude and sweep of constitutional morality is not confined to the provisions and literal text which a Constitution contains, rather it embraces within itself virtues of a wide magnitude such as that of ushering a pluralistic and inclusive society, while at the same time adhering to the other principles of constitutionalism. It is further the result of embodying constitutional morality that the values of constitutionalism trickle down and percolate through the apparatus of the State for the betterment of each and every individual citizen of the State.[37]

While this approach gives primacy to individual rights, the courts must nonetheless decide conflicts that arise between religious freedom of religious denominations and the constitutional guarantees of equality and dignity to individuals. To do this, the courts employ the doctrine of essentiality – essential religious practice – to balance between the two.[38]

The Supreme Court in *Mahendran*[39] applied this doctrine in order to assess whether the practice of barring the entry of women was an essential religious practice. It concluded that even if the celibacy of the Lord could be established, the practice of exclusion was not prescribed in any of the relevant religious texts. Moreover, it observed that such age-groups of women were not barred completely, but were barred for specific months during the year. There were multiple instances which showed that the entry of women of menstruating age was allowed throughout the year except during the Mandalam, Makalavilakku and Vishu seasons.[40] As such, the Court concluded that as the practice was not uniform, it could not be held as being obligatory in nature. Moreover, applying the principles laid down in *Avadhuta II*,[41] the Court found that the fundamentals of the religion would not undergo any change if the practice were to be discontinued.

ii. Religious Denomination Status

The Board also argued that the Temple was protected under religious denomination status guaranteed by Article 26 of the *Constitution*. The Supreme Court observed that the rights of a 'denomination' have to be differentiated from those of an 'individual' and that the former must be strictly viewed as denominational in nature, applying the

[35] ibid.
[36] *Navtej Singh Johar Navtej Singh v Union of India*, Writ Petition (Criminal) No 76 of 2016.
[37] ibid.
[38] *Sabarimala* (n 4).
[39] See *S Mahendran v The Secretary, Travancore Devaswom Board, Thiruvananthpuram and Others* (n 11).
[40] Mandalam–Makara vilakku season (November–January) and Vishu (April). see D Das Acevedo, 'Pause for Thought: Supreme Court's Verdict on Sabarimala' (2018) 53 *Economic and Political Weekly* 12.
[41] See *Commissioner of Police v Acharya Jagdishwarananda Avadhuta* (2004) 12 SCC 770.

threefold test for a religious denomination set out in *Shirur Math*[42] and later applied in *Devaru*,[43] *SP Mittal*[44] and *Avadhuta I*,[45] which required: (i) the existence of a religious sect or body; (ii) a common faith shared by those who belong to the religious sect and a common spiritual organisation; and (iii) the existence of a distinctive name. The fundamental character of a denomination involves a common faith, a common organisation and a distinct commonality with religion that forms the basis of its identity.

iii. The Barring of Entry to Women

It was also specifically contended that barring the entry of women on the basis of customs contravened Article 17 of the Indian *Constitution*. The Board countered that Article 17[46] cannot be extended to gender issues, being confined only to caste-based untouchability. It is unclear how the framers of the *Constitution* intended the term 'untouchability' to apply. Nonetheless, the Court concluded that the purpose of the term meant that untouchability in all its forms must be abolished.[47] This is so because the *Constitution* is the custodian of social justice, is intended to ensure equality within the social order and serves as a document to be used in guiding the moral trajectory so as to uphold the values of equality, liberty, fraternity and justice.[48] Thus, any form of discrimination or stigmatisation resulting in inequality and practices which violate human dignity is unacceptable; 'untouchability' cannot be confined to any single form and, as such, Article 17 serves as a guarantee against exclusion of any form. Here, the notions of purity and pollution associated with menstruation are embedded in the Brahmanical[49] practices, constituting a stigma born of a patriarchal system – the treatment of women during this period resulting in *untouchability*,[50] invoking Article 17.

iv. Doctrine of Ultra Vires

Section 3 of the *Kerala Hindu Place of Public (Authorisation of Entry) Act 1965*[51] works to invalidate a prohibition on entry of a Hindu in places of worship; because Hindu women form a class or section under this law, any provision which may ban entry to

[42] See *The Commissioner, Hindu Religious Endowments, Madras v Sri Lakshmindra Thirtha Swamiar of Sri Shirur Mutt* (n 25).

[43] See *Sri Venkataramana Devaru and Others. v State of Mysore and Others* (n 26).

[44] See *SP Mittal v Union of India* (1983) 1 SCC 51.

[45] See *Acharya Jagdishwaranand Avadhuta v Commissioner of Police, Calcutta* (1983) 4 SCC 522.

[46] See *Constitution of India 1950*, art 17.

[47] See *Sabarimala* (n 4); Constituent Assembly Debates (29 November 1948).

[48] *Sabarimala* (n 4).

[49] 'Brahmin' is a person who belongs to the upper priestly class in India. See M Keppens and J de Roover, 'The Brahmin, the Aryan, and the Powers of the Priestly Class: Puzzles in the Study of Indian Religion' (2020) 11(4) *Religions* 181; TS Ramesh Bairy, *Being Brahmin, Being Modern: Exploring the Lives of Caste Today* (Routledge, 2010).

[50] Members of certain lower castes were considered untouchables in India. See M Aktor, R Deliège and T Khair, *From Stigma to Assertion: Untouchability, Identity and Politics in Early and Modern India* (Museum Tusculanum Press, 2010).

[51] *Kerala Hindu Place of Public (Authorisation of Entry) Act 1965*, s 3.

that class may be exempted by section 3. But two criteria must first be fulfilled: (1) the palace of worship is a temple; and (2) the temple has been founded to achieve the goals of a religious denomination.

The Supreme Court held that the devotees of the Lord did not satisfy the above criteria and that the Temple of Sabarimala was not a religious denominational one. It therefore concluded that the notifications restricting women of a particular age group did not satisfy the requirements laid down under the law; in fact, they infringed the rights of all Hindu women who were thus barred. As such, the notifications were ultra vires to the *Constitution*.

Moreover, Rule 3(b) of section 3 of the *Kerala Hindu Place of Public (Authorisation of Entry) Act 1965*[52] places a restriction on entry of women if they are already placed under such restrictions by custom or usage. Interestingly, section 4(1)[53] of the same *Act* grants power to the person in charge to make rules and regulations relating to rites and ceremonies. This not an absolute power and the proviso does impose a bar on discrimination of any kind against a Hindu if they belong to a particular class/section. Considering the fact that such a proviso grants access to all Hindus including women, Rule 3(b) becomes controversial and contentious. It cannot give precedence under the guise of custom or usage and lay down restrictions that infringe the rights of a particular class/section of Hindu women. Therefore, Rule 3(b) was also ultra vires.

v. Conflict between Customs, Personal Law and Narasu

It is clear that personal laws, custom and usage were of paramount importance in *Sabarimala*. In an earlier case, *Narasu*,[54] the Supreme Court considered the relationship between these concepts in the context of Article 13,[55] which provides as follows:

> 3(1) All laws in force in the territory of India immediately before the commencement of this Constitution, in so far as they are inconsistent with the provisions of this Part, shall, to the extent of such inconsistency, be void.
>
> (2) The State shall not make any law which takes away or abridges the rights conferred by this Part and any law made in contravention of this clause shall, to the extent of the contravention, be void.
>
> (3) In this article, unless the context otherwise requires –
>
> (a) 'Law' includes any Ordinance, order, bye-law, rule, regulation, notification, custom or usage having in the territory of India the force of law;
>
> (b) 'laws in force' includes laws passed or made by a Legislature or other competent authority in the territory of India before the commencement of this Constitution and not previously repealed, notwithstanding that any such law or any part thereof may not be then in operation either at all or in particular areas.
>
> (4) Nothing in this article shall apply to any amendment of this Constitution made under article 368.[56]

[52] ibid s 3, r 3(b).
[53] ibid s 4(1).
[54] *State of Bombay v Narasu Appa Mali*, AIR 1952 Bom 84. See I Jaisingh, *The Ghost of Narasu Appa Mali is Stalking the Supreme Court of India* (Lawyers Collective, 2018).
[55] *Constitution of India 1950*, art 13.
[56] ibid art 13.

The question thus arose as to whether customs and usages were 'laws in force' and, if so, whether they withstood the application of Chapter III of the *Constitution*. Justice Chagla[57] observed:

> Custom or usage is deviation from personal law and not personal law itself. The law recognises certain institutions which are not in accordance with religious texts or are even opposed to them because they have been sanctified by custom or usage, but the difference between personal law and custom or usage is clear and unambiguous.[58]

Justice Chagla concluded that personal law would not fall under the purview of 'laws in force' under Article 13(1). However, other members of the Court disagreed. Justice Gajendragadkar, for instance, thought that[59] that if the above notion were to be accepted, then untouchability, which forms the basis through custom and usage, would fall under such a definition. This would render Article 17 obsolete.[60]

Since *Narasu*, the Supreme Court in *Puttaswamy*[61] emphasised the debates of the Constituent Assembly as relevant to determining the restrictions which might be placed on individual liberty by the state.[62]

In *Sabarimala*, the Supreme Court emphasised that the *Indian Constitution* is socially reformative, being aimed at protecting the dignity of the individual. The Court referred to the South African *Constitution*, noting that dignity:

> [R]equire[s] a complete reconstruction of the state and society, including a redistribution of power and resources along egalitarian lines. The challenge of achieving equality within this transformation project involves the eradication of systemic forms of domination and material disadvantage based on race, gender, class and other grounds of inequality. It also entails the development of opportunities which allow people to realise their full human potential within positive social relationships.[63]

The Court raised these questions concerning the *Indian Constitution*:

> At the heart of transformative constitutionalism is a recognition of change. What transformation in social relations did the Constitution seek to achieve? What vision of society does the Constitution envisage? The answer to these questions lies in the recognition of the individual as the basic unit of the Constitution. This view demands that existing structures and laws be viewed from the prism of individual dignity. Did the Constitution intend to exclude any practice from its scrutiny? Did it intend that practices that speak against its vision of dignity, equality and liberty of the individual be granted immunity from scrutiny? Was it intended that practices that detract from the transformative vision of the Constitution be granted supremacy over it?[64]

In this case, the Court answered each of these questions in the negative.

[57] *Narasu* (n 54) [15] (Chagla J).
[58] ibid.
[59] ibid (Gajendragadkar J).
[60] ibid.
[61] *KS Puttaswamy v Union of India* (2017) 10 SCC 1.
[62] See *Sant Ram v Labh Singh* (1964) 7 SCR 756.
[63] ibid.
[64] ibid 100.

C. The Majority Judgment of Chandrachud J

Justice Chandrachud adopted an innovative approach to mediating the relationship between the religious denomination of an institution and the individual rights of citizens pursuant to Chapter III of the *Indian Constitution*. On the essential practice test, Chandrachud J observed that[65] it would not be appropriate for the judiciary to interpret religious texts and scripts. The Supreme Court quoted Gautam Bhatia:[66]

> While it is true that Article 26(b)[67] makes groups the bearers of rights, as pointed out above, the Constitution does not state the basis of doing so. It does not clarify whether groups are granted rights for the instrumental reason that individuals can only achieve self-determination and fulfilment within the 'context of choice' provided by communities, or whether the Constitution treats groups, along with individuals, as constitutive units worthy of equal concern and respect. The distinction is crucial, because the weight that must be accorded to group integrity, even at the cost of blocking individual access to important public goods, can only be determined by deciding which vision the Constitution subscribes to.[68]

In determining the essentiality of the religious denomination, the Court could do no more than offer an external perspective. As such, it adopted the two-stage formula outlined by Jaclyn L Neo:[69]

> Accordingly, there would be a two-stage test in adjudicating religious freedom claims that adopts a more deferential approach to definition, bearing in mind … a workable approach to religious freedom protection in plural societies. In the first stage, as mentioned, the courts should accept a group's self-definition except in extreme cases where there is clearly a lack of sincerity, fraud or ulterior motive. At the second stage, the courts should apply a balancing, compelling reason inquiry, or proportionality analysis to determine whether the religious freedom claim is outweighed by competing state or public interest.[70]

This approach, the Court concluded, freed it from the burden of interpreting religious texts and doctrines. And because Articles 25(1)[71] and 26[72] are subject to public order, morality and health, any limitations placed upon the religious freedom of a denomination must undergo the two-stage test as a means of assessing the constitutionality of the limitations. The Court applied an anti-exclusion principle as a means of achieving this:

> [T]he state and the Court must respect the integrity of religious group life (and thereby treat the internal point of religious adherents as determinative of the form and content of religious practices) except where the practices in question lead to the exclusion of individuals

[65] See *Sabarimala* (n 4).
[66] ibid. See G Bhatia, 'Freedom from Community: Individual Rights, Group Life, State Authority and Religious Freedom under the Indian Constitution' (2016) *Global Constitutionalism* 351.
[67] *Constitution of India 1950*, art 26(b).
[68] ibid.
[69] JL Neo, 'Definitional Imbroglios: A Critique of the Definition of Religion and Essential Practice Tests in Religious Freedom Adjudication' (2018) 16 *International Journal of Constitutional Law* 574.
[70] ibid.
[71] *Constitution of India 1950*, art 25(1).
[72] ibid art 26.

from economic, social or cultural life in a manner that impairs their dignity, or hampers their access to basic goods.[73]

The Court asserted that the anti-exclusion principle would go a long way towards helping it in terms of excluding those practices that might violate Chapter III.[74] And while the Court seemed hesitant to establish a precedent in relation to this doctrine, it nonetheless held that a violation of fundamental rights, even by religious denominations, would be constitutionally impermissible as a form of social discrimination contrary to constitutional morality. Even if religious denominations were to enjoy such rights, they cannot be protected to the extent of countenancing the infringement of the fundamental rights enshrined in Chapter III.[75] For the Court, the primacy of the individual remained the fundamental principle of the Indian *Constitution*. The majority therefore concluded as follows:

1. The devotees of Lord Ayyappa did not constitute a religious denomination under Article 26.
2. Even if the exclusion of women was prescribed under religious texts, such exclusion could not supersede the constitutional values of liberty, equality and dignity enshrined under the *Constitution*; such practices violate constitutional morality.
3. This practice of exclusion of women who are menstruating is not an essential religious practice and therefore the Court could not legitimate that practice. This exclusion is tantamount to 'untouchability' and violates the constitutional order.
4. The notifications were ultra vires.
5. Rule 3(b) directly offends the fundamental rights of women who form a class/section.

D. The Dissent of Malhotra J

Justice Malhotra dissented,[76] adopting a narrow approach, which can be summarised as follows:[77]

1. Article 14[78] does not override Article 25.
2. Constitutional morality means that fundamental rights must be harmonised with other rights, including the right to practise religion, irrespective of whether such practices are rational or logical.
3. The Temple constituted a religious denomination pursuant to Article 26; because it is a question of both fact and law, the civil courts are competent to adjudicate such determinations.
4. Restrictions of entry of women, being 'limited', do not fall under Article 17.
5. Rule 3(b) does not contravene section 3 of the *Kerala Hindu Place of Public (Authorisation of Entry) Act 1965*.

[73] See *Sabarimala* (n 4).
[74] ibid.
[75] ibid.
[76] ibid (Malhotra J).
[77] ibid.
[78] *Constitution of India 1950*, art 14.

In reaching these conclusions, Malhotra J adopted a restrictive approach to untouchability, constitutional morality and essential religious practice. In relation to untouchability, she concluded that the restrictive practices for women failed to constitute a form of constituting untouchability that violated the constitutional prohibition. Similarly, Malhotra J considered the argument that constitutional morality requires the harmonisation of fundamental rights, irrespective of the practices being rational, to be absurd and flawed.

Finally, Malhotra J concluded that restrictions placed on menstruating women were 'limited' and thus were permissible due to the prerogative of the religious denomination to do so when custom or religious practice demands. She found such a practice to be 'essential', drawing upon *Shirur*,[79] *Adelaide Company*,[80] *Ratilal*,[81] *Durgah*,[82] *Devaru*[83] and *Avadhuta II*[84] to conclude that the religious practice had been followed by the Temple since time immemorial. Still, this ignored whether such a practice is discriminatory, irrational or superstitious. This opens the door to treating religious practices as 'essential or permissible' even though they may be irrational or superstitious. This trend could be dangerous; granting unfettered autonomy to the religious institutions and refusal to interfere with their practices could jeopardise individual rights. As held by the majority, the *Indian Constitution* is a socially reformative document and, as such, the courts must uphold the fundamental rights protected therein.

Sabarimala remains before the Supreme Court for final disposition pursuant to its review jurisdiction.[85] There is little doubt that however it is decided, the case will have far-reaching consequences for religious denominations across the country.

III. *Sharaya Bano*

The husbands of Sharaya Bano[86] and three others divorced them using an irrevocable form of Islamic divorce known as Talaq-e-Biddat.[87] This 'triple talaq' – three pronouncements of 'talaq', or 'divorce', are made either in one sentence or separately – is lawful, even though it would be sinful in the eyes of Islamic law and the Holy Quran.[88]

Indian Muslims are mainly divided into two sects: Shia and Sunni. The Sunnis are further classified into four schools: Hanafi, Maliki, Shafi'l and Hanbali.[89] And Hanafi Muslims constitute the dominant part of the Sunni Muslim[90] community in India.

[79] See *The Commissioner, Hindu Religious Endowments, Madras v Sri Lakshmindra Thirtha Swamiar of Sri Shirur Mutt* (n 25).

[80] See *Adelaide Company of Jehovah's Witnesses v Commonwealth* (n 22).

[81] See *Ratilal Panachand Gandhi v State of Bombay and Others* (n 24).

[82] See *Durgah Committee, Ajmer and Another v Syed Hussain Ali and Others* (n 27).

[83] See *Sri Venkataramana Devaru and Others v State of Mysore and Others* (n 26).

[84] See *Commissioner of Police v Acharya Jagdishwarananda Avadhuta* (n 41).

[85] Review Petition (Civil) No 3358/2018 in Writ Petition (Civil) No 373/2006.

[86] See *Shayara Bano* (n 5). See M Desai, 'A "Safe" Judgment: Religious Rather Than Constitutional Test' (2017) 52 *Economic and Political Weekly* 12.

[87] *Shayara Bano* (n 5).

[88] ibid.

[89] See L Takim, *Law: The Four Sunni Schools of Law: Overview* (Brill, 2009).

[90] See K Chitwood, *Sunni-Shi'a Divide* (Springer, 2019) 1517–18.

While Shia Islam has banned the triple *talaq*,[91] the practice is still used in the Hanafi school,[92] pursuant to the Hanafi laws,[93] which have been followed by the Indian Hanafi community for centuries.[94]

A. Controversy

This case was adjudicated by the Supreme Court of India pursuant to its *suo moto* or original jurisdiction. On 22 August 2017, the Supreme Court of India issued a 3:2 majority decision upholding the rights of Hanafi Muslim women pursuant to the *Constitution* and declaring the triple *talaq* to be unconstitutional.

B. The Majority Judgment: Kurian, Nariman and Lalith JJ

While the three members of the majority employed different approaches, each dealt broadly with two principal issues: (i) the legality of the impugned practices as a matter of personal law; and (ii) conflict between the triple *talaq* and the fundamental rights enshrined in Chapter III of the *Constitution*.

i. Conflicts within Personal Law

The majority was faced with the question of whether *Shamim Ara*,[95] a case which held the triple *talaq* to be invalid, was still good law in India. In order to reach a decision, the Supreme Court re-examined the tenets of section 2 of the *Shariat Act 1937*, which provides as follows:

> 2. Application of Personal law to Muslims[96]
>
> Notwithstanding any custom or usage to the contrary, in all questions (save questions relating to agricultural land) regarding intestate succession, special property of females, including personal property inherited or obtained under contract or gift or any other provision of Personal Law, marriage, dissolution of marriage, including talaq, ila, zihar, lian, khula and mubaraat, maintenance, dower, guardianship, gifts, trusts and trust properties, and wakfs (other than charities and charitable institutions and charitable and religious endowments) the rule of decision in cases where the parties are Muslims shall be Muslim Personal Law (*Shariat*).[97]

The Court observed that section 2 meant nothing more than that Sharia law is applicable to Muslims, although it may not regulate the triple *talaq*:

> In that view of the matter, I wholly agree with the learned Chief Justice that the 1937 Act is not a legislation regulating talaq. Consequently, I respectfully disagree with the stand taken by

[91] See *Shayara Bano* (n 5).
[92] ibid.
[93] ibid. See PJ Bearman, R Peters, and Vogel, 'The Islamic School of Law: Evolution, Devolution, and Progress' (2005) 20(2) *Journal of Islamic Studies* 259.
[94] *Shayara Bano* (n 5).
[95] ibid; see *Shamim Ara v State of UP* (2002) 7 SCC 518.
[96] *Muslim Personal Law (Sharait) Application Act 1937*, s 2.
[97] See *Shayara Bano* (n 5).

> Nariman, J that the 1937 Act is a legislation regulating triple talaq and hence, the same can be tested on the anvil of Article 14. However, on the pure question of law that a legislation, be it plenary or subordinate, can be challenged on the ground of arbitrariness, I agree with the illuminating exposition of law by Nariman, J. I am also of the strong view that the Constitutional democracy of India cannot conceive of a legislation which is arbitrary.[98]

In arriving at this assertion, the Court examined the four sources of Islamic law: the Quran, Hadith, Ijma and Qiyas. The Quran is considered to be the 'first source', while the others supplement it. Because these sources cannot run counter to the Quran and because the triple *talaq* emerges from the supplementary sources, being permissible only as an exception in unavoidable circumstances, it cannot form a part of the protected law.

The Court relied upon a number of its own precedents – *Furzund Hossein*,[99] *Jaiuddin Ahmed*,[100] *Rukia Khatun*,[101] *A Yousuf Rawther*,[102] *Mohammed Haneefa*,[103] *Zamrud Begum*,[104] *Praveen Akthar*[105] and *Nazeer*.[106] Each had relied on *Shamim Ara* and contributed to the law on *talaq* in India. In reaching its conclusion, the Court rejected the position which had been taken by Batchelor J in *Sarabai*,[107] who referred to the triple *talaq* as 'good in law, though bad in theology', a position itself challenged in *Fuzlunbi*.[108] The majority wrote:

> Before we bid farewell to *Fuzlunbi* it is necessary to mention that Chief Justice Baharul Islam, in an elaborate judgment replete with quotes from the Holy Quoran, has exposed the error of early English authors and judges who dealt with talaq in Muslim Law as good even if pronounced at whim or in tantrum, and argued against the diehard view of Batchelor, J. that this view 'is good in law, though bad in theology'. Maybe, when the point directly arises, the question will have to be considered by this Court but enough unto the day the evil thereof and we do not express our opinion on this question as it does not call for a decision in the present case.[109]

The majority therefore concluded that the triple *talaq* could not be legal, whether as a part of the Shariat or not.

ii. *The Triple* Talaq *and Fundamental Rights under Chapter III*

While they took divergent paths to conclude that the triple *talaq* was not legal, the majority agreed that the practice was unconstitutional as infringing the rights of Hanafi Muslim women in India.[110] The Court applied Article 25, applying *Shirur Mutt*, *Javed* and *Avadhuta* to hold that 'applying the aforesaid tests, it is clear that Triple Talaq is only

[98] ibid.
[99] See *Shayara Bano* (n 5); *Furzund Hossein v Janu Bibee* (1878) ILR 4 Cal 588.
[100] See *Shayara Bano* (n 5); *Jiauddin Ahmed v Anwara Begum* (1981) 1 Gau LR 358.
[101] See *Rukia Khatun v Abdul Khalique Laskar* (1981) 1 Gau LR 375.
[102] See *A Yousuf Rawther v Sowramma*, AIR 1971 Ker 261; *Shayara Bano* (n 5).
[103] See *Mohammed Haneefa v Pathummal Beevi*, 1972 KLT 512.
[104] See *Zamrud Begum v K Md Haneef and Another* (2003) 3 ALD 220.
[105] See *AS Parveen Akthar v The Union of India*, 2003-1-LW 370.
[106] See *Nazeer @ Oyoor Nazeer v Shemeema*, 2017 (1) KLT 300.
[107] See *Sarabai v Rabiabai* (1906) ILR 30 326 Bom 537.
[108] See *Furzund Hossein v Janu Bibee*, ILR (1878) 4 Cal 588.
[109] *Shayara Bano* (n 5).
[110] ibid.

a form of Talaq which is permissible in law, but at the same time, stated to be sinful by the very Hanafi school which tolerates it'.[111] Thus, the triple *talaq* could not form part of any essential religious practice.

Moreover, following *Acharya Jagdishwarananda*,[112] the fundamental nature of the Islamic religion, as seen through an Indian Sunni Muslim's eyes, will not change if this practice is unavailable. The Court observed that Hanafi jurisprudence itself treated the triple *talaq* as sinful; thus, it concluded, the triple *talaq* could not be saved by Article 25(1).[113]

In conclusion, the majority found the triple *talaq* to be illegal in the eyes of Islamic law or the Shariat because it contravened the spirit of the Quran. As such, it also violated the fundamental rights enshrined in Chapter III of the *Indian Constitution*.

C. The Dissent

The dissenting justices[114] hesitated to interfere with the Muslim personal laws; for them, the power to do so was not one bestowed upon the courts. They observed that religious denominations are empowered to act under their autonomy and, as such, the courts should refrain from interfering in this.

IV. Conclusion: The Indian Constitution and the Rights of Women

Chapter III of the *Indian Constitution* provides explicit protection for the rights of women and prohibits discrimination of any kind. Yet the courts have been hesitant to strike down laws that infringe those rights. Instead, the judiciary confers unfettered autonomy upon those who rely upon status as a religious denomination who continue to implement irrational and illegal practices in the guise of religion. Frequently, such religious practices fall within the scope of personal laws, which, whether Hindu or Islamic law, are predominately patriarchal. Some scholars call this system plurilegal – one in which the state may not have full jurisdiction over religious actors.[115]

The courts have always been cautious in dealing with such cases, which has placed the fundamental rights of women in serious jeopardy. Some scholars suggest that this constitutes a 'gender blind spot':

> [T]here always circulates in the public domain some version of the argument that, to be truly secular, India needs a UCC. But the question we must ask is, to what extent is the issue of

[111] See *Shayara Bano* (n 5). See *The Commissioner, Hindu Religious Endowments, Madras v Sri Lakshmindra Thirtha Swamiar of Sri Shirur Mutt* (n 25); *Javed v State of Haryana* (2003) 8 SCC 369; *Commissioner of Police v Acharya Jagdishwarananda Avadhuta* (n 41).

[112] See *Commissioner of Police v Acharya Jagdishwarananda Avadhuta* (n 41).

[113] Citing Sir D Fardunji Mulla, *Mulla: Principles of Mohomedan Law*, 20th edn (LexisNexis, Butterworths Wadhwa, 2013).

[114] *Shayara Bano* (n 5) (Kheher and Abdul Nazeer JJ).

[115] G Solanki, *Adjudication in Religious Family Laws: Cultural Accommodation, Legal Pluralism, and Gender Equality in India* (Cambridge University Press, 2011).

> the Uniform Civil Code about 'secularism'? Is it about the relationship between religious communities and the state? Is it not really about gender-injustice – that is, the constitutionally enshrined inequality between men and women? The fact is that all personal laws on *marriage*, and inheritance and guardianship of children, discriminate against women in some form or the other; surely, this should make the issue of the Uniform Civil Code visible in a different way? Should it not be debated as 'India cannot claim to be truly gender-just as long as discriminatory personal laws exist'? However, only feminists pose the question in this way.[116]

And some of the personal law of those claiming religious freedom itself denies the equality rights of women. The Shariat, for instance, fails to provide the right to a woman to practise the triple *talaq*.[117] Women are required to approach the law court. This may be discriminatory.

While the courts rarely attempt to redress this position, even if they did, the full import of Chapter III of the *Constitution* is yet to be settled, with little judicial treatment of the problematic interface of women's rights and religious freedom contained in personal law. Thus, *Sabaraimala* and *Shayara Bano* offered an opportunity for the Supreme Court to act decisively, an opportunity that may have been missed.

What might be lacking? There are three possibilities for reform.[118] First, feminist legal scholars look at the disputes in these cases through the lens of gender,[119] asserting that the personal laws allow for discriminatory practices against the interests of women.[120] These scholars do not argue for the unification of laws, but rather for cultural and religious accommodation of identity – for example, the Third World feminism debates.[121] Second, legal anthropologists investigate the complexities under state law, religious and personal rights, sociocultural practices and the debate on gender justice.[122] They conclude that India 'never had and most probably never will have a legal monopoly in the area of family laws'.[123] And, finally, some scholars explore the way in which religion itself may accommodate the rights of women within the context of personal laws.[124]

There is no doubt that the equality of women and the protection of their rights has a very long way to go in India. In taking those steps, the courts must lead the way in

[116] N Menon, *Seeing Like a Feminist* (Penguin, 2012) 151.

[117] KL Dryden, 'India's Highest Court Strikes Instant Divorce Law Available to Husbands Only: Previously Protected by Personal Law' (2019) 44 *North Carolina Journal of International Law* 85.

[118] ibid.

[119] ibid.

[120] ibid.

[121] See CT Mohanty, A Russo and L Torres, 'Introduction: Cartographies of Struggle: Third World Women and the Politics of Feminism' in CT Mohanty, A Russo and L Torres (eds), *Third World Women and the Politics of Feminism* (Indiana University Press, 1991). See also K Crenshaw, 'Demarginalizing the Intersection of Race and Sex: A Black Feminist Critique of Antidiscrimination Doctrine, Feminist Theory and Antiracist Politics' (University of Chicago Legal Forum, 1989) 139.

[122] M Hong Tschalaer, *Muslim Women's Quest for Justice: Gender, Law and Activism in India* (Cambridge University Press, 2017) 52.

[123] ibid.

[124] ibid; R Kumar, *The History of Doing: An Illustrated Account of Movements for Women's Rights and Feminism in India 1800–1990* (Kali for Women, 1993); CE Holmes, 'Conventions, Courts, and Communities: Gender Equity, CEDAW and Religious Personal Law in India' (2019) 54(7) *Journal of Asian and African Studies* 965.

harmonising the personal laws of religious groups with the *Constitution*. After all, as Chandrachud J[125] rightly observes, the *Indian Constitution* is a transformative document. As such, India cannot afford to countenance those practices that infringe the rights of women. Perhaps, with judgments like *Sabaraimala* and *Shayara Bano*, the first tentative steps on the journey towards harmonisation might have just begun.

[125] See *Sabarimala* (n 4).

19

Allcard v Skinner

Religious Influence and Undue Influence

CRAIG ALLEN

I. Introduction

Law and religion exhibit a dialectical interaction.[1] In many instances, law and religion cross over and fertilise one another.[2] The study of law and religion is furthered by examining both the religious and the non-religious dimensions of specific areas of law and legal doctrines.[3] In this chapter, I will demonstrate how *Allcard v Skinner*[4] has cross-fertilised both the religious and general understandings of when relational influence becomes unlawful following the equitable understanding of undue influence in the English and Australian courts.

Undue influence is a private law vitiating doctrine used to challenge financial transactions like contracts, inter vivos gifts and testamentary dispositions. It may seem that consideration of such a doctrine is out of place in a book such as this. However, the contribution of *Allcard* to the regulation of religious influence surrounding financial transactions in both jurisdictions, especially involving inter vivos gifts, has proven significant. The theological and religious foundations of equities intervention in cases exhibit a long historical pedigree, after all.[5] Examining the relationship between law and religion in *Allcard* informs how contemporary undue influence laws have developed just as much as it helps to explains the specific considerations of undue influence in religious contexts. In this sense, *Allcard* is a rare case within the study of law and religion; seldom has a case with a religious background had such a direct and long-lasting impact on a private law doctrine in both jurisdictions.

[1] J Witte Jr and FS Alexander (eds), *Christianity and Law: An Introduction* (Cambridge University Press, 2008) 1.

[2] ibid.

[3] P Edge, 'The Contribution of Law to Interdisciplinary Conversations on Law and Religion' in S Ferrari (ed), *Routledge Handbook on Law and Religion* (Routledge, 2015) 80.

[4] *Allcard v Skinner* (1887) 36 Ch D 145.

[5] See generally R Hedlund, 'The Theological Foundations of Equity's Conscience' (2015) 4(1) *Oxford Journal of Law and Religion* 119.

Prior to the development of religious and spiritual undue influence case law, English law had always held a deep concern about clergy members and other religious officials pressuring adherents into gifting land or leaving property through testamentary dispositions to religious institutions.[6] Canon law also shared this concern at one time.[7] Reported religious and spiritual undue influence cases heard before *Allcard* was decided in 1887 were uncommon and concerned disgraced former religious officials and exploitative conduct.[8] Undue influence was found in each of the three cases.[9]

Allcard demonstrated less obvious abuses of religious capital and was concerned with presumed undue influence and inter vivos gifts given to a closed religious sisterhood. The judgment remains the leading case on religious undue influence in England. More generally, it is defined as the locus classicus of undue influence.[10] Consequently, the judgment has retained a persuasive role in English law, as well as Australian law, and it is regularly cited by the highest courts in both jurisdictions.[11] *Allcard* has been examined by judges to assist in determining when religious influence becomes undue and how doctrinal elements of the test for undue influence should be applied. Beyond this, *Allcard* has proven significant to theoretical debates about the correct rationale for undue influence[12] and to scholars examining the concerns raised by the regulation of financial transactions motivated by religious faith.[13]

Despite the judgment's twofold contribution to understandings of presumed undue influence, *Allcard* arguably provides limited practical assistance for courts to effectively determine when religious influence, an inevitable part of any religious experience, becomes undue and thus unlawful. In this context, Hedlund has rightfully observed that: 'The religious context is rather unique in how it expects obedience without too

[6] Mortmain statutes were introduced from 1279 to protect the feudal aristocracy by limiting the abuse of religious power to acquire property from testamentary dispositions and later inter vivos gifts. The statutes restricted religious institutions from holding land and imposed restrictions on charitable organisations from acquiring land, and how donors and testators could make charity bequests. The last of these laws were repealed in 1960; see AH Oosterhoff, 'The Law of Mortmain' (1977) 27(3) *University of Toronto Law Journal* 259, 294–96.

[7] Canon law included *restitutio in integrum*, which allowed parties to undo transactions where they had been disadvantaged by it – for example, where there was coercion. See R Hedlund, 'Undue Influence and the Religious Cases That Shaped the Law' (2016) 5(2) *Oxford Journal of Law and Religion* 301.

[8] See *Norton v Relly* (1764) 2 Eden 268, 28 ER 908; *Nottidge v Prince* (1860) 2 Giff 245; *Cocks v Manners* (1871) LR 12 Eq 574, 581; *Lyon v Home* (1868) LR 6 Eq 655 (concerning spiritual influence).

[9] *Norton v Relly* (n 8); *Nottidge v Prince* (n 8); *Cocks v Manners* (n 8) 581.

[10] AP Bell, 'Abuse of a Relationship: Undue Influence in English and French Law' (2007) 15(4) *European Review of Private Law* 557, fn 7.

[11] In the House of Lords, now the UK Supreme Court, see *Barclays Bank plc v O'Brien* [1993] UKHL 6, [1993] 4 All ER 417; *Royal Bank of Scotland plc v Etridge (No 2)* [2001] UKHL 44, [2001] 3 WLR 1021 (the leading case). In the High Court of Australia, see *Johnson v Buttress* [1936] HCA 41 (the leading case); *Commercial Bank of Australia Ltd v Amadio* [1983] HCA 14; *Thorne v Kennedy* [2017] HCA 49.

[12] See P Birks and CN Yin, 'On the Nature of Undue Influence' in J Beatson and D Friedmane (eds), *Good Faith and Fault in Contract Law* (Clarendon Press, 1997); M Chen-Wishart, 'Undue Influence: Vindicating the Relationships of Influence' (2006) 59(1) *Current Legal Problems* 231; P Saprai, *Contract Law without Foundations: Toward a Republican Theory of Contract Law* (Oxford University Press, 2019) 102–23.

[13] See P Ridge, 'The Equitable Doctrine of Undue Influence Considered in the Context of Spiritual Influence and Religious Faith: *Allcard v Skinner* Revisited in Australia' (2003) 26(1) *University of New South Wales Law Journal* 66; S Degeling, 'Undue Influence and the Spiritual Economy' in K Barker et al (eds), *Private Law and Power* (Hart Publishing, 2017).

much question, though submission to the institution is generally voluntary. It poses a very difficult legal question.'[14] Of all the cases of this nature, *Allcard* most distinctly underlines the challenges of regulating abuses of religious capital resulting in financial gains in hard cases where there is no clear evidence of exploitation. This concern applies equally to contemporary litigation in England[15] and Australia.[16] Although such litigation has and continues to occur very infrequently in England, there have been five reported religious undue influence cases since the turn of the twentieth century,[17] and of the three which were decided on the substantive issue of undue influence, each case was successfully argued.[18] A similar theme is found in the Australian jurisprudence;[19] in the six cases decided by the Supreme Courts of the Australian legal territories since 2000, all judgments have found that undue influence produced the challenged transactions.

The chapter first outlines the facts of *Allcard* and the first instance and Court of Appeal judgments of the Court of Chancery. Subsequently, it examines the general contributions of the judgments to the regulation of undue influence. The discussion then moves on to examine the legacy of the Court of Appeal judgment on the regulation of gifts motivated by religious faith following the current tests for presumed undue influence. This analysis establishes why *Allcard* is a landmark case in law and religion, and explains why courts should closely re-engage with the reasoning of the Chancery judges to reach more principled decisions on defendant liability in religious undue influence cases.

II. *Allcard v Skinner*

In 1887, when *Allcard* was decided, English society was greatly suspicious of religious sisterhoods,[20] which were akin to Catholic convents.[21] The nineteenth-century religious norms of English society generally considered that sisterhoods relied on their vows and rules to steal, abuse or single out undutiful daughters for their benefit.[22] In this time of great social stigma, the defendant in *Allcard* was therefore incredibly unlikely to retain the gifts received that were challenged for undue influence.

[14] Hedlund (n 7) 308.

[15] ibid.

[16] See Ridge (n 13); Degeling (n 13).

[17] *Chennells v Bruce* (1939) 55 TLR 422; *Tufton v Sperni* [1952] 2 TLR 516; *Catt v Church of Scientology Religious Education College Inc* (2001) CP Rep 41; *Hollis v Rolfe* [2008] EWHC 1747, [2008] 7 WLUK 681; *Kliers v Schmerler* [2018] EWHC 1350 (Ch), [2018] 4 WLUK 57. For similarly reasoned spiritual cases where undue influence was found, see *Roche v Sherrington* [1982] 1 WLR 599; *Nel v Kean* [2003] 2 WLUK 467; *Azaz v Denton* [2009] EWHC 1759 (QB), [2009] 7 WLUK 568; *Curtis v Curtis* [2011] EWCA 1602, [2011] 11 WLUK 381.

[18] See *Chennells* (n 17); *Tufton* (n 17); *Kliers* (n 17).

[19] *Quek v Beggs* (1990) 5 BPR 11,761; *Illuzzi v Christian Outreach Centre* (1997) Q ConvR 54-490; *McCulloch v Fern* [2001] NSWSC 406; *Hartigan v International Society for Krishna Inc* [2002] NSWSC 810; *Khan v Khan* [2004] NSWSC 1189.

[20] See C Smith, '*Allcard v Skinner* Revisited: Historical Perspectives on Undue Influence' in E Cooke (ed), *Modern Studies in Property Law Volume III* (Hart Publishing, 2005) 136, 136–40.

[21] See Hedlund (n 7) 308–09.

[22] Smith (n 20) 140–51.

The claimant was introduced to an Anglican religious sisterhood called the Sisters of the Poor by her priest, Reverend Nihill, the Vicar of St Michaels in Shoreditch, London in 1868, when she was 26 years old. The sisterhood operated in Finsbury in North London and was administered by the Church of England.[23] By formally joining the sisterhood in 1870, the claimant intended to further her religious wellbeing and help the charitable causes of sisterhood, which provided for the poor. She held multiple positions in the sisterhood between 1870 and 1879. From 1871, she started to donate large sums of money and railway stocks to the defendant, known as Mother Superior, who led the sisterhood. The property gifted had been inherited by the claimant after the death of her wealthy father in 1868. The largest gifts were made between 1871 and 1874. At the time those gifts were made, the claimant was a professed member, which required her to agree to the sisterhood's rule of obedience and the vow of poverty. The money received by the defendant was used to further the religious and charitable practices of the sisterhood, which had been agreed to by both parties at the time. The defendant held on to the railway stocks on behalf of the sisterhood. Later in 1879, the claimant renounced her beliefs and left the sisterhood to join the Church of Rome because she had become increasingly dissatisfied with her life at the sisterhood.[24] In 1885, she sought to recover the value of the gifts totalling £10,171[25] on the grounds of undue influence.

Counsel for the claimant argued that 'spiritual influence is the most subtle of all, and there was produced and maintained in this lady such a state of mind and subjection as to invalidate any gift made by her to the person exercising that influence'.[26] Considering what undue influence required, counsel submitted that the test is 'how the intention was produced' and referred to *Huguenin v Baseley*[27] to support that understanding,[28] reasoning that:

> [The defendant's] object [was] to efface absolutely the free will of the individual and to substitute the will of the lady superior, and the result is, that the individual becomes a mere cipher and does automatically and in obedience to the will of the lady superior what she is directed to do. The law requires that gifts made under such circumstances shall not be upheld unless the donor had competent independent legal advice.[29]

Competent advice was considered to amount to legal advice. This argument was based on the determination of the role advice in previous cases.[30] Since the claimant had not received such advice during the party's influential relationship, the gifts were argued to have been unduly influenced.[31]

[23] ibid.
[24] *The Times* (1 February 1887), www.thetimes.co.uk/archive/article/1887-02-01/3/3.html#.
[25] This is roughly estimated to be worth £1,346,171.30 in 2020; see www.officialdata.org/uk/inflation/1887?amount=10000.
[26] *Allcard* (n 4) 150.
[27] *Huguenin v Baseley* (1807) 14 Ves Jun 273.
[28] *Allcard* (n 4) 150.
[29] ibid 153.
[30] ibid.
[31] ibid.

Counsel for the defendant replied: 'This is not a case, like *Huguenin v Baseley*, of a person using her influence for her own benefit … In all the reported cases the undue influence has been exerted for the benefit of the donee.'[32] Counsel cited several examples of previous case law, most significantly *Nottidge v Prince*,[33] a successfully proved case of religious undue influence against the leader of the Agapemonites, as evidence of this understanding of undue influence.[34] Counsel argued that the gifts could not be revoked years after the money had been spent with the claimant's approval because she was bound by the defences of laches and acquiescence. When leaving the sisterhood, the claimant was independent of spiritual influence. In addition, counsel submitted that even if such influence existed at a time prior to this, the claimant had received advice from her brother that allowed her to reflect on her beliefs and the nature of the gifts.[35] Accordingly, the claimant had failed to show that the gifts had been unduly influenced.[36]

At first instance, the Court of Chancery examined six gifts of money made to the defendant from 1871 to 1876, valued at £8,500. The claimant did not seek to recover other gifts, some of which were of considerable value.[37] Justice Kekewich decided that the gifts had not been unduly influenced. Emphasis was placed on the gifts made by cheque in September 1871 in reaching this conclusion.[38] Justice Kekewich considered the timing of the gifts alongside the state of the relationship between the parties at each stage in time.[39] The most significant stage in the party's relationship was found to be when the claimant initially became aware of the sisterhood and its vows and rules. It was held that this indicated that the claimant had acted without undue influence and had made the gifts based on 'intelligent intention' and external advice from her brother, a practising barrister.[40] Justice Kekewich did not discuss a distinction between presumed and actual undue influence explicitly, and the relationship was not subjected to a presumption of influence. In finding that there had been no undue influence, Kekewich J noted his efforts to remain impartial to the religious beliefs of the sisterhood:

> I have endeavoured, to the best of my ability, to treat this as a question of law, regardless of feelings which might otherwise sway the judgment, and, so far as I could control thoughts or command language, I have endeavoured to express my conclusions so as to avoid wounding susceptibilities or causing pain to any person directly or indirectly interested in the matter in hand.[41]

The claimant subsequently appealed this decision. The Court of Appeal judgment was limited to two gifts of railway stock made to the defendant in 1874. The judgment created the first distinction in expressions of influence. Lord Justice Cotton submitted that there were two categories of undue influence – one that gave rise to a presumption

[32] ibid 152.
[33] *Nottidge v Prince* (1860) 2 Giff 245.
[34] *Allcard* (n 4) 152.
[35] ibid.
[36] ibid 151.
[37] ibid 175.
[38] ibid 167–68.
[39] Also highlighted by Bowen LJ in the Court of Appeal judgment (ibid 191).
[40] ibid 167.
[41] ibid 168.

of influence and one now known as actual undue influence – which required some fraud or coercion on behalf of the defendant.[42] A presumption of influence was held to have arisen between the parties because of the religious circumstances of their relationship.[43] Lord Justice Lindley stated that 'religious influence is the most dangerous and the most powerful'.[44] He also considered that the vow of poverty and the rule of obedience did not require the claimant to gift her property to the sisterhood; it could also have been donated to the poor.[45] It was nevertheless concluded that the claimant must have felt some obligation to gift some of the property to the sisterhood and that she would feel that the defendant expected this of her.[46]

Interestingly, Bowen LJ submitted that '[t]his is a case of great importance. There are no authorities, which govern it',[47] but this is inaccurate. Since 1764, the Court of Chancery had decided several cases relating to the question of whether religious influence had reached the level of undue influence.[48]

Lord Justice Cotton held that in cases of this nature, a court could interfere based on public policy to prevent the influential relationships from being abused rather than any wrongful act committed by defendants.[49] Adding to this, Bowen LJ elaborated on when equity's intervention would be justified in religious cases:

> It is plain that equity will not allow a person who exercises or enjoys a dominant religious influence over another to benefit directly or indirectly by the gifts which the donor makes under or in consequence of such influence, unless it is shewn that the donor, at the time of making the gift, was allowed full and free opportunity for counsel and advice outside the means of considering his or her worldly position and exercising an independent will about it ...[50]
>
> This is not a limitation placed on the action of the donor; it is a fetter placed upon the conscience of the recipient of the gift, and one which arises out of public policy and fair play.[51]

The Court of Appeal examined the parties' relationship over the full course of their interactions in more detail than Kekewich J, even though the appeal was limited to the gifts made in 1874. Disputing the approach of Kekewich J, Bowen LJ contended:

> It seems to me that the case does not turn upon the fact that the standard of duty was originally created by the Plaintiff herself, although her original intention is one of the circumstances, no doubt, which bear upon the case, and is not to be neglected. But it is not the crucial fact. We ought to look, it seems to me, at the time at which the gift was made, and to examine what was then the condition of the donor who made it.[52]

Several factors were examined by the Court of Appeal before a decision was reached. A leading factor relied on was that the claimant had not received sufficient independent

[42] ibid 171–72.
[43] ibid 171.
[44] ibid 184.
[45] ibid 177.
[46] ibid.
[47] ibid 180.
[48] See *Norton v Relly* (n 8); *Nottidge v Prince* (n 8); *Cocks v Manners* (n 8) 581; *Lyon v Home* (n 8).
[49] *Allcard* (n 4) 171.
[50] ibid 190.
[51] ibid.
[52] ibid 191.

advice prior to making the gifts or joining the sisterhood[53] and could not seek such advice without the defendant's consent.[54] In addition, the defendant had ended up controlling the claimant's contact with the outside world.[55] The rule that adherents of the sisterhood could not seek advice outside of the sisterhood was treated as suspicious by the court because it could be used 'in a very tyrannical way, and so as to result in intolerable oppression'.[56] Also, the claimant had expressed a desire to leave the sisterhood on various occasions, but was told by the defendant that she was bound to the sisterhood for life.[57] The claimant continued living with the sisterhood on each occasion.

However, other factors were considered by the Court of Appeal in support of the defendant's plea that the gifts had not been unduly influenced. First, there was no excessive pressure found in the defendant's conduct during the parties' relationship.[58] Lord Justice Lindley confirmed that no pressure had been put on the claimant when entering into or subsequently living at the sisterhood and that all religious obligations followed by the claimant were consented to voluntarily.[59] Second, the gifts had not been used for the defendant's personal gain.[60] Third, the claimant only asked for her money back in 1885, six years after leaving the sisterhood, when she was in need of money.[61]

Furthermore, the judges were sensitive to the religious circumstances of the case. Lord Justice Bowen reasoned:

> It is a question which must be decided upon broad principles, and we have to consider what is the principle, and what is the limitation of the principle, as to voluntary gifts where there is no fraud on the part of the Defendant, but where there is an all-powerful religious influence which disturbs the independent judgment of one of the parties, and subordinates for all worldly purposes the will of that person to the will of the other … It seems to me that persons who are under the most complete influence of religious feeling are perfectly free to act upon it in the disposition of their property, and not the less free because they are enthusiasts.[62]

Considering the significant stigma experienced by religious sisterhoods at the time, Lindley LJ was conscious of the emotional connection between the claimant's religious beliefs and the necessity of donating substantial gifts to enhance spiritual growth:

> It is important, however, to bear in mind that the fetter thus placed on the Plaintiff was the result of her own free choice. There is no evidence that pressure was put upon her to enter upon the life which she adopted. She chose it as the best for herself; she devoted herself to it, heart and soul; she was, to use her own expression, infatuated with the life and with the work. But though infatuated, there is no evidence to shew that she was in such a state of mental imbecility as to justify the inference that she was unable to take care of herself or to manage her own affairs.[63]

[53] ibid 173 (Cotton LJ).
[54] ibid 184.
[55] Including the claimant's correspondence with her brother on general and financial matters: ibid 178–79 (Lindley LJ).
[56] ibid 178 (Cotton LJ).
[57] ibid 176 (Lindley LJ).
[58] ibid 179–80, 186.
[59] ibid 178.
[60] ibid (Cotton LJ).
[61] ibid 180.
[62] ibid 189.
[63] ibid 178.

Similarly, Cotton LJ noted the possibility of changes to the claimant's religious beliefs and financial situation after the donations were made:

> She had devoted herself and her fortune to the sisterhood, and it never occurred to her that she should ever wish to leave the sisterhood or desire to have her money back. In giving away her property as she did she was merely acting up to her promise and vow and the rule of the sisterhood, and to the standard of duty which she had erected for herself under the influences and circumstances already stated.[64]

The Court of Appeal ultimately held that the defendant could not disprove the presumption of influence. It proved too difficult for the defendant to show evidence that the gifts were free of undue influence. However, relief was denied due to the time lapse between the claimant leaving the sisterhood and making the claim.[65]

Allcard is a perfect illustration of a court's formidable task of determining when religious influence motivating gifts becomes undue and unlawful. The Court of Appeal was aware of this great difficulty, and it seems that the Chancery judges were concerned about the possible impact the decision could subsequently have on religious gifts made to religious institutions of any background. Given the Court of Appeal's difficulties in reaching a decision, a presumption of influence was considered a strongly justified element of the law on undue influence, especially in religious cases. The usage of the presumption was intended to protect vulnerable religious donors from being taken advantage of by religious figures, but also to take account of the religious circumstances agreed to by donors. Further, the decision reveals the difficulties facing religious defendants seeking to bring evidence to disprove the presumption of influence when independent advice has not been received by donors, even if the defendant has not taken advantage of their faith and enthusiasm.

Temporality was also an inherent factor in the decisions. Changes in influence and to the religious grounding of the party's relationship were assessed in different ways in the two judgments. At first instance, Kekewich J treated the claimant's initial decision to join the sisterhood and the advice received before some of the earlier gifts were made as the determinative factors in not finding undue influence. This approach fails to recognise or understand the importance of changes in influence over time in relationships. Arguably, Kekewich J placed too much weight on the parties' relationship at the beginning and failed to examine how that influence could have subsequently become undue. Such an approach unfortunately freezes the analysis of influence in time at the earliest possible stage in the relationship and fails to adequately protect the claimant's interests later on. In contrast, in the Court of Appeal judgment, Bowen LJ disputed this approach (as discussed above), which indicates a more temporally nuanced approach to the reasoning of when religious influence becomes undue.

The two judgments affirmed that religious influence can easily be abused because of its subtle and powerful impact on an enthusiastic donor's motives gift property. The judgments also highlighted how religious institutions that commonly accept donations or gifts from adherents are vulnerable to undue influence challenges because of the inevitable influence and the sorts of relationships of religious figures and adherents.

[64] ibid.
[65] ibid 172 (Cotton LJ).

The Court of Appeal judgment showed much greater caution about over-regulating and under-regulating the religious influence that inevitably motivates such transactions. If undue influence was not found in *Allcard*, the doctrine might not have adequately protected vulnerable parties in subsequent cases because of a particular court's respect for more favourably viewed religious institutions. In contrast, based on the same judgment, a religious institution could be wrongly stripped of gifts where a court considered that a religious official took advantage of a donor's religious enthusiasm without effectively showing this to be an accurate description of the party's relationships.

Ultimately, the Chancery judges engaged specifically with the religious context of the case, but neither judgment made a clear determination about when religious influence becomes undue. Consequently, when courts apply *Allcard*, the locus classicus of presumed undue influence,[66] the equitable doctrine does not sufficiently guard against either of the two negatives consequences just mentioned relating to the rebuttal stage of presumptions of undue influence and the issues concerning temporal assessments of relationships. Even when courts rely less on the ruling in *Allcard* in religious cases, the same concern still arises because of *Allcard*'s impact on the contemporary tests for presumed undue influence more generally in English and Australian law.

III. *Allcard's* Doctrinal Contributions

In England, it is generally considered that undue influence defies accurate definition.[67] In *Etridge*, for instance, Lord Clyde submitted: 'It is something which can be more easily recognised when found than exhaustively analysed in the abstract.'[68] Beyond considering the propriety of influence and when a transaction is motivated by a person's free will, Lord Nicholls stated: 'The circumstances in which one person acquires influence over another, and the manner in which influence may be exercised, vary too widely to permit of any more specific criterion.'[69] Even though there is no exact definition, Sir Martin Nourse observed in *Hammond v Osbourne*:[70] 'The doctrine of presumed undue influence is now very well settled and ought to be well understood.'[71] The requirements of both actual and presumed influence are set by the Court of Appeal judgment in *Allcard* and more recently by the House of Lords in *Etridge*.[72]

Allcard firstly established a distinction between two expressions of undue influence, as already briefly mentioned.[73] However, the two expressions have now been restated by the House of Lords in *Etridge*,[74] a case concerning eight joined appeals by homeowners who successfully challenged the legality of surety agreements on mortgaged property that they had signed on behalf of their husbands. Actual undue influence

[66] See Bell (n 10).
[67] *Bullock v Lloyd's Bank* [1955] Ch 317, 324 (Vaisey J).
[68] *Etridge* (n 11) [92].
[69] ibid [7].
[70] *Hammond v Osbourne* [2002] EWCA Civ 885.
[71] ibid [24].
[72] *Evans v Lloyd* [2013] EWHC 1725 (Ch) [36] (Keyser QC).
[73] *Roche* (n 17) 606–07 (Slade J).
[74] *Etridge* (n 11).

requires the defendant's express conduct to overpower a person's free will,[75] which can include some form of fraud or coercion.[76] It is hard to prove and is more commonly used to challenge testamentary dispositions. *Allcard* has not really inspired this sort of undue influence and so there is no need to examine it further.

Presumed undue influence examines relational influence and imposes a presumption of influence, which can subsequently be rebutted by defendants by showing that a transaction was of the parties' free will. It is an equitable doctrine used to challenge inter vivos gifts and contractual bargains,[77] and is more commonly argued. *Allcard* affirmed that automatic presumptions of influence apply to relationships between religious advisors and adherents. Automatic presumptions now also apply to a broader range of status-based relationships[78] that are typically described as being of a fiduciary nature.[79] Claimants must prove a relationship of trust and confidence existed when status-based relationships are not applicable. In order for a presumption of influence to crystallise, claimants must also prove that a transaction 'calls for an explanation' because it is not explicable by the nature of the party's relationship.[80] This part of the presumption analysis is directly inspired by *Allcard*. Justice Lindley made a distinction between small and large gifts made to defendants; where 'the gift is so large as not to be reasonably accounted for on the ground of friendship, charity, or other ordinary motives on which ordinary men act',[81] influence is presumed.

Defendants can rebut presumptions of influence to prove the lawfulness of transactions. In *Inche Noriah v Sheik Allie Bin Omar*,[82] Lord Hailsham LC held that in order to do so, the defendant must satisfy the courts 'that the donor was acting independently of any influence from the donee and with full appreciation of what he was doing'.[83] More specifically, the House of Lords affirmed in *Zamet v Hyman*[84] that evidence relied on by defendants must show that donors acted with 'full, free and informed thought' when making the challenged transaction.[85] Such reasoning was later accepted by the House of Lords in 2002 in the *Etridge* judgment, where it was also held that it is a question of fact determined on the evidence whether the presumption of influence has been rebutted by defendants.[86]

The most common way for defendants to rebut the presumption of influence is to show that donors or promisors received independent advice prior to the challenged transaction.[87] As demonstrated above, the lack of advice in *Allcard* was an

[75] ibid [103] (Lord Hobhouse).
[76] *Re Edwards* [2007] EWHC 1119 (Ch), [2007] 5 WLUK 72.
[77] For example, surety agreements; see *Etridge* (n 11).
[78] For example, between trustees and beneficiaries, parents and children, medical advisers and patients, and solicitors and clients: Law Commission, Consultation Paper 231, *Making a Will* (2017) [7.40].
[79] R Flannigan, 'Presumed Undue Influence: The False Partition from Fiduciary Accountability' (2015) 34(2) *Queensland University Law Journal* 205.
[80] *Etridge* (n 11) [22]–[24] (Lord Nicholls).
[81] *Allcard* (n 4) 185.
[82] *Inche Noriah v Sheik Allie Bin Omar* [1929] AC 127 (PC).
[83] ibid 135.
[84] *Zamet v Hyman* (1961) 1 WLR 1442.
[85] ibid 1444, 1446, 1450 (Lord Evershed).
[86] *Etridge* (n 11) [20] (Lord Nicholls).
[87] See Law Commission (n 78) [7.49].

essential element in determining when influence became undue. This approach has since been expressly followed by the Court of Appeal in *Hammond*.[88] If a presumption of influence is not rebutted, the transaction is void and the most typical remedy awarded is rescission.

Australian jurisprudence features similar definitional comments made by the High Court of Australia (the highest court of appeal in the Australian legal states) conveying a lack of demand for a specific definition for undue influence. In *Thorne v Kennedy*,[89] a case concerning an undue influence challenge to a pre-nuptial agreement by the wife of the defendant, Gordon J relied on Lindley LJ's comment that 'no court has ever tried to define undue influence' before concluding that: 'It is neither possible nor desirable to provide an all-encompassing description of a court's jurisdiction to grant relief on the ground of undue influence.'[90]

The tests for both expressions of undue influence in Australian law are set by *Johnson v Buttress*.[91] The claimant appealed a finding of undue influence alleged by the son of the deceased donor, the executor of his father's estate. The claimant had looked after the business affairs of the deceased, who at one time was gifted some land. At that time, the donor was aged 67, illiterate and had not received legal advice about the transaction. At first instance, the trial judge held that undue influence had caused the transfer. On appeal, the High Court of Australia held that the tribunal judge was correct to find that the transaction had been unduly influence because the defendant could not rebut the presumption of influence. Chief Justice Latham based his understanding of presumed undue influence on the Court of Appeal's reasoning in *Allcard*, which has since been confirmed in *Thorne*.[92] He explained:

> Where certain special relations exist, undue influence is presumed in the case of such gifts … Wherever the relation between donor and donee is such that the latter is in a position to exercise dominion over the former by reason of the trust and confidence reposed in the latter, the presumption of undue influence is raised.[93]

Citing *Allcard*, the High Court submitted that certain categories of relationships involve 'protected persons',[94] which included religious adherents involved in religiously influential relationships, and persons seeking advice from solicitors and physicians acting in their professional capacity.[95] For a presumption of influence to arise, claimants must also show that challenged transactions cannot be explained by 'ordinary motives'[96] and are 'not readily explicable by the relationship of the parties'.[97]

[88] After considering the judgments of Cotton LJ and Bowne LJ in *Allcard* (n 4) at length (see [42]–[47]), Ward LJ concluded: 'Independent advice is thus usually the crucial evidence going to the rebuttal of the presumption' (at [49]).
[89] *Thorne* (n 11).
[90] ibid [84], citing *Allcard* (n 4) 183.
[91] ibid. The understanding of actual undue influence is very similar to the English test – see *Johnson* (n 11) 134 – but is not one substantially inspired by *Allcard*. This explains why I do not consider it any further here.
[92] *Thorne* (n 11) [24], [34], fn 48 (Kiefel CJ).
[93] *Johnson* (n 11) 119.
[94] ibid 124 (Starke J).
[95] ibid 119 (Latham CJ).
[96] *Thorne* (n 11) [34] (Kiefel CJ), citing *Allcard* (n 4) 185 (Lindley LJ).
[97] ibid citing *Etridge* (n 11) [21] (Lord Nicholls).

Defendants can rebut presumptions of influence in the same way as in English law by showing that transactions are 'voluntary and a well-understood act of the mind' of donors.[98] On this basis, the Australian test is also based on determining whether a transaction was freely entered.[99] An important means of doing so is to demonstrate that the donor received independent advice.[100]

IV. *Allcard's* Impact on Contemporary Regulation

Allcard has clearly had a significant impact on the general doctrinal and judicial understandings of when relational influence becomes undue. *Allcard*'s contribution to the regulation of religious influence surrounding financial transactions is arguably less explicit. The judgments of English and Australian courts have arguably not furthered *Allcard*'s application in contemporary settings in a meaningful way. This has led to scholarly commentary specifically focused on the concerns about the suitability of the test for presumed undue influence in religious and spiritual cases.[101]

More specifically in English law, *Allcard* has had little substantive impact on contemporary religious cases beyond establishing that religious and spiritual advisors are part of a status-based relationship that does not require proof of sufficient trust and confidence. In the five reported cases decided since 2000, limited weight has generally been placed on the specific religious contexts involved in cases, or the challenges of regulating religious influence raised in *Allcard* many years ago.[102] Courts have not re-examined the concerns of the Chancery judges concerning how difficult it is to determine the lawfulness of influence in religious contexts. Instead, in contemporary presumed undue influence cases,[103] the test is considered by courts in a general sense with no regard to the claimant's initial consent to their religious experience and whether there had been any degree of pressure at this point in the party's relationships. This omission in judicial reasoning was also made in *Kliers v Schmerler*.[104] The claimant challenged the lawfulness of the influence of family members, the defendants, and a rabbi's advice to sign a mortgage agreement. The influence and advice were motivated by the beliefs of a particular Hasidic sect that the claimant was part of in London, which was described by Mr MH Rosen QC as a 'patriarchal body'.[105] The claimant consented to those beliefs and practices at one stage and then left the faith and later challenged the transaction for undue influence. The High Court established undue influence without assessing the claimant's former beliefs in any depth.

[98] *Johnson* (n 11) 123 (Latham CJ), quoting Eldon LC in *Huguenin v Basely* (1807) 14 Ves 273.
[99] *Johnson* (n 11) 120 (Latham CJ).
[100] ibid 120.
[101] See Ridge (n 13); Degeling (n 13).
[102] *Catt* (n 17); *Hollis* (n 17); *Kliers* (n 17). For similarly reasoned spiritual cases where undue influence was found, see *Roche* (n 17); *Nel* (n 17); *Azaz* (n 17); *Curtis* (n 17).
[103] ibid.
[104] ibid.
[105] See *Kliers* (n 17) [35].

Furthermore, in contemporary cases, courts do not give any weight to the fact that the claimant's beliefs motivating gifts are likely to form part of a legally recognised belief system and are therefore significant to the motivations of a great number of gifts to religious institutions. The omission of courts to consider the effect of specific religious beliefs and practices on an adherent's motivations to make gifts similarly applies to cases involving spiritual movements.[106] In these cases, judgments have not made any real distinctions between the conduct of religious ministers and the manifestation of religious beliefs accepted by all followers of the same legally recognised religions.

In Australian legal states, *Allcard* has generally contributed more to judicial understandings of when religious influence becomes undue. The Court of Appeal judgment has been cited regularly in religious undue influence cases by courts seeking to make principled judgments on whether religious undue influence has motivated challenged transactions. The most notable example of this is *Hartigan v International Society for Krishna Inc.*[107] The claimant, a follower of Hare Krishna, gifted her family home worth $87,000 to the founders of a Hare Krishna community after reading religious scriptures on conceptions of 'giving'. The transaction was completed even after the defendants had informed the claimant that the gift was too large and that she had misunderstood the community's meaning of giving. The transaction was overseen by the defendant's agents, who were not members of the community. *Allcard* was significant to Bryon J's reasoning who assessed the judgments of Cotton LJ and Bowen LJ.[108] Justice Bryson subsequently found that the defendants had unduly influenced the claimant's donation because it was not a fully voluntary decision, even though there were no signs of exploitative conduct exerted on the claimant or impropriety from the defendants.[109] The size and improvidence of the gift were both highly significant factors to this finding.[110] Close consideration was also given to the interaction of religious teachings and undue influence based on the reasoning in *Allcard*.[111]

However, more generally, courts in both jurisdictions have more generally either failed to properly engage with the judgments in *Allcard* in a consistently justified way or have omitted to do so entirely. The concerns discussed by both Kekewich J at first instance and the Court of Appeal in *Allcard* have therefore not been suitably addressed by the courts in both jurisdictions. In practice, this means that it is difficult to understand how courts determine when religious influence becomes undue in a principled way. Following a universal approach, it is questionable how courts consistently reach principled outcomes, given the types of relationships and motivations for gifts in religious cases that are not present in non-religious cases. There are numerous challenges with regulating religious influence in a general way without considering the specific religious relationships of the parties and their beliefs motivating religious practices.[112]

[106] See *Chennells* (n 17); *Nel* (n 17); *Azaz* (n 17); *Curtis* (n 17).
[107] *Hartigan* (n 19).
[108] ibid [32]–[33].
[109] ibid.
[110] ibid [36]–[37].
[111] ibid [30].
[112] For instance, all gifts, regardless of value, should be capable of being challenged for undue influence. Lord Nicholls' reasoning (discussed above) about this feature of the test is arguably unprincipled since the

I now focus on three challenges relating to the tests for presumed undue influence that are compounded in religious cases. My analysis helps to justify why *Allcard* should inspire the regulation of religious influence as much as it has inspired the tests for presumed undue influence in both jurisdictions.

An overarching challenge concerning when religious influence becomes undue relates to the rationale for presumed undue influence.[113] Courts have affirmed that the rationale is based on the donor's impaired will, as noted above. However, it is not always clear when someone's will has been sufficiently impaired for relief to be justified in cases where there is clear evidence of consent and no signs of exploitation. *Allcard* is a prevalent part of these rationale discussions.[114] In particular, Chen-Wishart has described *Allcard* as a 'clean case' because of the absence of obvious unlawful influence, but believes it is still right to infer undue influence– as in *Allcard* – if the claim had been brought sooner.[115] However, in the rationale debates, the most developed accounts of undue influence do not make any meaningful references to the potential differences that may exist between a finding of undue influence in religious contexts and a finding of undue influence in a more general doctrinal sense.[116] Instead, the leading rationale premised on a claimant's impaired will, which most closely captures the reasoning of the House of Lords in *Etridge*, makes 'an implicit judgment about the normative acceptability of the transaction[s]'[117] in *Allcard*. This critique is also an accurate description of how the presumed undue influence tests operate in practice in religious cases for the two reasons examined below.

First, it is unclear what the role of independent advice is at the rebuttal stage of cases.[118] Such ambiguity is more likely to have a detrimental effect on the judgments of religious cases.[119] In the case law of both jurisdictions, there are two interpretations on this. One view contends that if legal advice is received by donors or promisors, but is not heeded and followed, where it is seen as independent and relevant to the transaction by courts, a presumption of influence can still be rebutted by defendants.[120] On the other hand, another view submits that unless independent advice is followed by donors or promisors, it is almost impossible for the presumption to be rebutted by defendants.[121] It is important to determine how advice operates in religious cases because improvident gifts

wrongfulness of the defendant's conduct is the same. Persuasive arguments have been made suggesting that this part of the test should be abandoned. See *Evans* (n 72) [42], [63] (Keyser QC); and M Haughey, 'The Fiduciary Explanation for Presumed Undue Influence' (2012) 50(1) *Alberta Law Review* 145.

[113] Ridge (n 13) 67.

[114] Chen-Wishart (n 12) 238.

[115] ibid 237.

[116] A slight exception is Birks and Yin's account ((n 12) 67), which considers that: 'Religious enthusiasm … might be thought to be distinct from dependence. But there are no further discussions of the possible differences between what might amount to religious undue influence and how this may differ to general instances of undue influence.'

[117] Chen-Wishart (n 12) 238.

[118] Ridge (n 13) 88.

[119] ibid 84.

[120] In *Hartigan* (n 19) [31], Bryon J cited *Watkins v Coombs* [1922] HCA 3, 194 (Isaacs J) to support this view. This view is also echoed by Lord Nicholls in *Etridge* (n 11) [20].

[121] R Meagher et al, *Equity: Doctrines and Remedies*, 4th edn (LexisNexis Australia, 2002) [15]–[135], citing *Powell v Powell* [1900] 1 Ch 243, 246.

motivated by religious faith may be the leading reason why donors ignore legal advice.[122] Furthermore, as considered by Kekewich J in *Allcard*, external legal advice might be distrusted and seen as an evil temptation.[123] If the second view mentioned is favoured in hard cases, religious defendants will face an ever more challenging task when rebutting presumptions of influence.

Second, and closely related to the previous analysis, it is necessary to develop understandings about the significance of the improvidence of religiously motivated gifts.[124] It is unclear whether improvidence is enough for a gift to be set aside by English courts in particular,[125] which gives rise to a possibility of incompatibility between religious and legal conceptions of gift-giving.[126] The incompatibility is produced by the English 'calls for a transaction' requirement and also the Australian 'ordinary motive' standard included in the tests for presumed undue influence. Judges may consider that the amount of money or property gifted cannot be explained by ordinary motives and thus fail to consider religious viewpoints associated with religiously motivated gift-giving. Judicial scrutiny is likely to be much stricter where the donor holds strong religious beliefs or where religious practices are viewed as particularly severe.[127] The threshold test of what constitutes ordinary motives can be considered as an extension of the problem identified in law and religion scholarship by Bradney when family law imposes objective moral standards that do not match up to the standards of obdurate believers.[128] In cases like *Allcard*, gifts cannot be explained by ordinary motives, but can be explained by religious motives. Consequently, the two requirements of the presumption stage of the presumed undue influence tests do not have any filtering effect in religious cases. In practice, this means that religious defendants are more likely to unfairly face the difficult task of rebutting presumptions of influence. In hard cases, the difficulties are compounded further where no independent advice has been received prior to the challenged gift.

V. Conclusion

The facts of *Allcard* are still as applicable to many religious experiences of adherents today. It is not unusual for religious beliefs to involve vows of poverty and rules of obedience to religious figures. Many religions require, or at least expect to, receive donations or tithes as part of common religious practices. Accordingly, the challenge of deciding the legality of religious influence surrounding financial transactions has not become less relevant to contemporary religious practices and institutions. The legal challenge has certainly not evaporated despite the efforts of courts and scholars.

[122] Ridge (n 13) 84.
[123] *Allcard* (n 4) 159.
[124] Ridge (n 13) 83.
[125] ibid 83.
[126] ibid 84–85.
[127] ibid 84.
[128] A Bradney, 'Faced by Faith' in P Oliver et al (eds), *Faith in Law: Essays in Legal Theory* (Hart Publishing, 2000) 90 – for example, Roman Catholic adoptions agencies that reject applications from homosexual couples wishing to adopt a child.

Allcard has proven significant in relation to how English and Australian courts regulate relational influence and, to a lesser extent, religious influence. Therefore, it is undoubtedly a landmark case in law and religion. However, the rationale and procedural challenges mentioned in this chapter confirm why English and Australian courts should re-assess *Allcard* and take the concerns of the Chancery judges about regulating religious influence more seriously. Smith has rightfully argued that: 'Perhaps such uncritical use of this case risks the perpetuation of religious and social concerns, stereotypes and prejudices which should arguably have no place in the formulation of the modern law.'[129] Re-evaluating *Allcard* with reference to the contemporary tests for presumed undue influence and jurisprudence will reinvigorate an often-forgotten area of law that is important to the regulation of specific forms of religious financing.

One possible means of doing so is to reinvigorate the rationale debates by introducing an account that gives greater focus to the contexts and grounding of relational influence. The predominant focus of such an account should be religious and spiritual relationships that involve a shared belief system between donors and donee that require gifts or donations in exchange for religious services.

A more pragmatic approach could also be pursued by the courts of both jurisdictions. Courts could seek to add further explanation to when a donor's will has been impaired and how this can alter over time, given the potential for changes to relationships and influence. Such developments could help to address when religious influence becomes undue by elaborating on the role of independent legal advice and the improvidence considerations examined. As a result of judicially led developments to understandings of presumed undue influence, religious institutions would be less vulnerable to such challenges to property gifted by adherents. Consequently, this expression of undue influence is less likely to be used as a generous and unjust returns policy by aggrieved former adherents seeking rescission of large gifts made to religious institutions.

[129] Smith (n 20) 153.

INDEX

www.ingramcontent.com/pod-product-compliance
Lightning Source LLC
Chambersburg PA
CBHW071304180926
51613CB00001B/120
9781509950140